53-9024

S0-AYF-099

EUROPEAN COMPOSERS TODAY

EUROPEAN COMPOSERS TODAY

A Biographical and Critical Guide

Compiled and Edited by
DAVID EWEN

WITHDRAWN
NAZARETH COLLEGE
LIBRARY

THE H. W. WILSON COMPANY
NEW YORK   1954

31468

Copyright 1954
By The H. W. Wilson Company

———

Printed in the United States of America
Library of Congress Catalog Card No. 53-9024

780.92
Ewe

INTRODUCTION

EUROPEAN COMPOSERS TODAY is a biographical and critical guide to more than a hundred European composers who have exerted the greatest influence upon, and who have been the richest contributors to, the music of the twentieth century.

Since it is a companion volume to the previously-published AMERICAN COMPOSERS TODAY * (together, these two volumes replace the long out-of-print COMPOSERS OF TODAY, originally issued in 1934), it follows the pattern set by the earlier American volume.

Composers who have been writing music after January 1, 1900, are included; consequently many of those represented in this volume are no longer alive, and a few belong to the traditions and backgrounds of the late nineteenth century rather than to those of the twentieth. Selection of composers for inclusion in the present book was based upon (1) the importance of their works; (2) the frequency with which these works are heard in the concert hall or opera house, over the radio, and on phonograph records; (3) the interest which the American music public has in these composers. Musicians of exclusively local significance have, then, been omitted.

Several world-famous composers like Bartók, Stravinsky, and Schoenberg were born in Europe and first became famous there. However, since they migrated to this country or to South America after 1933 and remained permanently, they were regarded as American composers and were discussed in AMERICAN COMPOSERS TODAY. These men, consequently, are not included in this volume. Cross-references in the text indicate who they are.

Most of the material in this volume was procured directly from first-hand sources—from the composers themselves. During an extended trip to Europe in 1952, I was able to meet many of these people personally, and to tap them for all the information I required. For the supreme patience and the whole-hearted cooperation I encountered, I wish here and now to express my gratitude. But for that patience and that cooperation, this volume would surely have been less informative and less accurate. These direct and personal meetings enabled me to include several significant European composers about whom little or no information is available in this country.

I would like to express my indebtedness to Nicolas Slonimsky for his advice and criticism after a fastidious reading of the manuscript. I am also grateful to *Musical Courier* and *Etude* for the loan of several photographs.

The pronunciation of unusual or difficult names is indicated in footnotes to the biographies. The system of marking used follows Webster's *New International Dictionary.*

D. E.

* Published in 1949.

October 1953

Wilson ~June '54 ~ 4.00

CONTENTS

EUROPEAN COMPOSERS TODAY

Jean Absil *1893-*

JEAN ABSIL, contemporary Belgian composer, was born in Péruwelz, Hainaut, on October 23, 1893. At the Brussels Conservatory he received first prize in organ, harmony, and fugue, after which he studied orchestration and composition privately with Paul Gilson.

In 1921 Absil's First Symphony won the Prix Agniez, and one year after that his cantata *La Guerre* won the second Prix de Rome. These and other early works, as Joseph Dopp noted in *La Revue Musicale,* "were composed according to scholastic principles" in which the inspiration still submitted "to abstract rules and academic form."

After 1929, beginning with the String Quartet No. 1, Absil arrived at a style with which he was to produce his most important works. Coming into contact with the music and principles of such modernists as Schoenberg and Hindemith, Absil freed himself from the constrictions of traditional harmony and rhythm, allowing himself complete independence through the use of polytonality, atonality, and polyrhythms. His music grew complex and austere. But it was marked by the skill and inventiveness with which he utilized modern resources in expressing his ideas. His works were now performed extensively throughout Europe, and won several major awards (including the Prix Rubens in 1934 and tne Prix Ysaÿe in 1938). In reviewing a performance of Absil's Concerto for Piano and Orchestra in 1939, Florent Schmitt referred to the composer as "one of the leaders of the contemporary movement in Belgium, if not all of Europe" (*Le Temps*).

In a detailed analysis of Absil's style, Joseph Dopp wrote in the *Revue Musicale* article quoted above: "His music, informed by deep emotion, is remarkable for its spontaneity, originality, and for purity of style. . . . His music is contrapuntal throughout. He goes very far in the matter of irregular meters. . . . He uses discords as consonances freely, but his music is always tonal or modal. . . . He uses many new scales. . . . The description of his technique

JEAN ABSIL

and methods might suggest that his music is mainly cerebral, too abstract, deliberately calculated. In actual fact, it is profoundly human, quite accessible."

In 1923 Absil became director of music at the Academy of Etterbeek, and in 1931 professor of fugue at the Brussels Conservatory. He has also been president of the Société Nationale des Droits d'Auteurs and one of the founders of the *Revue Internationale de Musique.*

MAJOR WORKS:

Ballets—Le Miracle de Pan, op. 71, 1949; Épouvantail, op. 76, 1951.

Chamber Music—String Quartet No. 1, op. 5, 1929; String Quartet No. 2, op. 13, 1934; Quintet for Winds, op. 16, 1934; String Trio, op. 17, 1935; String Quartet No. 3, op. 19, 1935; Piano Quartet, op. 33, 1938; Trio No. 2 for Strings, op. 39, 1939; Fantaisie, for quartet with piano, op. 40, 1939; Philatélie, cantata for four voices and fifteen instruments, op. 46, 1940; String Quartet, No. 4, op. 47, 1941.

Choral Music—Three Choruses, for three-part women's voices, op. 6, 1932; Three Choruses, for four-part men's voices, op. 14, 1934; Les Bénédictions, cantata for soloists, chorus, and orchestra, op. 48, 1941; Le Bestiaire, five pieces for a cappella quartet, op. 59, 1944; Zoo, seven pieces for a cappella quartet, op. 64, 1944; Le Zodiaque, symphonic variations for chorus with piano, op. 70, 1949.

Opera—Fanson, musical farce, op. 64, 1945.

Absil: ăb-sēl′

Orchestral Music—Symphony No. 1, op. 1, 1921; La Mort de Tintagiles, tone poem, op. 3, 1926; Rapsodie sur des Thèmes Populaires Flamands, op. 4, 1928; Concerto for Violin and Orchestra, op. 11, 1933; Five Pieces, for small orchestra, op. 23, 1936; Symphony No. 2, op. 25, 1936; Concerto for Piano and Orchestra, op. 30, 1937; Rhapsody No. 2, op. 34, 1938; Concertino for Cello and Orchestra, op. 42, 1942; Serenade, op. 44, 1940; Variations Symphoniques, op. 50, 1942; Concerto for Viola and Orchestra, op. 54, 1942; Rapsodie Roumaine, for violin and orchestra, op. 56, 1943; Symphony No. 3, op. 57, 1943; Jeanne d'Arc, tone poem, op. 65, 1945.

Piano Music—Three Impromptus, op. 10, 1932; Sonatina, op. 27, 1937; Three Pieces, op. 32, 1938; Suite Pastorale, op. 37, 1939; Bagatelles, op. 61, 1944; Suite, op. 62, 1944; Hommage à Schumann, op. 67, 1946.

Vocal Music—Five Melodies, for voice and string quartet, op. 12, 1933; Nostalgie d'Arabella, poem for contralto and several instruments, op. 22, 1936; Phantasmes, for contralto, saxophone, viola, piano, and percussion, op. 73, 1950.

ABOUT:
La Revue Musicale, October-December 1937.

Isaac Albéniz *1863-1909*

BECAUSE Albéniz' greatest works were written after 1900, he has been included in this volume of twentieth-century composers.

He was born in Camprodón, Catalonia, on May 29, 1863. Few composers lived a life so full of adventure and incident as he. After being taught the elements of the piano by an older sister, he made a public appearance in Barcelona when he was only four years old. Skeptics in the audience were so sure that some mature artist was playing, concealed behind the drawn curtains, that the curtains had to be opened to prove that nobody was backstage. He was brought to Paris two years later, and for nine months he studied with Marmontel to prepare for entering the Conservatory. But in the middle of the entrance examinations, for which he had prepared so carefully, he suddenly took a ball out of his pocket and threw it with all his might at the mirrors in the examination hall, and then fled from the room.

Denied admission because of this episode, he was brought back to Madrid, where he was enrolled in the Conservatory. He had not been a student for a long while before he suddenly ran away from school, secretly boarding the first train he could get out of Madrid. En route, the Governor of the

Escorial noticed him, became interested in him and brought him to his own home. The governor arranged to have him perform at the town casino. Then, stuffing the boy's pockets with coins, he made Albéniz promise to return home. At the first station, Albéniz deserted the Madrid-bound train and boarded another going in the opposite direction. For the next few months he wandered from one Spanish city to another—an eight-year-old minstrel, earning his living by playing the piano. At last, homesick, he decided to return home. But on the way he was attacked and robbed of all his savings. The humiliating prospect of going home without a single peseta to show for his travels changed his mind. His wanderings continued. For another two years he passed from city to city giving performances on the piano. Then when he finally returned home it was with accumulated funds and with an established reputation.

For a while he studied and worked hard. Then once again he ran away. This time he reached the southern port of Cadíz. Apprehended by the local governor, who insisted that he return home, Albéniz was detained as a runaway until train time. Somehow he managed to escape. He stowed away aboard the ship *España*, which carried him across the Mediterranean, out into the Atlantic, and toward Puerto Rico. From Puerto Rico he went on to Cuba and from there north to the United States. He appeared publicly everywhere and was able to save a great deal of money.

His wanderlust sated, he returned to Europe for the purpose of studying music intensively. He entered the Leipzig Conservatory and for a while was a diligent student with Jadassohn and Reinecke. But the old restlessness returned like a recurrent disease, and once again he was on the move.

A chance meeting with Count Guillermo Morphy, who was greatly impressed by his ability, resulted in an endowment from Alphonso XII, King of Spain. Albéniz now became a pupil of François Gevaert in Brussels. But he chafed under the discipline of formal study.

Tragedy brought Albéniz to his senses. In a moment of schoolboy bravado, he made a pact with a friend: they would enjoy themselves to the full and then commit suicide. One morning Albéniz discovered that his

Albéniz: äl-bā'nēth

friend had taken the pact all too seriously, and had committed suicide. For weeks, Albéniz was a victim of depression. He emerged from it determined to mend his ways.

He went to Weimar in 1878, where he met and played for Franz Liszt. Then he undertook an extended concert tour through Spain, and to Cuba, Mexico and South America.

Up to this time, Albéniz had written only trivial pieces for the piano and some scores for popular operettas. He was convinced that his talent lay in his piano playing. But a meeting with the venerable Spanish musician, Felipe Pedrell, was to have a profound influence on his future. Pedrell, sometimes described as "the father of Spanish music" was a scholar who had done considerable research in old Spanish music, particularly folk music. It was Pedrell's belief that every Spanish composer should write *Spanish* music, rooted in the folk songs and dances of the country, and interpreting Spanish backgrounds. Pedrell convinced Albéniz of two things: he was henceforth to devote himself to composition rather than to playing the piano; and he was to aspire towards the creation of a serious national art.

Albéniz went to live in Paris in 1893, where he met Debussy and assimilated Debussy's advanced thinking about harmony. In 1899 Albéniz wrote a piano piece called *Catalonia,* his first serious effort to interpret his native land in tones. He orchestrated the piece, and it was successfully introduced at a concert of the Société Nationale de Musique in 1899—Albéniz' official debut as a composer.

He did not remain long in Paris. In 1900 he returned to his native land. Misfortune now haunted him. His wife succumbed to an incurable disease and was a chronic invalid; he himself was ill and frequently in pain.

He permitted neither tragedy nor personal suffering to interfere with his work. Indeed, during these terrible years he produced his greatest works, and those by which he is best known: the *Iberia* suite, for the piano, and *Navarra,* which he had left unfinished and which was completed by Déodat de Séverac.

Iberia, written between 1906 and 1909, is made up of twelve piano pieces in four

ISAAC ALBÉNIZ

books. The pieces evoke the sights and sounds of Spain: its exotic towns and harbors; its sensuous song and throbbing dance; its feast days and ceremonials; its exciting suburbs, taverns, and gypsy haunts. Five sections of *Iberia* were orchestrated by Enrique Fernández Arbós: *Evocación, El Corpus Christi en Sevilla, El Puerto, Triana,* and *El Albaicín.*

Individual sections of other suites for the piano are also celebrated for their impressions of Spanish scenes and backgrounds. In the nocturne "Córdoba," from *Cantos de España,* we have a picture of an Andalusian city with a Moorish background; "Sevillana," from *Suite Española,* brings us the poignant strains of a gypsy song; *Navarra* has the pulse- and heart-beat of the Spanish dance.

Modern Spanish music can be said to have been born with music such as this. Pedrell may have been the first to raise the torch of Spanish national music, but it was Albéniz who carried it, lighting the way for the Spanish composers who followed him (Granados, Turina, and Manuel de Falla). Pedrell was the theorist; it was Albéniz who put theory into practice.

The inspiration for Albéniz' best music was always some aspect of Spanish life; the materials he used were the rhythms of the Spanish dance and the languorous melodies of the Spanish gypsy song. Subject matter and idiom are so inextricably blended together that to listen to his music is to feel at once the very essence of Spain and its people.

"That in which Albéniz is inimitable," wrote G. Jean-Aubry in *La Musique et les Nations*, "is the atmosphere he creates around a theme, the living scenery with which he surrounds the 'melodic personage'—a word, a song, or a murmured confession. The method of Albéniz, if one can use such a word with regard to him, is almost inscrutable. It obeys only subtle and personal laws. An expressive counterpoint, always ductile and full of movement, supports his themes, plays with them or crosses them. The parts seem at times inextricably intermingled, and suddenly all is again resolved in lucidity."

Isaac Albéniz died in Cambo-les-Bains, in the French Pyrenees, on May 18, 1909. His body was brought to Barcelona, where—to the music of Fauré's Requiem and the funeral marches of Chopin, Beethoven, and Wagner—it was buried in the southwest churchyard.

MAJOR WORKS:

Choral Music—Cristo.

Operas—Enrico Clifford, 1895; Pepita Jiménez, 1896; Merlin, 1897-1906.

Orchestral Music—Catalonia, rhapsody, 1899.

Piano Music—Six Spanish Dances; Rapsodia Cubana; Rapsodia Española; Recuerdos de Viaje; Serenata Española; Chants d'Espagne; First Spanish Suite; Second Spanish Suite; España; Cantos de España (including (Córdoba); Suite Española (including Sevillana); Tango in D major; Iberia, four volumes; Navarra.

ABOUT:

Chase, G., Music of Spain; Collet, H., Albéniz et Granados; Van Vechten, C., In the Garret, Jean-Aubry, G., La Musique et les Nations.

Musical Times (London), December 1917; Musical Quarterly, January 1929.

Franco Alfano *1876-*

F RANCO ALFANO, composer of Italian operas, was born at Posilippo, near Naples, on March 8, 1876. His studies took place at the Naples Conservatory (with Serrao and De Nardis) and at the Leipzig Conservatory (with Jadassohn). His musical horizon was broadened in Germany through contact with German music. Solidity of form and an inventive harmonic language, found

FRANCO ALFANO

in several piano pieces published in Germany, betray the impact of this influence.

His first opera, *Miranda*, written in 1896, was poorly received. So was its successor, *La Fonte di Enscir*, which came two years later. But with *Risurrezione*, written when he was only twenty-seven, and introduced in Turin in 1904, he suddenly became famous. Dramatic and lyrical, *Risurrezione* (which is based on the novel of Tolstoy) carried on brilliantly the traditions of Italian opera. Referring to it as a "remarkable opera," Irving Schwerké wrote further in his book *Kings Jazz and David* that "the significant aspects of the score are the utilization of Russian themes without imitative purports, the poetic melancholy which pervades the work as a whole, the richness of the harmonic fabric, and the exalted characterization of the persons of the drama."

With the operas that followed, Alfano fulfilled the soaring promises of *Risurrezione*. *L'Ombra di Don Giovanni* (Milan, 1914), *La Leggenda di Sakuntala* (Bologna, 1921), and *Madonna Imperia* (Turin, 1927) were distinguished additions to the contemporary opera repertory. In these operas, Alfano established a style of his own in which the lyricism of the Italian school was successfully blended with the developed orchestration and harmonic writing of Wagner.

Indicative of his importance in Italian opera was the fact that when Giacomo Puccini died in 1924, Alfano was called upon to complete the master's last opera, *Turandot*. He fulfilled this assignment with such taste and fidelity to the composer's style that *Turandot*, as heard today, remains an integrated work defying detection as to where Puccini left off and Alfano took over.

In 1919 Alfano became director of the Liceo Musicale in Bologna. He held that post for seven years, then became director of the Liceo Musicale of Turin. Since 1937 he has been the director of the Rossini Conservatory in Pesaro.

MAJOR WORKS:

Chamber Music—Sonata for Violin and Piano, 1922; Sonata for Cello and Piano, 1924; 3 string quartets.

Operas—Miranda, 1896; La Fonte di Enscir, 1898; Risurrezione, 1904; La Leggenda di Sakuntala, 1921; Madonna Imperia, 1927; Cyrano de Bergerac, 1935; Il Dottor Antonio, 1949.

Orchestral Music—Suite Romantica, 1908; Symphony in E major, 1909; Symphony No. 2 in C minor, 1932.

ABOUT:

Schwerké, I., Kings Jazz and David; Musical Times (London), March 1921.

Hugo Alfvén *1872-*

H UGO ALFVÉN, Swedish composer, was born in Stockholm on May 1, 1872. After receiving preliminary training at the Stockholm Conservatory, he earned his living by playing the violin in various orchestras. A government stipend enabled him to continue his violin study with César Thomson in Brussels. In 1900 he was the recipient of a second stipend (the Jenny Lind), allowing him to travel and study for three years in Germany and France.

Back in his native land, he became teacher of composition and orchestration at the Stockholm Conservatory. In 1910 he was appointed musical director of the Royal University of Upsala, a post held until 1939. As a conductor of its chorus he traveled extensively throughout Europe, giving choral concerts. He visited the United States in 1938.

Walter Niemann once described Alfvén as the "only important symphonic composer

Courtesy of Etude
HUGO ALFVÉN

of the Swedish modern school." This was shortly before World War I. Indicative of Alfven's high station in the musical life of his country are the two awards he received in recognition of his services: the Wurttemberg Gold Medal, and the Swedish medal, "Litteris et Artibus."

In his best-known works for orchestra, Alfvén reveals himself to be a romanticist who has been strongly influenced by Brahms. His rhapsodies are the works of a nationalist who has skillfully employed Swedish folk melodies and dance rhythms. The most famous of these rhapsodies is the *Midsummer Vigil* (*Midsommarvaka*), inspired by the St. John's Eve festival revel in small Swedish towns. This work is built out of folk song and dance materials from the Schleswig-Holstein region of Germany.

This rhapsody was adapted into a ballet, *La Nuit de Saint-Jean*, and introduced in Paris by the Ballets Suédois, on October 25, 1925. Outstandingly successful, it was heard 134 times during that first season, and 119 times more in the next three years. Louis Schneider remarked that the ballet recreated "the personality of a people."

Alfvén has also written several fine symphonies, the first of which was completed when he was only twenty-five years old. An unidentified Swedish critic has said of Alfvén's symphonies that their "solidity and complexity of polyphonic style excite admiration."

MAJOR WORKS:

Chamber Music—Elegy, for horn and piano; Sonata in C, for violin and piano.

Choral Music—Baltic Exposition Cantata, op. 33; Ode on Gustavus Vasa, for soloists, chorus, and orchestra.

Orchestral Music—Symphony No. 1 in F minor, op. 7, 1897; Symphony No. 2 in D major, op. 11, 1899; The Bells, for baritone and orchestra, op. 13; Midsummer Vigil, rhapsody, op. 19; Ein Skargardssagen, tone poem, op. 20; Symphony No. 3 in E major, op. 23, 1905; Upsala Rhapsody, op. 24; Festspiel, op. 25; Drapa, op. 27; Symphony No. 4 in C minor, op. 39, 1919; Symphony No. 5 in A minor, 1952.

Stage Music—Den Bergtagna, pantomime, op. 37, 1923.

ABOUT:

Etude, March 1953.

Hendrik Andriessen *1892-*

HENDRIK ANDRIESSEN, Dutch composer, was born in Haarlem, on September 17, 1892, the son of a well-known organist and composer. He studied organ with Louis Robert and De Pauw, and composition with Bernard Zweers. His earliest works were primarily for the voice, revealing the influence of French composers. Eventually he realized a style of his own, particularly in his church music, in which contrapuntal skill was combined with intensity of expression and rhapsodic feeling.

Andriessen has distinguished himself in various musical activities other than the creative. From 1934 to 1939 he was organist at the Utrecht Cathedral where his performances and improvisations gave him an eminent place among contemporary organists. He has had a long and fruitful career as teacher and educator, first at the Amsterdam Conservatory, then at the Utrecht School of Music and the Utrecht Conservatory, finally (since 1949) as head of the Hague Royal Conservatory. He is also known as concert pianist, lecturer, and writer on musical subjects.

When the Dutch government, to celebrate the fiftieth anniversary of the reign of Queen Wilhelmina, commissioned him to write an opera in 1948, there was considerable surprise in Dutch music circles. Up to that time Andriessen had written nothing for the stage but had achieved his reputation in church music. With a text by Jan Engelman, based on an episode in Ovid's *Metamorphoses*, Andriessen produced an important opera, *Philomela*, successfully introduced at the Holland Music Festival at Amsterdam on June 23, 1950. In reporting the event for the *New York Times*, Daniel Schorr wrote that the work "looks like one of the most successful contemporary Dutch productions, ranking with some of the best musical theatre of the day."

Hendrik Andriessen's brother, Willem, is also an eminent musician—director of the Amsterdam Conservatory since 1937, and a talented pianist and composer.

MAJOR WORKS:

Chamber Music—Sonata for Violin and Piano, 1932; Trio, 1939; Pastorale, for flute, viola, and piano, 1942.

Choral Music—Missa Sponsa Christi, 1928; Qui Habitat, motet for a cappella chorus, 1933; Missa Diatonica, for a cappella chorus, 1935; Magnificat, 1937; Two Madrigals, 1940; Missa Christus Rex, 1942; Missa Lauda Sion 1944; Te Deum Laudamus, 1946; Missa Solemnis, 1946

Opera—Philomela, 1949.

Orchestral Music—Symphony No. 1, 1930; Ballade van den Merel, for narrator and orchestra, 1936; Symphony No. 2, 1937; Capriccio, 1941; Symphony no. 3, 1946; Ballet Suite, 1947; Concerto for Organ and Orchestra, 1950; Étude Symphonique, 1952.

HENDRIK ANDRIESSEN

Andriessen: än-drē'sĕn

Kurt Atterberg *1887-*

Th. Modin

KURT ATTERBERG

K URT ATTERBERG, one of Sweden's most distinguished composers, was born in Gothenburg, on December 12, 1887. He was graduated from the University of Gothenburg in 1907, and afterward attended the Royal Swedish Technical School as preparation for an engineering career. Music had always been a major interest. Atterberg combined engineering studies with a training in music, being a pupil at the Royal Conservatory in Stockholm in the class of Johann Andreas Hallen, and after that studying privately with Max von Schillings in Germany.

For several years, Atterberg served as engineer at the Stockholm Naval Station. From 1912 to 1937 he served in the Register Bureau at the Royal Patent Office, and from 1937 to 1940 he was its director. He devoted himself to various musical activities as well. He was conductor of the Dramatic School in Stockholm from 1913 to 1922; became music critic of the Stockholm *Tidningen* after 1919; toured Europe as a guest conductor following World War I.

At last a government subsidy enabled him to give up engineering for music. He continued his work as critic, conductor, and composer. In 1940 he became secretary of the Royal Academy of Music at Stockholm.

As a composer, Atterberg has been highly prolific. No other Swedish composer has had so many works published and performed at so early an age. Few other composers have been performed so extensively both in and out of Sweden. His major works include operas, ballets, and symphonies, as well as numerous compositions for choral and chamber-music groups. His writing has been described as "temperate, Nordic, neo-romantic . . . with a strong feeling for form and colorful orchestration."

Some of Atterberg's most popular works have drawn melodic and rhythmic materials from Swedish folk sources. One of these is the Symphony No. 4, in G minor, introduced in Stockholm in 1919. The two principal themes of the first movement have an identifiable folk character, while the last movement is filled with Swedish dance rhythms. The most famous of Atterberg's works is *A Värmland Rhapsody*, written in 1933 to honor Selma Lagerlöf, celebrated Swedish novelist, on her seventy-fifth birthday. This rhapsody is entirely based on Swedish folk melodies indigenous to the region associated with Lagerlöf's masterwork, *Gösta Berlings Saga. A Värmland Rhapsody* was introduced over the Swedish Radio on Selma Lagerlöf's birthday, November 20, 1933.

In 1928 Atterberg achieved international fame—and notoriety. His Fifth Symphony was entered in an international competition sponsored by the Columbia Phonograph Company to commemorate the centenary of Franz Schubert's death. It won the first prize of $10,000 and was performed by many of the world's leading orchestras. Some critics— Ernest Newman was one—pointed out how derivative Atterberg's music was, singling out actual quotations from works by Elgar, Glazunov, Rimsky-Korsakov, Dvořák, and other composers. Atterberg's rebuttal to this charge rocked the world of music. In an article entitled "How I Fooled the Music World," published in the *Musical Digest* (February 1, 1929), Atterberg admitted that he had been guilty of such quotations, insisted that these borrowings had been deliberate, and revealed that he had intended his symphony to be a satire on so-called connoisseurs of Schubert. In short, said Atterberg, he had

Atterberg: ăt'tĕr-bĕr-y'

planned his work not as a serious artistic production, but as a hoax.

MAJOR WORKS:

Ballets—Per Svinaherde, op. 9; The Foolish Virgins, op. 17.

Chamber Music—String Quartet, op. 11; Suite, for string quartet, op. 29.

Choral Music—Requiem, op. 8.

Operas—Härward der Harfner, op. 12, 1918; Bäckahästen, op. 24, 1924; Fanal, op. 35, 1932; Aladdin, op. 43, 1941; The Storm, op. 49, 1947.

Orchestral Music—Symphony No. 1 in B minor, op. 3, 1911; Overture, op. 4; Symphony No. 2 in F major, op. 6, 1913; Concerto for Violin and Orchestra, op. 7; Symphony No. 3, Pictures from the West Coast, op. 10, 1916; Symphony No. 4, op. 14, 1918; Concerto for Cello and Orchestra, op. 21; Symphony No. 5, Funereal, op. 20, 1922; Rondeau Retrospectif, op. 26; Symphony No. 6, in C major, op. 31, 1928; A Värmland Rhapsody, op. 36; Suite No. 4, Turandot; Suite No. 5, Baroque; Suite No. 6, Oriental Legend; Symphony No. 7, Romantic, op. 45, 1942; Symphony No. 8, op. 48, 1944.

LOUIS AUBERT

Louis Aubert *1877*-

L OUIS FRANÇOIS MARIE AUBERT belongs with those contemporary French composers—among them are found Ravel and Schmitt—who drew their guidance and inspiration from Gabriel Fauré. Aubert was born in Paramé, Ille-et-Vilaine, on February 19, 1877. At the Paris Conservatory (where his teachers included Fauré, Diémer, Vidal, Lavignac, and D'Indy) he won several prizes. So superior was his talent at playing the piano that some of his teachers urged him to consider seriously the possibility of becoming a virtuoso. For a while Aubert concertized in France with some success. But composition appealed so strongly to him that, after a few years, he felt impelled to give up the concert stage for good so that he might have more time for creative work. By 1901, he had developed as a composer to the point where he was seriously considered for the Prix de Rome. Only the fact that he had been recently married disqualified him.

In 1902 Aubert began writing in the larger forms. A major work was *La Légende du Sang*, for narrator, chorus, and orchestra, giving evidence of his ripening talent.

Aubert has not been a prolific composer. His writing is in a poetic vein, highly atmospheric and emotionally sensitive. It is pol-

ished in its craftsmanship. One of his most famous works is the *Habanera* for orchestra, which scored a decided success when it was introduced in Paris on March 22, 1919. This work derives its name from the rhythm of the habanera, the rhythm growing and developing slowly throughout the entire piece. The music is not essentially an evocation of the Spanish dance, but rather an interpretation of a passage from one of Baudelaire's prose poems: "Let me breathe long, long, the fragrance of your hair."

Other distinguished works by Aubert include his opera, *La Forêt Bleue*, performed successfully both in Geneva and Boston in 1913; *Les Crépuscules d' Automne*, for voice and piano; *Nuit Mauresque*, for voice and orchestra.

During World War I, Aubert was organist at the St. Hippolyte Church in Paris. For many years after that he was a member of the faculty of the Paris Conservatory.

One of Aubert's works was inspired by World War II. It is called *Offrande*, for orchestra, written in 1947 as a tribute to "all victims of the war." Following its premiere in Luxembourg on November 11, 1947, it was heard in France and New York City.

MAJOR WORKS:

Ballets—La Momie, 1903; Chrysothémis, 1904; La Nuit Ensorcelée, 1922; Belebat, 1938.

Aubert: ō-bâr'

Chamber Music—Quintet, for piano and strings; Introduction and Allegro, for flute and piano, 1922; Sonata for Violin and Piano, 1927.

Opera—La Forêt Bleue, fairy opera, 1907.

Orchestral Music—Fantasy in B minor, for piano and orchestra, 1899; Six Poèmes Arabes, song cycle for voice and orchestra, 1907; Nuit Mauresque, for voice and orchestra, 1911; Suite Brève, 1912; Habanera, 1919; Dryade, 1924; Caprice, for violin and orchestra, 1925; Offrande, 1947.

Piano Music—Trois Esquisses, 1900; Sillages, three pieces, 1913.

Vocal Music—Crépuscules d'Automne, for voice and piano, 1910.

ABOUT:

Vuillemin, L., Louis Aubert et Son Œuvre.

GEORGES AURIC

Georges Auric *1899-*

GEORGES AURIC was born in the town of Lodève, Hérault, France, on February 15, 1899. When he was still a child, his family moved to Paris where he was brought up. Composition began early. When he was fifteen, he wrote three songs, *Interludes*, performed at a concert of the Société Nationale.

He began his music study at the Paris Conservatory, and continued it at the Schola Cantorum with Vincent d'Indy and Albert Roussel. His fellow pupils included Francis Poulenc, Darius Milhaud, and Germaine Tailleferre. All of them were influenced by Erik Satie, then very much the iconoclast in French music rebelling against excessive emotion, large forms, pretentious writing, and preciousness. Satie looked disapprovingly on composers who took themselves and their art too seriously, and felt that a much more human approach to art was called for. The younger men—Auric, Milhaud, Poulenc— would sit at their favorite Parisian café listening to Satie's theories and beliefs which, before long, they assimilated as their own. They took to writing music that was simple in approach, intimate in form and (through the absorption of music-hall tendencies) popular in appeal.

Their music was originally performed at a painter's studio in the Rue Huyghens, the first concert taking place on June 6, 1917. On January 15, 1918, a public concert of their works (together with works by two other young Frenchmen) was heard at Vieux Colombier in Paris. Some time after this

there appeared an album of piano pieces by Auric, Poulenc, Tailleferre, Milhaud, Honegger, and Durey. A review of this music, in *Comoedia* on January 16, 1920—written by Henri Collet—was entitled "The Five Russians and the Six French," even though the connection between the two groups was not altogether clear. It was as a result of this review, and its caption, that the sobriquet of "French Six" was henceforth applied to these young French composers; and it was as the "French Six" that these composers attracted considerable publicity.

"The reaction in which . . . colleagues of the Six all shared to a greater or less extent," explained Eric Blom, "led to a careful avoidance of anything savoring in the least of romantic sentiment and poetic delicacy. The result was music characterized by a love of plain statement and a frankness of humor sometimes bordering on pretension and vulgarity, but often not without a certain youthful charm."

Actually, the French Six was never an integrated school of composers in the way that the Russian Five was. It was true that all these six composers were united by their rebellion against existing tendencies, but this was a nebulous tie. Each composer had his own individual style and, almost from the very beginning, insisted on going in his own direction, uninfluenced by what his fellow composers were doing. Darius Milhaud emphasized this point in an article in *Anbruch*. "We, the Six, had different types of musical education, and this contributed to the independence of our individual thinking, taste and style. . . . In view of this, how can we be regarded as slaves of a single code of esthetics, one theory?" The career of the French Six was, therefore, of brief duration. After a few ventures in giving concerts collaboratively, and a single venture in writing music collaboratively, the six composers parted company.

After producing some notable songs, particularly on eight poems of Jean Cocteau in 1917, Auric turned to the ballet, the field in which he has since been most successful. His first attempt was a collaboration with four other members of the French Six— Honegger, Milhaud, Poulenc, and Tailleferre: *Les Mariés de la Tour Eiffel*, on a text by Jean Cocteau, commissioned by Serge Diaghilev, and introduced at the Théâtre des Champs Elysées on June 18, 1921. Auric's contribution to this strange enterprise was an overture, *The Fourteenth of July*, which —in Jean Cocteau's description—"evoked the powerful charm of the streets, the people on holiday, the little bandstands that resemble guillotines, and about which drums and cornets incite clerks and girls and sailors to dance. His soft trills accompany the miming in the same way that a circus orchestra repeats a tune interminably during an acrobatic act."

Without benefit of collaborators, Auric soon produced two important ballet scores for Diaghilev's Ballet Busse: *Les Fâcheux* (after Molière), introduced in Monte Carlo in January 1924, and *Les Matelots* (text by Boris Kochno), first seen on June 17, 1925. The music of both ballets was light, popular, occasionally satiric. Auric now produced other highly successful ballet scores, notably *La Pastorale* in 1926 and *La Concurrence* in 1931, both presented by the Ballet Russe.

Among Auric's more recent contributions to the ballet repertory are: *Le Peintre et Son Modèle*, based on the story of Pygmalion, introduced in Paris by Massine on November 16, 1949; *Phèdre*, his first serious subject, first performed by Tamara Toumanova at the Paris Opéra on May 23, 1950; *Les Chaises Musicales*, based on the old parlor game of musical chairs, seen in New York

in 1951; and *Coup de Feu*, introduced at the Paris Opéra on May 7, 1952, during the Exposition of the Masterpieces of the Twentieth Century.

Auric has written many distinguished scores for motion-pictures, including *Moulin Rouge*, starring José Ferrer. He has also contributed the music for films by Jean Cocteau, among them *Sang d'un Poète*, *La Belle et la Bête*, and *Orpheus*. In 1953 he won first prize at the Venice cinema festival for his score for Sartre's *La Putaine Respectueuse*.

Auric now has little sympathy for advanced tendencies in contemporary music, and looks disdainfully on such new musical systems as the twelve-tone technique of Schoenberg. "It is all very well to escape from the classical tonal system," he has said. "But to bind oneself to a system still more rigid—that is simply terrible." His musical sympathies reach far into the past, to the fifteenth and sixteenth centuries.

MAJOR WORKS:

Ballets—Les Fâcheux, 1923; Les Matelots, 1925; La Pastorale, 1926; La Concurrence, 1931; Le Peintre et Son Modèle, 1949; Phèdre, 1950; La Pierre Enchantée, 1950; Les Chaises Musicales, 1951; Coup de Feu, 1952; Chemin de Lumière, 1952.

Chamber Music—Sonata for Violin and Piano, 1937; Trio, for oboe, clarinet, and bassoon, 1938.

Choral Music—Songs on Fifteenth Century Poems, for four a cappella choruses, 1942.

Opera—Path to the Light, 1951.

Orchestral Music—Overture, 1937.

Piano Music—Sonata, 1931.

Vocal Music—Three Interludes, 1914; Eight Poems of Jean Cocteau, 1917; Five Poems of Gerard de Nerval, 1925; Three Poems of Léon Paul Fargue, 1940; Five Poems of Paul Éluard, 1941; Three Poems of Max Jacob, 1946.

ABOUT:

Milhaud, D., Notes Without Music.

Hank Badings 1907-

HANK BADINGS, Dutch composer, was born in Bandoeng, Java, on January 17, 1907. Some early study of the violin was followed by five years of training in composition with Willem Pijper. He combined his musical interests with the study of engineer-

Badings: bä′dĕngz

HANK BADINGS

ing at the Technical University in Delft, receiving his diploma *cum laude* in 1931.

From 1935 to 1937, Badings was a demonstrator at the Delft Technical University. Then, abandoning engineering entirely for music, he accepted the post of professor at the Amsterdam Music Lyceum. He has since held several other major posts as teacher and educator: professor at the Rotterdam Conservatory; director of the Music Lyceum at The Hague; and director of the government Conservatory at The Hague.

His early works were marked by a tragic expression that permeates not only the slow movements of his symphonies and chamber-music works, but also the heroic fast movements. This preoccupation with tragedy is evident also in his choice of melancholy texts for songs: poems by Copla, Vildrac, Rilke, and Dullaert.

Gradually, a lighter and gayer mood was injected into his writing, apparent in his ballet *Orpheus and Eurydice* and in his comic opera *Love Intrigues*. From 1941 on this lighter touch was combined with greater economy of materials, transparency, and simplification of style. However, even the more complicated works written before 1941 are agreeable to listen to, since he always combined advanced thinking in harmony and counterpoint with spacious and emotional melodies. In 1946 Badings was brought up on charges of wartime collaboration with the

Nazis. He was found guilty, and for two years barred from all professional activities. These charges were later reexamined, and Badings was completely exonerated.

MAJOR WORKS:

Ballet—Orpheus and Eurydice, 1941.

Chamber Music—Quintet for Wind Instruments, 1929; Sonata No. 1 for Violin and Piano, 1933; Trio, 1934; Quartet No. 2, for strings, 1935; Sonata No. 2 for Violin and Piano, 1939; Sonata for Violin Solo, 1940; Sonata for Cello Solo, 1941; Quartet No. 3, for strings, 1943; Trio, for oboe, clarinet, and bassoon, 1943; Trio, for two violins and viola. 1945; Trio, for three oboes, 1945; Quartet for Brass Instruments, 1947.

Choral Music—Honestum Petimus Usque, for soprano, male chorus, female chorus, and orchestra, 1937; Apocalypse, oratorio, 1942.

Operas—Love Intrigues, comic opera, 1941; The Night Watch, 1943.

Orchestral Music—Symphony No. 1, 1930; Symphony No. 2, 1932; Symphony No. 3, 1934; Symphonic Variations, 1937; Tragic Overture, 1937; Heroic Overture, 1938; Concerto for Piano and Orchestra, 1939; Songs of Life and Death, for tenor and orchestra, 1940; Symphony No. 4, 1943; Concerto No. 3 for Violin and Orchestra, 1944; Concerto No. 4 for Violin and Orchestra, 1946; Overture, 1948; Concerto No. 2 for Cello and Orchestra, 1948; Songs on Texts by Copla, for contralto and orchestra, 1948; Symphony No. 5, 1948; Ballad: Symphonic Variations on a Dutch Folksong, 1950.

Piano Music—Suite, 1930; Sonatas Nos. 1-6, 1934-47.

Vocal Music—Three Songs on texts from Boutens' Lentemaan, for contralto, with flute, clarinet, violin, viola, and cello, 1931; Three Duets, for soprano, contralto, and strings, 1948; Songs with piano accompaniment.

Sir Granville Bantock *1868-1946*

SIR GRANVILLE BANTOCK was born in London on August 7, 1868. His father, a well-known surgeon and gynecologist, intended him first for chemical engineering, then for the Indian Civil Service. Since Granville Bantock did not at first appear to be particularly musical he did not dispute his father's wishes. A few lessons in harmony and counterpoint at Trinity College, however, convinced him that he wanted to be a professional musician. In 1889 he entered the Royal Academy of Music. Talent, combined with industry, enabled him, after a single term, to win the Macfarren Scholar-

Elliott & Fry

SIR GRANVILLE BANTOCK

ship for composition, of which he was the first recipient.

During his student days at the Academy, Bantock wrote several works, including a ballet suite, *Rameses II*, and a dramatic cantata, *The Fire-Worshippers*. Already there was in evidence his later passion for oriental subjects.

In 1893, on a little less than fifteen pounds, he founded the *New Quarterly Musical Review* which, under his editorship, became a leading journal of musical opinion for a period of three years. At this time, he supported himself by conducting orchestras for musical shows in the provinces. After the *Review* suspended publication, Bantock devoted himself more intensively than before to conducting. In 1897 he became musical director at the Tower in New Brighton, where he conducted band concerts intended for dancing and light entertainment. Bantock added strings, and before long startled his audiences by including on his programs the serious works of leading British composers; indeed, on several occasions he directed all-British programs. In 1898 he founded the New Brighton Choral Society, and some time after this became director of the Runcorn Philharmonic Society and the Liverpool Philharmonic.

In 1898 he married Helen F. Schweitzer, a gifted poetess, who not only supplied him with the lyrics for some of his best songs, but was also the inspiration for one of his finest orchestral works, *Helena Variations*.

It was not until the turn of the century that Bantock achieved recognition as a composer. In 1909 he completed *Omar Khayyam*; parts of this work were introduced at the Birmingham Triennial Music Festival. The entire work was heard at festivals in Cardiff and Leeds, and after that in London and Vienna. The rich oriental flavor of melody and harmony and the striking orchestral colors made a deep impression.

The oriental influence is evident in many other Bantock works. But it is not the only one in his music. A great variety of influences is found in the extensive repertory of his works: Scotch (*Hebridean Symphony* and the opera *The Seal Woman*); pagan (*The Great God Pan* and the *Pagan Symphony*); biblical (*Vanity of Vanities, Saul, Christus*, and the music for *Pilgrim's Progress*); Elizabethan (the songs). Whatever the influence, the style remained sensuous and exotic, touched with modern idioms. His music, which is mostly programmatic, is richly harmonized and orchestrated, is filled with spacious melodies, and is highly imaginative. He always aimed for—and usually realized—a poetic, objective beauty. Sidney Grew wrote: "His best music comes at suggestions of evening, heavy odors, aspects of physical beauty, flowers of various types, passion in a state of repose, and languid yearning."

Of Bantock's many works for orchestra, the best include the *Hebridean Symphony* and the comedy overture inspired by Ernest Dowson's fantasy, *Pierrot of the Minute*. His most distinguished works for chorus include the *Omar Khayyam* and *Vanity of Vanities*.

Bantock also distinguished himself as an educator. He succeeded Sir Edward Elgar as professor of music at the University of Birmingham. After that he became principal of the Midland Institute School of Music, also in Birmingham. In his sixty-fifth year he returned to his alma mater, Trinity College, to join its music faculty. He was knighted in 1930.

During the last decade of his life, Bantock traveled extensively, making several trips around the world to fulfill his office as wandering examiner for Trinity College. In his seventieth year he flew from New York to Barbados to conduct examinations. He died in London of pneumonia on October 16, 1946.

Bantock was notorious for his unconventional dress. The newspapers once remarked that he was probably the first man to attend a University faculty meeting in corduroys. He detested formal evening wear. Once when compelled to wear a high hat for a public function, he returned home and smashed it in silent rage. His favorite attire was that of an oriental sheik; visitors coming to see him often found him dressed in oriental splendor from head to foot.

MAJOR WORKS:

Ballets—Egypt, 1892; The Enchanted Garden, 1916.

Chamber Music—Sonata in F major, for violin and piano; Sonata for Cello and Piano.

Choral Music—The Fire Worshippers, cantata, 1892; Time Spirit, rhapsody for chorus and orchestra, 1902; Omar Khayyam, 1909; Prometheus Unbound; Atalanta in Calydon, choral symphony, 1912; The Vanity of Vanities, choral symphony, 1914; Pilgrim's Progress, 1928; Christus, oratorio; King Solomon, for narrator, chorus, and orchestra, 1937.

Opera—The Seal Woman, 1924.

Orchestral Music—Helena Variations, 1900; Thalba, the Destroyer, 1900; Hudibras, 1902; The Witch of Atlas, 1902; Thorvema's Dream, for narrator and orchestra, 1903; Lalla Rookh, 1903; The Great God Pan, 1903; Pierrot of the Minute, comedy overture, 1908; Dante and Beatrice, 1910; Overture to a Greek Tragedy, 1911; Fifine at the Fair, 1911; Hebridean Symphony, 1915; Pagan Symphony, 1916.

Piano Music—Old English Suite; Dramatic Sketches.

Vocal Music—Songs of the East (six albums).

ABOUT:

Anderton, O., Granville Bantock; Musical Opinion (London), December 1946; Musical Quarterly, July 1918; Musical Times (London), November 1946.

Elsa Barraine *1910-*

ELSA BARRAINE was born in Paris on February 13, 1910. Both parents were professional musicians. Her father was a cellist in the orchestra of the Paris Opéra, while her mother was a singer. Even before

Barraine: bă-rĕn′

Photo-Lipnitzki

ELSA   BARRAINE

she had learned to read or write, Elsa Barraine studied the piano. She started improvising soon after taking her first lessons, and by the time she was ten began composing serious works.

She attended the Paris Conservatory where her teachers included Dukas and Vidal. In 1928 she won the second Prix de Rome, and one year later the Prix de Rome.

Following her stay in Italy, she returned to Paris and earned her living writing music for the movies and the theatre, work which she considered sheer drudgery. She did not neglect more serious endeavor. *Trois Esquisses* was her first orchestral work to get a major performance; it was introduced in Paris by the Straram Orchestra in 1931. In 1937 she was commissioned to write *Fêtes des Colonies* for the Paris Exposition. A year after that the French government commissioned her to write the Second Symphony, which has been widely performed.

For a long time, Barraine combined creative work with hack jobs. "When I am broke," she explains, "I am willing to take any kind of a job at all." She has led choirs, served as sound engineer for a Paris radio station, done accompanying. Since 1946 she has abandoned virtually all activity that keeps her from writing music, living as best she can from the income of her serious works.

During World War II she did no composing whatsoever, devoting herself entirely to the Resistance movement. Only after the liberation of France did she return to music. She has since then written a Third Symphony, a ballet *(Le Mur)* produced by the Champs Élysées Ballet, and an orchestral work *(Le Fleuve Rouge)* commissioned by the French Radio. The *Ouvrage de Dame,* for wind quintet, was given in Paris in the spring of 1952 during the Exposition of the Masterpieces of the Twentieth Century.

She respects those composers who go in for experiments, but her own bent is for lyricism, and she expresses her deepest and inmost feelings within traditional forms.

MAJOR WORKS:

Ballet—Le Mur, op. 88, 1947.

Chamber Music—Ouvrage de Dame, for wind quintet, op. 64, 1939; Trio, for strings, op. 65, 1939.

Choral Music—Les Cinq Plaies, cantata, 1952.

Orchestral Music—Trois Esquisses, op. 27, 1931; Symphony No. 1, op. 28, 1931; Pogromes, tone poem, op. 38, 1933; Fantaisie Concertante, for piano and orchestra, op. 39, 1933; Three Hebrew Songs for Children (Bialik), for voice and orchestra, op. 43, 1935; Fêtes des colonies, op. 61, 1937; Symphony No. 2, op. 62, 1938; Avis, for chorus and orchestra, op. 66, 1944; Le Fleuve Rouge, variations, op. 71, 1945; Symphony No. 3: The Paris Insurrection, 1949.

Piano Music—Pièce, op. 16, 1929; Prelude, op. 24, 1930; Suite, op. 33, 1932; Nocturne, op. 36, 1933; Six Indicatifs, op. 101, 1950.

Vocal Music—Vocalise, op. 26, 1930; Silence sur la Vie, op. 80, 1946; Devant Notre Porte, op. 83, 1947; Elisabeth, op. 99, 1949.

Henri Barraud *1900-*

HENRI BARRAUD was born in Bordeaux, France, on April 23, 1900. While employed in his father's wine firm he began studying music by himself, then took lessons with a local teacher, Fernand Vaubourgoin. In 1926 he entered the Paris Conservatory where he studied with Aubert, Dukas, and Caussade. After his graduation he concentrated on creative work. Such early works as the *Poem,* for orchestra, written in 1934, and the *Concerto da Camera,* completed two years later, suggested his later mature style. Both works were impressionistic in their writing, rich in lyricism, poetic in content, and sound in construction.

Barraud: bă-rō′

Photo-Lipnitzki

HENRI BARRAUD

In 1937 Barraud served as director of music at the International Exposition in Paris, and led several performances at the Opéra Comique. On the day that he completed his Concerto for Piano and Orchestra, in August of 1939, a member of the Garde Mobile came to tell him to rejoin the Seventeenth Infantry Regiment at Mans, of which he was Reserve Lieutenant, and which had just been remobilized. Barraud served in the French army during World War II. After the defeat of France, he hid in Marseilles, where he was active in the Resistance movement.

Out of the experiences of World War II came one of Barraud's most poignant works, *Offrande à une Ombre,* for orchestra. This music reflects the grim spirit of the French patriot in time of war and duress. A correspondent for *Musical America* described the work as follows: "A long melodic line of lovely grace, freely drawn and contrapuntally treated, is followed by a tense war-like section, evoking the hero's part in the struggle, which ends abruptly with a drum roll and a tamtam crash clearly depicting the rendezvous with death." Barraud originally intended dedicating the composition to the memory of Maurice Jaubert, a French composer killed during the war. But his own brother had been shot by the Gestapo at the Camp of Souge on August 1, 1944, and Barraud extended his dedication to include him as well. *Offrande à une Ombre* was introduced in this country on January 10, 1947, by the St. Louis Symphony under Vladimir Golschmann.

One of Barraud's most ambitious works to date is the five-part oratorio, *The Mystery of the Holy Innocents,* based on a text from the third "mystery" of Charles Péguy. This oratorio was first heard over the Paris Radio on May 8, 1947, Manuel Rosenthal conducting. It was introduced to this country by the Boston Symphony Orchestra under Serge Koussevitzky on December 1, 1950.

Since the liberation of France, Barraud has served as director of music of the Radio-diffusion Française in Paris.

MAJOR WORKS:

Ballets—L'Astrologue dans le Puits; Le Diable à la Kermesse, 1943.

Chamber Music—Concerto da Camera, for thirty instruments, 1936; Trio, for oboe, clarinet and bassoon.

Choral Music—Mystery of the Holy Innocents, oratorio, 1947.

Opera—La Farce de Maître Pathelin, opéra-comique.

Orchestral Music—Final; Poem, 1934; Concerto for Piano and Orchestra, 1936; Le Feu; Suite pour une Comédie de Musset; Offrande à une Ombre, 1943; Overture to Numace, 1948; Preludes, for strings.

Piano Music—Preludes (two series).

Béla Bartók *1881-1945*

(See *American Composers Today*)

Sir Arnold Bax *1883-1953*

SIR ARNOLD TREVOR BAX was born in London on November 8, 1883. He was entered in the Royal Conservatory of Music in his seventeenth year, studying piano and composition with Matthay and Corder, respectively. His studies over, Bax devoted himself completely to composition. Being financially independent, he was never compelled to hold any official post, and could therefore indulge the luxury of allowing nothing to distract him from his creative work.

In 1910 Bax visited Russia, reflecting his impressions in several piano pieces. This

SIR ARNOLD BAX

visit to Russia also inspired his ballet, *The Truth about Russian Dancers,* to a scenario by Barrie, written in 1912-13. But a much more permanent and significant influence on Bax's creative thinking was the Celtic. Bax had Celtic blood in him; he had spent considerable time in Ireland; he was in personal contact with some of the most influential figures in the Celtic revival. Besides all this, he had an intense love for Irish folklore, culture, ideals. He began writing music in which Celtic spirit, design, color, and imagery were strongly evident.

His first Celtic work came in 1909, the beautiful tone poem, *In the Faëry Hills,* in which the dreams and colors of Irish lore are recreated in music. Another of Bax's celebrated Celtic tone poems was *The Garden of Fand,* written in 1916. But the most frequently heard and possibly finest of all these orchestral works was *Tintagel,* completed in 1917, evoking in music of great atmospheric beauty the image of Tintagel, a castle-crowned cliff as seen from the heights of Cornwall.

"The most pronounced characteristic of Celtic art is the sense of decoration and sharply defined imagery which they evince," wrote Leigh Henry of Bax's Celtic music in *Musical Opinion* (May 1926). "The outcome of that keen delight in color and sensatory stimuli which underlay the Celtic love of display and luxury was noted by Diodorus and Posidonius in the early historical records. This sense is markedly manifest even in the earliest Celtic proverbs, which embody a wealth of metaphorical imagery unequaled by any of the occidental race. . . . It is some such picturesque pageantry of vivid images that moves through the music of Arnold Bax."

Not all of Bax's music is inspired by Irish lore. In such works as the tone poem *November Woods,* the Quintet for Oboe and Strings, and the Third and Fourth symphonies, he is the poet and the romanticist—the "potential dreamer, the visionary, the nature lover," as Lawrence Gilman described him, who belongs not essentially "to this indurated and brass-bound age, but to an earlier and forgotten world of sensibility and beauty."

A man of extraordinary modesty, Bax lived in complete retirement, jealously guarding his privacy. He was knighted in 1937, and in 1942 he succeeded the late Sir Walford Davies as Master of the King's Musick. His autobiography, *Farewell My Youth,* appeared in 1942. He died in Cork, Ireland, on October 3, 1953.

MAJOR WORKS:

Ballets—The Truth about Russian Dancers (Barrie), 1913; Between Dusk and Dawn, 1917.

Chamber Music—Quintet for Piano and Strings, 1914-15; Sonata No. 2 for Violin and Piano, 1915; Four Pieces for Flute and Piano, 1916; Quartet No. 1 in G major, 1918; Sonata for Viola and Piano, 1921; Quartet for Piano and Strings, 1923; Quintet for Oboe and Strings, 1923; Quartet No. 2 in E minor, 1924; Fantasy Sonata for Harp and Viola, 1927; Sonata No. 3 for Violin and Piano, 1927; Nonet, 1931; Concerto for Flute, Harp, Oboe, and Strings, 1934; Quartet No. 3 in F major, 1936; Concerto for Bassoon, Harp, and String Sextet, 1936; Elegiac Trio, for harp, flute and viola; Legend Sonata for Cello and Piano, 1943.

Choral Music—Fatherland, for two sopranos, chorus, and orchestra, 1907; Enchanted Summer (Shelley), for tenor solo, chorus and orchestra, 1909; Mater Ora Filium, motet for unaccompanied chorus, 1922; St. Patrick's Breastplate, for chorus and orchestra, 1923; Walsinghame, for tenor, chorus, and orchestra, 1927; The Morning Watch, 1935.

Orchestral Music—In the Faëry Hills, tone poem, 1909; The Garden of Fand, tone poem, 1916; Symphonic Variations, for piano and orchestra, 1917; November Woods, tone poem, 1917; Tintagel, tone poem, 1917; Phantasy for Viola and Orchestra, 1920; Mediterranean, tone poem, 1921; Symphony No. 1 in E-flat minor, 1922; Symphony No. 2 in E minor, 1925; Symphony No. 3 in C major, 1929;

Overture, Elegy and Rondo, 1929; Overture to a Picaresque Comedy, 1930; Winter Legends, for piano and orchestra, 1930; The Tale the Pine Trees Knew, tone poem, 1931; Symphony No. 4 in E-flat major, 1931; Concerto for Cello and Orchestra, 1932; Symphony No. 5 in E minor, 1933; Symphony No. 6 in C minor, 1934; Rogues Comedy Overture, 1936; Concerto for Violin and Orchestra, 1937; Symphony No. 7 in A-flat major, 1939; Concerto for Orchestra with Piano (Left Hand), 1949.

Piano Music—A Mountain Mood, 1915; Sonata No. 1 in F-sharp minor, 1919; Sonata No. 2 in G minor, 1919; Sonata No. 3 in G-sharp minor, 1925; Paean, 1928; Sonata No. 4 in G major, 1932.

Vocal Music—A Celtic Song Cycle (McLeod), 1904; Five Irish Songs, 1921; Three Irish Songs (Colum), 1922.

ABOUT:

Bacharach, A. L. (ed.) British Music of Our Time; Bax, A., Farewell My Youth; Hull, R. H., A Handbook on Arnold Bax Symphonies; Musical Quarterly, April 1923.

Alban Berg *1885-1935*

ALBAN BERG was one of the major figures in the Schoenberg school of twelve-tone composition. He was born in Vienna on February 9, 1885. He had no formal musical training until he reached full maturity, even though he began composing when he was fifteen years old.

He became a government official in 1905, and only his leisure hours were devoted to musical interests. Meanwhile, in his nineteenth year he had met Arnold Schoenberg, then teaching in Vienna. Schoenberg's influence on the younger man was decisive. It was Schoenberg who converted Berg's musical pursuits from an avocation to a life's mission. Inspired by his teacher, Berg gave up his government position, and began an intensive period of study with Schoenberg. When Schoenberg went to Berlin, Berg followed him there.

Inevitably, Berg assimilated Schoenberg's theories, adopted Schoenberg's atonal style of composition, and became an apostle of musical expressionism. But this did not take place until Berg had gone through the growing pains of Wagnerism (Piano Sonata, op. 1, written in 1908) and French impressionism (String Quartet, op. 3, and Four Pieces for Clarinet and Piano, op. 5, both written in 1913).

Berg: bĕrk

On March 31, 1913, there took place the first public performance of some of Berg's music. Two numbers from the provocative *Five Songs for Orchestra*, op. 4, were heard in Vienna at a concert of the Academic Society for Literature and Music which was devoted entirely to the works of Schoenberg and his disciples. The concert developed into a riot.

During World War I, Berg served in the Austrian Army, despite his poor health. When the war ended, Berg returned to composition and resumed an ambitious project he had begun as early as 1914. Before the war, Berg had witnessed a performance of Georg Büchner's expressionistic play, *Wozzeck*, which made a profound impression on him. He saw the possibilities the play held for operatic treatment. By 1917 he had completed a workable libretto. With the war over, Berg had the leisure to write the music. He completed his score in 1920.

In 1924 three excerpts from the opera were introduced at the Frankfurt Music Festival. The unorthodox music aroused considerable dissension. So much attention did it attract, favorable as well as unfavorable, that the opera was accepted for performance by the Berlin State Opera. It was performed on December 14, 1925, Erich Kleiber conducting, and created a sensation. Some progressive-thinking musicians recognized it as a landmark in the evolution of opera. Most, however, found it unintelligible, and annihilated it with devastating criticism.

Berg provided the following explanation of his artistic purpose in writing *Wozzeck:* "Aside from the desire to create good music, to fill out—so to speak—the intellectual content of Büchner's immortal play, to translate his poetic idiom into a musical one, I intended, at the moment when I decided to compose the opera, nothing more than to bring to the theatre that which by right belongs to the theatre. I wanted to create music at every moment conscious of its responsibility to drama."

The celebrated musicologist Alfred Einstein has written the following illuminating analysis of the opera: *"Wozzeck* is ... from beginning to end both impressionistic and expressionistic. It is music drawn from Wozzeck's poor, worried, inarticulate, chaotic soul. It is a vision in sound. The

Trude Fleischmann
ALBAN BERG

orchestra is just like a bundle of nerves; at first sight it seems to consist only of confused strands, but it is actually a living organism. The events seem to be part of a dream; they are distorted as in some fantastic nightmare; even the folk-song element is distorted too. But even the noise proves to be expression, and the naturalism style. In the crucial scene, when Wozzeck becomes aware of Marie's infidelity, a chamber orchestra is used as well as the full orchestra, to represent the subconscious ideas of 'blood' and 'knife'—ideas with which Wozzeck toys for the first time. The chorus of sleeping soldiers is also a chorus of ghosts. The work is full of what lies behind and beneath our ordinary waking life. . . . What makes this work so unique and so convincing is that in this one particular case we have a composer whose technique from the first to the last is in perfect accord with his purpose of giving expression to the poem."

Wozzeck is complex, dissonant, unorthodox. It is unusual in its use of classical forms within the operatic framework; it is provocative in its orchestration; it is unconventional in its use of harrowing free-recitatives *(Sprechstimme)* in place of arias. Notwithstanding its strangeness and newness, *Wozzeck* was performed in opera houses throughout Europe. In ten years' time it was heard more than 150 times in twenty-eight different cities. It was introduced in the United States in 1931 under the direction of Leopold Stokowski, and it entered the repertory of the New York City Opera Company in 1952. It was heard at the Salzburg Festival in the summer of 1951, and one year later in Paris during the Exposition of Masterpieces of the Twentieth Century.

Berg did not produce many works after *Wozzeck*. He was too fastidious a craftsman and too exacting an artist to be prolific. But each work of his had originality, power, and sometimes compelling beauty. Most notable were the *Lyric Suite* (particularly impressive for the expressive and melodic way the twelve-tone system was used), the opera *Lulu* (which he left uncompleted, but which was introduced at the Municipal Theatre in Zurich on June 2, 1937), and the Concerto for Violin and Orchestra. The Concerto, one of the most deeply moving of his works, was written as an elegy to a young girl, a friend of the composer. But it turned out to be Berg's own requiem, his last piece of music. It was introduced by Louis Krasner in Barcelona on April 19, 1936.

Berg has been described as the romanticist of the twelve-tone technique. In this system a musical composition is built out of a row of twelve tones, each different and of equal importance, and none of which can be repeated till the others are used. There are various different and highly intricate ways in which the twelve tones can be used. This method has mathematical precision, but Berg has proved that it can also be made to express human feelings and deeply felt emotions. By doing this he has gone several steps beyond his teacher, Schoenberg, the father of the method.

All his life Berg was a frail and sick man. An unhappy love affair in his eighteenth year so disturbed his mental and physical makeup that henceforth he was to be in poor health. At twenty-three he suffered from bronchial asthma, from which he never completely recovered. Up to the end of his life, he paid periodic visits to hospitals and sanitariums.

His death, in Vienna on December 24, 1935, was caused by blood poisoning developed from an abscess on his back.

In *The Book of Modern Composers*, Paul A. Pisk portrayed Berg as follows: "Portraits of Alban Berg, revealing the propor-

tionate symmetry of his features and his tall, lean figure, bear a striking resemblance to those of Oscar Wilde. Even Berg's way of parting his hair, and his manner of dress, resembled those of the poet.

"Berg was not fond of the hectic life of the metropolis. . . . The composer was truly in his element in the Alpine district of Carinthia, where he spent a part of every year. In his earlier years he lived at the Berghof, a family estate near the Ossiach Lake; later on he made his home in his little cabin Waldhaus near the Wörther Lake. In this vicinity were beautiful mountains and two lovely villages.

"In Vienna, Berg made his quarters in a quiet street of a suburb, where he could always look at the green gardens and avoid the disturbance of the noise and dust of the city. . . .

"Berg's pleasant and gentle way of expressing himself was only the surface of his personality. Behind his good humor and light wit lay a profound philosophical mind as well as a creative imagination. He inclined towards mysticism. He believed in the symbolism of numbers, and was at home in the study of comparative religion."

MAJOR WORKS:

Chamber Music—String Quartet, op. 3, 1910; Four Pieces for Clarinet and Piano, op. 5, 1913; Chamber Concerto, for piano, violin, and thirteen wind instruments, 1925; Lyric Suite, for string quartet, 1926.

Operas—Wozzeck, 1921; Lulu, 1931.

Orchestral Music—Five Songs with Orchestra, op. 4, 1912; Three Orchestral Pieces, op. 6, 1914; Der Wein, concert aria, for soprano and orchestra, 1929; Concerto for Violin and Orchestra, 1935.

Piano Music—Sonata, op. 1, 1908.

ABOUT:

Ewen, D. (ed.) The Book of Modern Composers; Reich, W., Alban Berg; Thompson, O. (ed.) Great Modern Composers; Monthly Musical Record (London), February 1936; Musical Quarterly, October 1936; New York Times, March 30, 1952.

Sir Arthur Bliss *1891-*

ARTHUR BLISS was born in London on August 2, 1891. He received degrees in the arts and in music from Pembroke College, Cambridge. After this, he attended the Royal College of Music where his teachers included Stanford, Vaughan Williams, and Holst. His musical studies at the College came to an abrupt halt after one year because of the outbreak of World War I. During the entire war period Bliss was a commissioned officer. In 1916 he was wounded at the Somme, and two years after that gassed at Cambrai.

During his army service two of his early chamber-music works were performed, one of them receiving a prize at the War Emergency Concerts. Both works were published; after the war, Bliss destroyed the plates.

Bliss returned to music study by subjecting himself to severe discipline, and in a short period acquired a sound technique in composition. He wrote two major works of contrasting style, both successful. The first was the Rhapsody for soprano, tenor, flute, English horn, and string quartet, written in 1919. This was introspective and poetic music written with simplicity and refinement. Introduced at the International Society for Contemporary Music Festival at Salzburg, in 1923, the Rhapsody was acclaimed. In 1920 came his *Rout,* boisterous and satiric music for voice and ten instruments. "The success of *Rout* will long be remembered," wrote Norman Demuth. "It was like nothing else. Its novel conception and design, its amazing vitality, placed it and its composer immediately in the forefront and stamped him as a highly original mind."

In 1921 Bliss was appointed professor of composition at the Royal College of Music. He did not hold this post long. Since he was financially independent, he had no need to hold down any position for the sake of earning a living. He soon decided that he preferred devoting himself entirely to creative work, and to those pursuits that stimulated him creatively.

Between 1923 and 1925 Bliss lived in the United States, occupying himself with composition, conducting, and lecturing. He returned to this country for several additional visits, principally to write music for the films in Hollywood. His most significant film score came in 1935 for H. G. Wells's *Things to Come.* When World War II began, Bliss was in the United States serving as professor of music at the University of Southern California. He returned to England at the request of the British Broadcasting Corpora-

Wide World Photo
SIR ARTHUR BLISS

tion to become Assistant Director of Overseas Music, and after that Director of Music. He resigned the latter post in 1944.

Among Bliss's major works is a Concerto for Piano and Orchestra written in 1939 for the New York World's Fair and introduced there by Solomon and the New York Symphony under Sir Adrian Boult, on June 10, 1939. Dedicated to the "people of the United States," this Concerto is one of Bliss's most lyrical creations, a work sensitive in its beauty and delicate in its expression. Another frequently heard Bliss work is the *Music for Strings,* which preceded the Concerto by four years. This, too, is poetic and romantic music filled with original thinking.

Though Bliss has often been experimental, particularly in his use of form and in his harmonic language, he has always put beauty of sound and emotional expressiveness above originality. His music, as Alec Robertson once wrote, "is aristocratic. Physically it is entirely healthy and sane; mentally it is distinguished without being aloof; spiritually it is undenominational. It displays unvaryingly fine craftsmanship, a wit that has mellowed with the years, and . . . a note of almost Mediterranean passion and liveliness."

Bliss has stated his artistic principles as follows: "I believe that the foundation of all music is emotion, and that without the capacity for deep and subtle emotion a composer only employs half the resources of his medium. I believe that this emotion should be called into being by the sudden awareness of the actual beauty seen or by the vision of beauty vividly apprehended. I believe that the emotion resulting from apprehended beauty should be solidified and fixed by presenting it in a form absolutely fitting to it, and to it alone. If I were to define my musical goal, it would be to try for an emotion truly and clearly felt, and caught forever in formal perfection."

Arthur Bliss was knighted in 1950.

MAJOR WORKS:

Ballets—Checkmate, 1937; Miracle in the Gorbals, 1944; Adam Zero, 1946.

Chamber Music—Rhapsody, for soprano, tenor, flute, English horn, bass, and string quartet, 1919; Conversations, for seven instruments, 1919; Sonata for Viola and Piano, 1927; Quintet for Oboe and Strings, 1933; String Quartet No. 1, 1941; String Quartet No. 2, 1950.

Orchestral Music—Rout, for soprano and chamber orchestra, 1919; Two Studies, 1920; Mêlée Fantastique, 1921; Colour Symphony, 1922; Concerto for Two Pianos and Orchestra, 1924; Hymn to Apollo, 1926; Introduction and Allegro, 1926; Serenade, for baritone and orchestra, 1929; Morning Heroes, symphony for mixed chorus, narrator, and orchestra, 1930; Music for Strings, 1933; Concerto for Piano and Orchestra, 1939; Phoenix March, 1945.

Opera—The Olympians, 1949.

Vocal Music—Madame Noy, for soprano and six instruments, 1918; Two Nursery Rhymes, for soprano, clarinet, and piano, 1921; The Women of Yueh, song cycle for soprano and chamber orchestra, 1923.

ABOUT:

Bacharach, A. L. (ed.) British Music of Our Time; Chesterian (London), March-April, 1935.

Benjamin Britten *1913-*

BENJAMIN BRITTEN was born in Lowestoft, Suffolk, England, on November 22, 1913. His father was a well-to-do dental surgeon, and his mother an excellent amateur pianist. Benjamin Britten was exceptionally precocious. He wrote songs before he could read or write. At nine he completed a string quartet and an oratorio; by the time he was sixteen, he had produced a symphony, six quartets, ten piano sonatas, and smaller works. Later on, he gathered some of the melodic ideas of these juvenile

efforts into a serious and mature composition called *Simple Symphony,* completed in 1934.

His academic study took place at Gresham's School, Holt, in Norfolk. His music study began with Frank Bridge (who exerted a powerful influence over him) and continued with John Ireland and Arthur Benjamin at the Royal College of Music in London between 1930 and 1933.

Immediately after leaving the Royal College of Music, Britten made his mark as a composer. Three major works were heard at three different festivals of the International Society for Contemporary Music, in 1934, 1936, and 1938, and all were outstandingly successful. The first was the *Fantasy Quartet,* for oboe and strings; the second, the Suite for Violin and Piano; the third—and one of his finest orchestral works to date— the *Variations on a Theme of Frank Bridge.* In these three works, Britten combined an extraordinary virtuosity with a rich creative imagination. When his Concerto for Piano and Orchestra was introduced in London in 1938 there were few to deny that its composer was one of the most promising and exciting creative figures to emerge in English music in many years.

Britten came to America in 1939, staying here for three years. Several important works were written in this country, the most notable being the moving *Sinfonia da Requiem,* introduced by the New York Philharmonic-Symphony under John Barbirolli on March 29, 1941. While in this country, Britten was commissioned by the Koussevitzky Foundation to do an opera. That opera was not written until Britten's return to England in 1942. (He was drawn back to his native land by a desire to help his countrymen in their resistance to the Nazis, even though he himself was an ardent pacifist.) While giving concerts in bomb-proof shelters and hospitals, Britten sketched the music of his opera; the text, prepared by Montagu Slater, was based on a poem of George Crabbe called *The Borough.*

That opera, named *Peter Grimes,* made Britten a composer of international importance. It was introduced in London on June 7, 1945, one of the most memorable musical events of the period. It was the first new opera heard in England in several years; it marked the reopening of the Sadler's Wells Theatre, closed for five years during the war. These circumstances, dramatic though they were, proved to be incidental to the salient fact that *Peter Grimes* was an opera of amazing force, originality, and beauty. There was a stirring ovation for the composer when the opera was over. The correspondent for the *New York Times* did not hesitate to call the work "a milestone in the history of British opera."

In a long and detailed analysis of the score in the London *Times*, Ernest Newman admirably described Britten's music. There were in the opera, he wrote, "lyrical episodes . . . a few passages for Grimes or Ellen Orford, the final scene of Peter's madness, the fine reflective 'trio' for the four female characters in the second act. . . . The great part of the stage action is carried out in a sort of song-speech that keeps as faithfully as possible to the accents and rise and fall of the easy flow of ordinary speech, while the orchestra 'points' up what is being said in a curiously effective way. Apart from the lyrical episodes . . . the main burden of intense emotional expression is laid in the orchestra, in a number of interludes which sum up the emotional significance of what has gone before or prepare us for what is to come. They are of great power and masterly musicianship."

The success of *Peter Grimes* was unparalleled in modern opera. It was heard hundreds of times throughout Europe (in eight translations) before coming to this country. Its American premiere took place at Tanglewood, in Lenox, Massachusetts, during the Berkshire Music Festival period, on August 6, 1946, Leonard Bernstein conducting. Two years later it was successfully presented by the Metropolitan Opera Association in New York.

The operas Britten wrote after *Peter Grimes* further emphasized what that opera had suggested so strongly: namely, that he was one of the major creative writers for the musical theatre in our day. In a vein similar to *Peter Grimes* though much smaller in dimensions and scope, was the grim and realistic *The Rape of Lucretia*, produced at Glyndebourne in 1946. In a comic and satirical vein was *Albert Herring*, first heard in 1947. *Let's Make an Opera*, which followed it, was functional music, intended to teach children how an opera is written and pro-

BENJAMIN BRITTEN

duced. *Billy Budd*, based on the famous story of Herman Melville, returned to the large structure and ambitious design of *Peter Grimes*. *Billy Budd* was an immense success when introduced at Covent Garden on December 1, 1951. One year later, Britten became the first composer commissioned to write an opera for a coronation in England. The opera was *Gloriana*, introduced in London on June 8, 1953, as part of the festivities attending the coronation of Queen Elizabeth II.

But Britten has not confined himself entirely to the opera. In 1948 he wrote an eloquent cantata, *Saint Nicholas*, and in 1949 he completed one of his most inspired works, the *Spring Symphony*, for soloists, chorus, and orchestra. The latter is a setting of fourteen English poems about the vernal season almost in the style of the old English madrigalists.

Francis Poulenc described Britten as a "model of a composer" because Britten never fails in his technical skill or debases good taste. His style has varied with the composition at hand—now dissonant and modern (*Peter Grimes*), now medieval (*Ceremony of Carols*), now broadly satirical (*Albert Herring*), now romantic and poetic (*Spring Symphony*), now simple and direct (*Let's Make an Opera*). The amazing thing is that, regardless of what idiom he uses, he never fails to be thoroughly convincing. Always is he the complete master of his form and style, writing with force and clarity.

Britten looks shockingly young for a man who has already assumed the position of a *grand maître* of opera. Indeed, he looks much younger than his actual age. The boyishness of his face is accentuated by his blond shock of curls, and the boyish spareness of his frame emphasized by his usually casual dress of baggy slacks, sweater, and sport jacket. He looks like a college undergraduate, or a young teacher in a small-town university. Only in his nervous tensions does he betray that his calling is more exacting than that of either a student or teacher. When he talks, his face is expressive with frequent grimaces. He seems incapable of repose. When alone, at work or in thought, he paces the room nervously. Even in speaking to a friend he will, at intermittent periods, suddenly spring from his seat and walk up and down as he talks. He enjoys most to drive his Rolls Royce through the English countryside at high speed. His usual manner of thinking out problems in composition, away from his desk, is to take lonely strolls along the beach in Adelburgh, Suffolk, where he lives.

MAJOR WORKS:

Chamber Music—Fantasy, for oboe, violin, viola, and cello, op. 2, 1932; Suite for Violin and Piano, op. 6, 1934; String Quartet No. 1, op. 35, 1941; String Quartet No. 2, op. 36, 1945.

Choral Music—Ballad of Heroes, for tenor or soprano, mixed chorus and orchestra, op. 14, 1939; Hymn to St. Cecilia, op. 27, 1942; A Ceremony of Carols, op. 28, 1942; Rejoice in the Lamb, festival cantata, op. 30, 1943; Saint Nicholas, cantata, op. 42, 1948.

Operas—Peter Grimes, 1945; The Rape of Lucretia, 1946; Albert Herring, 1947; Let's Make an Opera, children's opera, 1948; Billy Budd, 1950; Gloriana, 1953.

Orchestral Music—Simple Symphony, 1934; Variations on a Theme of Frank Bridge, op. 10, 1937; Concerto for Piano and Orchestra, op. 13, 1938 (revised 1945); Les Illuminations, for soprano or tenor, and string orchestra, op. 18, 1939; Kermesse Canadienne, op. 19, 1939; Sinfonia da Requiem, op. 20, 1940; Diversions, for piano, left hand, and orchestra, op. 21, 1940; Scottish Ballad, for two pianos and orchestra, op. 26, 1941; Prelude and Fugue, for eighteen-part string orchestra, op. 29, 1943; Serenade, for tenor, horn, and string orchestra, op. 31, 1943; A Young Person's Guide to the Orchestra, op. 34, 1945; Spring Symphony, for soloists, chorus, and orchestra, op. 44, 1949; Divertimento, 1951.

ABOUT:

Bacharach, A. L. (ed.) British Music Today; Ewen, D. (ed.) The Book of Modern Composers, rev. ed.; Mitchell, D. and Keller, H. (eds.) Benjamin Britten; White, E. W., Benjamin Britten; Musical Opinion (London), July 1949; Musical Times (London), March 1948.

Alfredo Casella *1883-1947*

ALFREDO CASELLA was born in Turin, Italy, on July 25, 1883, to a family of musicians. It is believed that the madrigalist Casella, spoken of by Dante in *The Divine Comedy,* was an ancestor. Alfredo's father was professor of the cello at the Turin Liceo Musicale; his mother was an accomplished pianist; his uncle was a well-known cello virtuoso.

In such a musical environment, Alfredo was inevitably brought into early contact with music. He was only four when he began studying the piano, and he was able to play the entire *Well-Tempered Clavier* only four years later. He also started composing. But music was not his only interest. He showed such an aptitude for chemistry and electricity that Galileo Ferraris, a friend of the family, was insistent that the boy be directed to scientific study. For a while, Alfredo wavered between his love for music and his bent for science. It was at the urging of Giuseppe Martucci, well-known Italian composer, that Casella finally decided to choose music over science.

In 1896 Casella was sent to Paris, where he entered the Conservatory. As a pupil of Diémer, Leroux, and Fauré he took prizes in piano playing and composition. He also came into personal contact with Ravel and Debussy, both of whom he came to admire profoundly. Despite this admiration, he took to writing music that was romantic rather than impressionistic. His first two symphonies, written in 1905 and 1909, stem from Mahler and Richard Strauss rather than the French composers then in vogue.

Casella achieved his first success with the rhapsody *Italia*, written in 1909 and introduced in Paris on April 23, 1910, the composer conducting. In this work Casella skillfully incorporated folk melodies from Sicily and Naples into a romantic effusion.

Casella: kä-sĕl'lä

After serving briefly on the faculty of the Paris Conservatory, Casella returned to Italy in 1915. He was now to emerge as the dynamic musician whose influence was strongly felt in many different ways. He succeeded Sgambati as professor of the piano at the Liceo Musicale Santa Cecilia; for many years he was prominent as a teacher of the younger generation of Italian composers. He toured extensively as both pianist and conductor, distinguishing himself in his performances of the contemporary repertory. He founded the Società Italiana di Musica Moderna, which spread propaganda for contemporary Italian music. (In 1923, this organization was renamed Corporazione delle Nuove Musiche, becoming the Italian section of the International Society for Contemporary Music.) He devoted himself to musicological research, eventually producing definitive works on the development of the piano and of the cadence, and creating new editions of Beethoven's Sonatas, Bach's *Well-Tempered Clavier*, and the piano music of Mozart. He became editor of a new music journal, *Musica d'Oggi*, which he wrote, edited, issued, and financed. He wrote criticisms in the Italian papers. He was, in short, indefatigable in devoting his inexhaustible energies for the cause of good music—especially good modern music.

But his many and varied activities, prolific though they were, did not keep him from composing. In 1913, with *Notte di Maggio*, his style evolved from the romantic to the modern, as he went in for unorthodox progressions, harmonies, tonalities. But his style was not completely crystallized until after the end of World War I, when he combined modern thinking with the forms and styles of the past. He wrote now in a neo-classical style in which a new Italian musical art makes its appearance, a fusion of the old and the new. He went to the music of the older Italian composers for melodic materials for extended orchestral works: to Paganini, for *Paganiniana*; to Domenico Scarlatti, for *Scarlattiana*. He exploited old Italian forms as in his *Partita*, for piano and orchestra, and the *Due Ricercari*, for piano. He simulated the simplicity, clarity, objectivity, and purity of the old Italian instrumental masters; yet he did not sacrifice modern devices and techniques.

ALFREDO CASELLA

Also in the neo-classical vein was his successful ballet, *La Giara*, based on a story of Pirandello, presented by the Swedish Ballet in Paris on November 19, 1924. As the composer himself explained, his intent here was "to unite in modern synthesis the old fundamental musical comedy of the Neapolitan school with the elements of Italian folklore, more particularly the Sicilian." Together with a fine sense for characterization, the score is outstanding for its robust melodies and ingratiating wit.

Casella's first tacit, then open, acceptance of the Fascist regime disappointed many of his friends outside Italy. They could not altogether reconcile Casella's personal integrity, idealism, and cosmopolitan viewpoint with his espousal of dictatorship. His readiness to serve at Fascist festivals and celebrations, they felt, was not easily condoned. They were particularly disconcerted at his willingness to use his own music as a means to further Fascist ideals, as in the case of the opera *Il Deserto Tentato* (written at the request of Mussolini) which mystically exalted the Italian conquest of Ethiopia. Indeed, one of his personal friends, Leon Kochnitzky, was so upset by Casella's devotion to fascism that in writing Casella's obituary he could not refrain from remarking that he "had more talent as a musician than character as a man."

The last years of Casella's life were difficult. He was seriously ill, often in great pain; he had to undergo four difficult operations. The entrance of Italy into World War II and the subsequent occupation of Italy by the Nazis added personal privations to physical ones. Yet, in spite of all this, he was still capable of doing an extraordinary amount of work. As he wrote to one of his friends: "I have written six studies for the piano and . . . finished a large edition of the *Well-Tempered Clavier* and the *Inventions* of Bach; also of the Chopin *Etudes*, all of whose works I am to edit. In addition, I have just finished an enormous undertaking: a large Missa Solemnis, *Pro Pacem*, for soprano, baritone, and orchestra, which I feel to be my best work up to now. You see that I have not been idle despite the adverse circumstances."

Alfredo Casella died in Rome on March 5, 1947.

In searching for the most distinguishing characteristic of Casella's best music, Georges Jean-Aubry came upon the quality of "sensibility." "One must be guarded against the word; those to whom it conveys merely a synonym for sentimentality, will not have grasped its meaning. But those to whom it means the faculty to create a perfect accord between sense and spirit which gives equal pleasure, or at least equal interest to both, will discover the real personality of Casella."

Casella wrote his memoirs in 1942, *I Segreti della Giara*.

MAJOR WORKS:

Ballets—La Giara, 1924; La Camera dei Disegni, 1940; La Rosa del Sogno, 1943.

Chamber Music—Five Pieces for String Quartet, 1920; Concerto for String Quartet, 1924; Sonata No. 2 in C major, for cello and piano, 1927; Serenata, for clarinet, bassoon, trumpet, violin, and cello, 1927; Sinfonia, for piano, cello, trumpet, and clarinet, 1932.

Operas—La Donna Serpente, 1931; La Faviola di Orfeo, one-act opera, 1932; Il Deserto Tentato, 1937.

Orchestral Music—Italia, rhapsody, 1909; Notte di Maggio, for voice and orchestra, 1913; Elegia eroica, 1916; Pupazetti, five pieces for marionettes, 1919; Partita, for piano and orchestra, 1924; Scarlattiana, for piano and orchestra, 1926; Concerto Romano, for organ and orchestra, 1926; Concerto in A minor, for violin and orchestra, 1928; Introduzione, Aria e Toccata, 1933; Concerto for Trio and Orchestra, 1933; Concerto for Orchestra, 1937;

Symphony No. 3, 1941; Paganiniana, 1942; Tre Canti Sacri, for baritone and orchestra, 1943; Missa Solemnis, for soprano, baritone, and orchestra, 1944.

Piano Music—Nine Pieces, 1914; Sonatina, 1916; Deux Contrastes, 1918; Eleven Pieces for Children, 1920; Due Canzoni Italiane, 1928; Due Ricercari sul Nome Bach, 1932.

ABOUT:

Musical Quarterly, July 1947.

Mario Castelnuovo-Tedesco 1895-

(See *American Composers Today*)

Gustave Charpentier 1860-

A SOLITARY work—the opera *Louise*—has earned for Gustave Charpentier a permanent niche in contemporary opera.

He was born in Dieuze, Lorraine, on June 25, 1860. When Germany annexed Lorraine after the Franco-Prussian War, the Charpentier family crossed the French border to Tourcoing. There Gustave began the study of music, showing unusual gifts from the very first. The necessity of earning a living made it impossible for him to devote himself exclusively to music. When he was fifteen, he took a job as accountant in a Tourcoing factory. His employer, a music lover, recognized the boy's unusual talent and did what he could to encourage it. He helped establish in Tourcoing an orchestra and a music society so that young Charpentier might get the necessary contact with music-making that his development required. As Charpentier's gift for music expression became more and more pronounced, the employer financed further study at the Lille Conservatory. There Charpentier won several prizes, and these awards led to a grant from the town of Tourcoing to enable him to enter the Paris Conservatory.

At the Paris Conservatory Charpentier entered the class of Massenet, under whose guidance he wrote the cantata *Didon*, which won the Prix de Rome. *Didon*, performed in Paris, Brussels, and Tourcoing, brought the young composer his first success.

During his stay in Rome Charpentier was inspired by his contacts with Italian life and geography to write his first orchestral work,

Charpentier: shăr-päN-tyā'

Impressions of Italy. This is the only work by Charpentier, other than *Louise*, still heard. The suite is a romantic, if conventional, travelogue; it was introduced by the Colonne Orchestra in 1892.

After returning to Paris, Charpentier rented a small room in Montmartre and lived the life of a bohemian. He interested himself in socialism, finding an outlet for his political enthusiasms in writing songs, with orchestral accompaniment, to texts propounding Socialist ideology. At the same time he worked on *Louise*, writing his own libretto around an incident he himself had witnessed: the illicit love of the painter Julien for the dressmaker, Louise, despite parental opposition. During the period that he was working on his opera (and he knew all the while that it would be his *magnum opus*) he suffered such poverty that he might literally have starved if a friendly proprietor of a nearby grocery had not provided him with unlimited credit of eggs, milk, and bread.

Charpentier peddled his opera ten years before it was finally accepted for performance. The opera managers found a great deal to praise in it, and would have accepted it at once if the composer had allowed alterations. One manager wanted the contemporary setting to be replaced by one of the past. Another wanted its realism to be less photographic. Still another sought a happy ending. To all such suggestions Charpentier turned a deaf ear, faithful to his original conception.

How justified he was in refusing changes became apparent on February 2, 1900, when the work was finally introduced at the Opéra Comique of Paris. A young and then unknown Scottish singer by the name of Mary Garden appeared in the title role as a replacement for the prima donna whose health broke down in the second act, and she appeared without the benefit of a single rehearsal. The success of the opera, and of its star, was phenomenal. There was a magnificent ovation for both the composer and the singer.

The opera retained its popularity. It was heard one hundred times in the first season; by 1935, it had been heard a thousand times in Paris alone. In 1908 it was introduced in New York, at the Manhattan Opera; in

GUSTAVE CHARPENTIER

1909 it was seen in London, at Covent Garden. The fiftieth anniversary of the premiere of the opera was celebrated at the Paris Opéra on February 28, 1950. A festive audience was present, including the President of France. In the final scene, Charpentier—now nearly ninety years old—took over the baton and led the opera to the very end, to receive as thunderous an ovation as that historic auditorium had experienced in its long history. On the occasion of this anniversary, President Auriol presented him with the grade of Grand Officer of the Legion of Honor at the Elysée Palace.

Louise is an important opera. As the first French opera to treat a realistic and contemporary subject with naturalism (a French counterpart of the "Verismo" movement in Italy), it was a milestone. It was also for its day daring in its harmonies and in its supple and expressive use of the recitative. But beyond its historic importance, *Louise* is an opera which (though sometimes faded) has never lost its ability to enchant audiences. It has a persuasive charm all its own, particularly in the way the city of Paris dominates the work. It is the personality of Paris, rather than that of Louise, which gives the opera its unique character: the sights, sounds, and the spirit of the city. Paris is found in the delightful Montmartre street vendors' cries which the composer incorporated so skillfully into his score. It is found in the evocative prelude to Act II, called "Paris Awakes," a miniature tone poem in which the city is radiantly portrayed. In such pages, *Louise* is much more than a tender love story of Louise and Julien; as one writer put it so well, it is the song of a city.

Charpentier wrote a second opera, a sequel to *Louise*. It was called *Julien*, and was introduced at the Opéra Comique on June 4, 1913. But it never equaled either the importance or the popularity of its predecessor. Charpentier has written virtually nothing since then, now satisfied that what he had to say he had already said in *Louise*. He remained a colorful and greatly admired figure in French music by virtue of his one opera.

Against the setting which he used so effectively in his masterpiece, Charpentier appears like a character he might have created in his own opera—with his bohemian dress, long hair, and beard. He is still living in the same way he did at the turn of the century, even in the same quarters near the Sacré Cœur which he had occupied as a young man.

Major Works:

Choral Music—La Vie du Poète, for soloists, chorus, and orchestra, 1892.

Operas—Louise, 1900; Julien, 1913.

Orchestral Music—Impressions of Italy, suite, 1890; Poèmes Chantés, for voice and orchestra, 1894; Impressions Fausses, for voice and orchestra, 1895; Serenade to Watteau, for voice and orchestra, 1896.

Vocal Music—Les Fleurs du Mal, for voice and piano, 1895.

About:

Peltz, M. E. (ed.) Opera Lover's Companion; Musical Quarterly, July 1939.

Luigi Dallapiccola 1904-

LUIGI DALLAPICCOLA, one of the first Italian composers to utilize the twelve-tone technique, was born in Pisino, Istria, on February 3, 1904. At the age of six he started studying the piano. In 1917, the Dallapiccola family moved to Graz, Austria, where Luigi heard performances of operas by Mozart and Wagner, a decisive influence

in convincing him to become a professional musician. Back in Italy, he studied harmony in Trieste from 1919 to 1922. Settling in Florence, which since then has been his home, he studied the piano with Ernesto Console and attended the Cherubini Conservatory. Since 1931, he has been a member of the faculty of that Conservatory, first as teacher of the piano, then in the department of composition.

Dallapiccola first attracted attention with works introduced at festivals of the International Society of Contemporary Music, between 1934 and 1939. In the best of these compositions—including the Partita, for orchestra, the Hymns, for three pianos, and *Tre Laudi*, for voice and chamber orchestra—modern techniques are admirably fused with a neo-classic approach. This is music in which, as a critic said of the three-piano Hymns, "thought gains victory over matter."

After 1939 Dallapiccola adopted the twelve-tone technique of Schoenberg. In this style he has produced some of his most important works, beginning with *Volo di Notte*, an opera based on the famous novel of St. Exupéry, *Night Flight*, introduced in Florence on May 18, 1940. One of the most important works in this technique was the ballet *Marsia*, which created a scandal when introduced in Italy in 1943 because of its unconventional score.

What Dallapiccola himself regards as one of his finest works is the one-act opera *Il Prigioniero*. The libretto, by the composer, is based on a short story of Villiers de l'Isle-Adam and a scene from Charles de Coster's *Ulenspiegel*. The action concerns the imprisonment of a Flemish Protestant in the sixteenth century during the struggle for liberation from the Spaniards. This theme had particular significance for the composer in view of Italy's struggle for freedom before, during, and immediately following World War II. Completed in 1948, this opera was introduced over the Turin Radio on December 4, 1949 and given its first stage presentation at the Florence May Music Festival on May 20, 1950. On March 15, 1951, it was heard for the first time in New York. "There are moments," wrote Howard Taubman in his review in the *New York Times*, "when this music rises to heights of tension. For the most part, it is somber,

Dallapiccola: dä-lä-pē′kō-lä

Whitestone
LUIGI DALLAPICCOLA

slow-moving, like something through a veil. Dallapiccola reserves his most eloquent writing for the orchestra. He is a master of vivid and moving tonal combinations. And when he combines his orchestra with chorus towards the end he achieves shattering effect. . . . In sum, this is a composer and a work of individuality."

Though Dallapiccola is, for the most part, faithful to atonality, he still manages to derive from tonality, or impressionism, or neo-classicism those stylistic elements that serve his artistic needs. A critic of the *New York Herald Tribune* put it this way: "Caring nothing for labels and trends, he takes freely from atonalism for its continuity devices, from impressionism for atmospheric collages, from tonality and consonance for their capacity to chart areas of arrival and departure, and to reconcile all tensions and dissonance in repose."

In the summer of 1951 Dallapiccola visited the United States for the first time to join the faculty of the Berkshire Music Center, in Lenox, Massachusetts (Tanglewood). He returned to this country, and to Tanglewood, in the summer of 1952. On August 16, 1952, Dallapiccola made his American debut as pianist when he appeared as soloist with the NBC Symphony Orchestra over the NBC network, in the American premiere of his Little Concerto for Piano and Orchestra.

On September 22, 1952, the first all-Dallapiccola program to be presented anywhere was given in Mexico City. With the composer present and participating either as conductor or pianist, a group of distinguished Mexican musicians presented six works from different periods of the composer's career.

MAJOR WORKS:

Ballet—Marsia, 1942-43.

Chamber Music—Divertimento in Four Studies, for soprano and five instruments, 1934; Tre Laudi, for voice and thirteen instruments, 1936; Chaconne, Intermezzo and Adagio, for solo cello, 1945; Due Pezzi for violin and piano, 1947.

Choral Music—Estate, for a cappella male chorus, 1932; Six Choruses from Michelangelo, 1936; Songs from Captivity, for chorus and percussion, 1941; Liriche Greche, 1945; Job, oratorio, 1950.

Operas—Volo di Notte, 1939; Il Prigioniero, 1947.

Orchestral Music—Partita, 1932; Rhapsody for Cello and Orchestra, 1937; Little Concerto for Piano and Chamber Orchestra, 1941; Due Pezzi, 1947; Tartiniana, divertimento for violin and chamber orchestra, 1949; Three Poems, for voice and chamber orchestra, 1949.

Piano Music—Hymns, for three pianos, 1935; Sonatina Canonica, after Paganini's Caprices, 1943; Quaderno Musicale di Anna Libera, 1952.

Vocal Music—Rencesvals, three fragments from La Chanson de Roland, for voice and piano, 1946; Quattro Liriche di Antonio Machado, for soprano and piano, 1948; Persian Songs, for woman's voice and two clarinets, 1952.

ABOUT:

Chesterian (London), July 1938; Monthly Musical Record (London), February 1937; New York Times, March 11, 1951.

Claude Debussy *1862-1918*

ACHILLE-CLAUDE DEBUSSY was born in Saint-Germain-en-Laye on the outskirts of Paris, on August 22, 1862. The poverty of the Debussy household dictated that Claude, three years old, be turned over to his godparent, a rich aunt. She saw to it that Debussy begin to study the piano early. When he revealed unusual talent she acquired for him a first-rate teacher in Mme. Mauté de Fleurville, one-time pupil of Chopin and friend of Wagner. Mme. de Fleurville prepared Debussy for his entrance

Debussy: dĕ-bü-sē'

CLAUDE DEBUSSY

examinations for the Paris Conservatory, which he passed successfully in October 1873.

Debussy remained at the Conservatory eleven years. Even in those days he would search for new harmonies and tonalities. Time and again he would amaze his fellow pupils and disconcert his teachers with improvisations that utilized progressions and harmonies outlawed by the textbooks. However, eventually even such diehard academicians as Marmontel and Durand were won over to Debussy because of his outstanding talent. Durand gave Debussy a prize in harmony, and passed him on to Guiraud's class in composition in preparation for the Prix de Rome. Marmontel did not hesitate to recommend Debussy for a desirable summer post as pianist to a noted Russian patroness —Mme. von Meck, none other than the mysterious "beloved friend," Tchaikovsky's fabulous benefactor. During the summer of 1880 Debussy traveled with Mme. von Meck and her family to Italy and Austria. The following two summers he lived at her estate in Russia.

Debussy continued to make admirable progress at the Conservatory. In 1884 (after two unsuccessful attempts) he won the Premier Prix de Rome for the cantata *L'Enfant Prodigue*.

Debussy was not happy in Rome. He chafed under the many restrictions imposed on winners of the Prix de Rome. He therefore terminated his stay there prematurely, but not before submitting to the Conservatory authorities three *envois*, as was demanded of every laureate. The third of these was *The Blessed Damozel* (*La Damoiselle Élue*) after Dante Gabriel Rossetti. The judges found in this work a fine poetic feeling, but they were disconcerted by the "vagueness" of Debussy's writing. On the whole, they considered it below Prix de Rome standards. Later critical opinion, however, placed it in a high position, as the first of the masterworks in which he gave strong indication of his coming powers, the first of his works in which his later unorthodox harmonic writing is foreshadowed and his later feeling for subtle atmosphere already in evidence.

Back in Paris, Debussy set up a home with the first of the women to play an important part in his life: Gabrielle Dupont, whom he playfully called "Gaby of the Green Eyes." She was his helpmate and companion for a decade, and during that time they appeared to be contented with their life together.

Debussy was now being subjected to several major influences which affected his creative growth decisively. One was his personal contact with the Symbolist poets (whose leader was Stéphane Mallarmé) and the impressionist painters (notably Renoir, Monet, and Manet). Through his friendship and conversations with these poets and artists, Debussy arrived at a musical esthetic of his own—musical impressionism—which adapted the principles of these two movements. Debussy now felt that it was not the subject of a musical work that was important but the impressions that the subject aroused; that it was not the content of a musical composition that was the first consideration of the composer but rather subtlety of effect, color, nuance, and atmosphere. Another influence on Debussy was Erik Satie, the eccentric French musician, whom Debussy met for the first time in 1891. Satie was repelled by the Gargantuan forms and the emotional excesses of German romantic music and sought a French art that went in for subtlety of suggestion and understatement within miniature forms.

Debussy's first important works were not slow in coming once his direction and purpose had been clarified by the Symbolists, Impressionists, and Satie. In 1893 he completed the Quartet in G minor, which was introduced on December 29 by the Ysaÿe Quartet. Most of the critics failed to appreciate it. but a handful—among them was Paul Dukas—sensed the presence of genius. Dukas wrote: "Debussy is one of the most gifted and original artists of the younger generation of musicians . . . a lyricist in the full sense of the term."

The Quartet was succeeded by the exquisitely sensitive orchestral prelude, *L'Après-midi d'un Faune*, inspired by the poem of Stéphane Mallarmé. So well did the audience like this remarkable work when it was introduced at a concert of the Société Nationale on December 22, 1894, that it had to be repeated the next day.

In 1899, Debussy married a dressmaker, Rosalie Texier, whom he nicknamed "Lily-Lilo." For a while he was singularly attached to her, even though she was of plebeian mentality and tastes. But the idyll was short-lived. He abandoned her three years after his marriage, for Emma Bardac, a banker's wife. He married Emma as soon as both his own and his beloved's divorces were obtained, and in 1905 a daughter was born to them, Debussy's only child, to whom he gave the pet name of Chouchou.

The major work to occupy Debussy during the closing decade of the nineteenth century was an opera which he intended as the antithesis for everything for which Wagner stood. It is believed that the idea to adapt Maurice Maeterlinck's sensitive drama *Pelléas et Mélisande* into an opera came to him from Satie. In any event, Debussy started working on the opera in 1892. He spent ten years on this project. (Meanwhile he completed another of his celebrated orchestral works, the trilogy *Nocturnes*.)

Debussy completed *Pelléas et Mélisande* in 1902, and it was introduced by the Opéra Comique on April 30 of the same year. Scandal preceded that performance; a veritable furor attended it. Maurice Maeterlinck had expected his mistress, Georgette Leblanc, to sing the role of Mélisande. When the role was assigned to Mary Garden, Maeterlinck sent a letter to the press vehe-

mently denouncing both the opera and its composer (whom he suspected of complicity in the act). Some of the opposition to the new opera, which was articulated in the antagonism of some of the critics and in the open hostility of many in the audience, was the direct result of Maeterlinck's machinations.

But the novel and revolutionary character of Debussy's opera was also responsible for much of the opposition. Here was an opera in which the aria was banished, to be supplanted by a recitative closely simulating speech; in which nothing ever happened, but whose effect was dependent on the most sensitive atmospheres and nuances; in which the orchestra frequently provided an exotic background; in which the harmonic writing and the tonalities were as iconoclastic as the lyricism. "All I heard," wrote Leon Kerst after the premiere, "for even when you don't understand a thing you can't go to the theatre without hearing something—well, all I heard was a series of harmonized sounds (I don't say harmonious) which succeeded one another, uninterruptedly, without a single phrase, a single motive, a single accent, a single form, a single outline. And to this accompaniment, unnecessary singers drone out words, nothing but words, a kind of long drawn-out monotonous recitative, unbearable, moribund."

In self-defense, Debussy explained his esthetic goal: "I have tried to obey a law of beauty which appears to be singularly ignored in dealing with dramatic music. The characters of the drama endeavor to sing like real persons, and not in an arbitrary language on antiquated traditions. Hence, the reproach leveled at my alleged partiality for monotone declamation, in which there is no melody. . . . To begin with this is not true. Besides, the feeling of character cannot be continually expressed in melody. Also, dramatic melody should be totally different from melody in general. . . . I do not pretend to have discovered anything in *Pelléas*; but I have tried to trace a path that others may follow, broadening it with individual discoveries which will, perhaps, free dramatic music from the heavy yoke under which it existed for so long."

It was not until four years after its premiere that Paris acclaimed *Pelléas et Mé-*

lisande. Repeated at the Opéra Comique the opera was now an unqualified success. Today, of course, it is accepted as one of the most important and original operatic creations since Wagner, a milestone in the evolution of the operatic form.

Oscar Thompson has pointed out that the unique position held by *Pelléas et Mélisande* in the lyric theatre is due to three principal reasons: "(1) the word setting, which enables the sung text to move with almost the naturalness of speech; (2) the suggestive background of the orchestra, which supplies for the drama what may be termed a tonal envelope, without constituting itself either an accompaniment for the singers or a series of symphonic expansions in competition with them; (3) the mood expressiveness of the score, which in its reticence and lack of emotional stress takes on the mystery of the other-worldly, and ends in being profoundly human in its sympathy and pathos."

Debussy was now one of France's most famous and provocative composers. Oblivious of both adulation and attack, he continued producing masterworks: piano compositions crowned by the two sets of Preludes written in 1910 and 1913, among the most significant piano music since Chopin; orchestral works, including *La Mer* and *Images*, the latter a set of three orchestral pictures containing the famous "Ibéria."

Oscar Thompson gives the following vivid word picture of the composer: "In manner Debussy was a being of many contradictions. One description refers to him as 'that very materially minded fellow,' 'that sleep-heavy creature,' 'always so taciturn unless he wanted to get a good address for procuring caviar, for which he was on the lookout and of which he was inordinately fond.' An interviewer for *Le Figaro* found that he smiled readily and spoke in a soft, melodious voice (not 'nasal' or 'sepulchral' this time) but was almost monastic in reserve. . . . Rarely on first meeting would he disclose anything of himself. While others talked, Claude would turn the leaves of a book or examine an engraving, listening but apparently not concentrating on what was said. Yet his eyes would take on a look of singular intensity when he was really inter-ested, and it was clear that although he was master of his comportment he had difficulty in controlling his emotions.

"When he turned to writing his thoughts, whether in personal letters or almost equally personal musical criticism, Debussy was a wit, if perforce a somewhat self-conscious one. . . . But writing was not the only quotidian affair of which he made a game. The virtuosity with which he rolled a cigarette in paper always devoid of glue without spilling the slightest speck of tobacco was a source of wonder and admiration to great and humble alike among the Parisians he encountered day by day. The opera he endured—if only now and then. But the circus! There he would have gladly gone every day. He could admire Mary Garden or Maggie Teyte. But the clowns! Debussy was like a child in his relish of their time-honored slapstick. The card game he enjoyed most was called bézique—Chinese bézique. When he played, Debussy would put his pipe beside him, as a cowboy of American-frontier times might have placed his six-shooter. He would cheat, more or less openly, turning down the tip of a card he might want to put in his hand later."

By the time he reached his fiftieth birthday, Debussy knew that he was a victim of cancer. The next nine years of his life were filled with intense pain accentuated by financial problems and the worry attending the outbreak of World War I. His mental and physical state affected the quality of his composition. He wrote three sonatas in which he tried writing in the classical forms of the seventeenth and eighteenth century French composers. There are here moments of the old imaginative powers, but these moments are few and far between. This music is primarily an imitation of some of the mannerisms that had made him famous.

Debussy died at his home in Paris on March 25, 1918, eight days after he had applied for a recently-vacated seat at the Académie de France.

He was a composer who produced masterworks. He was also a composer whose influence on the music of his generation was of incalculable significance. As Henri Prunières noted, he accomplished "a complete revolution in the musical art. . . . He invented new ways of associating chords hitherto regarded as discords, and used them to produce exquisite and delightful harmonies, and he disengaged the separate timbres of the orchestra by making one accentuate the value of the other, instead of combining them in confused masses. In this respect, his method is that of an impressionist painter who lays on his canvas primary colors, side by side, instead of mixing them on his palette. Debussy violated all conventional formulas, replacing them by new ones no less beautiful, and far more suitable for expression of those transient sensations and delicate emotions which he loved above all to portray. He was the incomparable painter of mystery, silence, and the infinite, of the passing cloud, and the sunlit shimmer of the waves—subtleties which none before him had been capable of suggesting. His power of expression is not less real for being always restrained and intolerant of excess and overemphasis, but its force is under the surface."

MAJOR WORKS:

Ballets—Jeux, 1912; La Boîte à Joujoux, 1913.

Chamber Music—Quartet in G minor, 1893; Rhapsody for Clarinet and Piano, 1910; Sonata for Cello and Piano, 1915; Sonata for Flute, Viola and Harp, 1915; Sonata for Violin and Piano, 1917.

Choral Music—La Damoiselle Élue, cantata, 1888.

Opera—Pelléas et Mélisande, 1902.

Orchestral Music—L'Après-midi d'un Faune, orchestral prelude, 1894; Nocturne, 1899; Danse Sacrée et Danse Profane, for harp and strings, 1904; Rhapsody for Saxophone and Orchestra, 1905; La Mer, 1905; Le Martyre de Saint-Sébastien, incidental music for a "Mystery," 1911; Images, 1912.

Piano Music—Pour le Piano, 1901; Estampes, 1903; Masques, 1904; L'Île Joyeuse, 1904; Suite Bergamasque, 1905; Images, two series, 1907; Children's Corner, suite, 1908; La Plus que Lente, 1910; Preludes, two books, 1910-13; Twelve Etudes, 1915; En Blanc et Noir, for two pianos, 1915.

Vocal Music—Mandoline, 1883; Paysage Sentimental, 1883; Clair de Lune, 1884; Cinq Poèmes de Baudelaire, 1889; Ariettes Oubliées, 1888; Trois Mélodies, 1891; Fêtes Galantes, two series, 1892-1904; Proses Lyriques, 1893; Chansons de Bilitis, 1897; Trois Ballades de François Villon, 1910; Trois Ballades de Stéphane Mallarmé, 1913.

ABOUT:

Harvey, H., Claude of France; Lockspeiser, E., Debussy; Myers, R., Debussy; Thompson, O., Debussy: Man and Artist; Vallas, L., Claude Debussy.

Marcel Delannoy 1898-

ALTHOUGH Marcel Delannoy played the piano well when he was nine years old, and revealed a genuine talent for improvisation soon afterwards, he was not at first destined for a musical career. He was born in La Ferté-Alais, France, on July 9, 1898. His father wanted him to be an engineer; other members of his family thought he should study architecture. During the early part of World War I he attended the École des Beaux Arts where he showed little enthusiasm for his studies. He was soon mustered into the army. One day in April of 1918, in the midst of a battle, Delannoy vowed that if he survived he would devote himself only to music after the war. The war ended, he proceeded to carry out the oath, even though living conditions were difficult. His first wife, Lisette Claveau, a fine musician, taught him the elements of harmony and theory as preparation for further study with Jean Gallon and André Gedalge. ("The music that first brought us together was destined to separate us at last," Delannoy has said of that first marriage. "We were divorced in 1923.")

His first major work was an opera based on a Flemish legend, *Le Poirier de Misère*. This work greatly impressed many Parisian musicians (including Honegger) who opened

François Pagès

MARCEL DELANNOY

Delannoy: dĕ-lă-nwä'

up for Delannoy his first opportunities. *Le Poirier de Misère* was produced at the Opéra Comique on February 21, 1927, and was successful. Some criticism was leveled at Delannoy that he was imitating Ravel, but this accusation was permanently discounted when Ravel himself came to the defense of the young composer.

Other major works gave further evidence of a creative talent of the first order: the ballet with singing, *Le Fou de la Dame,* heard at the International Society for Contemporary Music Festival in 1929; the String Quartet, also introduced at a concert of the International Society for Contemporary Music Festival, in 1932; and the Symphony, heard in Paris in 1934, under Pierre Monteux's direction.

In his earlier works, Delannoy leaned towards impressionism. Beginning with his Quartet he veered towards neo-classicism. The neo-classical bent has since been more and more pronounced and has become fully crystallized in the opera *Ginevra* (commissioned by the French government in 1938 and introduced at the Opéra Comique on July 25, 1942) in which the idioms of Cimarosa and Pergolesi are given contemporary treatment. Delannoy's music is essentially lyric, a fresh and engaging melodic gift being evident not only in his splendid songs but also in his operas and other major works. He aspires to be a composer deriving his material from popular sources in the way Manuel de Falla did.

Delannoy explains his views on modern music as follows: "I believe that a new system of music can be derived not from the use of atonality and dissonance but from the modern adaptation of the old ecclesiastical modes and from exploitation of international folklore. This allows for liberty without license, because it in no way compromises the laws regulating the association of sounds, while at the same time it increases incalculably the number of such associations."

MAJOR WORKS:

Ballets—Le Fou de la Dame, 1929; La Pantoufle de Vair (originally, Cendrillon), 1931; Les Noces Fantastiques, 1948.

Chamber Music—Rapsodie, for saxophone, trumpet, cello and piano, 1931; Quartet, 1932.

Operas—Le Poirier de Misère, 1927; Philippine, 1937; Ginevra, 1939; Puck, 1948.

Orchestral Music—Figures Sonores, for chamber orchestra, 1930; Symphony, 1934; Sérénade Concertante, for violin and orchestra, 1938; Concert de Mai, for piano and orchestra, 1950.

Frederick Delius *1862-1934*

FREDERICK DELIUS was born in Bradford, England, on January 29, 1862. His family was German and his name was entered in the birth registries as Fritz Theodore. As a child he showed unusual talent for music, playing the piano well by ear and making excellent progress in his studies of the violin. His father, however, did not encourage him in his musical activities. A successful wool merchant, the elder Delius wanted his son to enter his business. The boy was therefore sent to Germany for the study of the wool business. While there he heard a performance of Wagner's *Die Meistersinger,* whose impact on him was so great that then and there he vowed he would become a musician.

But first he had to suffer for two years in his father's business. At last he prevailed on his father to buy him an orange plantation in Solano, Florida. Delius became a plantation proprietor in 1884. He left its supervision to an overseer while devoting himself first to music study and after that to composition. His first work of major proportions—*Appalachia,* for chorus and orchestra—was based on an old slave tune he heard in Florida.

He was happy on his plantation. But the need for more intensive music study impelled him to leave it. For a while he taught music in Danville, Virginia. Then, after his father gave him his belated though still reluctant consent for music study, he went to Europe. He attended the Leipzig Conservatory, where his teachers included Sitt, Jadassohn, and Reinecke. In the winter of 1888 Grieg visited Leipzig, where he heard a performance of Delius' *Florida,* for orchestra. This work impressed the Norwegian composer so greatly that he used his influence to get Delius' father to provide Frederick with a generous subsidy to allow him to pursue his career in music.

Delius now went to Paris, where he assimilated its cultural life and devoted him-

Delius: dēl'yŭs

self more assiduously than ever to composition. In 1892 his first published work appeared: *Légende,* for violin and orchestra. This was followed by a tone poem, *Over the Hills and Far Away,* the Concerto for Piano and Orchestra, and an orchestral nocturne, *Paris: The Song of a Great City.* On May 30, 1899, there took place in London the first concert devoted entirely to Delius' music. It was not successful, and did little to promote his career.

After marrying Jelka Rosen in 1899, Delius settled in Grez-sur-Loing in France. This was his home for the remainder of his life. During the next decade and a half he produced a series of outstanding works which placed him among the foremost composers of his time. In 1901 he completed an opera, *A Village Romeo and Juliet,* the libretto prepared by his wife from a novel of Gottfried Keller. During the next two years he produced two major choral works: *Sea-Drift* and *A Mass for Life.* Then came the exquisite tone poems for orchestra, with which his name is identified: *Brigg Fair, In a Summer Garden, Summer Night on the River,* and *On Hearing the First Cuckoo in Spring.*

The music of these tone poems is pictorial. These works are sensitive paintings by a poetic temperament, their tranquil mood far removed from the turbulence of our times. One English critic described this music as "the autumn of the romantic sentiment, which found its morning in Beethoven and its noon in Wagner."

"Delius," wrote Cecil Gray, "is an artist before he is a musician; for him music is not merely a decorative craft, the skillful weaving together of a pleasant pattern of sounds, signifying nothing, but a creative art and the means to the apprehension and expression of the supreme realities of life."

"He found the basic material for his music in those of his sensations which appeal to all," wrote Bernard van Dieren in the *Musical Times* (August 1934). "Delius is not a Shakespeare and he is the more admirable for his understanding the character of his genius. . . . Delius' art is so completely satisfactory because while being definitely circumscribed it is so justly balanced. His music never undertakes to convey anything that does not belong to the adventures

FREDERICK DELIUS

of a very sensitive human spirit. To all that he touched he gave a new meaning, a new color, a new loveliness, and a new poignancy."

Recognition first came to Delius in Germany, where he became known as "Friedrich Delius." Performances of his works took place at the Lower Rhine Festival in 1905, the Tonkünstlerfest in Essen in 1906, and in Berlin in 1907. "I never dreamed," said Richard Strauss, "that anybody except myself was writing such good music."

Not until after World War I did Delius get the acclaim he deserved in his native land. That he was eventually honored was due in a large measure to the patient and passionate espousal of his music by such appreciative conductors as Sir Thomas Beecham.

Soon after World War I Delius' health suffered marked deterioration. At first he suffered from attacks of fatigue and inertia. After 1923 his health disintegrated to a point where paralysis and blindness set in. Delius accepted this terrible calamity with amazing serenity and fatalism. He enlisted the services of a young musician, Eric Fenby, who came to live with him and acted as an amanuensis. Painstakingly Delius dictated to Fenby his last works, note by note.

In 1929, though blind and paralyzed, Delius was brought to London to be present at a monumental festival of six concerts devoted to his major works. He was now accorded the full measure of homage his genius deserved and which had for so long a time been denied him. Appreciative essays by England's foremost music critics placed him with the great creative figures of the twentieth century. Oxford University bestowed on him an honorary degree.

Delius died at his home in Grez-sur-Loing on June 10, 1934. One year later his body was transferred to the churchyard in Limpsfield, in southern England. At the nearby church Sir Thomas Beecham led a concert of Delius' music.

In his admirable personal study of Delius, Eric Fenby singled out the following salient traits of Delius' character: "his intellectual isolation, his inhuman aloofness, his penetrating truthfulness, wholly indifferent thereby whether he hurt people or not, his utter contempt for the 'crowd,' and his all-embracing sufficiency. To these were added his colossal egotism, his dreadful selfishness, his splendid generosity . . . his equal indifference to money and honors, his exceptional refinement." Fenby further pointed out Delius' bent for excess. "If he must smoke, then he must smoke all day long; if he must have spinach, then spinach it had to be almost every meal. . . . There were no half-measures with Delius."

MAJOR WORKS:

Chamber Music—Sonata No. 1 for Violin and Piano, 1892; String Quartet No. 1, 1893; Sonata No. 2 for Violin and Piano, 1915; String Quartet No. 2, 1916; Sonata for Cello and Piano, 1917; Sonata No. 3 for Violin and Piano, 1930.

Choral Music—Appalachia, 1902; Sea Drift (Whitman), 1903; A Mass of Life (Nietzsche), 1905; Songs of Sunset (Dowson), 1907; Wander-er's Song, 1908; Requiem, 1916; A Poem of Life and Love, 1919; Songs of Farewell (Whitman), 1930.

Operas—Koanga, 1897; A Village Romeo and Juliet, 1901; Fennimore and Gerda, 1910.

Orchestral Music—Concerto in C minor for Piano and Orchestra, 1897; Over the Hills and Far Away, 1895; Nachtlied Zarathustra (Nietzsche), for baritone and orchestra, 1898; Paris: The Song of a Great City, nocturne, 1899; Cynara (Dowson), for baritone and orchestra, 1907; Brigg Fair, rhapsody, 1907; In a Summer Garden, fantasy, 1908; A Dance Rhapsody, No. 1, 1908; Summer Night on the River, 1911; On Hearing the First Cuckoo of Spring, 1912; A Dance Rhapsody, No. 2, 1916; Concerto for Violin, Cello and Orchestra, 1916; Concerto for Violin and Orchestra, 1916; Eventyr, ballad, 1917; A Song before Sunrise, 1918; Concerto for Cello and Orchestra, 1921; A Late Lark

(Henley), for tenor and orchestra, 1922; A Song of Summer, 1930; Idyll (Whitman), for soprano, baritone, and orchestra, 1932.

ABOUT:

Delius, C., Memories of My Brother; Fenby, E., Delius as I Knew Him; Heseltine, P., Frederick Delius; Hull, A. E., Delius; Hutchings, A., Delius.

Ernst von Dohnányi *1877-*

ERNST VON DOHNÁNYI was born in Pressburg, Hungary, on July 27, 1877. His father was professor of mathematics and physics at the local high school, and a good amateur cellist. He introduced his son to music. In 1885 the boy became a piano pupil of Karl Förstner. Four years after that Dohnányi enrolled in the Budapest Academy of Music where his teachers included Thomán (piano) and Koessler (composition). Before long, Dohnányi started writing ambitious works. By 1895 he had completed a mass, three string quartets, a sextet, and a piano quintet, the last of which was published.

During the summer of 1895 Dohnányi visited Brahms, bringing him the manuscript of his Piano Quintet. Brahms was greatly impressed with the music and used his influence to get the work performed. Soon after this performance, Dohnányi's reputation as a composer was established through the winning of the King's Prize for the Symphony in F major (1897) and the Bösendorfer Prize in Vienna for the Piano Concerto No. 1 (1899).

Following a short period of study of the piano with Eugene d'Albert, Dohnányi began his career as concert pianist by making a successful debut in Berlin on October 1, 1897. Tours followed, bringing him to all parts of the music world, including the United States, where Dohnányi made his debut in 1898. By the turn of the century, he was acclaimed as one of the out standing pianists of the day.

Dohnányi was also successful as a teacher. From 1905 to 1908 he taught the piano at the Berlin Hochschule, becoming full professor in 1908. In 1919 he became director of the Budapest Conservatory, and in 1934 the head of the Landesakademie. "As a teacher," wrote Edward Kilenyi, one of his pupils, "he was extremely non-committal, pre-

Dohnányi: dôĸ′nä-nyē

ferring to allow the pupil to develop rather than have the teacher do it for him, training the student to such a high degree of musical taste that he himself was conscious of his own errors of interpretation rather than having them pointed out to him by the teacher."

Dohnányi distinguished himself in still one other field, that of conducting. For thirty years he led the Budapest Philharmonic Orchestra. In 1925 he made several orchestral appearances in the United States.

Though Dohnányi has been creatively productive throughout his life, he is perhaps best known for the works of his youth and early manhood. His first Piano Quintet, the Suite in F-sharp minor for orchestra, and the *Variations on a Nursery Theme* (all written before 1914) are among his most frequently heard works. This is the music of a romantic who could not shake himself free from the influence of Brahms. In his respect for classical form, in his lack of emotional inhibitions, and in his expropriation of some of Brahms' melodic and rhythmic idiosyncrasies, Dohnányi proved himself to be a true disciple of the master. While this music is rarely original, it never fails to please concert audiences with its sound musicianship, charm, poetic ideas, and melodic freshness.

In a few of his works, Dohnányi (like his compatriots Bartók and Kodály) tried to achieve a national expression by exploiting melodic and rhythmic ideas from Hungarian folk music. Occasionally he produced forceful and original music in this vein. The most notable of his national works are the *Variations on a Hungarian Theme* and the *Ruralia Hungarica*, the latter written originally for the piano but later orchestrated by the composer.

In 1922 Dohnányi received the honorary title of Doctor of Music from the Budapest Academy, and the Corvin Lanz, the highest Hungarian decoration. He was also awarded the Officers' Cross of the French Legion of Honor.

Up to the time of the outbreak of World War II, Dohnányi was the dominant figure in Hungary's musical life. As Kilenyi wrote: "The musical life of Budapest centered around him." But Dohnányi did not permit

ERNST VON DOHNANYI

his many and varied activities, and his great fame, to rob him altogether of the quiet and the retirement he needed. "Sundays at his country home on the hillside," wrote Kilenyi, "were days of peaceful strolls through the gardens with the few intimate friends who came to visit him—of easy, vivacious conversations about all sorts of subjects—and permeating through it all, the personality of the man himself, his intense interest in everything that went around him from the flowers which he gardened daily to the newest bulletin just off the press." Dohnányi remained in his native land during the war. In 1946 and 1947 Dohnányi toured England, giving piano recitals, and assisting at performances of several major new works (including his Piano Concerto No. 3 and the Symphony in E major). The Symphony was introduced by the Chelsea Symphony Orchestra in London, Norman Del Mar conducting, on November 23, 1948. The critic of the London *Times* described the work as "overbrimming with the exuberant ripeness of decadent romanticism."

Dohnányi came to the United States in 1948, and one year later settled in Florida where he was appointed instructor at the Florida State College. One of his most recent works, the Concerto No. 2 for Violin and Orchestra, performed in 1952 by Frances Magnes and the New York Philharmonic-Symphony under Mitropoulos, revealed a return to the idioms of Hungarian folk music.

MAJOR WORKS:

Chamber Music—Quintet in C minor, for piano and strings, op. 1, 1895; String Quartet in A major, op. 7, 1899; Sonata in B-flat minor, for cello and piano, op. 8, 1899; String Quartet No. 2, in D-flat, op. 15, 1906; Sonata in C-sharp minor, for violin and piano, op. 21, 1912; Quintet No. 2, for piano and strings, op. 26, 1914; String Quartet No. 3, in A minor, op. 33, 1926; Sextet in C major, op. 37, 1935.

Choral Music—Missa in Dedicatione Ecclesiae, op. 35, 1930; Cantata, for chorus and orchestra, cp. 38.

Operas—Tante Simona, comic opera, op. 20, 1910; Ivar Turm, op. 30, 1917; The Tenor, comic opera, op. 34, 1919.

Orchestral Music—Concerto in E minor, for piano and orchestra, op. 5, 1898; Symphony in D minor, op. 9, 1901; Concertstück for Cello and Orchestra, op. 12, 1904; Suite in F-sharp minor, op. 19, 1909; Variations on a Nursery Theme, op 25, 1913; Concerto in D minor, for violin and orchestra, op. 27, 1915; Festival Overture, op. 31; Minutes Symphoniques, op. 36, 1931; Suite en Valse, op. 39, 1942; Symphony No. 2 in E major, op. 40, 1944; Concerto No. 2, for piano and orchestra, op. 42, 1946; Concerto No. 2, for violin and orchestra, op. 43, 1948; Concertina for Harp and Orchestra, op. 45, 1952.

Piano Music—4 Pieces, op. 2, 1896; Valses, for four hands, op. 3, 1897; Variations and Fugue on a Theme by E. G., op. 4, 1897; Passacaglia, op. 6, 1899; 4 Rhapsodies, op. 11, 1903; Winterreigen, 10 bagatelles, op. 13, 1905; Humoresken, in the form of a suite, op. 17, 1907; 3 Pieces, op. 23, 1913; 6 Concert Études, op. 28, 1916; Variations on a Hungarian Folksong, op. 29, 1916; Ruralia Hungarica (also for orchestra, op. 32b), op. 32a, 1924; 6 Pieces, op. 41, 1945; 12 Études, op. 44, 1950.

Vocal Music—6 Lieder for Baritone, op. 14, 1905; Im Lebenslenz, six songs, op. 16, 1907; Two Songs for Baritone and Orchestra, op. 22, 1912.

Sem Dresden *1881-*

SEM DRESDEN is an outstanding creative figure in Dutch music, and one of Holland's vital forces in disseminating propaganda for contemporary music.

He was born in Amsterdam on April 20, 1881. He studied harmony with Roeske, counterpoint with Bernard Zweers, and composing and conducting with Hans Pfitzner. Both Zweers and Pfitzner were romantics; it was due to their influence that Dresden's early works were marked by romantic writing in the Germanic vein. From

SEM DRESDEN

romanticism, Dresden passed to impressionism. By 1916 he had evolved his own idiom in which modern techniques and styles predominate.

His most important works show a predilection for simplicity, clarity, and economy of means. His forms are transparent and balanced; his harmonic writing concise and powerful. His music is particularly noteworthy for its rhythmic ingenuity—with its change of meters and displacement of accents—a rhythm derived not from classical or romantic literature but from the music of the polyphonic era.

Dresden has also distinguished himself as critic, conductor, and teacher. In 1918 he became music critic of the *Groene Amsterdammer,* and in 1923 of the *Telegraaf.* From 1924 to 1937 he directed the Amsterdam Conservatory, and after 1937 was head of the Royal Conservatory of The Hague. In 1931 he was elected president of the Dutch section of the International Society for Contemporary Music. He was also made president of the state commission of education in 1945. Over a period of many years he has conducted numerous choral societies.

MAJOR WORKS:

Chamber Music—Sonata for Cello and Piano, 1916; Sonata for Flute and Harp, 1918; Sextet No. 3, for flute, oboe, clarinet, bassoon, horn, and piano, 1920; First String Quartet, 1924; Sonata

No. 2 for Cello and Piano, 1942; Trio, 1943; Sonata for Violin Solo, 1943; Suite for Cello Solo, 1947.

Choral Music—Chorus Tragicus, 1927; O Kerstnacht, for mixed chorus, 1939; Chorus Symphonicus, 1944; Gelukkig Is het Land, for mixed chorus and brass band, 1948.

Orchestral Music—Four Vocalises, for mezzosoprano and orchestra, 1935; Concerto No. 1 for Violin and Orchestra, 1936; Sinfonietta, for clarinet and orchestra, 1938; Concerto for Oboe and Orchestra, 1939; Concerto No. 2 for Violin and Orchestra, 1941; Concerto for Piano and Orchestra, 1946; Seven Pieces, for school orchestra, 1949; Concerto for Flute and Orchestra, 1950.

Piano Music—Three Pieces, 1944.

Paul Dukas *1865-1935*

PAUL DUKAS was born in Paris on October 1, 1865. Though he revealed unmistakable musical gifts from early childhood, it was some time before he received formal training. Meanwhile, he learned by himself what he could about the piano, composition, and solfeggio.

In 1881 he finally entered the Paris Conservatory. He remained there eight years, a pupil of Dubois (harmony) and Guiraud (composition). It did not take him long to prove himself. In 1883 and 1884 he wrote two highly gifted orchestral overtures, *King Lear* and *Goetz von Berlichingen*. He continued to distinguish himself. In 1886 he won first prizes in counterpoint and fugue, and in 1888, second Prix de Rome with *Velleda*. There were disappointments, too—the major one being his failure to win the Prix de Rome in 1889 with *Semele*.

Military service interrupted his studies. This period was, however, not altogether wasted. Deprived of textbooks and exercises, he went to the classical scores for further study. This intensive absorption with the music of the past gave Dukas a consummate understanding and command of form and technique.

Dukas's first important success as composer came with the overture *Polyeucte*, introduced by the Lamoureux Orchestra in Paris on January 23, 1892. The reviewer for the *Guide Musical* went so far as to say that this work was "one of the most remarkable of recent years." Five years later came the Symphony in C major, introduced in Paris on January 3, 1897, under the direction of

Photo-Lipnitzki
PAUL DUKAS

Paul Vidal. "It is distinguished by a youthful ardor which does not exclude a style of lofty feeling and a strong structure," wrote Gustave Samazeuilh.

The work that made Dukas famous was not slow in coming. On May 18, 1897, the Société Nationale introduced *The Sorcerer's Apprentice (L'Apprenti Sorcier)* under the composers direction. It was a sensation. This orchestral scherzo was a musical adaptation of the whimsical ballad by Goethe, *Der Zauberlehring*. The music interpreted the story with such wit, and such skill in approximating the precise musical equivalent of every mood, character, and action, that it has never lost its immense popularity with audiences young and old. It was successfully made into an animated cartoon by Walt Disney in his film *Fantasia*.

Two other major works by Dukas are the opera *Ariane et Barbe-bleue* and the "danced poem" *La Péri*. The opera, on a text by Maurice Maeterlinck, is an adaptation of the Bluebeard tale. Dukas here renounced the Wagnerian principles and style, then so much in vogue, to produce a work subtle in its suggestions and delicate in its impressions. Some French critics regard *Ariane et Barbe-bleue* as one of the most important works in the French lyric theatre since Debussy's *Pelléas et Mélisande*. It was introduced at the Opéra Comique on May 10, 1907, and was well re-

Dukas: dü-kä'

ceived. Gabriel Fauré wrote in *Figaro* : "This music of Paul Dukas, so clearly delineated, so sharp and eloquent—does it not throw more light on the personages of the drama, who walk in a somewhat imprecise atmosphere and express themselves in a similarly imprecise manner?" In 1911 *Ariane et Barbe-bleue* was seen at the Metropolitan Opera House in New York.

La Péri was written in 1910 for the dancer Mlle. Trouhanowa, who introduced it successfully in Paris on April 22, 1912.

Dukas produced few works after 1910. Supercritical of himself and his music—and perhaps a bit contemptuous of public opinion —he did not try to get those few works either performed or published, and just before his death he destroyed some of them.

He devoted himself primarily to teaching, becoming professor of orchestration at the Conservatory in 1910. In 1918 he succeeded Debussy as member of the Conseil de l'Enseignement Supérieur. From 1927 to the time of his death he was professor of composition. He was also music critic for the *Revue Hebdomadaire* and the *Gazette des Beaux Arts,* and the editor of the complete works of Rameau.

Paul Dukas died in Paris on May 17, 1935. A few months before his death he was chosen to succeed the late Alfred Bruneau at the Académie des Beaux Arts.

Major Works:

Ballet—La Péri, "danced poem," 1910.

Chamber Music—La Villanelle, for horn and piano, 1906.

Opera—Ariane et Barbe-bleue, 1907.

Orchestral Music—Polyeucte, overture, 1891; Symphony, 1896; The Sorcerer's Apprentice, scherzo, 1897.

Piano Music—Sonata in E-flat minor, 1901; Variations, Interlude, and Finale, on a theme by Rameau, 1903; Prélude Élégiaque, 1909; La Plainte au Loin du Faune, 1920.

Vocal Music—Sonnet de Ronsard, for voice and piano, 1924.

About:

Samazeuilh, G., Paul Dukas; La Revue Musicale (Paris), May-June 1936.

Gottfried von Einem *1918-*

GOTTFRIED VON EINEM, best known for his opera *Dantons Tod,* was born in Bern, Switzerland, on January 24, 1918. He was the son of the Austrian military attaché. Immediately after World War I, the family settled in Holstein and went on frequent trips to different parts of Europe. Attendance at several of the Salzburg festivals and association there with such eminent musicians as Bruno Walter and Toscanini encouraged him to pursue a career in music. He arrived in Berlin in 1938 expressly to study with Paul Hindemith, an ambition that was not realized because Hindemith was evicted from the Third Reich. Von Einem studied instead with Boris Blacher and worked for a while at the Berlin Staatsoper, where he was able to get an intimate and first-hand understanding of the technique of opera performances. He also concentrated on composing, producing a few works which received major performances. Most noteworthy were the *Capriccio for Orchestra,* introduced by the Berlin Philharmonic under Leo Borchard in 1943; the Concerto for Orchestra, given its first performance by the Berlin Staatsoper Orchestra under Herbert von Karajan in 1944; and the ballet *Princess Turandot,* first seen in Dresden also in 1944.

Because of his undisguised hostility to the Nazi regime, Gottfried von Einem suffered disparaging reviews at the hands of Nazi critics, Worse still, at one time he and his mother were seized by the Gestapo and imprisoned for several months. In 1945 he left Germany, settling near Salzburg, where he has lived ever since, making his home in a medieval watchtower. In Salzburg he began working on his *magnum opus,* the opera *Dantons Tod,* under the guidance of his teacher, Boris Blacher. This opera is based on a play of Georg Büchner (one of whose dramas also provided Alban Berg with a notable text, that of *Wozzeck),* and, as its title indicates, is set during the period of the French Revolution, its central theme being the rise and fall of the revolutionary Danton during Robespierre's reign of terror. *Dantons Tod* was introduced at the Salzburg Festival on August 6, 1947 (the first year the festival was resumed after World War II) and was an outstanding success. However,

Von Einem: fŏn ī'nĕm

Gondi

GOTTFRIED VON EINEM

its style proved so eclectic, that some Austrian wits were tempted to remark: *"Nicht von Einem, sondern von Vielen"*—"Not from one man, but from many."

"The score," wrote Everett Helm in *Musical America*, "is in keeping with his impersonal concept of the story. It is descriptive and it is dramatic, but it is never sentimental. The musical form ... depends directly on the action and is a commentary on it. . . . Each scene is composed as a separate unity; even the brief introduction with which the opera begins has its own musical material, independent of what follows. The first three and the last three scenes are connected by orchestral interludes, which bridge the changes in mood and cover the changes of scenery. . . . The vocal writing ... is in keeping with the basic naturalistic-poetic conception. . . . Most of the opera is written in a kind of melodic recitative that approximates the accents of everyday speech but is still far enough removed from it to preserve the poetic quality of Büchner's language. In the more impassioned passages, von Einem employs an arioso style; but nowhere is there a true aria. . . . A large part of *Dantons Tod* consists of dialogue, with two or more persons, and frequently the chorus as well, participating. . . . The music is predominantly tonal and is never systematically atonal, but the constant shifting of key often obscures the feeling of a tonal center."

Gottfried von Einem's second opera was *Der Prozess*, based on *The Trial*, by Franz Kafka. Like *Dantons Tod*, this opera was first seen at the Salzburg festival, during the summer of 1953.

Gottfried von Einem visited the United States early in 1953 as a guest of the State Department to study the American musical scene. On April 16, the New York Philharmonic-Symphony under Mitropoulos gave the American premiere of *Orchestra Music* with the composer in the audience.

MAJOR WORKS:

Ballet—Princess Turandot, 1942; Pas de Cœur, 1952.

Chamber Music—Sonata for Violin and Piano.

Operas—Dantons Tod, 1946; Der Prozess, 1950.

Orchestral Music—Capriccio for Orchestra, 1943; Concerto for Orchestra, 1944; Orchestra Music, 1948; Serenade, for double string orchestra, 1949.

Vocal Music—Eight Hafs-Lieder; Five Songs from the Chinese.

ABOUT:

Musical America, May 1951.

Sir Edward Elgar *1857-1934*

SIR EDWARD ELGAR was born in Broadheath, near Worcester, England, on June 2, 1857. He was the son of the organist of St. George's Roman Catholic Church in Worcester. As a boy, Elgar disclosed an insatiable appetite for music. He began studying by himself harmony, counterpoint, the violin, and organ, and spent hours memorizing the scores of operas and symphonies. His father, however, wanted him to study law. In his sixteenth year, therefore, Elgar was sent to London where for three years he concentrated on legal studies. Then he suddenly decided to return home and to concern himself exclusively with music. He served as the concertmaster of a local orchestra, played in a woodwind quintet, gave concerts on the violin, and sometimes substituted for his father at the church organ. In 1879 he was back in London, this time to study the violin with Adolf Pollitzer. Five lessons

Elgar: ĕl'gĕr

convinced him that he was not meant to be a violin virtuoso. Back again in Worcester, he served as pianist and conductor of the Worcester Glee Club and as bandmaster of the Worcester Lunatic Asylum. He also wrote functional pieces, one of which had the droll title of *Quadrille for an Eccentric Orchestra.* In 1885 he succeeded his father as organist of St. George's Church, his first important musical post.

In 1889 he married his pupil, Caroline Alice Roberts, a woman of outstanding intelligence and drive. She was destined to shape his career. It was due to her influence that Elgar decided, soon after his marriage, to abandon his varied and scattered musical assignments for serious creative work. He established his home in London, and, encouraged by his wife, began writing music in larger forms and more ambitious in scope than heretofore. In 1890 he completed the first such work, a concert overture, *Froissart.*

The disturbances of a great city, Elgar found, were not conducive to sustained creative work. In 1891 he moved on to Malvern. There he wrote several important choral works, including four cantatas, some of them being performed at major English festivals.

Fame arrived with two of Elgar's greatest works. The first was the *Variations on an Original Theme* (or, as it is now better known, the *Enigma Variations*) for orchestra, written in 1899. Each variation was intended by Elgar as a portrait of one of his own friends, one of these variations even being a self portrait. "The enigma," Elgar said, "I shall not explain—its 'dark saying' must be left unguessed." But that enigma is believed to be a hidden theme which though never actually heard *could* accompany each of the variations.

The melodic freshness and beauty and the emotional exuberance of the *Enigma Variations* impressed the celebrated conductor Hans Richter. He introduced this work in London on June 19, 1899, and then gave it several performances in other countries. Its success was both immediate and outstanding; for the first time the attention of the English music world was focused on Elgar.

But Elgar scored an even greater success with his oratorio *The Dream of Gerontius*, completed in 1900, based on the poem of Cardinal Newman. Consisting of a series of lyric and dramatic episodes describing the doctrine of purgatory as found in Catholic teachings, this oratorio was music filled with mysticism, vivid imagery, and melodic beauty. Ernest Newman said of it: "The work is of the first order almost throughout. Its detail work is poignant and convincing, while as a whole it has the homogeneity, the rounded completeness of vision, that only comes when the artist sees his picture through and through in one white heat of imagination."

The Dream of Gerontius was introduced at the Birmingham Festival on October 3, 1900, Hans Richter conducting. But its success did not come until a year later when the work was heard at the Lower Rhine Festival. It was a triumph. Richard Strauss described it as a "masterpiece." From this time on, the oratorio was acclaimed wherever and whenever it was heard. In short order it became almost as popular with English audiences as Handel's *Messiah* and Mendelssohn's *Elijah.*

Elgar was now one of England's most celebrated composers. Bernard Shaw went so far as to say that he "holds the same position in English music as Beethoven in German music." Others regarded him as the greatest composer to emerge in England since the time of Purcell.

In 1901 Elgar wrote a set of marches called *Pomp and Circumstance* (the phrase "pomp and circumstance" being taken from *Othello*). The first of these marches, in D major, has become as intimately associated with the British Empire as "God Save the King." When Edward VII heard the rousing and majestic melody (to which Laurence Housman subsequently wrote the lyric, "Land of Hope and Glory"), he exclaimed: "This tune will go round the world." With the writing of these patriotic marches, Elgar became the unofficial musical laureate of his land. For the coronation of Edward VII he was commissioned to write an Ode, and three years after that he was knighted.

During the next decade Elgar produced several major orchestral works The most important of these were two symphonies, the Concerto for Violin and Orchestra, the Introduction and Allegro for strings, the symphonic study *Falstaff* and the concert overture *Cockaigne.*

During World War I Elgar joined the Hampstead Division as special constable and after that volunteered in the Hampstead Reserve. He also enlisted his music in the war effort by setting war poems to music, writing two large works on martial subjects, and producing *Polonia* for the purpose of raising funds for Polish relief. After the war Elgar returned to serious creative work. He now became more objective in his writing, more reserved, leaning towards slighter forms and more concentrated expressions. He completed several interesting chamber-music works.

Elgar's wife died in 1920. This was such a crushing blow to him that he felt he could no longer write any music. Not the persuasion of his close friends, nor even an appointment as Master of the King's Musick in 1924, could bring him back to his work table. When he finally did return to composition, he was brought back to it by his patriotism. George V was stricken by a serious illness in 1929. Elgar wrote a Christmas carol as a prayer for his recovery. This was the first piece of music he had written in nine years. He now spoke of continuing his work where it had been interrupted, planning a third symphony. Meanwhile, in 1931, he received one of the highest honors the crown could bestow on a composer, that of baronetcy.

In January 1934 Elgar suffered from an attack of sciatica which necessitated an immediate operation. He never recovered. His health degenerated quickly after the operation. He died at his home in Worcester on February 23, 1934. One of his last requests was that no one attempt to complete or publish his third symphony.

It is quite true, as some critics have said of him, that Elgar was never a highly original composer. But at its best, his music has great charm, is filled with warm lyricism, and has engaging sentiments and beauty of sound. John F. Porte wrote: "His vein of tender sentiment was perhaps the most lovable of all its kind in music, and shared by that of Schubert. Elgar never shows us a soul that is seared or tortured, for while he can feel, he does not despair. An extreme sensitiveness to poetic ideas or reflections is a part of

Herbert Lambert
SIR EDWARD ELGAR

Elgar's thought, but this is always counter-balanced by a breezy reaction, a throwing aside as it were of anything which might lead to doubt; it is the ascendant spirit, the strong faith in himself, the blessing of common pluck, which never failed him."

Elgar had no set method of working. He conceived music at all times, while walking, playing, even while conversing with friends. He was usually scribbling ideas on paper, guarding the scraps carefully, and referring to them when he worked on major compositions. He worked easily and swiftly; ideas came to him copiously; and the task of working out these ideas seemed effortless.

Elgar's personality has been sketched as follows: Shaw once pithily described Elgar as a typical English country gentleman. Like many English country gentlemen, Elgar was tall, erect, and well built. He kept himself aloof in the company of strangers, suspicious of people he did not know well. To friends, however, he was open, generous, and warm-hearted. His fine sense of humor (he had an especially quick tongue for puns) and his genial disposition were known to all who knew him well. He had the English country-man's love of the outdoors. Dressed in informal rough clothing, he often took long walking tours or bicycle trips. He loved flowers, woods, brooks, country paths. Chopping wood and clearing away brushwood was play. He also liked to fish.

MAJOR WORKS:

Chamber Music—Sonata in E minor, for violin and piano, op. 82; Quartet in E minor, for strings, op. 83; Quintet in A minor, for piano and strings, op. 84.

Choral Music—The Black Knight, cantata, op. 25, 1893; The Light of Life, oratorio, op. 29, 1896; King Olaf, cantata, op. 30, 1896; Caractacus, cantata, op. 35, 1898; The Dream of Gerontius, oratorio, op. 38, 1900; The Apostles, oratorio, op. 49, 1903; The Kingdom, oratorio, op. 51, 1906.

Orchestral Music—Variations on an Original Theme (Enigma Variations), op. 36, 1899; Pomp and Circumstance, six marches, op. 39, 1901; Cockaigne, concert overture, op. 40, 1901; Introduction and Allegro, for string quartet and orchestra, op. 47, 1905; In the South, concert overture, op. 50, 1904; Symphony in A-flat, op. 55, 1908; Elegy, for string orchestra, op. 58, 1910; Concerto in B minor, for violin and orchestra, op. 61, 1910; Symphony in E-flat, op. 63, 1911; Falstaff, symphonic study, op. 68, 1913; Concerto in E minor, for cello and orchestra, op. 85, 1919; Nursery Suite, 1931.

ABOUT:

Maine, B. Elgar: His Life and Works; Porte, J. F., Elgar and His Music; Powell, R., Edward Elgar; Reed, W. H., Elgar as I Knew Him; Shera, F. H., Elgar's Instrumental Works.

Georges Enesco *1881-*

GEORGES ENESCO

G EORGES ENESCO, Rumania's foremost living musician, was born in Liveni, on August 19, 1881. A village musician taught him the elements of notation. Before long, the child Enesco was writing music; by the time he was seven years old he produced several rondos and sonatas for the piano.

His father recognized his son's musical talent. He took the seven-year-old boy to Vienna to enter him in the Conservatory. The Conservatory director, Joseph Hellmesberger, was so impressed with the child that he had him live in his own home. One of the celebrated Viennese musicians Enesco met during this period was Johannes Brahms. Enesco's admiration for the master developed into adulation, an adulation expressing itself in the boy's instinctive attempt to imitate Brahms's style.

After winning prizes in violin-playing and harmony at the Vienna Conservatory, Enesco went to Paris to complete his studies at its Conservatory. Once again he won the highest honors: in violin-playing, counterpoint, and fugue. His teachers (who included Marsick, Massenet, Fauré, and Gedalge) spoke of him as a "genius." Through their influence, performances of Enesco's early works were arranged. In 1897 there took place in Paris a concert devoted entirely to Enesco's music. One year later, on February 6, 1898, Édouard Colonne directed the premiere of Enesco's *Poème Roumain* at a Chatelet concert.

Not until a decade later did Enesco become famous. On February 7, 1908, Pablo Casals directed in Paris the world premiere of Enesco's most celebrated works, the two Rumanian Rhapsodies. They were instantaneously successful and forthwith established Enesco as the major musical voice of Rumania.

Meanwhile, beginning in 1900, Enesco was making his mark as a concert violinist. He distinguished himself for the wide range of his musicianship and his penetrating interpretative insight. Recognition of his virtuoso abilities became complete when he was appointed court violinist to the Queen of Rumania.

Just before the outbreak of World War I, Enesco settled in Bucharest. He now became one of the most vital and influential of Rumanian musicians. He conducted the Bucharest Philharmonic Orchestra; he organized concerts of modern music; he founded a prize for young Rumanian composers. He was indefatigable in his efforts to bring recognition to talented young musicians of his native land.

When the war ended, Enesco established himself in Paris. He was to live for the next few decades in an apartment in the Rue de Clichy, returning to his native land at least once a year. During this period, he toured the music world in the triple role of violinist, conductor, and composer. His first appearance in the United States was made on January 19, 1923, when he was heard as soloist with the Boston Symphony Orchestra.

During World War II, Enesco lived on a large farm in Sinai, near Bucharest. The difficult years found him tending his stock, and doing some composing. When the Soviets took over Rumania, they made an exception in Enesco's case by confiscating only two thirds of his farm, permitting him to retain the other third.

On November 10, 1946, Enesco returned to the United States after an absence of almost a decade. During this tour, he received the Grand Cross of the Order of Loyal Service from the Rumanian ambassador to the United States, for his lifelong service to Rumanian music.

Enesco has written music in many different styles. An early work like the Symphony No. 1 is Brahmsian in its romanticism. The Suite No. 2, for orchestra, is in a neo-classic vein, and the opera *Oedipe* uses experimental tonalities and quarter tones. But Enesco is best known and best loved for those works built around folk idioms. Utilizing the songs and dances of his native land with brilliant virtuosity, Enesco has produced several works indigenous to Rumania, and yet, in their skillful rhythmic and harmonic techniques, personal with him. Whether or not he writes in a folk vein, Enesco is always the musician of impeccable taste, a consummate technician, a fine and sensitive poet. His style is as aristocratic as is his personality; he has always served the highest interests of his art faithfully, with humility, without ostentation. Lawrence Gilman once put it well when he wrote: "He remains a man of dignity and gentle ways, modest and genuine and simple, magnanimous and poised, wise and humorous and humane, close to the roots of universal things."

31468

Speaking of his method of writing music, Enesco has said: "Melodic ideas come into my head years, sometimes, before I utilize them. Yet in that time my method of treating them may be very different from what it would have been at their conception. Still I can always put an old idea to account. I compose very slowly because I believe that to be the best way. If you work slowly and carefully, even if you do not achieve great results, you at least achieve sincere ones. . . . Much as I enjoy writing for orchestra, I find no end of pleasure in writing for the piano— writing orchestrally for it, as it were."

In 1946 Enesco was married to Princess Cantacuzene. This was his second marriage. They live for the greater part of the year in a comparatively modest three-room apartment in Paris.

Enesco has always had an enormous capacity for work. When he is not on tour, his workday is a long one, beginning soon after dawn and ending long after midnight. Time must be found for several hours of composition, practicing on the violin, playing the piano (he is an accomplished pianist), studying new scores. "Nothing else exists for me but work," he told an interviewer. "I'm just a musician, and a humble one. My happiness is at the writing table, composing. Outside of my music, I'm like an ostrich that hides under the wing. I have no hobbies. I just happen to live like a bourgeois."

Enesco has also achieved significance as a teacher of the violin, having held master classes in violin in several leading conservatories in Europe and the United States. His most famous pupil is Yehudi Menuhin.

Major Works:

Chamber Music—Sonata No. 2, in F minor, for violin and piano, op. 6, 1901; Octet in C major, op. 7; Quartet in D major, for piano and strings, op. 16; Sonata No. 3 in A minor, for violin and piano, op. 25, 1926; Quintet for Piano and Strings; Quintet in D minor, for strings, op. 30, 1944; Impressions d'Enfance, for violin and piano.

Opera—Oedipe, 1931.

Orchestral Music—Poème Roumain, op. 1, 1897; Suite in C major, op. 9; Symphony No. 1, in E-flat major, op. 13, 1904; Rumanian Rhapsodies, Nos. 1 and 2, in A major and D major, op. 11, 1907; Symphony No. 2, in A major, op. 17, 1915; Symphony No. 3, in C major, 1919; Suite No. 3, in A major, Villageoise, op. 27, 1939; Symphony No. 4, in E minor, 1940; Symphony No. 5; Overture on Motifs in the Rumanian Character, op. 32, 1948.

Piano Music—Suite No. 2, in D major, op. 10; Pièces Impromptus, op. 19; Sonata in F minor, op. 24.

Vocal Music—Seven Songs (Marot), op. 15; Three Songs (Gregh), op. 18.

Manuel de Falla *1876-1946*

(See *American Composers Today*)

Gabriel Fauré *1845-1924*

GABRIEL URBAIN FAURÉ was born in Pamiers, Ariège, on May 12, 1845, the son of simple village people. As a boy, he played the organ, which he learned by himself. His intensive musical education took place at the École Niedermeyer, where one of his teachers, Camille Saint-Saëns, was a profound influence. On leaving the school in 1866, Fauré began his professional career. He became organist in Rennes, Brittany. After four years, he returned to Paris and held several important organ posts including those at the Notre Dame de Cligancourt, St. Honoré d'Église, St. Sulpice, and the Madeleine. During this long and successful period as organist, Fauré first turned to teaching. At first he taught composition at the École Neidermeyer, then accepted a similar post at the Conservatory. In 1905 he succeeded

G. L. Manuel

GABRIEL FAURÉ

Fauré: fô-rā′

Dubois as director of the Conservatory, holding the position for fifteen years. His importance as a teacher can partially be measured by the stature of some of the pupils who studied with him and have since expressed their indebtedness to him: Ravel, Schmitt, Roger-Ducasse, Aubert, Nadia Boulanger, Enesco, Vuillermoz, Koechlin.

Fauré first emerged as a composer with a group of songs published in 1865. These early songs had a tender beauty and an emotional restraint which gave indications of Fauré's later mature lyric style. Maurice Ravel wrote: "The personality of Fauré is apparent in his first songs. The seductiveness of his melodic contour does not cede to the subtlety of harmonies in these pieces."

The song-form remained one of Fauré's happiest mediums of artistic expression, among the most treasurable items in contemporary French music. He was a consummate master of its form, artist *par excellence* in producing fresh and tender melodies, refined and sensitive atmospheres, and translating the most elusive suggestions of the poetic text into tones. He wrote about a hundred songs, the last appearing two years before his death. Among the most celebrated are "Après un Rêve," "Sylvie," "En Prière," "Les Roses d'Ispahan," "Au Cimitière," "Soir," and "Prison," as well as such song cycles as *La Chanson d'Ève* and *L'Horizon Chimérique*.

Fauré's first major work in a large form was his *Requiem*, written in 1887 and introduced at the Madeleine church one year later. It is not only one of Fauré's masterpieces, but one of the most poignant works in French music. "Nothing purer, clearer in definition has been written," wrote Nadia Boulanger. "No exterior effect alters its sober and rather severe expression of grief, no restlessness troubles its deep meditation, no doubt strains its spotless faith, its gentle confidence, its tender and tranquil expectancy."

Fauré has also written within the chamber-music forms. His beautiful Sonata in A major, for violin and piano, written in 1876, is music that exemplifies the new type of French music foreshadowed by Franck and developed by Fauré, Chausson, and Debussy; it is tender, passionate, rich in imagination. With the Quartet in C minor, for piano and strings, completed in 1879, French chamber music is said to come fully into its own. Fauré's later chamber works—the Piano Quintet, op. 89, and the String Quartet, op. 121—tap new veins of expression. "Never did a creative artist present us with subtler and more powerful achievements," wrote Vuillermoz.

In his music the spirit of ancient Greece was fused with advanced musical thinking. The serenity, refinement, and beauty of Fauré's writing sometimes makes us forget that his style and techniques were sometimes highly advanced. Twenty years before Debussy, Fauré suggested the syntax of impressionism, while his harmonic construction is often original and even daring. And yet, the Hellenic spirit of his art is ever predominant. Julien Tiersot put it this way: "Perhaps it is not enough to recognize in him a Greek musician revived in our twentieth century; but it is the spirit of Hellenism, as well as its forms, which is reborn in him. . . . He, too, thrusts himself beyond the spheres in order to bring back pure beauty."

In 1909 Fauré was elected to the Académie des Beaux-Arts. Thirteen years later he became the object of national tribute. A testimonial concert of his music was given by national decree; he was honored by the Sorbonne; he was promoted to the highest class in the order of the Legion of Honor. To these honors, and to official tributes, Fauré reacted with humility and modesty.

He died in Paris on November 4, 1924. Not until seven years after his death did his son reveal the fact that Fauré had been suffering from deafness during the last twenty years of his life, a condition the composer had kept a dark secret for fear of jeopardizing his post at the Conservatory.

MAJOR WORKS:

Chamber Music—Sonata No. 1, in A major for Violin and Piano, op. 13, 1876; Piano Quartet No. 1, op. 15, 1879; Elegy, for cello and piano, op. 24, 1883; Piano Quartet No. 2, op. 45, 1886; Quintet for Piano and Strings, op. 89, 1906; Sonata No. 2 for Violin and Piano, op. 108, 1917; Sonata No. 1 for Cello and Piano, op. 109, 1918; Quintet No. 2 for Piano and Strings, op. 115, 1921; Sonata No. 2 for Cello and Piano, op. 117, 1922; Trio in D minor, op. 120, 1923; String Quartet, op. 121, 1923.

Choral Music—Les Djinnes, for mixed chorus and orchestra, op. 12, 1875; La Naissance de Vénus, mythological scene for chorus and orchestra, op. 29, 1882; Madrigal, op. 35, 1884; Requiem, op. 48, 1887; Tantum Ergo, for soloist and chorus, op. 55, 1890; Ave Verum, op. 65, 1894.

Operas—Prométhée, op. 82, 1900; Pénélope, 1912.

Orchestral Music—Ballade, for piano and orchestra, op. 19, 1881; Romance, for violin and orchestra, op. 28, 1882; Symphony in D minor, op. 40, 1884; Pelléas et Mélisande, suite, op. 80, 1897; Fantaisie, for piano and orchestra, op. 111, 1919; Masques et Bergamasques, suite, op. 112, 1918.

Piano Music—5 Impromptus, op. 25, 31, 34, 91, 102, 1883-1910; 13 Barcarolles, op. 26, 41, 44, 66, 70, 90, 96, 101, 104, 105, 116, 1883-1921; 4 Valse Caprices, op. 30, 38, 59, 62, 1883-1894; 13 Nocturnes, op. 33, 36, 37, 63, 74, 97, 99, 104, 119, 1883-1922; 9 Preludes, op. 103, 1911; Mazurka, op. 32, 1883; Dolly, six pieces for four hands, op. 56, 1896 (orchestrated by H. Rabaud); Theme and Variations, op. 73, 1897; Huit Pièces Brèves, op. 73, 1897.

Vocal Music—Chant d'Automne, Rêve d'Amour, and L'Absent, op. 5; Aubade, Tristesse, Sylvie, op. 6; Après un Rêve, Hymne, and Barcarolle, op. 7; Nell, Le Voyageur, Automne, op. 18, 1880; Aurore, Fleur Jetée, Le Pays des Rêves, Les Roses d'Ispahan, op. 39, 1884; Noël, Nocturne, Clair de Lune, op. 43, 1887; Larmes, Au Cimitière, Spleen, La Rose, op. 51, 1889; Cinq Mélodies de Verlaine, op. 58, 1889; La Bonne Chanson (Verlaine), op. 61, 1892; Prison, Soir, op. 83, 1900; La Chanson d'Ève, op. 95, 1910; Le Jardin Clos, op. 106, 1918; Mirages, op. 113, 1919; C'est la Paix, op. 114, 1920; L'Horizon Chimérique, op. 118, 1922.

ABOUT:

Faure, G., Gabriel Fauré; Rostand, C., L'Œuvre de Gabriel Fauré; Suckling, N., Fauré.

Jean Françaix 1912-

JEAN FRANÇAIX came from a family of professional musicians. He was born in Le Mans, France, on May 23, 1912. His father was the director of the Le Mans Conservatory; his mother, the organizer of a splendid women's choral group. Jean Françaix began to study music early, and showed marked talent from the very first. At the age of four he started improvising at the piano. Before very long, he began writing music. His first published work appeared when he was ten years old, in 1922—a piano suite entitled *Pour Jacqueline*, written one year earlier to celebrate the first walking steps of his little cousin.

His music study took place in his father's Conservatory where he won several prizes. In his tenth year, he began making regular trips to Paris to study harmony and composition with Nadia Boulanger and piano with

Françaix: fräN-sä'

NAZARETH COLLEGE
LIBRARY

Photo-Lipnitzki

JEAN FRANÇAIX

Isidor Philipp at the Paris Conservatory. In 1930 he won first prize in piano at the Conservatory.

Two of his works received important performances in 1932. On June 21 his *Bagatelles*, for string quartet and piano, was introduced at a festival of the International Society for Contemporary Music in Vienna. On November 6 his Symphony was presented in Paris by the Orchestre Symphonique under Pierre Monteux. Both works were exceptionally well received. Hardly past his twentieth birthday, Français was already regarded by some French critics as one of the most promising composers to emerge in France after World War I.

Several other significant works fulfilled the promise of his earlier compositions. The most important of these were two works for piano and orchestra. The first was the Concertino for Piano and Orchestra, written in 1934, and introduced by the composer and the Lamoureux Orchestra under Morel on December 15 of the same year. The other work was the Concerto for Piano and Orchestra, completed in 1936, and first heard in Berlin on November 8 of that year, the composer appearing as soloist.

Français is a neo-classic composer who has been profoundly influenced by Stravinsky, whom he regards as the greatest of all twentieth-century composers (and whom he resembles physically). Français goes in for smaller forms, briefly stated ideas, economical instrumentation and harmonization; he often fills his music with ironic or acid statements. His touch is light, his style is graceful, his manner suave and engaging.

In 1938 Français visited the United States for the first time. He made his American debut on February 11 with the New York Philharmonic-Symphony, under Nadia Boulanger, in a performance of his own Concerto for Piano and Orchestra. The sparkle and wit of his music inspired praises among the New York music critics, one of whom spoke of him as "the white hope of French music."

At the time of this visit, Français confided to an interviewer his aims as a composer: "It is important that a composer should be of his country and that he should try to translate the spirit of his country into music, eliminating the faults and emphasizing the great qualities. In other respects, my ideal is to write music that is absolutely personal, that belongs to myself and not to anybody else. One should not deliberately declare that one adheres to this or that school or is influenced by this or that composer. One is influenced largely unconsciously, but one's chief conscious interest should be in personal expression."

In May 1950 Français's opera *La Main de Gloire* received its world premiere at the Bordeaux Music Festival in France. It is based on a story of Gerard de Nerval, the libretto prepared by the composer himself. Reviewing the opera, Henri Barraud wrote in *Musical America*: "It is one of the most original stage works produced in France in a long time."

An earlier opera, *L'Apostrophe*, was in a highly satirical vein. It scored a huge success when introduced at the Holland Music Festival in Amsterdam on July 1, 1951. So effective was Français's satire, wrote a correspondent in the *New York Times*, "that even the non-French speaking section of the audience often was lured into laughter by the caprices of the score."

On September 11, 1951, the New York City Ballet presented a new ballet entitled *À la Français*, a setting of the Serenade for Twelve Instruments.

Major Works:

Ballets—Scuola di Ballo (adapted from the music of Boccherini), 1933; Les Malheurs de Sophie, 1935; Le Roi Nu, 1935; La Lutherie Enchantée, 1936; Le Jeu Sentimental, 1936; Verreries de Venise, 1938; Le Jugement du Fou, 1938; Demoiselles de la Nuit, 1948.

Chamber Music—Bagatelles, for string quartet and piano, 1931; Sonata for Two Violins and Cello, 1933; Serenade for Twelve Instruments, 1934; Trio in C major, for violin, viola, and cello; Le Diable Boiteux, for tenor, bass, and fifteen instruments, 1937; Quintet, for woodwind.

Choral Music—L'Apocalypse de Jean, oratorio, 1942.

Operas—L'Apostrophe, 1940; La Main de Gioire, 1948.

Orchestral Music—Symphony, 1931; Concertino for Piano and Orchestra, 1932; Concerto for Piano and Orchestra, 1936; Musique de Cour, suite for flute, violin, and orchestra, 1937; Le Jugement du Fou, suite, 1939; Symphony for Strings, 1948; Le Cantate de Méphisto, for bass and strings, 1952.

PAUL GILSON

Paul Gilson *1865-1942*

PAUL GILSON, one of the major musical figures of Belgium, was born in Brussels on June 15, 1865. He spent his childhood in Ruysbroeck, on the outskirts of Brussels, where his family moved when he was five years old. There he received his first instruction in music from the village organist, August Cantillon. Later on, he studied the piano, harmony, and counterpoint with Duyck. After the family returned to Brussels, Gilson met the eminent Belgian teacher and theorist, Gevaert, who became interested in him. Largely as a result of Gevaert's urging, Gilson entered the Brussels Conservatory in 1886. He remained there three years. In his last year at the Conservatory Gilson won the Prix de Rome with the cantata *Sinai*.

Gilson was appointed professor of harmony at the Brussels Conservatory in 1889. He held this post for two decades. From 1904 to 1909 he also taught theory at the Antwerp Conservatory.

Gilson's success as a composer was first realized in 1892 with the premiere of his symphonic sketches, *La Mer*, based on poems of Eddy Levis. It was heard at the Concerts Populaires under Joseph Dupont's direction and was acclaimed. It has since then remained one of Gilson's best known works.

La Mer was followed by two other major works: an opera, *Alva*, and an oratorio, *Francesca da Rimini*, both introduced in Brussels in 1895. With these two works, Gilson's position as one of Belgium's major composers was solidified.

From 1901 to 1914 Gilson combined his activities as teacher and composer with that of writing music criticism for the Belgian newspapers and for the journal which he edited, *La Revue Musicale Belge*. He abandoned teaching in 1909 when he received an appointment as Inspector of Musical Education, succeeding Edgar Tinel.

Influenced to a degree by the music of the "Russian Five," Gilson's works are rhythmically vital, aglow with instrumental colors, and intense and passionate in their expression.

His influence on his younger contemporaries has been far-reaching. His extraordinary culture, sympathetic tolerance to all styles, and natural gifts for pedagogy were qualities which drew to him many of Belgium's most talented young composers, including Poot, Bourguignon, Bernier, and many others. They studied under him and received from him the direction and purpose they needed in the development of their own careers.

Gilson was the author of several important theoretical works including *Les In-*

tervalles, Le Tutti Orchestral, and *Traité d'Harmonie.* He died in Brussels on April 3, 1942.

MAJOR WORKS:

Ballet—La Captive.

Chamber Music—2 string quartets; Scènes Rustiques, for string quartet; Concertstück and Scherzo, for three trumpets, Humoresques, for woodwind and horns; Septet.

Choral Music—Sinai, cantata; Francesca da Rimini, oratorio; Le Démon, oratorio.

Operas—Alva; Marines; Princess Sunshine; A Brigand's Love.

Orchestral Music—La Mer; Italia; Fanfare Inaugurale; Rapsodie Canadienne; Scotch Rhapsody; 2 concertos for saxophone and orchestra; La Destinée; 3 overtures; 8 suites.

Umberto Giordano *1867-1948*

UMBERTO GIORDANO was one of Italy's outstanding twentieth-century opera composers. He was born in Foggia on August 27, 1867. His father, an artisan, wanted him to follow in his trade. But Umberto's obvious musical talent combined with the protests of music-loving friends to convince the father to allow the boy to study music. Giordano's first teacher was Gaetano Briganti in Foggia. Making exceptional progress under Briganti, Giordano was sent

UMBERTO GIORDANO

Giordano: jôr-dä′nō

to the Naples Conservatory where he remained nine years.

Giordano wrote his first opera, *Marina,* while he was still a Conservatory student. He entered it in the Sonzogno contest in 1889. He failed to win the prize (that honor went to Mascagni's *Cavalleria Rusticana*). But he attracted the interest of the powerful publisher Sonzogno, who commissioned him to write a new opera. That work, *Mala Vita,* was first seen in Rome on February 21, 1892, and was moderately successful. Giordano subsequently revised the work, and retitled it *Il Voto;* in this new version it was introduced in Milan in 1897.

Fame came at a time when Giordano had reached the lowest ebb in his fortunes. The operas he had written up to 1896 were either outright failures or moderate successes, and they had failed to lift him out of his poverty and obscurity. He was in a state of depression and stifling discouragement. "This is my last card," he said of the opera he was then writing. "If this opera is not a success, I shall play no more."

The "last card" proved to be the ace of trumps: *Andrea Chenier.* The effective libretto by Luigi Illica was centered around the character of André de Chenier, a French poet during the period of the Revolution who was guillotined. For this "story with a historical setting" (as the composer designated his opera), Giordano wrote a score that was romantic in the best Italian tradition. He filled his music with large arias, stirring declamations, and big scenes. *Andrea Chenier* was introduced at La Scala in Milan on March 28, 1896. It was an immediate triumph. Overnight, Giordano found himself an established composer. Other great opera houses presented the work with immense success: the Academy of Music in New York in 1896; the Berlin Royal Opera in 1898; and Covent Garden in London in 1904.

Besides making Giordano famous, *Andrea Chenier* was responsible for the composer's happy marriage. The authenticated story is as follows: Giordano, while still impoverished and comparatively unknown, was courting the daughter of a Milan hotel proprietor. The latter, a friend of the great Verdi, confided to the master that his daughter was in love with a composer, adding that he would not object to the match if he were sure that the composer had talent. Verdi promised to pass on the merits of the young musician. One day, while Giordano was absent in Naples, the hotel proprietor removed from Giordano's room the uncompleted score of *Andrea Chenier* and showed it to Verdi. Verdi later returned the manuscript to the hotel proprietor with the following note: "You may safely confide your daughter to the man who composed a work like this."

Giordano wrote several operas after *Andrea Chenier*. A few were successful, among them *Fedora* (adapted from the famous play of Sardou and introduced at La Scala on November 17, 1898); *Madame Sans-Gêne* (derived from the play of Sardou and Moreau and, like *Andrea Chenier*, utilizing the background of the French Revolution, and first seen at the Metropolitan Opera House in New York on January 25, 1915); and *La Cena delle Beffe* (first performed at La Scala on December 20, 1924).

What R. A. Streatfeild wrote of Giordano is undoubtedly valid: "In his music the usual theatrical tricks for extorting applause too often take the place of a sincere expression of emotion." But it is also true that, together with his obvious theatricalism, Giordano brought to his operas a wonderful fund of melody and a sound instinct for building climactic scenes. He was not an original composer, but his best operas are effective theatre.

Giordano was the recipient of many honors; he was made a Chevalier of the Legion of Honor in France, a Commander of the Crown of Italy, and a member of the Italian Academy. He died in Milan on November 12, 1948.

MAJOR WORKS:

Operas—Mala Vita (Il Voto), 1892; Andrea Chenier, 1896; Fedora, 1898; Siberia, 1904; Madame Sans-Gêne, 1915; Giove a Pompei, 1921; La Cena delle Beffe, 1924; Il Re, 1929.

Alexander Glazunov *1865-1936*

ALEXANDER GLAZUNOV was born in St. Petersburg on August 10, 1865. His father was a publisher. When Glazunov was nine years old, he began to study the piano with Elenkovsky, formerly his mother's teacher. "At home we had a great deal of music," Glazunov revealed later in life, "and everything we played remained firmly in my memory, so that, awakening in the night, I could construct, even to the smallest details, all that I had heard earlier in the evening." He also had the gift of learning a piece of music, note by note, after a single reading. His aptitude in theory and harmony was no less marked. Before he was thirteen he started writing chamber and orchestral music.

When Elenkovsky left St. Petersburg in 1878, Glazunov went to Balakirev for advice, direction, and some instruction. Balakirev was so impressed with the boy's talent that he brought one of his compositions to Rimsky-Korsakov. Rimsky-Korsakov recalled the event in his autobiography: "It was an orchestral score written in childish fashion; the boy's talent was indubitably clear." Glazunov became Rimsky-Korsakov's pupil in 1880. "He was a charming boy with beautiful eyes," the teacher wrote. "Elementary theory and solfeggio proved unnecessary for him, as he had a superior ear. . . . After a few lessons in harmony, I took him directly into counterpoint, to which he applied himself zealously. . . . His musical development progressed not by the day, but literally by the hour."

He had been only a year and a half with Rimsky-Korsakov when he completed his first symphony. It was introduced at a concert of the Free School of Music, Balakirev conducting, on March 29, 1882. When Glazunov came to the stage to take his bows —a sixteen-year-old boy dressed in a schoolboy uniform—the appreciative audience was shocked to learn that the symphony was the work of one so young. It was described by César Cui as "frightening in its precocious maturity." So good was this work that there were some authorities who suspected that it was actually the work of Rimsky-Korsakov.

He now began composing in earnest and did not lack for attention. The most influential musicians of St. Petersburg sang his praises. Balakirev called him "the little Glinka"; Stassov spoke of him as "our young Samson"; some students at the Conservatory, in presenting him with a wreath, designated him as "our Hermann and Cazeneuve"— Hermann and Cazeneuve being two popular magicians of the day. Among Glazunov's

Glazunov: glä-zŏo-nôf'

ALEXANDER GLAZUNOV

works of his apprentice period—and they were performed and published—were two string quartets, two overtures on Greek themes, and the symphonic poem *Stenka Razin*.

In 1884 Glazunov went on an extended trip throughout Europe. In Weimar he met Franz Liszt, whom he admired and who was to be won over completely by the young man's ability. Liszt praised Glazunov's First Symphony; and when Glazunov wrote a second symphony he dedicated it to Liszt's memory. Glazunov's international stature was growing. At the Paris Exposition of 1889, his Second Symphony and *Stenka Razin* were performed with great success. In 1892 the Columbian Exposition in Chicago commissioned him to write a work expressly for it—the *Triumphal March* for chorus and orchestra. In 1896 he visited England and directed successful performances of his works. By 1900 he was acknowledged to be one of the great creative figures in Russian music—and he was only thirty-five years old at the time.

But the twentieth century saw a sharp decline of Glazunov's significance as a composer. He who had been acknowledged a genius in his youth, and a composer of international prestige in his maturity, became a "has been" in the closing decades of his life. Glazunov wrote his last symphony in 1906. Then, for the next sixteen years he wrote by fits and starts, and little that was of value. He was honored as a teacher and a musical figure. But as a composer, he was recognized outside Russia only for a handful of works, all of them written in early manhood.

Glazunov's career as a teacher began in 1899, when he conducted a class in instrumentation at the St. Petersburg Conservatory. In 1905 he became director of the Conservatory, holding this post until 1922. He exercised a profound influence on his pupils, many of whom were accused of succumbing to "Glazunovichina"—writing in the Glazunov style.

As a protégé of Balakirev and a pupil of Rimsky-Korsakov, Glazunov acquired the ideals and principles of the national school of Russian composers known as the "Russian Five." Glazunov's early works, the most notable being *Stenka Razin*, were expressions of nationalist ideals, and it may be said with justification that Glazunov was the last of the famous nationalists.

But even as a nationalist composer, in the tradition of the "Five," Glazunov represented reaction. Time and again he disappointed Rimsky-Korsakov and the others by his adherence to German structure and stylistic procedures. As he continued writing, Glazunov's music became so increasingly reactionary that it was said of him that he entered the future backwards. He preferred adhering to the classic forms and filling these forms with traditional melodies and harmonies that fell pleasingly on the ear.

Though Glazunov was not completely in sympathy with the Revolution in Russia, he remained and held several positions. For a while he served as kind of musical emissary in France, Germany, and Austria to report back on musical activities there. He continued as director of the St. Petersburg (from 1924, Leningrad) Conservatory. He helped organize an opera studio and a students' orchestra, and did what he could to promote the musical life of the Soviet Union. Growing dissatisfaction with the Soviet Union led him to leave his country for good. In 1928 he went to Paris, which was to remain his home for the rest of his life. One year later he visited the United States, making his first appearance in this country on November 21, conducting the Detroit Symphony Orchestra in a program of his own works. He died in Paris on March 21, 1936.

Dmitri Tiomkin has written the following informal sketch of Glazunov: "Either he was very lively or very silent. Although he inherited considerable wealth from his ancestors that enabled him to live well (up to the time of the Revolution), he was never so happy as in simple bohemian apartments. . . . His particular hobby was his old family coach, a strange-looking vehicle which he used in summer and winter. With a long black cigar, a big black tie and robust figure dressed in the manner of Turgenev's or Tolstoy's novels, he was an outstanding figure. . . . Utter modesty and spiritual democracy were his watchwords at home and in school. As a rule, he spoke little in society, but when he was aroused on a particular subject he could be brilliantly conversational. . . . There was in him much of the hospitable Russian merchant, who loves to entertain his visitors, or, in the good old days, treat them to a glass of tea or vodka."

MAJOR WORKS:

Ballets—Raymonda, op. 57, 1897; Ruses d'Amour, op. 61, 1898; The Seasons, op. 67, 1899.

Chamber Music—Quartet No. 2, in F major, op. 10, 1884; Novelettes, for string quartet, op. 15, 1888; Quatuor Slave in G major, op. 26b; Suite, for string quartet, op. 35, 1894; In Modo Religioso, quartet for brass, op. 38; String Quintet, op. 39, 1895; Quartet No. 4, in A major, op. 64, 1899; Quartet No. 5, in D major, op. 70, 1900; Elegy, for string quartet, op. 105, 1929; Quartet No. 6, op. 106; Quartet No. 7, op. 107.

Choral Music—Triumphal March, for chorus and orchestra, op. 40, 1892; Coronation Cantata, for soloists, chorus, and orchestra, op. 56; Cantata, for women's chorus, soloists, and two pianos, op. 63; Memorial Cantata, for soloists, chorus, and orchestra, op. 65; Hymn to Pushkin, for women's chorus, op. 66, 1899; Requiem, 1930.

Orchestral Music—Symphony No. 1, in E major, 1881; Overture on Greek Themes, op. 3, 1884; Second Overture on Greek Themes, op. 6, 1885; Suite Caractéristique, op. 9, 1887; Stenka Razin, symphonic poem, op. 13, 1884; Symphony No. 2, in F-sharp major, op. 16, 1886; The Forest, symphonic poem, op. 19, 1888; Wedding March, op. 21, 1888; Une Fête Slave, symphonic sketch, op. 26a, 1888; The Sea, symphonic fantasy, op. 28, 1888; Rhapsodie Orientale, op. 29, 1889; The Kremlin, op. 30, 1890; Symphony No. 3, in D major, op. 33, 1890; Le Printemps, symphonic sketch, op. 34, 1892; Chopiniana, suite, op. 46, 1894; Symphony No. 4, in E-flat major, op. 48, 1893; Cortège Solennel, op. 50, 1894; Scènes de Ballet, suite, op. 52, 1894; Symphony No. 5, in B-flat major, op. 55, 1895; Symphony No. 6, in C minor, op. 58, 1895; Pas de Caractère, op. 68, 1900; Intermezzo Romantico, op. 69, 1901; Symphony No. 7, in F major, op. 77,

1900; Ballade, op. 78, 1902; Suite from the Middle Ages, op. 79, 1903; Scène Dansante, op. 81, 1904; Concerto in A minor for Violin and Orchestra, op. 82, 1904; Symphony No. 8, in E-flat major, op. 83, 1905; Le Chant du Destin, dramatic overture, op. 84, 1907; Two Preludes, op. 85, 1908; A la Mémoire de Gogol, symphonic prologue, op. 87, 1909; Esquisses Finnoises, op. 89, 1909; Introduction et la Danse de Salomé, op. 90, 1909; Concerto No. 1, in F minor, for piano and orchestra, op. 92, 1911; Karelian Legend, op. 99, 1915; Concerto No. 2, in B major, for piano and orchestra, op. 100, 1920; Concerto Ballata, in C major, op. 108, 1930; Concerto in E-flat major, for alto saxophone and string orchestra, op. 109, 1934.

Piano Music—Three Etudes, op. 31; Nocturne, op. 37; Grande Valse de Concert, op. 41; Trois Morceaux, op. 49; Two Impromptus, op. 54; Prelude and Fugue, op. 62; Theme and Variations, op. 72, 1901; Sonata in B-flat major, op. 74; Sonata No. 2, op. 75; Suite for Two Pianos, 1920; Four Preludes and Fugues, 1922.

ABOUT:

Calvocoressi, M. D., and Abraham, G., Masters of Russian Music; Montagu-Nathan, M., Contemporary Russian Composers.

Reinhold Glière 1875-

REINHOLD GLIÈRE, Soviet composer of Belgian ancestry, was born in Kiev on January 11, 1875. Some music study took place in his native city, but formal and systematic training was delayed until his maturity. In his twentieth year Glière entered the Moscow Conservatory, where his teachers included Taneiev, Arensky and Ippolitov-Ivanov. He was an outstanding student, winning a gold medal in composition. While still at the Conservatory, he started writing chamber-music works, one of which, a Sextet, was published.

In 1902 his Symphony No. 1 was performed by the Russian Musical Society in Moscow and was severely criticized. This convinced him that he needed more study. For the next two years he traveled in Germany, devoting himself to intensive study in Berlin. The influence of this German period is apparent in his Symphony No. 2, written in 1907, filled as it is with German romanticism instead of the Russian nationalism that characterized his music before his German travels. He also started writing in an impressionist vein, as in the tone poem *The Sirens*, which came one year after the Second Symphony.

Glière: glē-âr′

REINHOLD GLIÈRE

He was obviously groping for a style that would satisfy his artistic ends. When that style was finally crystallized, it combined romanticism with nationalism. It is in this vein that he produced his most successful work, completed in 1911, the Symphony No. 3, subtitled *Ilia Mourometz*. To the present day it is Glière's most frequently heard major work. In this symphony Glière went for his inspiration to the twelfth-century Russian folk legend, glorifying the hero, Ilia Mourometz. Rich in orchestral effects, vivid in its harmonizations, filled with exotic colors and atmospheres, dynamic with dramatic surges and sweeps, this symphony never fails to have a powerful impact on audiences. When it was introduced in Moscow in 1912, in a performance by the Russian Musical Society under Emil Cooper, it was an instantaneous success. Soon after this it won the Glinka Prize.

In 1913 Glière became professor of composition at the Kiev Conservatory, becoming its director one year later. It was largely due to his efforts, that this institution became one of the foremost in Russia. In 1920, Glière joined the faculty of the Moscow Conservatory.

During World War I Glière was for the most part non-productive as a composer. After the war and the Revolution in Russia, he became fired with the ambition of making his music glorify the ideals and aims of the Soviet regime. Thus, in 1926-27, he wrote the first ballet employing a social theme. That ballet was *The Red Poppy*, which achieved an overwhelming success in the Soviet Union after its premiere at the Bolshoi Theatre in Moscow on June 14, 1927. The "Russian Sailors' Dance" (*"Ekh Yablochko"*) has become extremely popular in this country. Since then, Glière produced many works which paid tribute to the Soviet regime, including *For the Festival of the Comintern*, the *March of the Red Army*, and *Twenty-five Years of the Red Army*.

During World War II Glière's music echoed and interpreted many different aspects of the war effort. As he wrote in an appeal to American musicians on July 6, 1941, "we Soviet composers, together with the people, are employing the medium of our art to help the Red Army wage its struggle against the brutal enemy." In 1941 he wrote an orchestral overture, *Friendship of the Nations*, a tribute to the collaboration of the Allies in the war. This was followed by the *War Overture* ("a declaration of the fighting principles of the three great powers"), the patriotic marching song, "Hitler's End Will Come" (written in 1941 in anticipation of the event), and the *Victory Overture* (celebrating the defeat of Nazi Germany).

Indicative of Glière's high station in the Soviet Union was the winning of the Stalin Award (the highest prize a composer can receive) not once but twice. The first time took place in 1948 with the String Quartet No. 4. Two years later Glière won the Award again with the ballet, *The Bronze Horseman*. It is significant to remark that Glière's position in the Soviet Union rose because of the indictment of the Central Committee of the Communist Party in 1948 of the "dissonance makers" and "decadent formalists" (see Prokofiev).

MAJOR WORKS:

Ballets—Chrysis, op. 65, 1912; Cleopatra, ballet-melodrama, 1925; The Comedians, 1922-30; The Red Poppy, 1926-27; The Bronze Horseman, 1950.

Chamber Music—Sextet, for strings, op. 1, 1900; String Quartet No. 1, op. 2, 1900; Octet, for strings, op. 5, 1900; Sextet, No. 2, for strings, op. 7, 1902; Sextet No. 3, for strings, op. 11, 1904; String Quartet No. 2, op. 20, 1905; String Quartet No. 3, op. 67, 1928; String Quartet No. 4, 1948.

Operas—Shakh-Senem, 1923-25; Rachel, 1943.

Orchestral Music—Symphony No. 1, op. 8, 1899-1900; Symphony No. 2, op. 25, 1907; The Sirens, symphonic poem, op. 33, 1908; Symphony No. 3, Ilia Mourometz, op. 42, 1909-11; Two Poems, for soprano and orchestra, op. 60, 1924; Cossacks of Zaporozh, symphonic poem, op. 64, 1921; Trizna, symphonic poem, op. 66, 1915; Imitation of Jezekiel, symphonic poem, for narrator and orchestra, 1919; For the Festival of the Comintern, fantasy for wind orchestra, 1924; March of the Red Army, for wind orchestra, 1924; Concerto for Harp and Orchestra, 1938; Friendship of Nations, overture, 1941; For the Happiness of the Fatherland, overture, 1942; Concerto for Coloratura Soprano and Orchestra, 1942; Twenty-Five Years of the Red Army, 1943; Victory Overture, 1945; Concerto for Cello and Orchestra, 1946.

Piano Music—More than 200 pieces for the piano.

Vocal Music—More than 150 songs.

EUGENE GOOSSENS

Eugene Goossens *1893-*

EUGENE GOOSSENS was born in London on May 26, 1893. He comes from a family of musicians. Both his grandfather and his father were operatic conductors of renown. His brother, Leon, is an internationally celebrated oboist, while two of his sisters are professional harpists.

Eugene was ten years old when he entered the Bruges Conservatory. Three years after that he continued his music study at the Liverpool College of Music. In 1907 he went to the Royal College of Music in London on a scholarship, his teachers including Stanford (composition) and Rivarde (violin). Subsequently, Goossens won the silver medal of the Worshipful Company of Musicians and was made Associate of the Royal College of Music.

Upon graduating from the Royal College, Goossens served his orchestral apprenticeship in the Queen's Hall Orchestra, then conducted by Sir Thomas Beecham. After becoming Beecham's assistant, Goossens was selected, in 1916, to direct the premiere of Stanford's opera, *The Critic*. His success influenced him to consider conducting as a career, but he did not become a full-fledged conductor until 1921, when he founded his own orchestra and gave six subscription concerts in London. He made such a good impression that he was forthwith invited by many major orchestras to serve as a guest conductor. He also conducted the London performances of the Rus-

sian Ballet, and guest performances of the Carl Rosa Opera Company.

Goossens came to this country for the first time in 1923 to serve as conductor of the Rochester Philharmonic Orchestra. He remained permanent director of that organization for eight years. In 1931 Goossens succeeded Fritz Reiner as musical director of the Cincinnati Symphony Orchestra. He held this post until 1947. In that year he transferred his activities to Australia to become conductor of the Sydney Symphony Orchestra and director of the New South Wales Conservatory of Music.

Goossens first attracted attention as a composer during World War I, when two trios were performed at the War Emergency Concerts. These and other chamber-music works betrayed a tendency towards modern idioms. He first came to the notice of American music lovers with a Sinfonietta, performed in this country in 1922. Since then, his works have been frequently performed in the United States by symphony orchestras and chamber-music ensembles. His two operas, both on texts by Arnold Bennett, have been successfully performed in London: *Judith* in 1929 and *Don Juan de Mañara* in 1937.

Cyril Scott analyzed Goossens' style as follows in *Music and Letters* (October 1931): "He is a highly creative harmonist,

Goossens: go͞o′s′nz

but not merely a harmonist, for he does not scorn to avail himself of structural, contrapuntal, and melodic devices. He is not afraid of certain ugliness, and he is not afraid—and this requires even more courage —of beauty. He is furthermore at various moments witty, grotesque, hard, soft, pathetic, exotic, passionate. . . . Like all true artists, he is a prodigious inventor of effect, this element being noticeable even in his piano works."

Goossens composed his First Symphony in 1939, and it was introduced the following season by the Cincinnati Symphony under his own direction. This is one of Goossens' most important works to date, and is particularly noteworthy for its beautiful slow movement and the wit and orchestral brilliance of the Scherzo. Another major work is the *Phantasy Concerto*, written for José Iturbi and introduced by that pianist with the Cincinnati Symphony Orchestra. Goossens described this work as "in reality a four-movement concerto in miniature, written in compressed sonata form and with the movements interlocked."

Goossens has provided the following self-portrait: "Outside an occasional game of golf, I indulge in no kind of sport or sporting interest, though I formerly much enjoyed fencing. Most of all, I enjoy being left alone (though I am not what is known as unsociable), in preference with a good book. Architecture has always absorbed me and at one time I used to sketch every interesting building I could find. I like sword-fishing and anything connected with the sea. I would rather idle around a harbor than anything else I know. I have also driven a steam locomotive, and never lose an opportunity to accept a ride.

"My secretary tells me, concerning my mannerisms and habits, that I am a telephone artist, by which she means that I must draw designs when I speak over the telephone—a necessity I try to avoid like the plague. She also tells me that I cannot go anywhere without a cane, of which I have quite a collection. I find a Tudor house with some adjoining elm trees more fascinating to keep company with than the club bore.

"It bores me intensely to conduct and otherwise prepare a performance of any of my works (subsequent to the first performance, of course). The reason for this is that I would much rather devote my time to studying someone else's music and rehearsing it. My enjoyment has always been in writing the work, but I never write a work with thoughts of its performance in view, except insofar as purely practical considerations are concerned."

MAJOR WORKS:

Ballet—L'École en Crinoline, 1921.

Chamber Music—Phantasy Quartet, for strings, op. 12, 1916; Rhapsody for Cello and Piano, op. 13, 1916; String Quartet No. 1, op. 14; Sonata No. 1 for Violin and Piano, op. 21, 1918; Quintet for Piano and Strings, op. 23a; Lyric Poem, for violin and piano (also orchestra), op. 24, 1921; Three Songs, for voice and string quartet, op. 26; Phantasy Sextet, for strings, op. 35, 1923; Sextet for Strings, op. 37, 1925; Pastoral and Harlequinade, for flute, oboe, and piano, op. 39, 1924; Fantasy, for wind instruments, op. 40, 1927; Octet for strings, 1927; Sonata No. 2 for Violin and Piano, 1931; String Quartet No. 2, 1940.

Choral Music—Silence, for chorus and piano, op. 31, 1921.

Operas—Judith, 1925; Don Juan de Mañara, 1937.

Orchestral Music—Tam O'Shanter, op. 17a, 1916; The External Rhythm, symphonic poem, op. 27, 1920; Sinfonietta, op. 34, 1922; Rhythmic Dance, 1927; Concertino for Double String Orchestra, 1929; Two Nature Poems, 1937; Concerto for Oboe and Orchestra, 1938; Pastoral and Bacchanal, 1938; Symphony No. 1, op. 58, 1939; Cowboy Fantasy, 1943; Symphony No. 2, 1944; Phantasy Concerto, for piano and orchestra, 1944; Concerto for Violin and Orchestra, 1948.

Piano Music—Kaleidoscope, op. 18, 1918; Four Conceits, op. 20, 1917.

ABOUT:

Goossens, E., Overture and Beginners: A Musical Autobiography; Music and Letters, September 1931; Victor Record Review, July 1941.

Enrique Granados *1867-1916*

ENRIQUE GRANADOS Y CAMPINA was born in Lérida, Spain, on July 27, 1867. Revealing talent for music, he was given instruction at the piano at an early age; before several years passed he was marked for a career as virtuoso. But like his famous compatriots Albéniz and Manuel de Falla, Granados soon came under the influence of Felipe Pedrell, distinguished Spanish musicologist and father of Spanish nationalism in music. Pedrell induced Granados to turn

Granados: grä-nä'dōs

completely to the creative field. Granados received his most important instruction in harmony and composition from Pedrell as well as the ambition to write music in an authentic Spanish style.

When he was twenty years old, Granados went to Paris to enter the Conservatory. Typhoid fever prevented him from taking the necessary entrance examinations. Although he never did get into the Conservatory, Granados remained in Paris for two years, absorbing its musical influences.

Returning to Spain Granados gave a successful piano recital in Barcelona on April 20, 1890. Despite his success as a virtuoso, Granados had no intention of neglecting composition. He began writing music for the piano, successfully combining Spanish traits in composition with the fullest resources of piano technique; it is sometimes suggested that Granados is the creator of modern Spanish music for the piano. Among the notable piano works produced by Granados before 1900 were four volumes of *Spanish Dances,* in which every element of Spanish folk dance has been caught; this music, in the words of J. B. Trend, has "stateliness, elegance, finish, and an extraordinary sense of poetry."

On November 12, 1898 Granados' first opera, *María del Carmen,* was successfully introduced in Madrid. He subsequently wrote several other operas. The most important of these was *Goyescas,* which grew out of a remarkable set of six piano pieces (two books). Each of these pieces represented a scene from one of Goya's famous paintings revealing the picturesque Goyesque period of eighteenth-century Madrid. Granados himself introduced both books of piano pieces at a recital in Barcelona on March 11, 1911. Shortly after this, the idea occurred to him that the Goyesque period, and the music he had written about it, might be the basis for an effective opera. Without considering any particular libretto, he set to work on the entire score. And not until he completed his music did he call on Enrique Periquet to prepare a text. Against the colorful background of eighteenth-century Spain, Periquet prepared an effective story of love, jealousy, and death.

Granados' score is perhaps most notable for its skillful and effective use of Spanish

ENRIQUE GRANADOS

dances, which are woven into the texture and give it much of its brilliant color. But one number in the opera is preeminently famous, and is the most popular piece written by Granados—the "Intermezzo." Strange to report, this fragment—through which the name of the opera is kept alive—was not originally a part of the score. During the rehearsal of the opera it was suggested to Granados that an instrumental intermezzo was called for, and he wrote it hurriedly and incorporated it into his opera.

The premiere of *Goyescas* was originally set for the Paris Opéra. But the outbreak of World War I prevented this, and the first performance was transferred to the Metropolitan Opera in New York. This took place on January 28, 1916. Despite the war, Granados came to the United States to attend the premiere, and he won great acclaim. A huge bronze wreath was presented to the composer when the performance was over.

"The music," wrote Richard Aldrich in the *New York Times,* "is Spanish, coming from the brain and the heart of a real Spaniard. . . . Nor does he fall into the easy commonplaces to which Spanish tunes and rhythms are so often a tempting invitation. There is here something deeper, more profoundly felt. . . . Mr. Granados has a rich and unconventional harmonic feeling. . . . His harmonic scheme is elaborate and gives a peculiar distinction, warmth and brilliancy to his style. The music has a haunting power. . . . It is genuine and vital."

An invitation to play for President Wilson at the White House proved fatal to Granados. Delaying his return to Europe by a week in order to fill this engagement, Granados was aboard the *Sussex*—sailing from Folkestone to Dieppe—which was torpedoed by the Germans on March 24, 1916.

One would search in vain in Granados' music for the originality of a Manuel de Falla. Granados never attempted to exploit modern devices or seek new colors and effects. He was quite content to write in the traditional manner of the nineteenth-century Germans. But he did this, at times, with elegance and stately grace; his best works make up in charm and appeal what they lack in individuality. To the personality of Spanish folk music he brought romantic feeling and poetry. His one identifying trait as a composer, as J. B. Trend remarked, was to "ramble on" in his music, "making his points by repetition (like a Spanish poet), and saying the same things in a number of delightful and decorative ways."

MAJOR WORKS:

Chamber Music—Serenata, for two violins and piano, 1913; Oriental, for oboe and strings.

Choral Music—Chant des Étoiles, for chorus, organ, and piano.

Operas—María del Carmen, 1898; Goyescas, 1916.

Orchestral Music—Elisenda, suite for piano and small orchestra, 1912; Navidad, suite; Suite Arabe; Suite Gallega; La Nit del Mort, symphonic poem.

Piano Music—Twelve Spanish Dances (four books); Six Pieces on Spanish Popular Songs; Goyescas (two books).

Vocal Music—Canciones Amatorias (seven songs), 1914; La Maja Dolorosa (three songs); other songs for voice and piano.

ABOUT:

Chase, G., Music of Spain; Trend, J. B., Manuel de Falla and Spanish Music.

Alexander Gretchaninoff *1864-*

(See *American Composers Today*)

Paul Hindemith *1895-*

(See *American Composers Today*)

Gustav Holst *1874-1934*

GUSTAVUS THEODORE VON HOLST was born in Cheltenham, England, on September 21, 1874. His great-grandfather, a musician, had emigrated from Sweden to England in 1807.

Gustav's mother, formerly a concert pianist, taught the boy to play the piano. This instruction was supplemented with lessons on the organ, and, before long, Gustav was able to officiate as organist in the local church. In 1893 he went to London for intensive music study, enrolling at the Royal College of Music where, after two years, he won a scholarship in composition. As a Conservatory student he wrote the music for an operetta which reflected his enthusiasm for Sir Arthur Sullivan. But a much more important influence on Holst was that of Wagner, whose style he emulated in several early works.

While still at the Conservatory, Holst suffered an attack of neuritis which compelled him to give up the study of the piano. He turned to the trombone. When his Conservatory schooling ended, he played the trombone in the orchestra of the Carl Rosa Opera Company. Other orchestral posts followed. In 1903, he assumed his first job as a teacher of music. During the next two decades, Holst taught music at the St. Paul's Girls' School (of which he was musical director), Morley College, and the Royal College of Music.

During World War I, he was sent by the YMCA to Salonika, Constantinople, and points in Asia Minor to help organize musical activities among the British troops stationed there.

In February 1923 Holst fell off a platform in Reading, England. The effects of this accident at first seemed slight, and he did not hesitate to fulfill contractual obligations to visit the United States and deliver some lectures at the University of Michigan at Ann Arbor. But when he was back in England, in 1924, his physical condition began to deteriorate markedly. He had to give up his work as teacher, lecturer, and conductor. For the next decade he lived in London, in comparative seclusion and frequently in poor health, working exclusively on his compositions. In 1932 he felt well

Holst: hōlst

enough to visit the United States a second time. He now directed the Boston Symphony in a concert of his own works and lectured at Harvard University. Illness (duodenal ulcers) prevented him from accepting other American engagements.

He died in London on May 25, 1934.

Literature was one of several important influences on Holst's creative development. At first, he was inspired by Walt Whitman and William Morris, and after that by Sanskrit writings. During this Sanskrit phase, which began about 1905, he wrote a chamber opera (*Savitri*), a grand opera (*Sita*) and several other works in which the poetry and mysticism of Eastern philosophy prevailed strongly and gave his musical writing an exotic character.

The Sanskrit phase passed about 1913. Holst now produced some of his finest and most famous works, including the *St. Paul's Suite*, and *The Planets*, a suite for orchestra.

The *St. Paul's Suite* was written in 1913 for the St. Paul's Girls' School orchestra. In this the influence of the English folk song is prominent. In the earlier movements the music derived its character and style from idioms of English folk music, while in the last movement two actual folk songs are quoted, "Greensleeves," and "Dargason."

An even more famous work is *The Planets*, which came in 1916. This music, as the composer has explained, "was suggested by the astrological significance of the planets. . . . If any guide to the music is required, the subtitle to each piece will be found sufficient. . . . For instance, Jupiter brings jollity. . . . Saturn . . . not only physical decay but also a vision of fulfillment. Mercury is the symbol of the mind, etc." *The Planets* was introduced as a private concert in 1918. Five movements were performed by the London Philharmonic in 1919, while the entire suite of seven movements was given by the same orchestra one year later. Brilliant in its orchestration, dramatic in its sonority and climaxes, picturesque in its harmonies, and vividly descriptive, *The Planets* enjoyed an immediate and lasting success.

After World War I, Holst was drawn into greater seclusion and instropection by his illness. His daughter described him at the time as "sitting huddled over the fire, sinking lower and lower into a gray region where

Elliott & Fry

GUSTAVE HOLST

thought and feeling had ceased to exist and the spirit itself was numb. . . . His mind was closed in gray isolation. He had sunk . . . into that cold region of utter despair."

This separation from the outside world brought greater austerity, economy, and restraint to his musical writing. At the same time he began experimenting with the writing of non-harmonic counterpoint and free tonalities. Lean and spare though his music now became, it was also filled with occasional strength and passion. In this new vein he wrote in 1929 the *Twelve Songs,* on lyrics by Humbert Wolfe, and the Concerto for Two Violins and Orchestra.

"Holst's weaknesses," wrote Ralph Vaughan Williams in *Music and Letters* (July 1920), "are the defects of his qualities—occasionally his magnificent technique masters him and the end gets lost in the means. Sometimes he spoils the noble simplicity of his work by an unnecessary piece of elaboration; at other times, the very individuality of his thought which requires such a personal technique causes a flaw in his work. . . . But the very fact that these lapses are noticeable only goes to show how individual his music is. As time goes on, the discrepancies get fewer and fewer, and his style gets maturer and maturer, simpler and more individual, and this individuality shows in all his music ; whether it is in the extreme harmonic and rhythmic thought of *The Planets* or the absolute simplicity of *The Four Carols*, his signature is plain on every page."

MAJOR WORKS:

Ballet—The Golden Goose, choral ballet, op. 45, 1927.

Chamber Music—Quintet for Piano and Strings, op. 3, 1896; Suite in E-flat major, op. 10, 1900.

Choral Music—King Estmere, old English ballad for chorus and orchestra, op. 17, 1903; Choral Hymns from Rig-Veda, op. 26, 1908; The Cloud Messenger, ode for chorus and orchestra, op. 30, 1910; Two Eastern Pictures, for women's chorus and harp, 1911; Hecuba's Lament, for contralto, women's chorus and orchestra, op. 31, no. 1, 1911; Hymn to Dionysus, for women's chorus, op. 31, no. 2, 1911; Two Psalms, for chorus, strings, and organ, 1912; Dirge for Two Veterans, for men's chorus and brass band, 1914; Three Hymns, for chorus and orchestra, op. 36a, 1916; Ode to Death, for chorus and orchestra, op. 38, 1919; Choral Symphony, op. 41, 1923; The Evening Watch, motet, op. 42, 1924.

Operas—Sita, op. 23, 1906; Savitri, op. 25, 1908; The Perfect Fool, op. 39, 1921; At the Boar's Head, musical interlude, op. 42, 1924; The Tale of the Wandering Scholar, op. 50, 1929.

Orchestral Music—Walt Whitman Overture, op. 7, 1899; Cotswolds Symphony, op. 8, 1900; Indra, symphonic poem, op. 13, 1902; The Mystic Trumpeter, for soprano and orchestra, op. 18, 1904; Song of the Night, for violin and orchestra, op. 19a, 1905; Marching Song and Country Song, for small orchestra, 1906; Songs of the West, op. 21a, 1907; Somerset Rhapsody, op. 21b, 1907; Songs Without Words, op. 22, 1906; Beni Mora, oriental suite, op. 29a, 1910; Invocation, for cello and orchestra, op. 29b, 1911; St. Paul's Suite, for string orchestra, 1913; The Planets, suite for large orchestra and voices, op. 32, 1916; Japanese Suite, op. 33, 1916; Fugal Overture, op. 40, no. 1, 1922; Fugal Overture, for flute, oboe, and strings, op. 40, no. 2, 1923; Egdon Heath, symphonic poem, op. 47, 1927; Concerto for Two Violins and Orchestra, op. 49, 1929.

Piano Music—Two Folk-Song Fragments, op. 46, 1927.

ABOUT:

Holst, I., The Music of Gustav Holst; Rubbra, E., Gustav Holst.

Arthur Honegger *1892-*

A RTHUR HONEGGER'S parents were Swiss, coming from Zurich to the French seaport town of Le Havre to set up a business. It was there that Honegger was born in March 10, 1892. From his mother, a good amateur pianist, he acquired a love for the sonatas of Beethoven and his first piano lessons. A local teacher, Sautreuil, taught

Honegger: ō-nĕ-gâr'

him the violin, while an organist, Martin, gave him some lessons in harmony.

When Honegger was sixteen years old, he entered his father's business. But the boy's interest lay elsewhere. His father soon decided to send him to Zurich for further music study at the Conservatory. Its director, Friedrich Hegar, recognized the boy's talent and was influential in convincing Honegger's father to consent to an intensive preparation for a professional career. For two years Honegger studied at the Zurich Conservatory. He returned to France in 1912 and entered the Paris Conservatory where his teachers included Gedalge, Widor, and D'Indy. But his studies at the Conservatory were temporarily interrupted in 1914 when Honegger had to return to Switzerland to complete a year of military training prescribed by Swiss law for all its citizens; for, despite his French birth, Honegger was and still is a citizen of Switzerland.

While still a Conservatory student, Honegger wrote several songs. Some of these were performed in a small hall in Paris on July 13, 1916, Honegger's debut as a composer. More ambitious works followed: the Toccata and Variations for piano, which was introduced by Andrée Vaurabourg on December 15, 1916; the First String Quartet; a Sonata for Violin and Piano; and an orchestral overture to Maurice Maeterlinck's *Aglavaine et Sélysette*. The stylistic influences of Debussy, Ravel, and Richard Strauss are apparent in these early works.

On January 19, 1918, there took place in a Paris studio the first concert to be devoted entirely to Honegger's works. At the end of the year, on December 3, Honegger's first orchestral work, *Le Dit des Jeux du Monde*, was heard at the Théâtre du Vieux Colombier. However, Honegger did not become widely known in France until he became identified with a young group of French composers which came to be known as "The French Six" (see Auric). After Honegger joined this group, his music achieved great circulation and attracted attention. But Honegger was never really a party to the accepted artistic goals of "The Six." Their interest in jazz and music-hall idioms never absorbed his attention, though he did make a brief excursion into that sort of style with his Concertino for Piano and Orchestra, written in 1924, and introduced in Paris by Andrée Vaurabourg on May 23, 1925. Nor could he adopt the fetish for neo-classic simplicity. Strong-willed and artistically independent, Honegger listened to the esthetic ideals of his colleagues and to their music, and went his own way in the directions to which his artistic conscience led him.

Characteristic of his independent thinking was the fact that his first great success was realized with a work that adhered to the traditions and styles of the past: the oratorio *King David*. Written in 1921, and introduced in the same year in Switzerland, it was immediately received with enthusiasm. Two years later, Honegger reorchestrated this work, and in the new version it was soon heard in Winterthur, Paris, New York, Zurich, and Rome.

King David made Honegger a favorite son of the conservative wing of French composers. But with the cacophony and harmonic ruggedness of *Pacific 231*, written in 1923, Honegger was rejected by the conservatives and embraced by the *avant garde*.

His style was crystallized in such subsequent works as the opera *Judith*, and the Concerto for Violoncello and Orchestra. His language became passionate, rugged, and freely dissonant. It had a strong rhythmic force; the contrapuntal writing was frequently linear. Yet lyricism was not sacrificed. In analyzing Honegger's music of the 1920's, Guido Pannain remarked that its lyricism was one of its most salient qualities, a lyricism "sometimes instinct with joy and praise, sometimes touched with a melancholy that expresses itself in songs of winged sweetness. The vivid score of *King David (Le Roi David)* is steeped in the poignancy of a racial, a national heart cry. The same motive kindles the frenzied vocalism of *Judith*. Honegger in this mood is a poet of the human voice raised in song."

Lyrical abundance combined with strength of idiom—this, and an occasional tendency towards mysticism and religious feeling—are found in Honegger's later works. The most notable of these are the Symphony for Strings, the Symphony No. 3 ("Liturgique"), the dramatic oratorio, *Joan of Arc at the Stake (Jeanne d'Arc au Bûcher)*, and the Symphony No. 5. All of these works have been performed with considerable success

H. S. Babbitt, Jr.

ARTHUR HONEGGER

in this country. In 1929 Honegger visited the United States for the first time, appearing as a guest conductor of many leading American orchestras in performances of his works.

During World War II Honegger remained in Paris, seeking escape from the war and the Nazi occupation by writing music. It is the opinion of Willi Reich that the Symphony for Strings, completed in 1941, reflects Honegger's mood and feelings during this trying period. Soon after the liberation of Paris, there took place in Paris the premiere of Honegger's *Chant de Libération*, to a text of Bernard Zimmer, commemorating that historic event. That work had been written in 1942, during the Nazi occupation, in anticipation of the liberation.

Honegger visited this country a second time in July 1947, to conduct classes in composition at the Berkshire Music Center at Tanglewood, in Lenox, Massachusetts. Poor health made it impossible for Honegger to complete this assignment.

Honegger once wrote as follows about his artistic principles: "I attach great importance to musical architecture, which I should never want to be sacrificed for reasons of a literary or pictorial order. My model is Bach. . . . I do not seek, as do certain impressionists, the return of harmonic simplicity. I find on the contrary that we should use the harmonic materials created by the schools which preceded us, but in a different way—as the base of lines and rhythms."

Honegger's wife is the gifted pianist Andrée Vaurabourg, who introduced some of his early works, and who for many years taught piano at the École Normale. Their only child, a daughter, has shown no particular desire to follow in the footsteps of her parents. Honegger's own extra-musical interests include boats and locomotives.

MAJOR WORKS:

Ballets—Skating Rink, 1921; Sous-Marine, 1924; Amphion, 1929; Semiramis, 1934; The Song of Songs, 1938; L'Appel de la Montagne, 1944.

Chamber Music—String Quartet, 1917; Sonata No. 1 for Violin and Piano, 1918; Hymn, for ten strings, 1920; Sonata for Cello and Piano, 1920; Sonata for Viola and Piano, 1920; Rhapsody, for two flutes, clarinet, and piano, 1921; Sonatine for Clarinet and Piano, 1922; Sonatine for Violin and Cello, 1932; String Quartet No. 2, 1936; String Quartet No. 3, 1937; Quartet for Piano and Strings, 1938; Concerto da Camera, for flute, English horn, and strings, 1948.

Choral Music—Le Roi David, oratorio, 1921; Cris du Monde, for soloists, chorus, and orchestra, 1931; Jeanne d'Arc au Bûcher, dramatic oratorio, 1935; La Danse des Morts, oratorio, 1938; Nicolas de Flue, dramatic legend, for mixed chorus, children's chorus, and orchestra, 1939; Chant de Libération, for baritone, chorus, and orchestra, 1942.

Operas—Judith, 1925; Antigone, 1927; Amphion, melodrama, 1928; L'Aiglon (with Ibert), 1937.

Orchestral Music—Pastorale d'Été, 1920; Horace Victorieux, symphony, 1921; Chant de Joie, 1922; Pacific 231, 1923; Incidental Music to The Tempest, 1923; Concertino for Piano and Orchestra, 1924; Incidental Music to Phaedra, 1926; Rugby, 1928; Concerto for Cello and Orchestra, 1929; Symphony, 1930; Mouvement Symphonique No. 3, 1933; Prelude, Arioso, Fughetta on the Name of Bach, for strings, 1933; Nocturne, 1939; Symphony for Strings, 1941; L'Appel de la Montagne, suite, 1944; Symphony No. 3, Liturgique, 1946; Sérénade à Angélique, 1946; Symphony No. 4, Deliciae Basilienses, 1946; Prelude, Fugue, and Postlude, 1948; Symphony No. 5, 1950; Suite Archaïque, 1950; Monopartita, 1951; Symphony No. 6, 1953.

Vocal Music—Chanson de Ronsard, for voice, flute, and string quartet, 1924; Fièvre Jaune, 1933.

ABOUT:

Bruyr, J., Honegger et Son Œuvre; Gerard, A. H., Honegger; Milhaud, D., Notes without Music.

Jacques Ibert *1890-*

JACQUES IBERT was born in Paris on August 15, 1890. His father wanted him to become a businessman. He himself hoped to be an actor, and in his boyhood he attended dramatic school for a while. The study of music was for a long time followed spasmodically. He did not enter the Paris Conservatory until he was twenty-one years old. By this time he had given up his boyhood ambition to become an actor. At the Conservatory, in classes including Honegger and Milhaud, he had to make up for lost time, since his musical background was far less adequate than that of his fellow students. But he made up the lost ground quickly, aided by such sympathetic teachers as Gedalge, Roger-Ducasse, and particularly Gabriel Fauré. He now became conscious for the first time of a powerful urge to create his own music.

Music study was interrupted in 1914 when, with France at war, Ibert became an officer in the Navy. But his study was resumed in 1919 with Paul Vidal and was climaxed by the writing of the cantata *Le Poète et la Fée*, his first work utilizing an orchestra.

Ibert's debut as a composer took place soon after his return from Italy, where he had spent three years as the winner of the Prix de Rome. It was the symphonic poem inspired by the Oscar Wilde poem, *The Ballad of Reading Gaol*, which Ibert had completed in Italy and which was introduced at a Colonne concert in Paris on October 22, 1922. Ibert did not have to wait long after this for acclaim. In 1922 he wrote the

JACQUES IBERT

Ibert: ē-bâr'

orchestral suite *Escales,* stimulated by a Mediterranean cruise. *Escales* is a three-movement suite, each movement being a picture of a Mediterranean port. This work was introduced by the Concerts Lamoureux in Paris on January 6, 1924, with outstanding success. It not only made Ibert known; it also became his most popular work. "I have written twenty important works since *Escales,*" Ibert told an interviewer sadly many years later. "But always, when they speak of Ibert, they talk about *Escales!*" But those twenty works that followed *Escales* made Ibert one of the most respected composers in France.

In 1937 Ibert became director of the Académie de France in Rome, the first musician ever to hold this post. After World War II he also became assistant director of the Paris Opéra. Since then he has spent part of the year in Paris and part in Rome filling these two important offices. In 1950 he visited the United States for the first time to teach master classes in composition at the Berkshire Music Center in Tanglewood, in Lenox, Massachusetts. His presence in Tanglewood inspired the American premiere of his charming satirical four-act opera, *Le Roi d'Yvetot,* which he had written in 1927.

There are two opposing stylistic tendencies in Ibert's music. The first is satirical. After all, Ibert came to the fore when a great deal of attention was lavished on members of the so-called "French Six" (see Auric); some of them were his personal friends. The inclination of the "French Six" towards levity and flippancy is echoed in a work like *Divertissement* which indulges in tongue-in-the-cheek irony and malicious and witty musical quotations and parodies. This is Ibert's lighter side. The more serious, and the more important, is the neo-impressionistic music—sensitive and aristocratic, filled with the artistic subtleties, nuances, and refinements of the impressionistic art at its best.

A sizable percentage of Ibert's works are for the theatre: operas, ballets, even music for motion pictures. He has never forgotten his boyhood dream of being an actor. "I am still a man of the theatre," he will say. An opera like *Le Roi d'Yvetot* is more or less conventional. But Ibert has also attempted experimental theatrical forms. In 1950 the Paris Opéra presented an unorthodox opera, *The Knight Errant* (based on *Don Quixote*) calling for one hundred and twenty singers and a mammoth orchestra. In its ingenious union of spoken declamation, song, and the dance, *The Knight Errant* was regarded by many French critics as a successful effort to evolve a new lyric form.

Henri Prunières once wrote of Ibert: "He is a true musician who is acquainted with all the resources, all the subtleties of his art. None better than Ibert knows how to make the most of a melodic idea. He delights in the stark style. . . . Also to be admired . . . is the perfect taste, the tact, which enables him to avoid all shoals."

MAJOR WORKS:

Ballets—Les Rencontres, 1924; Les Amours de Jupiter, 1945; Triumph of Chastity, 1950.

Chamber Music—Jeux, for flute and piano, 1923; Deux Mouvements, for two flutes, clarinet, and bassoon, 1922; Concertino da Camera, for alto saxophone and eleven instruments, 1935; Three Pieces, for string quartet, 1938; Trio, for harp, violin, and cello.

Choral Music—Le Poète et la Fée, 1919; Chant de Folie, 1924.

Operas—Andromède et Persée, 1920; Angélique, 1927; Le Roi d'Yvetot, 1927; L'Aiglon (with Honegger), 1937; Barbe-Bleue, 1943; The Knight Errant, 1949.

Orchestral Music—Ballad of Reading Gaol, symphonic poem, 1921; Escales, suite, 1922; Féerique, symphonic scherzo, 1925; Concerto for Cello and Wind Instruments, 1925; Divertissement, 1931; Concerto for Flute and Orchestra, 1934; Overture for a Fête, 1944; Symphonie Concertante, for oboe and string orchestra, 1949.

Piano Music—Histoires, ten pieces (including The Little White Donkey).

Vocal Music—Deux Stèles Orientales (Segalen), for soprano and flute, 1925; Chansons de Vildrac; La Verdure Dorée.

ABOUT:

The New York Times, July 9, 1950.

Vincent D'Indy *1851-1931*

PAUL MARIE THÉODORE VINCENT D'INDY was born in Paris on March 27, 1851. His mother died while he was still a child, and he was brought up by his grandmother, a fine amateur musician, who gave him his early training at the piano. Though

D'Indy: dăɴ-dē'

Henri Manuel

VINCENT D'INDY

his father hoped he would become a lawyer, he did not stand in the way of an intensive musical education. When he was eleven, D'Indy became a piano student of Diémer. Two years after that he studied harmony with Lavignac. Later on he entered the piano class of Marmontel.

The Franco-Prussian War temporarily interrupted his musical activities. D'Indy volunteered in the 105th Regiment, and saw active service in the battle of Val-Fleuri on December 16, 1870, when he led a bayonet charge.

When the war ended, D'Indy returned to Paris and to music. His first published pieces—four *Romances sans Paroles* and the song, *Angoisse*—appeared in Paris in 1871. In 1872 he came into personal contact with César Franck (then professor of organ at the Conservatory) whom he had met briefly one year earlier. D'Indy showed Franck a piano quartet he had recently written. Franck was so enthusiastic about it that he urged the young man to enter the Paris Conservatory and round out his music studies there. However, the routinized study of the Conservatory irritated and oppressed the young musician. He refused to remain there, and entreated Franck to accept him as a private pupil. The master consented, and guided D'Indy through his final studies in composition.

Franck had a far-reaching influence on the younger man. From Franck, D'Indy acquired not only certain stylistic traits of writing music, but also that high-minded idealism and integrity which had always characterized Franck's career and which were also to distinguish D'Indy's life. In later years D'Indy returned the debt to his teacher by writing an authoritative and critical study of Franck.

In 1873 D'Indy traveled to Germany, spending several months with Franz Liszt in Weimar. He then proceeded to Vienna to meet Brahms, but the meeting, when it finally took place, was a disappointment: D'Indy was too much in awe of Brahms to be articulate, and Brahms was too busy at the time to be patient with and tolerant of a young worshiper.

From 1875 to 1879 D'Indy served as chorus master of the Colonne Orchestra. Meanwhile, his works were being heard. As early as 1871 there had taken place a performance of a movement from his First Symphony at the Concerts Populaires in Paris. The first movement of another symphony, *Jean Hunyade*, was heard at a concert of the Société Nationale de Musique on May 15, 1875, and the remaining movements were given by the Colonne Orchestra one year after that.

In 1876 D'Indy, now a passionate Wagnerite, made a pilgrimage to Bayreuth to attend the premiere of the entire *Ring* cycle. For many years after that, up to and including 1891, D'Indy returned each summer to Bayreuth to pay homage at the Wagnerian shrine.

The first of D'Indy's masterworks came in 1886. It was the *Symphonie Cévenole* (*Symphony on a French Mountain Theme*) based on a mountain air the composer had heard in the Cevennes mountain region in the French Alps. Introduced on March 20, 1887, by the Lamoureux Orchestra, it was received with enthusiasm, and went a long way in establishing the reputation of its composer. Equally tremendous acclaim came to D'Indy with his opera *Fervaal*, written between 1889 and 1895, and introduced in Brussels on March 12, 1897. After the premiere Camille Bellaigue wrote: "Whoever you be, here is your master; whatever your hopes, here must you bow and surrender."

Among the other major works by D'Indy to solidify his position as a preeminent French composer were the exotic and compelling *Istar*, a set of variations for orchestra, first heard in Brussels on January 10, 1897, the delicate nature-poem *Jour d'Été à la Montagne* (*Summer Day in the Mountains*), written in 1905 and first heard on February 18, 1906, in a performance by the Colonne Orchestra, and the Symphony No. 2 in B-flat major, completed in 1904, and performed by the Lamoureux Orchestra on February 26, 1904.

In these works the disciple of César Franck reveals that he has profited well from his contacts and lessons with the masters. Like Franck, D'Indy frequently used the cyclic form, which, through the skillful repetition of thematic material throughout an entire work, provides integration. Like Franck, D'Indy favored spiritual utterances, for music that was emotionally controlled, subtle in mood, delicate in its suggestions and trenchant in intellectual content.

"It is true," said Philip Hale, in his *Boston Symphony Programme Notes*, written while the composer was still living, "that D'Indy uses his head, not loses it, in composition; that his music will never be popular with the multitude; it lacks an obvious appeal. . . . It is not sugary; it is not theatrical. To say that it is cold is to say that it is not effusive. D'Indy does not gush. Nor does he permit himself to run with a mighty stir and din to a blatant climax. . . . He respects his art and himself, and he does not trim his sails to catch the breeze of popular favor. There is a nobility in his music; there is to those who do not wear their heart on their sleeve true warmth. There is a soaring of the spirit, not a dropping to court favor."

In 1893, invited by the French government to be a member of a committee to reform the Paris Conservatory, D'Indy proposed so revolutionary a plan that the professors of that institution united against it. The fierce opposition succeeded in frustrating the work of the committee. Reform did not come to the Conservatory for several years; but when it did, D'Indy accepted a post as professor of conducting.

But his far-sighted and progressive theories on musical education had to be put into effect elsewhere. In 1894 he helped found the Schola Cantorum, originally a school for the study of church music. Six years after the founding, the program of this institution was extended to include every phase of music. As one of its directors, and as one of its principal teachers, D'Indy left an indelible impression on contemporary French music. Over a period of several decades, most of the principal French composers, including Satie, Honegger, Auric, and Roussel, came under his influence.

D'Indy was also an influential member of the Société Nationale de Musique, which Franck had helped to organize in 1871 for the purpose of encouraging the performance of contemporary music. When Franck died in 1890, D'Indy became the president of the Société.

Vincent D'Indy visited the United States twice, in 1905 and in 1921, on each occasion directing American orchestras in successful performances of his works.

In January 1931 D'Indy directed a performance of his *Symphony on a French Mountain Theme*, on which occasion he received one of the most impressive ovations of his entire career. He died soon after that, in Paris, on December 2, 1931. To his impressive achievements as composer, teacher, theorist, and conductor must be added those of biographer and editor.

"My life," D'Indy once wrote, "is carefully regulated. I get up early, I work as a matter of fact, I am unable to remain idle for ten minutes. I am orderly, my manuscripts are rather clean." He did most of his composing at the country home he loved so well, in Ardèche. Like Beethoven (whom he admired more than any other composer of the past) he loved nature, and all his holidays were spent in the country.

"An artist," D'Indy wrote, "must have at least faith, faith in God and faith in his art; for it is faith that disposes him to learn and by his learning to raise himself higher and higher on the ladder of being, up to his goal, which is God. An artist should practice hope; for he can expect nothing from the present. He knows that his mission is to serve, and to give his work for the life and teaching of the generation that will come after him. An artist should be inspired by a splendid charity —'the greatest of these.' To love should be his aim in life; for the moving principle of all creation is divine and charitable love."

D'Indy was fond of the following epigram, which he quoted frequently: "Only the heart can engender beauty."

MAJOR WORKS:

Chamber Music—Quartet in A major, for piano and strings, op. 7, 1878; Trio, for piano, clarinet, and cello, op. 29, 1887; String Quartet No. 1, op. 35, 1890; String Quartet No. 2, op. 45, 1897; Chansons et Danses, for seven wind instruments, op. 50, 1898; Sonata for Violin and Piano, op. 59, 1904; Quintet, for piano and strings, op. 81, 1924; Sonata for Cello and Piano, op. 84, 1925; String Sextet, op. 92, 1929; String Quartet No. 3, in D-flat major, op. 96, 1930; Trio No. 2, for piano, violin and cello, op. 98, 1930.

Choral Music—Sainte Marie-Magdaleine, cantata, op. 23, 1885; Sur la Mer, for women's voices and piano, op. 32, 1888; Pour l'Inauguration d'une Statue, cantata, op. 37, 1893; L'Art et le Peuple (Hugo), for four-part male chorus, op. 39, 1894; Ode à Valence, for soprano and chorus, op. 44, 1897; Six Chants Populaires Français, for unaccompanied chorus, op. 90, 1928; Six Chants Populaires Français, second series, for unaccompanied chorus, op. 100, 1931.

Operas—Le Chant de la Cloche, dramatic legend, op. 18, 1883; Fervaal, lyric drama, op. 40, 1895; L'Étranger, lyric drama, op. 53, 1901; La Légende de Saint-Christophe, lyric drama, op. 67, 1915; La Rêve de Cynias, lyric comedy, op. 80, 1923.

Orchestral Music—Jean Hunyade, symphony, op. 5, 1875; La Forêt Enchantée, symphonic legend, op. 8, 1878; Wallenstein, symphonic trilogy, op. 12, 1879; Symphony on a French Mountain Theme, Symphonie Cévenole, op. 25, 1886; Fantaisie, for orchestra with oboe solo, op. 31, 1888; Incidental Music to Karadec, op. 34, 1890; Tableaux de Voyage, op. 36, 1891; Istar, symphonic variations, op. 42, 1896; Médée, suite, op. 47, 1898; Symphony No. 2 in B-flat major, op. 57, 1903; Jour d'Été à la Montagne, op. 61, 1905; Souvenirs, tone poem, op. 62, 1906; La Queste de Dieu, descriptive symphony, op. 67, 1917; Sinfonia Brevis de Bello Gallico, op. 70, 1918; Le Poeme des Rivages, op. 77, 1921; Diptyque Méditerranéen, op. 87, 1926; Concerto for Piano, Flute, Cello, and String Orchestra, op. 89, 1927.

Piano Music—Petite Sonate, op. 9, 1880; Poème des Montagnes, op. 15, 1881; Quatre Pièces, op. 16, 1882; Sarabande and Minuet, op. 24, 1885; Nocturne, op. 26, 1886.

Vocal Music—Clair de Lune, op. 13, 1880; L'Amour et le Crâne, op. 20, 1884; Lied Maritime, op. 43, 1896; La Première Dent, op. 48, 1898; 90 Chansons Populaires du Vivarais, op. 52, 1900; Mirage, op. 56, 1903; Les Yeux de l'Aimée, op. 58, 1904; Vocalise, op. 64, 1908.

ABOUT:

Borgex, L., Vincent d'Indy, Sa Vie et Son Œuvre; Burk, J. N. (ed.) Philip Hale's Boston Symphony Programme Notes; Rolland, R. Musicians of Today; Vallas, L., Vincent d'Indy, la Jeunesse; Musical Quarterly, April 1932.

John Ireland *1879*-

JOHN IRELAND was born in Bowden, Cheshire, on August 13, 1879. Both his parents were literary: his father was the editor of a Manchester newspaper, and his mother became known as an author and literary critic.

Showing unusual talent for music from childhood on, John Ireland was encouraged in his music study. In 1893 he was enrolled in the Royal College of Music, where he remained eight years, and where his teachers included Stanford (composition) and Cliffes (piano). After leaving school, Ireland started composing seriously, his first model being Brahms. Later on Ireland recognized how derivative was the music of this period and he destroyed much of what he had written and refused to allow the rest of it to be published.

The first work with which he was willing to identify himself was the *Phantasy Trio*, written in 1906. The structural logic still betrays a certain indebtedness to Brahms. But the purification and increasing sensitivity of his style reveals a new influence: impressionism. In this vein Ireland produced his first important works. In 1909 he won the Cobbett Prize for the Violin Sonata in D minor. Four years after that he produced his first important orchestral and piano works: the orchestral prelude *The Forgotten Rite*, and a set of piano pieces entitled *Decorations*. By 1917 his reputation was established with a second Sonata for Violin and Piano. When this sonata was introduced in London in 1917, it scored an immense success. Frank Bridge wrote to the composer: "Its power is tremendous. . . . Personally I am convinced it is not only a landmark in your own history but also in contemporary music. . . . I feel proud that any one of us has produced such a work."

One of the most important influences on Ireland's creative life has been his love of nature. Extremely sensitive to the beauty of the countryside, Ireland has time and again been inspired by nature to write some of his finest music. His early orchestral prelude, *The Forgotten Rite* (still one of his best works), treats the "mystical aspects of nature," as Rosa Newmarch pointed out; so does the orchestral rhapsody, *Mai-Dun*,

JOHN IRELAND

which came eight years later. The haunting *Legend*, for piano and orchestra, evokes the country that surrounded the cottage in Sussex Downs, where it was written. *Sarnia*, a set of three piano pieces, is a portrait of the Channel island of Guernsey, where for many years Ireland lived and worked.

Another stimulus has been literature. Ireland has responded particularly to the writings of Arthur Machen. Thus the *Legend* is dedicated to Machen, and *The Scarlet Ceremonies*, for piano, is prefaced with a Machen quotation. Ireland has also set to music poetry by Symonds, Housman, Hardy, Shakespeare, Blake, Arthur Symons, and Rupert Brooke.

In Ireland's more recent works there has been no radical change of style. He writes today as he did yesterday: with economy and precision while injecting the red blood of vital rhythms and robust sonorities into his music. Philip Heseltine, in a letter to John Ireland, pointed out the "steady development along wholly personal lines" found in Ireland's music from 1908 on, and noticed in the later works "the logical development of a style that was already very individual."

When World War II came in 1939, Ireland was living in comparative seclusion on the island of Guernsey. He succeeded in escaping from the island in June 1940, just before the Nazis took over, carrying away

with him the manuscript of his latest but then still uncompleted work, *Sarnia*.

For many years Ireland was professor of composition at the Royal College of Music. In 1924 he was elected Honorary Fellow of the College.

Major Works:

Chamber Music—Phantasy Trio, in A minor, 1908; Sonata No. 1 for Violin and Piano, 1909, Sonata No. 2 for Violin and Piano, 1917; Trio No. 2, in E major, 1917; Sonata No. 3 for Violin and Piano, 1920; Sonata for Cello and Piano, 1923; Phantasy Sonata for Clarinet and Piano; String Quartet in D major; String Quartet in C minor; Sextet for Strings; Trio No. 3, 1938; Sonata for Clarinet and Piano, 1943.

Choral Music—Mass in Dorian Mode; Vexilla Regis; Psalm 42; These Things Shall Be (Symonds).

Orchestral Music—The Forgotten Rite, prelude, 1913; Mai-Dun, rhapsody, 1921; Midsummer, overture; Tritons, prelude; Pelleas and Melisande, orchestral poem; Concerto for Piano and Orchestra, 1930; Legend, for piano and orchestra, 1933; A London Overture, 1936; Concertino pastorale, for string orchestra, 1939; Epic March, 1942; Overture Satyricon, 1946.

Piano Music—Decorations, 1913; Rhapsody, 1915; Three London Pieces, 1919; Sonata No. 1, 1920; Ambeley Wild Brooks, 1921; Sonatina, 1928; Sonata No. 2 in C minor; Greenways, 1938; Sea Idyll; Sarnia 1941; Three Pastels; The Scarlet Ceremonies.

Songs.

About:

Bacharach, A. L. (ed.) British Music of Our Time.

Gordon Jacob *1895-*

GORDON JACOB was born in Upper Norwood, near London, on July 5, 1895. His father was an official in the Indian Civil Service. At the age of eight Gordon Jacob began studying the piano, and after taking a few lessons he started composing. From 1908 to 1914 he attended Dulwich College, where he studied first the classics, then science. He also took lessons on the piano and played the timpani and other percussion instruments in the school orchestra.

During World War I he served as a lieutenant in the Queen's Royal West Surrey Regiment. He was taken prisoner by the Germans in 1917. In the prison camp he conducted a tiny orchestra for which he arranged all the music, both classical and popular.

Hughes

GORDON JACOB

After the war Jacob entered the Royal College of Music, where he studied composition with Stanford and Vaughan Williams, conducting with Adrian Boult, theory with Howells, and piano with George Thalben Ball. At the college Jacob was awarded both the Foli Scholarship and the Sullivan Prize. Soon after leaving college, he became a member of its faculty, as professor of composition, orchestration, and theory, a position he has held since that time. He has also taught at Morley College and Birkbeck College. In 1945 he was appointed examiner for degrees at London University and the University of Wales. After World War II Jacob curtailed many of his activities as a teacher to devote himself more extensively to composition.

Jacob first attracted attention as a composer when his Concerto for Piano and Orchestra was introduced in London by Arthur Benjamin and an orchestra directed by Sir Henry J. Wood in May 1927. Other important works followed: a String Quartet in 1927; the ballets *The Jew in the Bush* and *Uncle Remus*, presented by the Vic-Wells Company in 1928 and 1930, respectively; several orchestral works including the Concerto for Oboe and Orchestra and the Variations on an Original Theme heard in 1934 and 1936 respectively. Later works include a Sinfonietta, two symphonies, and a Clarinet Quintet.

"His style," wrote Robin Hull, in *British Music of Our Time,* "takes liberal but not extravagant account of latter-day harmonic resources: at times, indeed, there is a refreshing flavor of acerbity about his pages, whose strongly individual sentiment indicates an equally strong aversion to sentimentality. He possesses the rare merit of refusing to add a single note to his scores beyond the exact limits of what he wishes to express. This quality makes for a satisfying terseness."

Jacob is particularly known for his gift at instrumentation. He has made excellent orchestral arrangments of music by Handel, Byrd, Gibbons, Vaughan Williams, Holst, and Elgar, and has arranged ballet scores for the Sadler's Wells Ballet Company. He has also written an important book, *Orchestral Technique.*

In divulging his beliefs as a composer, Jacob has emphasized the importance of a sound technique together with an independence from current fashions. "A composer should be progressive in his outlook while retaining belief in tonality and classical forms." His favorite composers of the past include Bach, Haydn, Mendelssohn, Schumann, Glinka, and Rimsky-Korsakov; among the twentieth-century composers he prefers Elgar, Stravinsky, and Sibelius.

Apart from music, his interests include gardening, animals, birds, science, literature, and painting. As he says, he likes "a quiet life and time to work and think" and dislikes "pose and talking about music, except to fellow musicians, intellectualism, snobbery, and superiority."

He was awarded the John Collard Fellowship of the Worshipful Company of Musicians, 1943-46.

MAJOR WORKS:

Ballets—The Jew in the Bush, 1923; Uncle Remus, 1930.

Chamber Music—String Quartet, 1927; Quartet for Oboe and Strings, 1938; String Quartet No. 2; Quintet for Clarinet and Strings, 1942; Shakespearean Sketches, for string trio, 1945.

Choral Music—Donald Caird, for chorus and orchestra, 1935.

Orchestral Music—Concerto for Piano and Strings, 1926; Concerto for Oboe and Strings,

1933; Variations on an Original Theme, 1936; Sinfonietta, 1943; Symphony for Strings, 1944; Symphony, 1945.

ABOUT:

Bacharach, A. L. (ed.) British Music of Our Time.

Leoš Janáček *1854-1928*

LEOŠ JANÁČEK, sometimes described as the "Mussorgsky of Moravia," was born in Hukvaldy, Moravia, on July 3, 1854, the ninth of fourteen children. His father earned only a meager living as a schoolmaster, and his family knew abject poverty. In his tenth year Leoš became a chorister in the community church of the Austin Friars at Brünn where he studied music with the choir director, Krizkowski.

When Janáček's father died in 1866, Leoš began earning his living by giving music lessons. He soon went to Prague to study at the College of Organ Playing. This was a period of great hardship for the young musician. He lived in a perpetually cold attic; he had little to eat. Deprivations, however, did not depress him since he could concentrate on musical activity. Besides teaching and studying he wrote articles on music.

In 1875 Janáček was back in Brünn instructing at the Teachers School. Three years later he visited Leipzig and Vienna, and briefly attended conservatories in both cities. When he returned to Brünn he became one of the most vital musical figures in Moravia. He founded and directed two important musical institutions: the Organ School (which was taken over by the state in 1920) and the Conservatory of Brünn. He also established and conducted public concerts.

The first of three visits to Russia took place in 1896. Janáček became a great admirer of all things Russian. He studied the language and devoured its literature. The impact of that country and its literature on his music was immense, many of his works having been inspired by Russian subjects.

Janáček also devoted himself to the study and collation of Moravian folk songs and dances. It was as a result of this study that he evolved a musical system of his own, the elements of which were to be found in

LEOŠ JANÁČEK

Moravian folk music: In an article published later in his life, Janáček explained his theories on the "melodies of the language," demonstrating how the melody and rhythm of speech varies with different people and with different backgrounds and conditions. He came to the conclusion that musical expression must be founded upon these positive melodic and rhythmic speech elements.

His style became crystallized with the opera *Jenufa*, which he started sketching twenty-seven years before it was completed. *Jenufa* is a folk opera, deriving text and music from Moravian peasant life. Completed in 1902, it was introduced at the Brünn Opera on January 21, 1904, under the name *Jezi Pastorkyna (Her Stepdaughter)* and was a failure. Twelve years after that, on May 26, 1916, the opera was revived as *Jenufa* by the Prague Opera, and two years later it was seen at the Vienna Opera. In both these revivals, the opera was outstandingly successful; Janáček, unknown to the outside world up to this time, suddenly became an international musical figure.

The strength of Janáček's idiom in *Jenufa* stems from the stark, savage melodies. "Like Mussorgsky," wrote Vaclav Stepan, "Janáček rejects all intellectual elements. He uses no polyphony, no thematic construction and development. . . . His passion and

Janáček: yă′nä-chĕk

dramatic touch, penetrating and concise, accomplishing amazing effects especially when the milieu of the drama is so near to him." And Rosa Newmarch wrote: "Janáček's musical language is never stereotyped. Its strong personal note is always varied by methods and nuances appropriate to the subject at hand."

Besides *Jenufa,* Janáček is most frequently remembered for two fine orchestral works. One of these is a rhapsody, *Taras Bulba,* based on the celebrated story of Gogol. *Taras Bulba* was introduced in 1928 by the Leipzig Gewandhaus Orchestra under Bruno Walter. The second orchestral work is the Sinfonietta, originally a series of fanfares for brass instruments written to be performed at an open-air athletic meet in Prague. Subsequently Janáček gave his fanfares an extended and symphonic treatment, called them Sinfonietta, and had the new work introduced by the Czech Philharmonic Orchestra in Prague in May 1926.

In 1925 Janáček was given an honorary degree by the University of Brünn. One year later he was honored in England. On the occasion of his seventieth birthday, a cycle of his operas was presented in Prague and Brünn.

A cold caught in the Hukvaldy forests developed into pneumonia. Rushed to the Moravian Hospital, in Ostrau, Janáček failed to recover. He died there on August 12, 1928. Ten years after his death extensive cycles of his works were performed throughout the length and breadth of Czechoslovakia.

MAJOR WORKS:

Chamber Music—A Fairy Tale, for cello and piano, 1908; Piano Trio, 1908; Sonata for Violin and Piano, 1914; String Quartet No. 1, 1923; Youth, sextet for wind, 1924; Concertino for Piano, Two Violins, Clarinet, Horn, and Bassoon, 1925; String Quartet No. 2, 1928.

Choral Music—My Lord Have Mercy Upon Us, for quartet, double chorus, and orchestra, 1897; Amarus, for solo, mixed chorus, and orchestra, 1901; Four Moravian Choruses, for male voices, 1904; At the Inn of Solan, for solo, male chorus, and orchestra, 1912; The Eternal Gospel, for solo, chorus, and orchestra, 1914-15; Kaspar Rucky, for women's voices, 1922; Teacher Halfar, for male chorus, 1923; The Wandering Madman (Tagore), for soprano and male chorus, 1924.

Operas—Sarka, 1887; The Beginning of a Romance, 1894; Jenufa, 1902; Fate, 1905; The Housewife Maid; The Excursions of Mr. Broucek, 1914; Kate Kabanova, 1921; The Cunning Little Vixen, 1923; The Markopoulos Affair, 1924; From the House of the Dead (completed by Bakala), 1928.

Orchestral Music—Suite for String Orchestra, 1877; Idyll, for string orchestra, 1880; Taras Bulba, rhapsody, 1917; The Ballad of Blanik, 1920; Sinfonietta, 1926.

Piano Music—Variations on an Original Theme, 1879; Vallachian Dances, 1888; National Dances of Moravia, three books, 1891-93; By. Overgrown Tracks, 1901; Sonata, 1905; Moravian Dances, two books, 1912; In the Threshing House, 1913.

Vocal Music—Song of Spring, for voice and piano, 1897; The Folk Poetry of Hukvaldy in Song, 1899; A Garland of Moravian Folksongs, two books, 1892, 1901; Folk Nocturnes, 1916; Songs of Silesia, 1920; Songs of Childhood.

ABOUT:

Brod, M., Leoš Janáček; Miller, D., Leoš Janáček.

Joseph Jongen 1873-1953

JOSEPH JONGEN, one of the outstanding musicians of present-day Belgium, was born in Liége, on December 14, 1873. All his musical schooling took place at the Liége Conservatory. In 1894, he received the 1,000 franc prize of the Royal Academy of Belgium for a string quartet. One year later he won the second Prix de Rome and the Royal Academy prize for a trio. And in 1897 he received the Prix de Rome for the cantata *Comala.*

For the next four years, Jongen traveled throughout Europe. During this period he wrote a Symphony which was introduced in 1900 at the Concerts Ysaÿe in Brussels. He also completed a Concerto for Cello and Orchestra, a Concerto for Violin and Orchestra, and a Piano Quartet, the last performed by the Société Nationale de Musique in Paris in 1903.

Upon returning to Belgium, Jongen became professor of harmony and counterpoint at the Liége Conservatory. When war broke out in Europe, in 1914, he migrated to and settled in England.

After the war, Jongen was back in Belgium, resuming his work at the Liége Conservatory. He resigned this teaching post in 1920 to become professor of counterpoint and fugue at the Brussels Conservatory. In 1925 he was appointed director of this Conservatory, maintaining this position until 1939, when he was succeeded by his brother.

Jongen: yông'ĕn

Photo-Belge
JOSEPH JONGEN

From 1919 to 1926 Joseph Jongen was also active as conductor of the Concerts Spirituels in Brussels, which were responsible for introducing many new works by notable French, Belgian, and Italian composers.

Jongen's music is delicate in style, sensitive in feeling, and finely wrought. It is characterized by subtle statements and suggestions rather than by big impressions and effects. Though impressionism makes itself felt in some of his best works, Jongen was more indebted to Franck than to Debussy. Charles van den Borren wrote: "From the purely expressive point of view, he soars, in most of his work (especially in slow movements), in an atmosphere of nostalgic revery or cheerful well-being in full accord with his own character and with the idealism of his native soil."

Jongen produced more than a hundred works in virtually every branch of musical composition. The refinement of his style found its aptest medium in chamber music, and it was here that he wrote some of his finest works.

Jongen died at his home near Liége on July 14, 1953.

MAJOR WORKS:

Ballet—S'Arka, op. 36, 1910.

Chamber Music—String Quartet No. 1, op. 3, 1894; Trio, op. 10, 1897; Piano Quartet, op. 23, 1902; Sonata No. 1 for Violin and Piano, op. 27, 1903; Trio No. 2, op. 30, 1907; Sonata No. 2 for Violin and Piano, op. 34, 1909; Sonata for Cello and Piano, op. 39, 1912; String Quartet No. 2, op. 50, 1916; Two Serenades, for string quartet, op. 61, 1918; String Quartet No. 3, op. 67, 1921; Rhapsody, for piano and wind instruments, op. 70, 1922; Concerto for Flute, Violin, Viola, Cello and Harp, op. 71, 1923; Two Pieces, for four cellos, op. 89, 1929; Quintet No. 1, for wind instruments, op. 93, 1933; Two Sketches, for string quartet, op. 97, 1932; Prelude and Chaconne, for string quartet, op. 101, 1934; Duo Sonata, for violin and cello, op. 109, 1941; Quartet for Saxophones, op. 122, 1942; Concerto for Wind Quintet, op. 124, 1942; Trio No. 3, op. 135, 1948.

Choral Music—La Meuse, for unaccompanied men's voices, op. 26, 1902; Chant Pastoral, for women's voices and piano (or orchestra), op. 42, 1913; La Légende de St. Nicolas, for children's voices and piano (or small orchestra), op. 100, 1933; Hymne a la Meuse, cantata, 1938; La Cigale et la Fourmi, for children's voices, op. 118, 1941; Mass, for chorus, organ, and orchestra, op. 130, 1946; Il Était un Berger, for children's voices and orchestra, 1947.

Opera—Felyane, 1907.

Orchestral Music—Symphony, op. 15, 1898; Concerto for Violin and Orchestra, op. 17, 1899; Concerto for Cello and Orchestra, op. 18, 1900; Adagio Symphonique, for violin and orchestra, op. 20, 1901; Fantaisie sur Deux Noëls Wallons, op. 24, 1902; Lalla-Roukh, symphonic poem, op. 28, 1904; Prélude et Danse, op. 31, 1907; Clair de Lune et Soleil à Midi, op. 33, 1903; Deux Rondes Wallonnes, op. 40, 1912; Impressions d'Ardenne, op. 44, 1913; Concertino for Trumpet and Orchestra, op. 41, 1913; Suite for Viola and Orchestra, op. 48, 1915; Tableaux Pittoresques, op. 56, 1917; Sarabande Triste, op. 58, 1918; Poème Heroïque, for violin and orchestra, op. 62, 1919; Prélude Élégiaque et scherzo, op. 66, 1920; Petite Suite, op. 75, 1924; Hymn, for organ and strings, op. 78, 1924; Symphonie Concertante, for organ and orchestra, op. 81, 1926; Passacaille et Gigue, op. 90, 1929; Suite No. 3, in the old style, op. 93, 1930; Triptyque, op. 103, 1936; Overture-Fanfare, op. 110, 1939; Allelulia, op. 112, 1940; Ouverture de Fête, op. 117, 1941; Concerto for Piano and Orchestra, op. 127, 1943; Bourrée, 1944; Concerto for Harp and Orchestra, op. 129, 1944; In Memoriam, op. 133, 1947; Ballade, Hommage à Chopin, op. 136, 1949.

Piano Music—Serenade, op. 19, 1900; En Forme de Valse, op. 43, 1913; Suite en Forme de Sonata, op. 60, 1918; Trois Études de Concert, op. 65, 1920; 13 Préludes, op. 69, 1922; Petite Suite, op. 75, 1924; Pensée Élégiaque, op. 82, 1926; Sonatine, op. 88, 1929; Dix Pièces, op. 96, 1932; First Ballade, op. 106, 1936; 24 Little Preludes, op. 116, 1941; Second Ballade, op. 119, 1941; Bourrée, op. 123, 1942; Third Impromptu and Mazurka, op. 126, 1943.

Vocal Music—Deux Vocalises, 1928; Deux Chants sans Paroles, 1923; La Musique (Baudelaire), 1949.

ABOUT:

Chesterian (England), December 1923; Revue Musicale (Paris), July 1923.

Dmitri Kabalevsky *1904-*

DMITRI KABALEVSKY was born in St. Petersburg on December 30, 1904, the son of a civil servant. Early in his life he revealed a bent for music by playing the piano by ear when he was only six and soon after that by trying to write his own music. However, he did not begin intensive study until his fourteenth year. At that time his family moved to Moscow. There Kabalevsky entered the Scriabin Music School, where for four years he studied with Vassilenko and Catoire. His study was completed at the Moscow Conservatory with Miaskovsky and Goldenweiser. Upon his graduation, in 1930, his name was inscribed on an honor plaque in the front hall of the Conservatory.

While he was still a music student, in 1925, he filled a government post as a teacher in a children's school. This post impelled him to write some charming pieces expressly for children, including the *Children's Songs* and *From Pioneer Life.* When his own schooling ended, Kabalevsky taught at the Scriabin Music School, and after that he was appointed professor of composition at the Moscow Conservatory.

In 1930 Kabalevsky wrote a Sonatina for piano. But his first major work did not come until two years later, when he wrote his Symphony No. 1 to commemorate the fifteenth anniversary of the Revolution in Russia. From this time on, Kabalevsky's music served to interpret the political and social ideals of the Soviet Union. He derived much of his creative stimulation from the historic and cultural traditions of his land and its people.

Kabalevsky's first successful work was completed in 1934, the Symphony No. 2. (Actually this was Kabalevsky's Third Symphony, since a *Requiem for Lenin,* written in 1933, was designated by its composer as a "symphony.") While the Symphony No. 2 was essentially absolute music, it suggested man's salvation through his role as a collaborator in the reconstruction of society. It was introduced in Moscow on December 25, 1934, and was an immediate success. Since then, the work has been performed throughout the world of music and has become one of Kabalevsky's most frequently heard works; its American premiere took place

over the NBC network, on November 8, 1942, with Arturo Toscanini directing the NBC Symphony Orchestra.

Another important work came in 1937: the opera, *Colas Breugnon,* based on the novel of Romain Rolland. Here Kabalevsky drew his inspiration from French rather than Russian backgrounds. His melodies were modeled after French folk songs (although only one melody is an actual quotation). "The folk songs are highly successful," wrote Romain Rolland to the composer. "You have grasped their essence perfectly and have given them form in your music."

With his subsequent works for orchestra, chamber-music groups, and piano, Kabalevsky achieved a major position in Soviet music. In 1939 he was elected a member of the Presidium of the Organizing Committee of the Union of Soviet Composers. One year later he was given the Order of Merit. And in 1946 he received the highest award that can come to a Soviet composer when the Stalin Prize was conferred upon him for his String Quartet. It is significant to remark that Kabalevsky was one of the few leading composers in the Soviet Union to escape censure when the Central Committee of the Communist Party attacked Soviet musicians for their "decadence" and "formalism" in 1948 (see Prokofiev).

Courtesy of Musical Courier
DMITRI KABALEVSKY

Kabalevsky: kă-bă-lĕf′skē

Within traditional forms, Kabalevsky uses broad melodies, fully developed harmonies, and vigorous rhythms. His music is highly expressive and easily assimilable. Occasionally, Kabalevsky indulges in witty statements, as in the orchestral suite, *The Comedians,* written in 1938, and in the highly popular overture to *Colas Breugnon.*

MAJOR WORKS:

Ballets—Vasilek, 1938; Byvayte Zdorovy, 1940.

Chamber Music—String Quartet No. 1, 1946; String Quartet No. 2 in G minor.

Operas—Colas Breugnon, 1937; Near Moscow, 1942; The Family of Taras, 1947.

Orchestral Music—Poem of Struggle, 1932; Requiem for Lenin, for chorus and orchestra, 1933; Symphony No. 2, 1934; Concerto for Piano and Orchestra, 1935; Symphony No. 4, 1939; The Comedians, suite, 1939; My Great Country, for chorus and orchestra, 1942; People's Avenger, suite for chorus and orchestra, 1942; Concerto for Violin and Orchestra, 1948.

Piano Music—Two Sonatinas, 1930; 24 Preludes, 1944; Sonata No. 2, 1945; Sonata No. 3, 1946.

ABOUT:

Abraham, G., Eight Soviet Composers.

Aram Khatchaturian *1903-*

ARAM KHATCHATURIAN was born in Tiflis, Armenia, on June 6, 1903. Though he showed an early interest in music, and particularly the folk songs and dances of his native land, it was not until later in life that he was able to receive adequate training. His father, a bookbinder, was too poor to pay for a musical education. Up until his twentieth year Khatchaturian knew almost nothing about theory or the musical repertory.

In the fall of 1923 he entered the Gnesin School of Music in Moscow to study the cello. Two years later he joined the composition class. No sooner had he learned some of the elements of composition than he took to writing his own music. His first piece was a *Dance,* for violin and piano, written in 1926, and it was good enough to be published. It is particularly significant to note that in this maiden creative effort there are qualities of Khatchaturian's mature style. As Gerald Abraham noted, "a fresh and spontaneous vein of melody inspired by the

ARAM KHATCHATURIAN

folk music of Transcaucasian peoples" is found in this *Dance,* together with "a tendency to loose, rhapsodic structure, a keen rhythmic sense, and a love of warm, colorful sound effects."

In 1929 Khatchaturian entered the Moscow Conservatory. He developed rapidly under such sympathetic teachers as Miaskovsky and Vassilenko. In 1932 he wrote a Trio, for clarinet, violin, and piano, and one year after that a *Dance Suite,* for orchestra. Both works revealed increasing self-assurance in technique and a growing maturity of style. Khatchaturian emerged as an important composer in 1934 with the Symphony No. 1, written to honor the fifteenth anniversary of Soviet Armenia. Introduced in Moscow in 1935, the work attracted considerable attention and enthusiasm. Victor Belaiev wrote: "It is a great work by reason of its contours and proportions. Interesting and imposing in its sonority, it is distinguished by the broad treatment of its musical ideas."

Other major works followed which extended and magnified Khatchaturian's importance as a composer. The Concerto for Piano and Orchestra, introduced by the composer in Moscow in 1937, became instantly popular in the Soviet Union. To this day it is one of Khatchaturian's most famous and frequently heard large works. The Concerto for Violin and Orchestra, in 1940, and

Khatchaturian: kǎ-chǎ-tōō′ryǎn

the ballet *Gayané,* in 1942, both won the much-coveted Stalin Prize. He also received the Order of Lenin for "outstanding services in the development of music in his native Armenia" and had his name inscribed on an honor plaque in the hall of the Moscow Conservatory.

The two orchestral suites which the composer prepared from *Gayané* have enjoyed considerable popularity. One of the numbers from the Suite No. 1 has been particularly successful—the "Sabre Dance." The first time the Suite No. 1 was played in New York City (at a concert at the Lewisohn Stadium), the "Sabre Dance" aroused such a demonstration that it had to be repeated. It was largely through the appeal of this one dance that the Columbia recording of the first suite became (according to *Billboard*) the best-selling classical album soon after its release in 1947. "Sabre Dance" was soon heard continually over the radio, in performances by most radio orchestras, and in a piano transcription by Oscar Levant, which he popularized. It became a juke-box favorite and for many months assumed the status of a nation-wide popular "hit."

Despite the official honors that came his way, and his high station in Soviet music, Khatchaturian was the object for vigorous denunciation by the Central Committee of the Communist Party in its wholesale condemnation of Soviet composers on February 10, 1948 (see Prokofiev). This attack on Khatchaturian is particularly amazing in view of the fact that his music has always had wide universal appeal, is based on folk sources, and is easily appreciated on first hearing—in short, music which cannot be said to be guilty of either "anti-popular trends" or "bourgeois formalism." However, Khatchaturian publicly admitted that the criticism of the Central Committee was justified and that henceforth he would write in a more acceptable vein.

The folk music of Armenia is the influence that is most strongly felt in Khatchaturian's music, stylistic elements of which have been assimilated in his writing. As his compatriot Dmitri Kabalevsky once wrote: "The especially attractive features of Khatchaturian's music are in its rootings in national folk fountainheads. Captivating rhyth-

mic diversity of dances of the peoples of Transcaucasia and inspired improvisations of *ashugs* (bards)—such are the roots from which have sprung the composer's creative endeavors. In the interlocking of these two principles there grew Khatchaturian's symphonism—vivid and dynamic, with keen contrasts, now enchanting in their mellow lyricism, now stirring in their tensity and dramatism."

Khatchaturian's wife is also a composer. Her music appears under the name of Nina Makarova.

MAJOR WORKS:

Ballets—Happiness, 1940; Gayané, 1941; Spartak, 1951.

Orchestral Music—Symphony No. 1, 1934; Concerto for Piano and Orchestra, 1935; Poem about Stalin, 1938; Incidental Music to The Masquerade, 1939; Concerto for Violin and Orchestra, 1940; Symphony No. 2, 1943; Russian Fantasy, 1945; Concerto for Cello and Orchestra, 1946; Overture—Poem, 1950.

Piano Music—Poem, 1927; Study in Ninths, 1927.

ABOUT:

Abraham, G., Eight Soviet Composers.

Zoltán Kodály *1882-*

ZOLTÁN KODÁLY was born in Keczkemét, Hungary, on December 16, 1882. His earliest musical experiences consisted of listening to the gypsy orchestra, the only "professional" music available in his town, and to the violin playing of his father, a station master who was a devoted musical amateur. When Kodály was eighteen years old he entered the Budapest Conservatory, where his principal teacher was Hans Koessler. He started composing immediately, his works strongly influenced by the styles of Brahms and Debussy.

From 1905 on, Kodály was inspired by his friend and compatriot, Béla Bartók, to devote himself to intensive research in the field of Hungarian folk music. They made numerous expeditions throughout Hungary, unearthing thousands of folk songs and dances, formerly completely unknown to the rest of the world. Many of these they edited and published. As a student at the University of Budapest, Kodály received his

Kodály: kô'dä-y'

doctorate with a thesis entitled *The Strophic Construction in Hungarian Folk Song.*

To the world outside of Hungary, the decorative, sinuous, and sentimental gypsy songs, exploited by Liszt and Brahms, have long stood for Hungarian folk music. But the researches of Kodály and Bartók proved that the indigenous music of Hungary had a far different character. It was more virile, more earthy, more brusque. Its rhythms had a savage and elemental power; its modal tonalities gave it an exotic character.

Like Bartók, Kodály was greatly influenced in his own musical writing by the style, character, and techniques of the Hungarian folk song and dance. M. D. Calvocoressi has summed up the stylistic traits of Kodály's music: "His music generally has a distinctly narrative character, even when not assuming the form of a kind of recitative. Its nature is that of a discourse rather than a meditation: a discourse very definite in tone, broadly and emphatically punctuated with sharp, sudden swerves and forcible repetitions which seem to aim at driving a point finally home before proceeding to the next. . . . Persistent repetition of a pattern, whether rhythmic or melodic arabesque, is a feature particularly conspicuous in Kodály's music." And these qualities are also found in the songs and dances of Hungary Kodály helped to rescue from obscurity.

Béla Bartók's description of Kodály's music follows: "A strong, broad-flowing melodic invention, a complete grasp of construction, and a certain leaning towards hesitating disintegration and melancholy. The expression of reckless revelry and wild intoxication is foreign to his individuality, which is of a predominantly contemplative nature. . . . Kodály's music . . . is not 'modern' in the current sense of the word. It has nothing in common with atonal, bitonal, or polytonal tendencies: everything remains based upon the principle of balanced tonality. Yet his musical language is entirely new and expresses musical ideas never before heard, thus proving that tonality is not yet completely exhausted."

Kodály wrote many notable works, largely in the field of chamber music, before he achieved his first major success. It came with the *Psalmus Hungaricus,* for solo,

ZOLTAN KODALY

chorus, and orchestra, written in 1923 to honor the fiftieth anniversary of the union of Buda and Pest, and commissioned by the city of Budapest. It was introduced in Budapest on November 19, 1923, and was a huge success. Translated into many different languages, it was subsequently heard throughout the world of music. Its text dated from the sixteenth century, and Kodály's music skillfully combined the old and the new, blending old Hungarian styles and idioms with contemporary techniques. Without becoming archaic, Kodály expressed the centuries-old culture of the Hungarian people. "His musical setting," wrote A. von Toth, "exhausts both the national and subjective elements of the poem and molds them into one perfect and homogeneous unit of great visionary beauty and of great lyric and dramatic strength."

Kodály's most famous work followed two years later. It was the folk opera, *Háry János,* completed in 1925, and presented in Budapest on October 16, 1926. Built around a fabulous character of Hungarian legend— Háry János, a notorious liar—the text was a merry tale for which Kodály provided music that was equally bright, sparkling, vigorous, and witty. The score of *Háry János* has become universally famous by virtue of the orchestral suite prepared by the composer and frequently heard at symphony concerts.

In his later works, notably the *Dances of Galanta,* the *Dances of Marosszék,* and the *Peacock Variations,* Hungarian folk art remains the source of the composer's inspiration. But from these folk materials Kodály always succeeds in developing a personal and individual art which has made him not only the leading composer of his land but also one of the most original figures in contemporary music.

In 1906 Kodály was appointed professor of composition at the Budapest Conservatory. A retiring person, he has lived out of the glare of the limelight, humbly serving music as a composer, teacher, and writer.

Kodály visited this country for the first time in the winter of 1946, as a delegate to the Congress of the International Confederation of Authors' Societies, held in Washington, D.C. While in this country, Kodály conducted the American concert premiere of his *Peacock Variations* with the Philadelphia Orchestra in Philadelphia.

During this visit, Kodály confided to Olin Downes of the *New York Times* his musical beliefs. "All music comes fundamentally from popular sources. As the culture of the people advances, the product becomes always more interesting and significant, but when the connection with ancestral sources is lost, the art enters the stage of decadence. . . . One of the most useless things a composer can do is to quote a few folk melodies in his score and think that in so doing he has created something national and genuine. This is no more the case, under such circumstances, than a bunch of flowers cut and put in vases on the shelf is a garden. The garden is made of seeds which have taken growth from the ground."

Major Works:

Chamber Music—String Quartet No. 1, op. 2, 1908; Sonata for Cello and Piano, op. 4, 1910; Duo for Cello and Violin, op. 7, 1914; Sonata for Unaccompanied Cello, op. 8, 1915; String Quartet No. 2, op. 10, 1917; Serenade, for two violins and viola, op. 12, 1920.

Choral Music—Evening, for mixed a cappella chorus, 1904; Psalmus Hungaricus, op. 13, 1923; Two Hungarian Folksongs, for a cappella female chorus; Ave Maria, 1935; Te Deum, 1935; Ode to Franz Liszt, 1936; Missa Brevis, 1945.

Operas—Háry János, 1925-26; The Spinning Room, lyric scenes, 1931-32; Czinka Panna, 1943.

Orchestral Music—Summer Evening, 1906; Ballet Music, 1925; Theatre Overture, 1927; Dances of Marosszék (also for piano), 1929-30; Dances of Galanta, 1933; Peacock Variations, 1939; Concerto for Orchestra, 1940; Funeral Music for the Dead of the War, 1946; Concerto for Viola and Orchestra, 1947.

Piano Music—Nine Pieces, op. 3, 1910; Seven Pieces, op. 11, 1917-18.

Vocal Music—Eneksza, op. 1, 1921; Seven Songs, op. 6, 1923; Five Songs, op. 9, 1915; Three Songs, op. 14, 1929; Hungarian Folk Songs, ten volumes, 1929-32.

About:

Mellers, W., Studies in Contemporary Music; New York Times, November 3, 1946.

Ernst Krenek *1900-*

(See *American Composers Today*)

Paul Le Flem *1881-*

PAUL LE FLEM was born in the Breton town of Lézardrieux (Côtes du Nord), France, on March 18, 1881. His grandparents were Breton peasants who could not speak a word of French. His father was a small functionary in the local government.

As a boy, Paul Le Flem did nothing to distinguish himself. But he was known to have a pleasing voice and could be counted on to sing in tune. He explains that the death of his father was the emotional shock to bring him to music. From that time on he felt the need for musical expression as keenly as for food. Such study as he received came from experimenting at the piano and reading texts. He acquired enough of a technical equipment to write a symphonic poem in his sixteenth year, *Eponine et Sabinus,* inspired by his Latin studies. It was performed by his school orchestra. With the ardor of youth, he entered it in a Paris competition. Guy Ropartz wrote him saying that while there was some promise in the work "you still know nothing. It is necessary to learn!"

When he was eighteen, Le Flem went to Paris and divided his time between the Sorbonne and the Conservatory. At last he was compelled to make a choice between philosophy, in which he had been specializing at the Sorbonne, and music. Music won out.

What he describes as the second great emotional shock of his life to influence his

Le Flem: lẽ flĕm′

musical development came in 1902 with the hearing of Debussy's *Pelléas et Mélisande.* That opera suddenly opened for him new vistas of musical expression. Suddenly Le Flem became impatient with the conformism and pedantry he confronted at the Conservatory. He abandoned the Conservatory and went on to Moscow, where for the next eighteen months he devoted himself to study and composition.

Back in Paris, Le Flem enrolled in the Schola Cantorum to study composition with Vincent D'Indy and counterpoint with Albert Roussel. In 1906 he made his official debut as composer when his Sonata for Violin and Piano was performed at a concert of the Société Nationale de Musique. This work was regarded so advanced in its harmonic thinking that one critic condemned him for "breaking and plundering everything in making his entrance into the world of music." It is interesting to note, however, that Guy Ropartz—who had been so critical of his youthful work—now wrote him a long letter praising him enthusiastically and without reservation.

At about this time Le Flem completed his First Symphony. It had to wait twenty years for performance, though isolated movements were heard at concerts of the Société Nationale. Conductors in France turned it down so frequently that Le Flem was convinced the work was inferior. However, after one of his orchestral works, *Danses,* was successfully performed by Walter Straram at one of his orchestral concerts in 1927, Le Flem showed the conductor his early symphony. Straram was so impressed with it that he performed it in 1927 and scored a decisive success. The symphony was now heard in Copenhagen, Berlin, and Budapest, acclaimed wherever it was heard. When, in 1931, Albert Wolff presented in Paris a cycle of the most important symphonies by French composers, Le Flem's First Symphony was included.

Le Flem distinguished himself with two operas. The first was *Le Rossignol de St. Malo,* written in 1942, and soon after that successfully presented by the Opéra Comique in Paris; it has since then become a permanent fixture in the repertory of the Opéra Comique. In 1947 Le Flem completed his second opera, *La Magicienne de la Mer* (on

the same Breton legend used by Lalo for his opera *Le Roi d'Ys*). This opera was also successfully presented by the Opéra Comique.

Le Flem's earliest works were strongly influenced by Debussy. At that time his style was sensuous and impressionistic. Later on, he veered from Debussy to D'Indy, inheriting the latter composer's respect for form, preciseness of expression, and objectivity of approach. Le Flem has always utilized modern techniques, particularly in his harmony and tonality.

He has distinguished himself in several musical fields other than composition. In 1924 he served as chorus master of the Opéra Comique, and after that he was director of a successful choral group known as the Chanteurs de St. Gervais. He has taught counterpoint at the Schola Cantorum, written music criticism for *Comoedia,* and been associated in a technical capacity with the Paris Radio.

In 1935 Le Flem allied himself with a group of musicians which called itself "La Spirale." This group dedicated itself to propagandize new music. "La Spirale," which included Daniel Lesur, Messiaen, and Migot, gave its first concert, in Paris, on December 12, 1935.

Le Flem has confessed that the greatest single influence in his life has been Brittany, where he was born. His two operas are based on Breton legends, and some of his melodic ideas in other works are derived from Breton folk music. He has been active in bringing about a renaissance of Breton culture. He was a leading figure in a movement to restore the Breton language and to focus the attention of France on Breton art and thought. He was also responsible for having classical plays performed in Brittany before audiences comprising fishermen and peasants.

A fatalist by temperament, Le Flem remained in Paris during World War II and the occupation. He found escape from the turmoil of the times in composing.

MAJOR WORKS:

Chamber Music—Sonata for Violin and Piano, 1905; Quintet for Piano and Strings, 1909.

Choral Music—Crépuscule d'Amor, 1908; La Neige, 1912; La Procession, 1912; Vray Dieu, 1912; Lamento, 1920; Paysage, 1922.

Operas—Le Rossignol de St. Malo, 1942; La Clairière des Fées, 1943; La Magicienne de la Mer, 1947.

Orchestral Music—Symphony, 1907; Aucassin et Nicolette, for soloists, chorus, and orchestra, 1909; Danses, 1911; La Voix du Large, 1912; Fantaisie, for piano and orchestra, 1912; Pour les Morts, triptych, 1913; Évocation, for voice and orchestra, 1920; Hymne au Vin, 1925; La Fête du Printemps, 1937; Le Village, 1942.

Piano Music—Par Landes, 1907; Par Grèves, 1907; Vieux Calvaire, 1910; Chants des Genêts, 1910; Clair de Lune sous Bois, 1910; Danse Désuète, 1910.

Daniel Lesur *1908-*

DANIEL LESUR was born in Paris on November 19, 1908. His mother, a composer, introduced him to music early. At the age of four he was already trying to write music: whenever his father came home on leave from the army, during the period of World War I, Lesur always had new works written for the event.

He attended the Conservatory, where his teachers included Caussade, Tournemire, and Ferté. When his studies ended, Daniel Lesur became an organist at the church of Ste. Clotilde. Later on, he combined his activity as organist at the church of St. Benedict with the teaching of counterpoint at the Schola Cantorum.

Studio Reinesque
DANIEL LESUR

Lesur: lĕ-sür'

In 1935 Daniel Lesur allied himself with a group of composers (including Le Flem, Messiaen, and Migot) which called itself "La Spirale." This group was devoted to promoting and publicizing the music of young and unknown composers. The first concert of La Spirale, on December 12, 1935, included a chamber-music work by Lesur. A much more important performance of a work by Lesur took place the same year when Pierre Monteux directed in Paris the premiere of *Suite Française*, for orchestra.

One year later Lesur identified himself with still another school of young French composers, self-styled "La Jeune France" (see Messiaen). The aim of this school was to express the "new France" in music "as far removed from revolutionary formulas as from academic formulas." In his later works, Lesur revealed most strongly the influence of the contrapuntal composers of the past, in his use of both polyphony and classical forms. But to his contrapuntal writing, he has always brought a romantic spirit. "Music," he has said, "is an expressive and emotional art. I admire pure mathematics and I admire science—but they have nothing to do with music." Occasionally, another influence can be detected in his works, that of French folk songs, which he admires profoundly, and whose simplicity and charm he has tried to emulate in his own songs.

During World War II Daniel Lesur served in the army. Nevertheless, he found the time to write music. When the Nazis invaded France, he went to live in Geneva, where several of his works were performed. Since the liberation, Lesur has abandoned playing the organ in churches and teaching (except for a few private pupils) to concentrate on creative work. Occasionally, he appears over the Paris Radio to disseminate news about music and musicians during intermissions of radio concerts.

Lesur lives in an attractive part of Paris, in an apartment filled with paintings, for his greatest interest outside of music is art. Whenever he has the leisure time, he wanders about in galleries and museums.

MAJOR WORKS:

Ballet—L'Infante et le Monstre (with Jolivet), 1938.

Chamber Music—Suite, for string quartet, 1940; Suite, for piano and three strings, 1943;

Suite Médiévale, for flute, violin, viola, cello and harp, 1945-46; Variations, for piano and strings, 1950.

Choral Music—Ave Maria.

Orchestral Music—Hommage à J. S. Bach, for string orchestra, 1933; Suite Française, 1934-35; Passacaille, for piano and orchestra, 1937; Pastorale, for chamber orchestra, 1938; Ricercare, 1939; L'Étoile de Seville, suite, 1941; Variations, for piano and strings, 1943; Andrea del Sarto, symphonic poem, 1949.

Piano Music—Soirs, three pieces, 1922-29; Les Carillons, suite, 1930; Bagatelle, 1934; Pavane, 1938; Deux Noëls, 1939-40; Le Bouquet de Béatrice, five children's pieces for four hands, 1946-47; Le Village Imaginaire, for two pianos, 1946-47; Pastorale Variée, 1947; Ballade, 1948.

Vocal Music—Four Songs, 1933-39; Trois Poèmes de Cécile Sauvage, 1939; Deux Chansons de l'Étoile de Seville, 1941; L'Enfance de l'Art (Roy), 1942; Clair comme le Jour (Roy), 1945; Chansons Cambodgiennes, 1946-47; Berceuse à Tenir Éveillé (Obaldia), 1946-47.

ABOUT:

Musical America, July 1937.

Gustav Mahler *1860-1911*

MAHLER'S inclusion in this volume is justified by the fact that his most important works—including six of his nine symphonies—were written after 1900.

He was born in the Bohemian town of Kalischt, on July 7, 1860, the son of middle-class merchants. From the very beginning he disclosed an unusual sensitivity to music. The folk songs and military marches he heard around him fascinated him to such an extent that when he was four years old he started to reproduce them on an accordion he found at home. He lost all interest in the accordion when he discovered a piano in the attic of his grandmother's house. From that moment on, he applied himself slavishly to learn to play the piano; and when he acquired a certain facility he began creating his own melodies.

His passion for music was too intense to be ignored. His father had no objection to his devoting himself to music, but only on the condition that he had talent. To satisfy himself on his point, the elder Mahler took his son to Vienna in 1875 and had him play for Julius Epstein, professor at the Vienna Conservatory. Epstein had no hesitancy in pronouncing Mahler a talent of the first or-

Mahler: mä'lĕr

der and arranged for his admission into the Conservatory.

At the Conservatory his teachers included Epstein (piano), Robert Fuchs (harmony) and Franz Krenn (composition). He was at times a rebellious student who insisted on questioning the validity of the rules taught him. But he was also a brilliant student, winning prizes in piano playing and composition, and in his second year he was excused from the classes in counterpoint because he had already mastered that subject. At the Conservatory he started writing ambitious works, including a Symphony, a Violin Sonata, a Piano Quintet, and an opera. One movement of the Quintet was performed at the Conservatory on July 11, 1878. Later on, Mahler discarded all these youthful efforts.

After leaving the Conservatory, Mahler earned his living by conducting in small town theatres and music halls. He graduated into the opera house in 1882, when he was appointed to the conductorial staff of a small and poorly equipped theatre in Olmütz. His next assignment was hardly more satisfying —at the Kassel Opera. But as he developed, he was given more and more important assignments—first at the Prague Opera, then at the Leipzig Opera, and after that at the Budapest Opera. During these years of apprenticeship, Mahler was already beginning to give an indication of his later interpretative powers. A performance of Mendelssohn's *St. Paul* in Leipzig in 1885 and performances of operas by Mozart and Wagner in Prague and Budapest aroused considerable attention and enthusiasm for the authority, attention to detail, and consecration Mahler brought to every work he conducted.

In 1897 Mahler received his most important appointment up to that time, that of first conductor of the celebrated Vienna Court Opera. (He was soon elevated to the rank of music director.) In Vienna, his interpretative genius, combined with an indefatigable and almost maniacal pursuit after perfection, resulted in performances the like of which had rarely before been heard either in Vienna or other music centers. Mahler was relentless in his demand for the best that was in him and in all those who worked with him; where music was concerned, he was the unsparing dictator. He created a revolu-

From a bronze by Rodin

GUSTAV MAHLER

tion in costuming, scenery, and stage direction. He revitalized the repertory with many novelties and premieres, and he subjected many of the old operas to complete restudy and rehabilitation. He demanded that every opera—including the Wagnerian music dramas hitherto presented only with cuts—be given exactly as the composer had instructed. He dismissed instrumentalists and singers who could not rise to the standards he set. Everywhere he met opposition—he was hated because he was so ruthless and inexorable in his demands, and because he was a Jew—and he triumphed over it. He made the Vienna Court Opera the leading opera house in the world, and his ten-year period as its director the most resplendent epoch in its history.

"Pedantic, almost like a schoolmaster, in rehearsals, Mahler reached his full greatness in performance," Karl Weigl, who worked under Mahler in Vienna, wrote in *Musical Courier* (January 1948): "The day's work on details was then forgotten and melted away in the flaming fire that emanated from him. . . . He insisted on absolute accuracy in everything—the smallest time values and rests, changes in dynamics, tempo, phrasing, had to be exactly according to the composer's directions. He had no use for arbitrary 'interpretations' nor so-called 'tradition.' The famous saying that *'Tradition ist*

Schlumperei!' ('Tradition is sloppiness') was coined by Mahler. His scope as interpreter was practically unlimited. . . . As is well known he spared neither time nor effort to attain the utmost perfection. Indefatigable himself, he expected his associates to be likewise."

"Certainly no operatic theatre was ever directed on a more grandiose plan," wrote Max Graf, also from first-hand experiences. "I count the first year of Mahler's direction among the high points of the modern theatre. His performances were perfection itself. 'This is the greatest opera ever written,' Mahler would say of each opera he restudied; such was the enthusiasm with which he threw himself into his interpretations. This overwhelming enthusiasm was necessary to bring all his energy to bear upon the work in hand."

Though he achieved the heights as a conductor and musical director—and he knew it—he was not satisfied. More than that, he wanted to write great music, of a scope and dimensions, and filled with concepts, hitherto unrealized in music. He combined his herculean activity with the baton with unceasing creation. He completed his first major work, the song-cycle *Lieder eines Fahrenden Gesellen,* as early as 1884. His First Symphony came in 1888, followed six years later by his monumental Second Symphony, the *Resurrection.* Between 1900 and 1910 he wrote six symphonies, the song-cycles *Kindertotenlieder* and the Rückert Lieder, and *Das Lied von der Erde.*

He belonged with the neo-romantic composers in Germany and Austria who used huge structures and immense orchestral forces to expound elaborate programs frequently filled with philosophic or metaphysical concepts. As this writer has written in *The Complete Book of 20th Century Music*: "Mahler was a complex individual. His entire life was obsessed by inner turmoil, conflicts, spiritual doubts, *Weltschmerz.* Restlessly he searched for a meaning to life. And in his music he continually posed metaphysical questions. He sought to prove the meaning of life and death, to seek out the mysteries of nature. Above all else, he wanted to resolve the cosmic questions that troubled him. In a way his music is a spiritual autobiography."

The essence of his musical art is found in his nine symphonies (he started but never completed a tenth). They have been divided by Mahler students into three groups. The first four symphonies are subjective works in which, in Paul Stefan's words, the composer was involved in "a great and intensely personal struggle with the world and the universe." In the Fifth through the Eighth symphonies Mahler is a tone-poet. "As though moving in lofty spheres," wrote Stefan, "he has now mastered his own musical language, penetrating into it more intensely, spiritualizing it, so that he now no longer needs human language." In the Ninth Symphony—and in *Das Lied von der Erde,* which the composer liked to consider a symphony though he did not designate it as such —he has finished with his doubts and struggles; he has found peace and resignation as he bids the world farewell.

"What kind of music . . . are these symphonies of Mahler?" asks Ernest Newman in the London *Times.* He provides the answer: "His music is a highly personal matter: it is himself, and into each successive work he poured virtually his whole self. . . . There is the same attempt in each work to make it cover the whole of life, the same alternations or fusions of the ecstatic, the tragic, the gay, the naive, the complex, the philosophic, the ironic, the sardonic, frequently achieved by the same technical procedures—the piling of tension on tension, for example, followed by a sudden relaxation and then a recommencement of the process of strain and release. But the important point to be observed is that although these procedures resemble each other superficially they are subtly different from one work to another, both in their purposes and in their final result; and having a *raison d'être* each time, they must be played, and imaginatively appreciated, with a different mental nuance."

Because his esthetic aims were so pretentious, Mahler was subjected to continual abuse and vilification whenever one of his symphonies was performed. Not until the end of his life—at the premiere of his Eighth Symphony in Munich on September 12, 1910—did a work of his receive acclaim. Indeed, this opposition and antagonism to his music has continued long after his death.

To this day there are many critics who condemn Mahler's works for their bombast, garrulousness, and emotional extravagances, just as there are many other critics who find in his music nobility of thought, sublimity of concept, and shattering emotional impact.

Rejection as a composer by his contemporaries was not the only cross Mahler had to bear. At the Vienna Court Opera he continually confronted petty intrigues, jealousies, obstructions. He was struck by a personal tragedy when his little daughter died of scarlet fever in 1906. Ever after he was haunted by the consciousness of guilt that he had brought on this disaster by having written elegies for dead children (the *Kindertotenlieder*). Besides all this, he was not well—suffering from a serious heart condition that demanded that he conserve his energies.

By 1907 he knew he could stay at the Vienna Opera no longer. He accepted an offer to conduct at the Metropolitan Opera House in New York. After an eloquent performance of *Fidelio* in Vienna on October 15, 1907, Mahler left the Vienna Opera. Mahler made his American debut on January 1, 1908, in *Tristan and Isolde,* and the following season he combined his activity at the Metropolitan with conducting concerts during the season of the New York Philharmonic Orchestra. Still unsparing of himself—despite his heart condition—he finally collapsed physically in New York early in 1911. Suffering from a streptococcus infection, he was brought back to Paris for serum treatments. He sensed that he had not much longer to live, and he asked to be taken back to his beloved Vienna. He died there, just before midnight on May 18, 1911.

Bruno Walter—who for many years worked with Mahler and who, after Mahler's death, was one of his most devoted disciples and protagonists—provides us with the following interesting portrait of the composer in his biography: "Those who knew Mahler will recall how often his facial expression would suddenly change from cheerfulness to gloom. It seemed as if he were reproaching himself for having thoughtlessly forgotten to remember something that was sad. The significance of these attacks of melancholy . . . became clear to me only gradually. At the bottom of his soul lay a profound world-sorrow whose rising cold waves would seize him with an icy grip."

His intellectual interests, Walter goes on to say, were many sided. "The wealth and variety of his intellectual powers, the warmth of his emotions, and the firmness of his judgment were matched by the thematic inexhaustibility, vitality, and assurance of his speech. Mahler was fond of conversation, and had not the frequent fault of being inattentive when others were speaking. He was able not only to speak but to listen. He had the virtue of spending himself freely in conversation. . . .

"Referring to his outward conduct towards people, let me admit . . . that, from the standpoint of social conventions, it left much to be desired. He, whose heart was full of kindness, could be hard and cutting, violent and hot-tempered, cold and forbidding. He was, however, always sincere. Despite his dominating professional position, this son of nature was never able to acquire polish, nor the customary careless pleasantness of manner, neither had he any ambitions in that direction. His was a commanding personality which unconsciously demanded that others should adapt themselves to him; and they usually did."

Mahler was married to Alma Schindler in 1904. His widow subsequently became the wife of the famous writer Franz Werfel.

MAJOR WORKS:

Choral Music—Das Klagende Lied, for soloists, chorus, and orchestra, 1898.

Orchestral Music—Lieder eines Fahrenden Gesellen, song cycle with orchestra, 1884; Symphony No. 1, in D major, Titan, 1888; Symphony No. 2, in C minor, Resurrection, 1894; Symphony No. 3, in D minor, 1896; Symphony No. 4, in G major, Ode to Heavenly Joy, 1900; Symphony No. 5, in C-sharp minor, The Giant, 1902; Kindertotenlieder, song cycle with orchestra, 1902; Five Songs from Rückert, with orchestra, 1902; Symphony No. 6, in A minor, Tragic, 1904; Symphony No. 7, in E minor, Song of the Night, 1905; Symphony No. 8, in E major, Symphony of a Thousand, 1907; Das Lied von der Erde, song cycle with orchestra, 1908; Symphony No. 9, in D major, 1909.

ABOUT:

Engel, G., Gustav Mahler: Song Symphonist; Mahler, A. M. S., Gustav Mahler: Memories and Letters; Newlin, D., Bruckner, Mahler, and Schoenberg; Stefan, P., Gustav Mahler; Walter, B., Gustav Mahler.

Gian Francesco Malipiero *1882-*

GIAN FRANCESCO MALIPIERO was born in Venice on March 18, 1882. He was descended from a famous Venetian family which included several important musicians. His grandfather, Francesco Malipiero, had been a famous opera composer, in his day, considered by some the equal of Verdi; his father was a gifted pianist. Gian, then, moved in a musical environment which predestined a musical career for him.

An undisclosed family tragedy sent the Malipieros wandering out of Italy when Francesco was seven years old. During this period, father and son earned a living for the family by playing in small orchestras in Germany and Austria. In 1896 they came to Vienna, where a Polish nobleman was convinced of Gian's musical talent and financed his musical education. For one year Malipiero studied at the Vienna Conservatory. Returning, at last, to his native city, he became a pupil of Enrico Bossi at the Liceo Benedetto Marcello. When Bossi was appointed director of the Liceo Musicale in Bologna, Malipiero followed him there. Malipiero wrote his first orchestral work in Bologna, *Dai Sepolcri*.

In 1902 Malipiero came upon a library of manuscripts by old Italian composers. This discovery had a far-reaching effect on his development as a composer. So strongly was he attracted to the musical art of Italy's past that henceforth he devoted himself to research in this field. Ultimately he was to become one of the foremost living authorities on old Italian music. His definitive editions of the complete works of Monteverdi, and his editions of Vivaldi, Marcello, Cavalli, and other old masters, represent the highest type of musical research.

Occupied with his studies of old Italian music, Malipiero found that his own composition was being too strongly influenced by the old Italian styles. Dissatisfied with the kind of music he was writing, he went off to Paris in 1913. There he mingled with the leading musical personalities of the time: Debussy, Fauré, Stravinsky, Ravel, Manuel de Falla. He came into intimate contact with the most progressive musical ideas, techniques, and directions which helped him to

Malipiero: mä-lē-pyâ'rō

clarify his own creative problems and to arrive at a more flexible technique.

At about this time, a competition was announced in Italy for new works of music. Malipiero entered five compositions, four of them under pseudonyms. Four of these works won prizes. The discovery that the four winning works were by the same man aroused considerable antagonism and bitterness in Italian music circles, and for a while Malipiero was regarded with great hostility. When two of his works were publicly performed in Rome—*Canossa,* an opera, on January 24, 1914, and the symphonic poem *Arione* on December 12, 1913—a large segment of each audience had been organized to give voice to loud opposition in the theatre.

Shortly before World War I, Malipiero settled in the little town of Asolo, two hours' distance by automobile from Venice. This has remained his home ever since. For a while, he found complete escape from the gruesome realities of World War I. But the war ultimately caught up with him. In October 1917 the fleeing Second Army, pursued by the enemy, came to Asolo. Malipiero and his family (taking with them only two precious musical manuscripts) escaped and after a difficult and circuitous journey came to Rome.

The war had an influence on Malipiero's music. Indeed, the war inspired the first of his important works, the *Pause del Silenzio,* for orchestra. Consisting of seven pieces, each different in character, this work was intended by the composer to express the horror of war. It represented to one Italian critic, "shudders . . . cries, lamentations." Introduced at the Augusteo in Rome on January 27, 1918, Molinari conducting, it was a huge success.

After the war, Malipiero returned to his Asolo home. He lived in comparative seclusion, devoted to study, composition, and his editing chores. He emerged from his seclusion once a week to teach composition at the Liceo Benedetto Marcello in Venice. In 1939 he was appointed director of the Conservatory. Occasional interruptions also came when he traveled to England, France, and Germany to attend performances of his works. Though accepted and honored by the Fascist regime in Italy as one of the country's leading composers, Malipiero tried to

GIAN FRANCESCO MALIPIERO

ignore the political currents around him. On several occasions, however, he came into conflict with the authorities. His opera, *La Favola del Figlio Cambiato,* performed on March 26, 1934, was suppressed because it was judged "morally incongruous" with Fascist ideals.

In 1920 Malipiero's *Rispetti e Strambotti,* for string quartet, won the Elizabeth Sprague Coolidge prize of $1,000 in the United States. Utilizing the structure of two old Italian forms of poetry, and deriving its style from the cadences and strophes of Italian poetry, this one-movement quartet, descriptive of scenes of the Renaissance, recreated the atmosphere of an old Italian world with unique success.

The influence of old Italian music and culture is evident in other Malipiero works. Like so many of the early Italians, Malipiero is more dramatic than lyrical, more contrapuntal than homophonic. His melodies usually have the character of recitatives in the manner, say, of Monteverdi. The classical spirit of the Renaissance—its spirituality and its tranquillity—pervades his music, which, happily, blends these old atmospheres and mannerisms with contemporary techniques.

During World War II, Malipiero was personally involved in anti-Nazi activity. During the last stages of the Italian campaign, he and his wife (she was of British birth) gave shelter to an escaped British aviator who stayed in the bathroom on the attic floor. For several weeks the Malipieros were able to handle this extraordinary situation until a contact could be made with the partisans, who took the aviator to the hills and arranged his passage to England.

The war ended only a stone's throw from his very door, and miraculously his home escaped destruction. The Second World War, like the first, inspired an important work: the Symphony No. 4 ("In Memoriam") commissioned by the Koussevitzky Foundation and introduced by the Boston Symphony Orchestra under Koussevitzky on February 27, 1948. The tragedy suffered by Italians both during and immediately after the war is described in this work with compelling intensity.

MAJOR WORKS:

Ballet—Pantea, 1920.

Chamber Music—Rispetti e Strambotti, for string quartet, 1920; Stornelli e Ballate, for string quartet, 1923; Ricercari, for eleven instruments, 1925; Ritrovari, for eleven instruments, 1926; Sonata a Tre, for violin, cello, and piano, 1926; Cantari alla Madrigalesca, for string quartet, 1930; Epodi e Giambi, for oboe, violin, viola, and bassoon, 1932; String Quartet No. 4, 1934; String Quartet No. 5; Sonata a Cinque, for harp, flute, violin, viola, and cello, 1934; String Quartet No. 6; L'Arca di Noè, for string quartet, 1947; String Quartet No. 7.

Choral Music—San Francesco d'Assisi, mystery for soloists, chorus, and orchestra, 1920; La Principessa Ulalia, cantata, 1924; La Cena, oratorio, 1927; Passione, oratorio, 1935; Missa pro Mortuis, 1938; La Terra, 1946.

Operas—Canossa, 1913; L'Orfeide, cycle of three operas, 1921; Tre Commedie Goldoniane, cycle of three operas, 1923; Filomela e l'Infatuato, 1925; Merlino Maestro d'Organi, 1927; Il Mistero di Venezia, cycle of three operas, 1929; Torneo Notturno, 1929; La Favola di Figlio Cambiato, 1933; Giulio Cesare, 1935; Antonio e Cleopatra, 1938; La Vita è Sogno, 1940; I Capricci di Callot, 1941; L'Allegra Brigata, 1943.

Orchestral Music—Arione, for cello and orchestra, 1913; Ditirambo Tragico, 1917; Pause del Silenzio, 1917; Armenia, 1917; Impressioni dal Vero, Suites Nos. 1, 2, and 3, 1910, 1915, 1921; La Cimarosiana, 1922; Variazioni senza Tema, for piano and orchestra, 1924; L'Esilio dell' Eroe, 1930; Concerti, 1931; Sette Invenzioni, 1932; Quattro Invenzioni, 1933; Symphony No. 1, in Quattro Tempi Come le Quattro Stagioni; Concerto No. 1 for Piano and Orchestra, 1934; Il Commiato, for baritone and orchestra, 1934; Symphony No. 2, Elegiaca, 1936; Concerto No. 2 for Piano and Orchestra, 1938; Concerto for Cello and Orchestra, 1938; Vergilii Aeneis, symphony for voices and orchestra, 1944; Concertante in Eco, 1947; Symphony No. 5, for two pianos and orchestra, 1947; Symphony No.

6, Degli Archi, 1947; Symphony No. 7, Della Canzoni, 1948; Concerto No. 4 for Piano and Orchestra, 1949; Cinque Favoli, for voice and orchestra, 1950; Symphony No. 8, Dello Zodiaco, 1951.

ABOUT:

EWEN, D. (ed.) The Book of Modern Composers; Saminsky, L., Music of Our Day; Thompson, O. (ed.) Great Modern Composers.

Frank Martin *1890*-

FRANK MARTIN, one of Switzerland's most important composers, was born in Geneva on September 15, 1890, the son of a Protestant minister. He revealed a talent for music in his eighth year by writing little pieces. Martin began his intensive music study in 1906 with Joseph Lauber and continued with him for the next eight years. At the same time, he pursued his academic study at the Geneva College.

The first work by Martin to be performed publicly was *Poèmes Païens,* for baritone and orchestra, heard in 1911 at a festival of the Association of Swiss Musicians. The Association immediately took a keen interest in Martin and from this time on, until 1925, performed his works at its annual festival.

Between 1923 and 1925 Martin lived in Paris, where he associated himself with, and was influenced by, its many and varied musical currents. Then, returning to Geneva, he at once assumed an important position in the the musical life of his country. For ten years, between 1927 and 1937, he participated in a chamber-music group as pianist and harpsichordist. He founded the Technique Moderne de Musique, was music critic of the *Tribune de Genève*, and served as a member of the Board of Directors of the Association of Swiss Musicians. Later on, he became the director of the Dalcroze Institute of the Conservatory of Geneva, where he had been teaching for many years.

In his earliest works Martin revealed a healthy respect for tradition. His style was somewhat academic, and his harmonic and rhythmic language followed accepted patterns. But, as a critic of the *Schweizerische Musikzeitung* remarked about these early works, Martin "has only one goal . . . and that is the creation of a sensitive beauty. He has been condemned for his conservatism.

Martin: mǎr-tǎN'

But although the art of music has stood still with Martin in that no new realms of sound have been explored, it has been immeasurably enriched with a group of unpretentious works whose only claim to importance is that they bring the listener new worlds of beauty, and new, intense experiences."

The first phase of Martin's creative evolution came to an end in 1922 with the *Four Sonnets of Ronsard.* His two-year stay in Paris brought him into contact with the advanced thinking of many progressive French composers. Martin now started experimenting with new styles and techniques. He produced works like the *Trio on Popular Irish Melodies*, and a set of three symphonic movements entitled *Rythmes*, in which he exploited new resources of melody, tonality, and rhythm. In 1932 he arrived at a new phase of his creative development when he used themes composed of twelve notes. Between 1932 and 1937 he wrote several works in this idiom, among them a String Trio, a Symphony, and the *Rhapsody for Five Strings.*

By 1938 Martin had developed a style which satisfied him and with which he achieved both maturity and significance. His music now fused old elements and new and allowed him freedom to express himself with independence without completely abandoning tradition. In this vein he wrote his first important compositions, with which he was to win the respect of the entire music world: a series of Ballads, for various instruments; the cantata *Le Vin Herbé*, based on the Tristan saga; the oratorios *In Terra Pax* and *Golgotha*; and the *Petite Symphonie Concertante*, for piano, harpsichord, harp, and two string orchestras. Outstandingly successful were the *Petite Symphonie Concertante*, first heard in Zurich on May 27, 1946, and subsequently performed throughout the world, and *Le Vin Herbé*, first seen in an operatic version at the Salzburg Festival in 1948. These later works, wrote Jacques de Menasce, "are characterized by broad melodic lines of a chromatic nature, subtle harmonic and rhythmic patterns, and a sustained contrapuntal texture. The common denominator can be described as an organic blend of several methods, which as a composite make for an idiom that is clearly personal."

FRANK MARTIN

Many of Martin's important later works have been heard in this country. The *Petite Symphonie Concertante* was introduced to American audiences by the NBC Symphony Orchestra under Ernest Ansermet in 1948. In 1950 George Szell gave the American premiere of the Concerto for Seven Wind Instruments with the New York Philharmonic-Symphony. In 1952 the first American performance of *Golgotha* was given by the Dessoff Choirs, conducted by Paul Boepple, in New York. And in that same year Joseph Szigeti introduced to America the Concerto for Violin and Orchestra, the world premiere of which he had given in Basle on January 24, 1952.

In a French musical quarterly, *Polyphonie*, published in 1948, Frank Martin revealed his creative methods. Abraham Skulsky has summarized Martin's article as follows: "During the process of composition, he is totally involved in translating his will into concrete sounds and rhythms. . . . Only after he has completed it can the composer look upon his work simultaneously as an object and as a remembrance. . . . In his own mind he will be able to meditate on his work, knowing better than anyone else its weak and strong points. He will remember the things that came to him without effort and those that caused him trouble. He will seek to understand why certain aspects of the work resisted or misled him. This meditation is precious, because it will help him in his next works. Martin calls this meditation a technique of composition of a very special kind—the technique of inspiration. Acquiring this technique takes a long time; it is the art of provoking discoveries, the art of catching an idea at the right moment. . . .

"In discussing formulation of such meditation, Martin takes us back to the beginning of the creative process. Before he starts, the composer decides the general shape of the work, its dimensions, and its instrumental or vocal means. . . . Sometimes he can foresee certain elements; he may know clearly that the work will be a fugue, a passacaglia, or an allegro. . . . When the composer sits down to work, he looks for melodic and harmonic ideas that are most in accord with his first conception. In the words of Martin, those ideas are the raw materials, which do not depend upon the composer's will. . . . As he brings his technical knowledge to bear upon the initial ideas, the work becomes richer than he had imagined. . . . The success of the work depends upon his adequate use of the right ideas."

MAJOR WORKS:

Chamber Music—Sonata for Violin and Piano, 1913; Quintet for Piano and Strings, 1921; Trio on Popular Irish Melodies, for piano and strings, 1925; Rhapsody, for two violins, two violas, and double-bass, 1935; Trio, for strings, 1936; Ballads, for various instruments (saxophone, flute, piano, trombone, etc.).

Choral Music—Mass, 1926; Le Vin Herbé, chamber oratorio (also an opera), 1941; In Terra Pax, oratorio, 1944; Golgotha, oratorio, 1947.

Orchestral Music—Rythmes, 1928; Musique pour les Fêtes du Rhône, 1929; La Nique à Satan, for soloists, chorus, and orchestra, 1931; Guitare, 1933; Concerto for Piano and Orchestra, 1934; Danse de la Peur, for two pianos and small orchestra, 1936; Symphony, 1937; Ballade, for saxophone, string orchestra, piano and percussion, 1938; Petite Symphonie Concertante, 1945; Ballade, for cello and orchestra, 1949; Concerto for Seven Wind Instruments, Percussion and Orchestra, 1949; Concerto for Violin and Orchestra, 1951.

Piano Music—Eight Preludes, 1948.

Vocal Music—Der Cornet (Rilke), for alto and small orchestra, 1943; Six Monologues from Everyman (Hugo von Hofmannsthal), for baritone and piano, 1943; Cinq Chants d'Ariel, 1950; Four Sonnets of Ronsard.

ABOUT:

Musical America, August 1949; Musical Quarterly, April 1948; New York Times, January 13, 1952.

Jean Martinon *1910-*

JEAN MARTINON was born in Lyons on January 18, 1910. He attended the Conservatories in Lyons and Paris. His teachers included Roussel (composition) and Munch (conducting). Specializing in the playing of the violin, Martinon began his musical career as a violin virtuoso and as a performer in orchestras. Since composing interested him much more than the violin, he found himself devoting more and more of his time to creative work, and less of it to the concert stage. Between 1934 and 1936 he completed his first symphony, and in 1935 he wrote a Sinfonietta. Both of these works were extensively performed in France and helped to establish his reputation.

During World War II Martinon served in the French army. Captured by the Nazis, he was interned at Stalag IX. In camp he wrote a religious work, *Absolve Domine*, which he dedicated to French musicians who fell in the war, and which was performed at Stalag IX on November 2, 1940. He also completed one of the finest musical works to emerge out of the war. It was originally called *Stalag IX, ou Musique d'Exil*, its text (Psalm 136) prepared by a French priest who was also a prisoner. Renamed *Psalm of the Captives*, this work was introduced in Paris in 1942 under the direction of Charles Munch. The symbolism of the Hebrew captives lamenting their fate and crying out for vengeance did not escape the Parisian audience, at a time when Paris was occupied by the Nazis, and it acclaimed the composition. *Psalm of the Captives* was unanimously awarded the Prix de la Ville de Paris. In 1948 Martinon won another important award: the Béla Bartók Prize for his String Quartet.

It was the success of the *Psalm* that influenced Martinon to give up the violin for composition. But he was soon diverted into another musical activity. Called upon to conduct one of his own works, Martinon found so much satisfaction in working with an orchestra that he decided to become a conductor. He has since then directed most of the important French orchestras and has appeared as a guest with leading orchestras in England, Italy, Poland, and South America, in performances of his own and other com-

Martinon: măr-tē-nôN'

Seeberger

JEAN MARTINON

Orchestral Music—Sinfonietta, for piano, harp, strings, and percussion, 1935; Symphony No. 1, 1936; Concerto Giocoso, for violin and orchestra, 1942; Hymne à la Vie, 1944; Concerto Lyrique, for string quartet and small orchestra, 1944; Les Métamorphoses d'Ovide, 1945; Symphony No. 3, Irish, 1947.

Piano Music—Sonatine, 1940; Épilogue d'un Conte d'Amour, 1944; En Promenade, 1945; Ballade au Soldat Incassable, 1945; Introduction and Toccata, 1947.

Vocal Music—Humanité, 1931; Après Ma Journée Faite, 1932; Paysage Antérieur, 1939; Les Horizons Perdus, 1940; Agonisante, 1944; Les Vieux Matelots, 1944.

Bohuslav Martinu *1890-*

(See *American Composers Today*)

Pietro Mascagni *1863-1945*

posers' music. In 1946 he was appointed permanent conductor of the Bordeaux Orchestra.

Martinon's style has been largely influenced by his teacher Albert Roussel, and to a lesser degree by Bartók and Schmitt. New resources of tonality and harmony are tapped, but not to the point of sacrificing expressiveness. Whether he is writing abstract music or programmatically, Martinon fills his works with dramatic intensity and emotional impact. What one reviewer said of his *Hymne à la Vie* applies to Martinon's other works, too: "Fire, enthusiasm, and the joy of being alive are found in Martinon's music."

Martinon, who lives in the Montmartre district of Paris, is a devoted sportsman. He is particularly adept at skiing and mountain climbing.

MAJOR WORKS:

Chamber Music—Sonatine No. 1, for violin and piano, 1935; Sonatine No. 2, for violin and piano, 1936; Quintet, for wind, 1938; Trio, for woodwinds, 1940; Sonatine for Solo Violin, 1942; String Trio, 1943; Piano Trio, 1945; String Quartet, 1946.

Choral Music—Trois Chansons de Fernand March, for mixed voices, 1938; Chants Populaires Français, for men's voices, 1940; Appel de Parfum (Marial), for men's voices, 1940; Absolve Domine, motet, 1940; Psalm of the Captives, 1942; Motet à Saint Jean Baptiste de La Salle, 1941; Ode au Soleil Né de la Mort, for narrator, chorus and orchestra, 1945; Ambohimanga ou la Cité Bleue, 1946.

PIETRO MASCAGNI was born in Leghorn, Italy, on December 7, 1863. The long-accepted report that Mascagni's father, a baker, objected to his son's musical activities, and that Pietro had to study music secretly, has been discredited. In any event, when Pietro entered the Cherubini Institute in Leghorn, it was with his father's knowledge. Subsequently, Pietro's uncle subsidized the boy's continued music study.

While still a music student, Mascagni wrote a Symphony, for small orchestra, and a Kyrie, for chorus, both of which were performed at the Cherubini Institute in 1879. A cantata, *Filanda*, received honorable mention in a competition sponsored by the International Exposition of Music in Milan. An *Ode to Joy* attracted the attention of Count Florestano de Larderel, who was so impressed that he provided the funds for Mascagni to complete his musical education in Milan.

Mascagni was not happy at the Milan Conservatory. He was oppressed by the severe discipline; he detested the humdrum exercises in fugue and counterpoint. One day, he suddenly decided that he had had enough of academicism. He left the Conservatory and joined a traveling opera company as conductor. This was a trying period, for the hardship of continual travel was combined with intense poverty. At last Mascagni married and settled in Cerignola.

Mascagni: mäs-kä′nyē

Courtesy of Musical Courier
PIETRO MASCAGNI

There he supported himself by conducting a band (which he organized), teaching the piano, and serving as the director of a small local music school.

He was a humble and obscure musician when, in 1889, he read the news that the publisher Sonzogno was offering a prize for a one-act opera. Strongly attracted to a libretto derived from a Verga tale called *Cavalleria Rusticana*, Mascagni set to work on an operatic score with passionate intensity. When he finished, he felt so dissatisfied with the result that he refused to submit it in the competition. Without his knowledge, his wife despatched the manuscript to Sonzogno. And it won the first prize.

Few operas scored so decisively at their premieres as did this new opera by Mascagni, presented at the Costanzi Theatre in Rome on May 17, 1890. The composer took forty curtain calls. Outside the opera house, hundreds waited to cheer him when he left the theatre. Coming home, his house was so besieged by admirers who came to honor him that he could not gain admittance and had to be hoisted into his rooms through the window.

Cavalleria Rusticana succeeded in making Mascagni the man-of-the-hour in Italy. Parades were held in his honor; medals were sold with his picture. The town of Cerignola

made him an honorary citizen, and the King of Italy gave him the Order of the Crown.

Nor was the success of *Cavalleria Rusticana* a local phenomenon. By 1892, it was performed throughout Italy, and had been acclaimed in Paris, Berlin, London, and New York.

This opera was responsible for a new trend in Italian opera, known as "Verismo." "Verismo" favored everyday incidents and everyday characters instead of costume plays. This movement brought in a period of realism in opera—that of Leoncavallo, Charpentier, and Puccini. But if new trails for opera were blazed with the libretto of *Cavalleria Rusticana*, the score embodied the older traditions. The strength of the music rested in its rich fund of Italian arias and choruses. Some of the music in *Cavalleria* is commonplace; some of it is more contrived than inspired. But Mascagni was skillful in alternating the mood of his melodies; he had a fine feeling for dramatic declamation; and he had a sound instinct for climactic effects.

Now rich and famous as a result of the success of his one-act opera, Mascagni proceeded to write other operatic works. Though he produced several that were well received —notably *L'Amico Fritz* in 1891 and *Iris* in 1899—he never did succeed in duplicating the success of his first opera. As he himself remarked in reviewing his career: "It is a pity I wrote *Cavalleria* first, for I was crowned before I became king."

Mascagni was closely identified with the Fascist regime in Italy. He did what he could to glorify Italian fascism in his works. His last opera, *Nerone*—produced at La Scala on January 16, 1935—was a thinly disguised tribute to Mussolini and Fascist Italy. With Italy involved in World War II, Mascagni's fortunes hit their lowest ebb. His home was confiscated by the Socialists after the Nazis were driven out of Italy. His persistent arguments that he had never been a Fascist, had never interested himself in politics, and that politicians had been exploiting his name and his reputation without his consent, had failed to make much of an impression. The last years of his life were spent in poverty and disgrace. He died in Rome on August 2, 1945, of bronchial pneumonia and hardening of the arteries.

Mascagni was for many years a successful conductor. In 1902 he toured the United States in performances of his own works, and in 1911 he visited South America. In 1929, he was appointed successor to Toscanini as the musical director of La Scala, in Milan.

MAJOR WORKS:

Choral Music—Cantata for the Leopardi Centenary, 1898; Requiem in Memory of King Humbert, 1900; Inno del Lavoro, 1928; Inno degli Avanguardisti, 1929.

Operas—Cavalleria Rusticana, 1890; L'Amico Fritz, 1891; I Rantzau, 1892; Guglielmo Ratcliff, 1895; Silvano, 1895; Zanetto, 1896; Iris, 1898; Le Maschere, 1901; Amica, 1905; Isabeau, 1911; Parisina, 1913; Lodoletta, 1917; Il Piccolo Marat, 1921; Scampolo, 1921; Nerone, 1935.

ABOUT:

Peltz, M. E. (ed.) Opera Lover's Companion. Time, August 13, 1945.

NICOLAS MEDTNER

Nicolas Medtner *1880-1951*

NICOLAS MEDTNER, sometimes referred to as "the Russian Brahms," was born in Moscow on January 5, 1880. His father, who was of German origin, was the director of a Moscow factory. A lover of fine literature (particularly the Russian classics and Goethe), the elder Medtner instilled in his son an early appreciation for books. Nicolas' mother was the musician of the family, having at one time given concerts as a singer. And it was through her influence that the boy was drawn to music. He started learning the violin by himself, and before long founded a little orchestra which gave regular concerts in his home. He also began composing. When he was six, he received his first piano lessons. In his twelfth year he was enrolled in the Moscow Conservatory, where his teachers included Arensky, Taneiev, and Safonov. He made remarkable progress, receiving a gold medal in piano playing when he graduated and soon after that winning a trophy in the important Rubinstein Competition. He was also writing music good enough to be published: his first opus was *Eight Musical Pictures*, for the piano; his second, *Three Improvisations*, also for the piano.

In 1902 Medtner started his career as concert pianist. He toured Europe extensively and was acclaimed as an outstanding interpreter of classical literature. In the same year of 1902 he became a professor of the piano at the Moscow Conservatory. He held this position only a single year, preferring to devote his time to concert work and to composition. In 1918, however, he reassumed his post at the Conservatory, this time holding it for three years.

Though unsympathetic with the ideals of the Revolution in Russia, Medtner remained in his native land at the time, teaching and composing. In 1921 he decided to leave Russia for good. He began a world tour as pianist, performing many of his own works at his concerts. His American debut took place in Philadelphia on October 31, 1924, when he appeared as soloist with the Philadelphia Orchestra under Stokowski in his own Piano Concerto No. 1. For an extended period Medtner made his home in Germany and in France. In 1936 he settled permanently in England, which was to remain his home up to the time of his death.

Although Medtner wrote three piano concertos, three violin sonatas, and many songs, he is best known for his shorter pieces for the piano. In some cases he created his own forms. In his earliest piano works his indebtedness to Brahms is pronounced. If, in his later works, he finally succeeded in freeing himself from the stylistic mannerisms of Brahms, he never lost Brahms's respect

Medtner: mĕt'nĕr

for tradition, sound construction, and romantic expression. The newer idioms and techniques never interested Medtner. He preferred to continue along the road paved by the German romantic school of the late nineteenth century. He believed in singable melodies, well-sounding harmonies, deeply felt emotions. Occasionally his writing may get contrapuntally or rhythmically complex. But his music rarely fails to achieve a decided effect through its power, and sometimes even grandeur.

Ernest Newman wrote: "Medtner is another proof that it is possible to work in the ordinary harmonic medium—developing it in complexity, of course, according to the necessities of the idea—and yet convey an expression of complete originality."

His most famous works are those shorter Schumannesque pieces which he has given a variety of picturesque titles, and the forms of some of which he himself invented. These include the *Fairy Tales*, the *Musical Pictures*, and the *Romantic Sketches.* He has also written Marches, Arabesques, Novelettes, Improvisations, Etudes, Caprices, Moments Musicaux, etc. Of these forms, he is probably at his best in his *Fairy Tales.* Leonid Sabaneyev wrote in *Modern Russian Composers*: "His creative work is best characterized" by these pieces, "a type of composition invented by him and partly similar to the old romantic form of the Ballad. Medtner's *Fairy Tales* unquestionably belong not only to the best in his creative work, but to the production of romantic inspiration in general. But Medtner's romanticism is peculiar. It is not the romanticism of enchantment, but rather the romanticism of the grotesque. Medtner's fantastic world, which opens for us through the sounds of his *Fairy Tales*, is not the world of elves and witchery, but the poetry of ancient heroic legends, and most of all an echo of the underworld of Nibelungs, gnomes and mountain kings."

"There are certain outstanding qualities in Medtner that combine to make him one of the most striking figures in modern music," wrote Alfred J. Swan. "His style is firm, rigid, somewhat uncouth; his thought concentrated (note his favorite epithet 'concen-

trando'), severe, ascetic, graphical, rather than steeped in color, yet of haunting beauty and transparent purity; his rhythm invariably striking and characteristic."

Soon after World War II, Medtner acquired a powerful patron in the Maharajah of Mysore, who created a special endowment for the purpose of recording all of Medtner's works, many of them performed by the composer himself. In reporting this strange fact in the *New York Times*, Joseph Yasser added the following significant comment: "It is the first case in the annals of music where the entire creative output of a single composer will be engraved on phonograph records in his own interpretation, so far as his pianistic music is concerned."

Nicolas Medtner died in London on November 13, 1951.

Major Works:

Chamber Music—Sonata No. 1 in B minor, for violin and piano, op. 21; Sonata No. 2 in G major, for violin and piano, op. 44; Sonata No. 3, for violin and piano, op. 57.

Orchestral Music—Concerto No. 1, for piano and orchestra, op. 33; Concerto No. 2, for piano and orchestra, op. 50; Concerto No. 3, for piano and orchestra, op. 58.

Piano Music—Sonata in F minor, op. 5; Three Arabesques, op. 7; Five Fairy Tales, op. 8-9; Three Dithyrambs, op. 10; Sonata-Trilogy, op. 11; Two Fairy Tales, op. 14; Three Novelettes, op. 17; Two Fairy Tales, op. 20; Sonata in G minor, op. 22; Four Lyric Fragments, op. 23; Two Sonatas, op. 25; Four Fairy Tales, op. 26; Sonata—Ballade, op. 27; Sonata in A minor, op. 30; Three Pieces, op. 31; Eight Fairy Tales, op. 34-35; Forgotten Motives, three cycles, op. 38-40; Three Fairy Tales, op. 42; Improvisation, op. 47; Two Fairy Tales, op. 48; Three Hymns to Labor, op. 49; Six Fairy Tales, op. 51; Sonata Romantica, op. 53a; Sonata Minacciosa, op. 53b; Eight Romantic Sketches, op. 54; Theme and Variations, op. 55a; Sonata Idyll, op. 55b.

Vocal Music—Nine Goethe Songs, first series, op. 6; Three Heine Songs, op. 12; Twelve Goethe Songs, second series, op. 15; Six Goethe Songs, third series, op. 18; Five Songs (Nietzsche), op. 19; Eight Songs, op. 24; Seven Songs, op. 28; Seven Songs, op. 29; Six Songs, op. 32; Six Songs (Pushkin), op. 36; Five Songs, op. 37; Sonate-Vocalise, op. 41a; Suite Vocalise, in four movements, op. 41b; Four Songs, op. 45; Seven Songs, op. 46; Seven Songs (Pushkin), op. 52; Songs, op. 56.

About:

Holt, R., Medtner and His Music; Music and Letters, January 1927.

Olivier Messiaen *1908-*

OLIVIER EUGÈNE PROSPER CHARLES MESSIAEN is the most prominent member of the school known as "La Jeune France." He was born in Avignon on December 10 1908, the son of Cécile Sauvage, well-known poetess. On the occasion of her son's birth, Mme. Sauvage wrote one of her finest poems, *L'Âme en Bourgeon.*

Olivier soon proved to be exceptionally gifted in music. He began composing when he was seven years old, and soon after that he taught himself to play the piano. As a student at the Paris Conservatory, which he entered in 1919, his teachers included Dukas, Gallon, Dupré, Caussade, and Maurice Emmanuel. He won every prize within reach. During this period he made an extensive study of rhythm, not only rhythm in music but also (in his own words) "Hindu and Greek rhythms and the rhythms of the stars, atoms, bird songs and the human body." He has never lost this early fascination in rhythm and now describes himself as a *"rythmicien."*

In 1931 he was appointed organist at the Trinité in Paris. On February 19 of the same year he attracted attention as a composer with *Les Offrandes Oubliées*, an elaborate and highly original orchestral work, rich in religious feeling. From 1936 to 1939 he taught composition at the Schola Cantorum and the École Normale de Musique. In April 1941 he was appointed professor of harmony at the Paris Conservatory, and in 1947 he became professor of analysis, esthetics, and rhythm.

Meanwhile, he identified himself with a group of other young French composers in a school self-styled "La Jeune France," which he helped organize. This school made its official appearance on June 3, 1936, at a concert at the Salle Gaveau in Paris. Its manifesto appeared on the program: "As the conditions of life become harder, more and more mechanical and impersonal, music must bring ceaselessly to those who love it, its spiritual violence, and its courageous reactions. La Jeune France, reaffirming the title once created by Berlioz, pursues the road upon which the master once took his obdurate course. This is a friendly group of four

Photo-Lipnitzki
OLIVIER MESSIAEN

young French composers: Olivier Messiaen, Daniel Lesur, Yves Baudrier, and André Jolivet. La Jeune France proposes the dissemination of works youthful, free, as far removed from revolutionary formulas as from academic formulas. . . . The tendencies of this group will be diverse; their only unqualified agreement is in the common desire to be satisfied with nothing less than sincerity, generosity, and artistic good faith. Their aim is to create and to promote a living music."

Of these four composers, Messiaen has proved to be the most original thinker and the most forceful creator. His music is highly complex, utilizing polymodal and polyrhythmic devices, intricate rhythms derived from Hindu sources, and the modes and melodic lines of plain songs. It is invariably most strongly concerned with rhythm. "The rhythmic pattern of a work is more interesting to me than the melodic or harmonic," he wrote. He delights in transposing melodic, harmonic, and structural devices rhythmically, thus writing rhythmic fugues and canons. In some of his works he has different instruments carry on independent and characteristic rhythmic patterns which appear and reappear in the work as *Leitmotifs* do in a Wagnerian opera. He has written a rhythmic "dictionary" containing identifiable rhythms found in Greek, Eastern, and Western music.

Messiaen: mĕs-yäN′

What is surely his most ambitious treatment of rhythm is his symphony, *Turangalîla*, which he wrote in 1948 on a commission from the Koussevitzky Foundation and which was introduced in Boston on December 2, 1949, by the Boston Symphony Orchestra under Leonard Bernstein. The basic element of this mammoth symphony, which is in ten movements, is rhythm. The composer explained that the work was written in "a very special rhythmic language, and makes use of several new rhythmic principles, including non-reversible rhythms, asymmetric rhythms, augmentations with several rhythmic identities, rhythmic modes, etc."

Messaien has clarified the influences that have shaped his career: "my mother, the poetess, Cécile Sauvage; my wife, the composer, Claire Delbos; Shakespeare; Claudel; Reverdy and Éluard; Hello and Dom Columba Marmion (dare I speak of the Holy Scriptures, which contain the only Truth?); birds; Russian music; the great *Pelleas and Melisande;* plain song; Hindu rhythms; the mountains of Dauphiné; and, finally, all that pertains to stained glass windows and rainbows."

The profoundest influence of all is the Catholic Church. Deeply religious, Messiaen has made his music the voice of his inmost spiritual and religious feelings. Most of his works are neo-mystic, drawing their programs from Catholic liturgy or Scriptures. They are all reverent, filled with mysticism. *L'Ascension (The Ascension),* written in 1934 as a suite for solo piano or organ but later adapted for orchestra, consists of Christ's prayers. *Les Offrandes Oubliées* carries in the printed score a paragraph to Christ on the Cross. Other major works expressive of Messiaen's deeply felt religious convictions include the *Trois Petites Liturgies de la Présence Divine (Three Little Liturgies in the Divine Presence),* for orchestra, the *Visions de l'Amen* for two pianos, and the *Vingt Regards sur l'Enfant Jésus,* for piano.

During World War II Messiaen served in the French army, and was interned as a prisoner of war in Silesia. In the prison camp he completed a major work, *Quatuor pour la Fin du Temps (Quartet for the End of Time).* "Only music," he said, "made me survive the cruelty and horrors of the camp."

In July 1949 Messiaen visited the United States for the first time, to teach special classes in composition at the Berkshire Music Center in Tanglewood, in Lenox, Massachusetts.

MAJOR WORKS:

Chamber Music—Quartet for the End of Time for violin, clarinet, cello and piano, 1941.

Choral Music—Cinq Rechants, for a cappella chorus, 1949.

Orchestral Music—Les Offrandes Oubliées, 1930; Hymne, 1932; L'Ascension, 1933; Poèmes pour Moi, 1937; Trois Petites Liturgies de la Présence Divine, 1944; Turangalila, symphony, 1948.

Organ Music—Apparition de l'Église Éternelle, 1932; La Nativité du Seigneur, 1935; Les Corps Glorieux, 1939.

Piano Music—Preludes, 1929; Visions de l'Amen, for two pianos, 1943; Vingt Regards sur l'Enfant Jésus, 1944.

Vocal Music—Chants de Terre et de Ciel, for soprano and piano, 1938; Harawi, Chant d'Amour et de Mort, for soprano and piano, 1945.

ABOUT:

New York Herald Tribune, September 23, 1945; New York Times, July 31, 1949.

Nikolai Miaskovsky *1881-1950*

NIKOLAI MIASKOVSKY was born in the fortress of Novogeorgievsk, near Warsaw (then in Russia), on April 20, 1881. His father was an engineer in the army who wanted his son to follow in his footsteps. Music, therefore, was little more than a hobby for Nikolai while he prepared himself for an engineering career at the Cadet School in Novogeorgievsk and then in St. Petersburg. He became an army engineer after completing his studies in 1899.

Meanwhile, music began to assume an increasingly important role in his life. A six-month course in harmony with Glière convinced him that he wanted to abandon engineering for music. He went to St. Petersburg in 1904, studied harmony and counterpoint with Kryzhanovsky, and started composing. Two years later, he entered the St. Petersburg Conservatory in the classes of Liadov and Rimsky-Korsakov.

Intensive composition was begun after his graduation from the Conservatory. He demonstrated without delay that he was a

Miaskovsky: myäs-kôf'skē

gifted composer. One of his earliest works, a Piano Sonata, was described by Prokofiev as possessing "nobility of material, carefulness of workmanship, and a general attractiveness which render it one of the most interesting sonatas of modern times."

During World War I Miaskovsky served in the Russian Army for three years. He was wounded and shell-shocked. When the war ended, he settled in Moscow, and in 1921 he became professor of composition at the Moscow Conservatory, a post held with great distinction until the end of his life. His pupils included Khatchaturian and Kabalevsky.

The revolution in Russia had a profound influence on Miaskovsky's creative development. Before then his music had been completely subjective. But after the Revolution he used his music not to express his personal reactions and his inmost feelings but to reflect the events happening in his country and the ideologies that set these events into motion.

Miaskovsky was a highly prolific composer. He wrote more symphonies than any other twentieth-century composer, twenty-seven in all. It is in the symphonic form that he has proved most successful and most important.

Nicolas Slonimsky divided Miaskovsky's symphonic output into four distinct periods: "The first period from the First to the Sixth Symphony is typical of his pre-revolutionary moods, introspective and at the same time mystical. . . . His second symphonic period, from the Seventh to the Twelfth Symphony, symbolizes a path from the 'subjective' to the 'objective,' from the individual to the collective. Without trying to be literal in programmatic descriptions of the life in the Soviet Union of that period, he nevertheless went for inspiration to the fields and factories of the country. . . . The third period, from the Thirteenth to the Eighteenth Symphony, represents a synthesis of subjective moods and objective realistic ideas. . . . The Nineteenth Symphony is the beginning of a new phase, almost utilitarian in character. Miaskovsky's symphonic writing here becomes more compact, more directly addressed to the masses."

The finest of these many symphonies is the Twenty-first, written in 1940 on a com-

NIKOLAI MIASKOVSKY

mission from the Chicago Symphony Orchestra. The premiere took place in Moscow under Alexander Gauck on November 16, 1940. When the work was given by the Chicago Symphony under Frederick Stock, five weeks later, it appeared under the title of Symphonie-Fantaisie. In 1941 this symphony won the Stalin Prize of 100,000 rubles. The Ninth String Quartet and the Concerto for Cello and Orchestra received the Stalin Prize, and the Twenty-seventh Symphony and Thirteenth String Quartet received this award posthumously.

When World War II came, it did not interrupt Miaskovsky's fertility as a composer. "I worked intensively in those days, even in bomb shelters," he wrote. "After completing three songs and two military marches, I conceived the idea of a Symphonic Ballad. It was finished in October, during the stern days of the Hitlerite offensive against Moscow. . . . Late autumn found me in Kabardino-Balkaria, a small Caucasian republic whose people have a wealth of wonderful songs and dances. Here, in the town of Nalchik, I wrote another symphony, my twenty-third, whose theme was inspired by Kabardino-Balkarian national music. Then I completed a string quartet in three movements, dedicated to the memory of those who perished for my country. It reflects one thought: the blood which has been spilled has not been in vain."

Though Miaskovsky long held a position of outstanding importance in Soviet music, he did not escape censure when the Central Committee of the Communist Party issued an official denunciation of leading Soviet composers in February 1948 (see Prokofiev). However, Miaskovsky was brought to task not for his music but for his teaching which, the committee said, injected "inharmonious music" into the Soviet educational system.

On August 9, 1950, the Moscow Radio announced that Miaskovsky had died that day.

MAJOR WORKS:

Chamber Music—Sonata No. 1 for Cello and Piano, op. 12, 1911; String Quartets, Nos. 1-4, op. 33, 1930; String Quartet, No. 5, op. 47, 1939; String Quartet No. 6, op. 49, 1940; String Quartet No. 7, op. 55, 1941; String Quartet No. 8, op. 59, 1942; String Quartet No. 9, op. 62, 1943; String Quartet No. 10; String Quartet No. 11; String Quartet No. 12; String Quartet No. 13; Sonata No. 2 for Cello and Piano, 1948.

Choral Music—Feather Grass, 1909; Wings of the Soviets, 1931; In Valor's Name, 1931; Planes Are Flying, 1931; Lenin, 1932; Karl Marx, 1932; Partisans, 1934; Song of the Order Guards, 1934; Glory to our Soviets, 1934; Fighting Orders, 1941; Kirov Is with Us, op. 61, 1942.

Orchestral Music—Symphony No. 1, in C minor, op. 3, 1908; Silence, symphonic poem, op. 9, 1910; Sinfonietta, op. 10, 1911; Symphony No. 2, in C-sharp minor, op. 11, 1911; Alastor, symphonic poem, op. 14, 1913; Symphony No. 3 in A minor, op. 15, 1914; Symphony No. 4, in E minor, op. 17, 1918; Symphony No. 5, in D major, op. 18, 1918; Symphony No. 6, in E-flat minor, op. 23, 1923; Symphony No. 7, in B minor, op. 24, 1922; Symphony No. 8, in A major, op. 26, 1925; Symphony No. 9, in E minor, op. 28, 1927; Symphony No. 10, in F minor, op. 30, 1927; Serenata in E-flat major, op. 32, no. 1, 1929; Sinfonietta, for strings, op. 32, no. 2, 1933; Concertino Lirico in G major, op. 32, no. 3, 1929; Symphony No. 11, in B-flat minor, op. 34, 1932; Symphony No. 12, in G minor, op. 35, 1932; Symphony No. 13, in B-flat minor, op. 36, 1933; Symphony No. 14, in C major, op. 37, 1933; Symphony No. 15, in D minor, op. 38, 1934; Symphony No. 16, in F major, op. 39, 1936; Symphony No. 17, in G-sharp minor, op. 41, 1937; Symphony No. 18, in C major, op. 42, 1937; Concerto for Violin and Orchestra, op. 44, 1938; Symphony No. 19, op. 46, 1939; Salutatory Overture, op. 48, 1939; Symphony No. 20, op. 50, 1940; Symphony No. 21, Symphonie-Fantaisie, op. 51, 1940; Symphony No. 22 in B minor, op. 54, 1941; Symphony No. 23 in A minor, op. 56, 1941; Symphony No. 24 in F minor, op. 63, 1942; Symphony No. 25 in D-flat minor, op. 64, 1947; Concerto for Cello and Orchestra, op. 66, 1945; Slavic Rhapsody, op. 71, 1947; Symphony No. 26 in E minor, op. 84; Symphony No. 27 in C minor, op. 85.

Piano Music—Sonata No. 1, op. 6, 1909; Sonata No. 2, op. 13, 1912; Frolics, 19 sketches, 1919; Sonata No. 3, op. 19, 1920; Whimsies, 6 sketches, op 25, 1922; Sonata No. 4, op. 27, 1924; Souvenirs, 6 pieces, op. 29, 1927; Yellowed Leaves, op. 31, 1928; Three Albums of Children's Pieces, op. 43, 1938; Sonatina, op. 57, 1942; Prelude and Rhapsody, op. 58, 1942.

Vocal Music—Sonnet (Michelangelo), op. 86, 1908; Premonitions, op. 16, 1913-14; Five Songs, for voice and piano, op. 20, 1921; Two Songs, op. 21, 1922; Faded Garland, op. 22, 1925; Twelve Songs, for voice and piano, op. 40, 1936; Three Sketches, for voice and piano, op. 45, 1938; Ten Songs, for voice and piano, op. 52, 1940.

ABOUT:

Ikonnikov, A., Miaskovsky: His Life and Work; Saminsky, L., Music of Our Day; American Quarterly on the Soviet Union, April 1938.

Georges Migot 1891-

GEORGES MIGOT was born in Paris on February 27, 1891. His father was a physician who had come to Paris from Franche-Comté, where he was able to trace back his ancestry to the early fifteenth century.

Since Migot's father planned a medical career for him, the boy received an intensive academic training at the University of Paris. Music, which meant a great deal to him, was relegated to a minor position in the boy's life. When Georges finally expressed the wish to abandon his academic study and to concentrate on music he encountered no serious opposition. After preparatory studies in harmony and counterpoint with Bouval and Ganaye, Migot entered the Conservatory in 1913, where his principal teachers included Vincent D'Indy and Widor.

It was during his student days at the Conservatory that Migot was first fascinated with and became immersed in the study of French music. He became convinced that French music preceded the music of other European nations. He has since remained a passionate advocate of French music, which he considers the best that the art of music has produced.

During World War I he served in the French army and was seriously wounded at Longuyon on August 24, 1914. For a while his life hung in balance. When that danger passed, it was feared he would be paralyzed for life. Something of a miracle took place, however. After a year of complete paralysis, Migot discovered one morning that he could move one of his limbs. For the next three

Migot: mē-gō'

From a pastel by Louis Baille
GEORGES MIGOT

He regards much of contemporary music as only so much noise and confusion.

During the past decade or more, Migot has devoted himself primarily to choral music, usually religious in theme (most of these works are based on different facets of Christ's life); they are invariably of epic proportions. He has given his works about Christ the name of *Christique*, and he refuses to consider them as either church or religious music. He explains that he has no religious dogma to propound. His aim here—as elsewhere—is to produce works of art that draw their interest and significance exclusively from musical values.

Migot lives alone in a book-filled apartment near the Conservatory. He describes himself as a "humanist," and he says his only interest, away from music, is books, particularly old French texts. He is the author of three volumes of critiques on music.

MAJOR WORKS:

Ballet—La Fête de la Bergère, 1925.

Chamber Music—Cinq Mouvements d'Eau, for string quartet, 1908; Le Paravent de Laque, for string quartet, 1909 (also for orchestra); Piano Trio; Quartet, for flute, violin, clarinet and harp; Piano Quintet, 1921; Le Premier Livre de Divertissements Français, for flute, clarinet, and harp, 1925; Trio, for oboe, clarinet, and bassoon, 1946.

Choral Music—Psaume XIX; St. Germain d'Auxerre, oratorio, 1935; Le Sermon sur la Montagne, oratorio, 1936; La Passion, oratorio, 1945; L'Annonciation, oratorio; La Mise au Tombeau, oratorio; La Résurrection, oratorio.

Opera—Le Rossignol en Amour, chamber opera, 1937.

Orchestral Music—Hagoromo, lyric and choreographic symphony, 1921; Les Agrestides, three symphonic frescoes, 1927; Le Jungle, for organ and orchestra, 1932; Two Preludes; Prélude, Salut, et Danse; Suite in Three Parts; Suite in Five Parts.

Piano Music—Préludes, two volumes; 12 Études de Concert; Le Zodaïque, twelve pieces, 1931; 2 Nocturnes Dantesques, 1937.

ABOUT:

Wolff, P., Georges Migot: La Route d'un Musicien.

years he walked on crutches. During convalescence, which at times was harrowingly painful, he turned for solace to composition. He has never completely recovered from his infirmity. For his heroism in battle he was awarded the Croix de Guerre.

During the period of his most intense physical suffering he produced his first major works and they won immediate recognition. In 1918 he received the Lili Boulanger Prize; in 1919, the Lapaulle Award for a Trio; in 1920, the Halphen Prize for a Piano Quintet; and in 1922, the Blumenthal Foundation Prize.

Migot has attempted writing music in the best French traditions of Guillaume de Machaut, the fourteenth century contrapuntist, and the lutenists and minstrels of that period. Migot's writing is primarily contrapuntal, consisting of horizontal lines of music, each one possessing a separate identity. His roots reach deep into the past; but so consummate is his technique and so vital is his expression that it does not fail to have what Pierre Wolff once described as "the fullness of human emotion."

Migot has never identified himself in any way with any of the contemporary schools of musical thought. He has a contempt for experiments of any kind in composition. "I do not play games with music," he has said. "I do not write experiments. I write music."

Darius Milhaud 1892-

DARIUS MILHAUD was born in Aix-en-Provence, on September 4, 1892. He took to music study early, and while still a boy played second violin in a string quartet. Intensive music first began at the College of

Milhaud: mē-yō'

DARIUS MILHAUD

Aix, and continued at the Paris Conservatory which he entered in 1909 and where his teachers included Leroux (harmony), Gedalge (composition), and Dukas (orchestration). As a Conservatory student he revealed a bent for composition by writing a Sonata for Violin and Piano in 1911, and a String Quartet in 1912, together with various songs and piano pieces. These early works showed derivative influences—sometimes that of Lekeu, most often that of Debussy. During this period, between the years of 1910 and 1915, Milhaud also completed his first opera, *La Brebis Égarée,* based on a text of Francis Jammes. This opera, in which the influence of Debussy is most noticeable, was performed a decade later, on December 15, 1923, at the Opéra Comique.

If these early works of Milhaud demonstrated any single fact it was that he was highly articulate. In some of this music he was also experimental. On occasion, the composer wrote several melodies simultaneously in different keys, his first excursion into the realm of polytonality in which he was later to travel freely. However, despite this occasional departure from traditional writing (with which the Conservatory authorities could hardly be expected to sympathize) Milhaud was an excellent student at the Conservatory. He won prizes in violin playing, fugue, and counterpoint. He planned competing for the Prix de Rome, but was thwarted by the outbreak of World War I, which brought his Conservatory schooling to a sudden and premature end.

Meanwhile, Milhaud had come into personal contact with the French poet Paul Claudel, whose verses he set to music and who became an intimate friend. When, in 1917, Claudel became the French ambassador to Brazil, he took Milhaud with him as an attaché at the Legation. In South America Milhaud collaborated with Claudel on several major works, the most important of which was the ballet *L'Homme et Son Désir,* which Milhaud completed in 1918. Milhaud also wrote music for several Claudel adaptations of the Greek tragedies of Aeschylus (*Agamemnon, Les Choéphores* and *Les Euménides*).

During his stay in Brazil, Milhaud became intensely interested in the melodies and rhythms of South American folk songs and dances. This interest led him to write some works in that style. One of the earliest of these was the popular *Saudades do Brasil,* in which the rhythms of South American dances, principally the tango, are brilliantly exploited in twelve attractive pieces. The South American influence is also found in a later work, the *Scaramouche* suite for two pianos. Another influence encountered by Milhaud in South America was American jazz, then performed widely throughout Rio de Janeiro. Milhaud produced several works in a jazz style, among them the ballet *Le Bœuf sur le Toit,* set in an American speakeasy, and *Caramel Mou,* a shimmy for jazz band. Milhaud's finest work in a jazz style was written in 1923, several years after Milhaud returned to Paris. It was the ballet *La Création du Monde,* the first successful attempt to utilize jazz style and techniques in a major serious work.

In 1919 Milhaud returned to France. He was soon identified with the then newly christened school of French composers known as "the French Six" (see Auric). But Milhaud's association with this group was, at best, tenuous. He protested being artistically identified with the other five composers, for all of whom he had a warm appreciation and personal affection. But Milhaud insisted that, in writing his own music, he had to follow the path pointed to by his conscience rather than some artistic creed. Indeed, Milhaud now began creating works so varied in style and approach that it would be futile to assemble them under a single artistic banner or to apply to them the identification of any single school.

Milhaud achieved considerable popularity, and in certain other quarters considerable notoriety, immediately after World War I for his works in a popular vein. In these compositions he brought such a personal charm, wit, an infectious vitality, and an original approach that they have artistic importance as well as popular appeal. But Milhaud's personality as a composer is perhaps more accurately mirrored in his more serious efforts: the symphonies; the quartets; the trilogy of operas on American subjects— *Maximilien, Christophe Colomb,* and *Bolivar,* which Virgil Thomson describes as a "monument of incomparable grandeur." Utilizing the most modern resources of harmony, counterpoint, and rhythm, Milhaud's serious works have an emotional intensity, a passion and vehemence, a concentration of speech and at times a grandeur of expression which place them with the major creations of our generation. Milhaud has invented no new forms or techniques; but as Paul Collaer noted, "he has enlarged the possibilities of musical language, broadened the scope of expression."

Milhaud's art, as Aaron Copland once wrote, is essentially lyrical. "His musical gift is clearly that of a lyricist. His musical nature impels him towards one end: a spontaneous outpouring of the emotions in terms of fine music. . . . Springing from a native lyricism, his music always sings. . . . The music flows so rationally that it seems to have been improvised rather than composed."

Milhaud has visited the United States on many occasions, the first time being in 1922, when he toured in the triple role of pianist, conductor, and lecturer.

He was in Paris when World War II began. His opera *Médée*—introduced in Antwerp on October 7, 1939—was the last work heard at the Paris Opéra before the Nazi occupation. Soon after the occupation, Milhaud fled to this country. He stayed here for the rest of the war years, assuming a teaching position at Mills College in California, and for one season holding a class in composition at Tanglewood, in Lenox, Massachusetts.

After the end of the war, Milhaud wrote his Symphony No. 3 to commemorate the liberation of France. A work of powerful emotional impact, it echoes the composer's feelings at this historic event. The war over, Milhaud returned to his native land to help supervise its musical activity. However, a part of his year is still spent in this country.

In 1950 Milhaud became the center of violent controversy in Paris as a result of the premiere of his opera *Bolivar,* introduced at the Opéra on May 12. Largely because of its excessive length (it took four hours for performance), a part of the audience expressed its resentment vocally at the premiere. The admirers of Milhaud were just as demonstrative, with the result that virtual pandemonium was let loose. This fight continued bitterly in the press for the next few days. Milhaud finally made drastic cuts in his opera without changing its structure.

During his stay in the United States, in the years of World War II, Milhaud was attacked by arthritis and virtually crippled. From then on he was confined most of the time to an armchair; when he walked he had to support himself on two canes. His infirmity did not interfere with his many activities. It did not even prevent him from directing the world premiere of his Symphony No. 2 with the Boston Symphony Orchestra on December 20, 1946, from a chair on the conductor's stand into which he was helped. Nor has it interfered with his subsequent travels to and from France.

MAJOR WORKS:

Ballets—L'Homme et son Désir, 1918; Le Bœuf sur le Toit, 1919; La Création du Monde, 1923; Salade, 1924; Le Train Bleu, 1924; Imagined Wing, 1944; Jeux de Printemps, 1944; The Bells, 1945; Jacob's Dream, 1949.

Chamber Music—Sonata No. 1 for Violin and Piano, 1911; String Quartet No. 1, 1912; Sonata for Two Violins and Piano, 1914; String Quartet No. 2, 1915; String Quartet No. 3, 1916; Sonata No. 2 for Violin and Piano, 1917; String Quartet No. 4, 1918; Sonata for Flute, Oboe, Clarinet, and Piano, 1918; String Quartet No. 5, 1920; Sonatina for Flute and Piano, 1922; String Quartet No. 6, 1922; String Quartet No. 7, 1925; String Quartet No. 8, 1932; String Quartet No. 9, 1935; Suite, for piano, violin, and clarinet, 1936; Suite, for oboe, clarinet, and bassoon, 1937; La Cheminée du Roi René, suite for woodwind quintet, 1939; String Quartet No. 10, 1940; Sonatine à trois, for violin, viola, and cello, 1940; Sonatina for Two Violins, 1940; Sonatina for Violin and Viola, 1941; String Quartet No. 11, 1942; Quatre Visages, for viola and piano, 1943; Sonata No. 1 for Viola and Piano, 1944; Sonata No. 2 for Viola and Piano, 1944;

Élégie, for cello and piano, 1945; Sonata for Violin and Harpsichord, 1945; Duo for Two Violins, 1945; String Quartet No. 12, 1945; String Quartet No. 13, 1946; Sept Danses sur des Airs Palestiniens, for eight instruments, 1946-47; String Quartet No. 13, 1946; String Quartets Nos. 14 and 15 (also played simultaneously as an octet), 1948-49; String Quartet No. 16, 1950; Quintet, 1951.

Choral Music—Psaume 126, 1921; Symphony for Vocal Quartet, Oboe, and Cello, 1923; Cantique du Rhône, 1936; Les Deux Cités, 1937; Cantate de la Paix, 1937; Les Quatre Éléments, cantata, 1938; Cantate de la Guerre, 1940; Bareschou-Schema, 1944; Prière pour les Morts, 1945; Six Sonnets, 1946; Sabbath Morning Service, 1947; Naissance de Vénus, cantata, 1949; Cantate des Proverbes, 1950.

Operas—Oreste, a trilogy of three operas (Agamemnon, Choéphores, Les Euménides), 1917-22; Les Malheurs d'Orphée, 1924; Le Pauvre Matelot, 1926; Christophe Colomb, 1928; Maximilien, 1930; Esther de Carpentras, opera-bouffe, 1937; Médée, 1938; Bolivar, 1943; David.

Orchestral Music—Cinq Etudes, for piano and orchestra, 1920; Serenade, 1921; Saudades do Brasil, 1921; Ballade, for piano and orchestra, 1921; 5 Symphonies for Small Orchestra, 1922; Three Rag Caprices, for piano and orchestra, 1922; Carnaval d'Aix, for piano and orchestra, 1926; Concerto No. 1 for Violin and Orchestra, 1926; Concerto for Viola and Orchestra, 1929; Concerto for Percussion and Orchestra, 1930; Concerto No. 1 for Piano and Orchestra, 1933; Concertino de Printemps, for violin and orchestra, 1934; Concerto No. 1 for Cello and Orchestra, 1934; Suite Provençale, 1936; Concerto for Flute, Violin and Orchestra, 1938; Fanfare, 1939; Symphony No. 1, 1939; Cortège Funèbre, 1939; Opus Americanum No. 2, 1940; Quatre Chansons de Ronsard, for voice and orchestra, 1941; Concerto for Clarinet and Orchestra, 1941; Four Sketches, 1941; Concerto for Two Pianos and Orchestra, 1941; Concerto No. 2 for Piano and Orchestra, 1941; Suite for Harmonica (also Violin) and Orchestra, 1942; Cain and Abel, for narrator and orchestra, 1944; Symphony No. 2, 1944; Le Bal Martiniquais, 1944; Concerto No. 2 for Cello and Orchestra, 1945; Concerto No. 2 for Violin and Orchestra, 1946; Symphony No. 3, 1946; Concerto No. 3 for Piano and Orchestra, 1946; Symphony No. 4, 1947; Concerto for Marimba and Orchestra, 1947; Kentuckiana, 1948; Concerto No. 4 for Piano and Orchestra, 1949; Les Amours de Ronsard, for vocal quartet and chamber orchestra.

Piano Music—Suite, 1913; Sonata No. 1, 1916; Printemps, suite, 1920; Scaramouche, for two pianos, 1937; Touches Noires, 1941; Touches Blanches, 1941; La Libertadora, for one or two pianos, 1943; La Muse Ménagère, 1944; La Libération des Antilles, 1944; Une Journée, 1946; Paris, for four pianos, 1948; Sonata No. 2, 1949.

Vocal Music—Poèmes Juifs, 1916; Poèmes de Francis Jammes, four albums, 1910-18; Les Soirées de Petrograd, 1919; Machines Agricoles, 1919; Catalogue de Fleurs, 1920; Chants Populaires Hébraïques, 1925; Le Voyage d'Été, 1940; Rêves, 1942; Chants de Misère, 1946.

ABOUT:

Collaer, P., Darius Milhaud; Milhaud, D., Notes Without Music; Musical Quarterly, April 1942.

Italo Montemezzi *1875-1952*

ITALO MONTEMEZZI, composer of the opera *The Love of Three Kings* (*L'Amore dei Tre Re*), was born in Vigasio, in the province of Verona, on August 4, 1875. His father, a successful engineer, directed his son towards engineering. After completing his high school education in Verona, Montemezzi went to Milan to enter the University. En route, he experienced a change of heart: he suddenly realized that he wanted most of all to become a musician even though, up to then, he had had no training. He took the entrance examinations for the Milan Conservatory and failed them. Not until his third attempt did he succeed in gaining admission. As a pupil of Saladino and Ferroni he worked hard and made up for lost time. He was graduated with honors. His graduating composition, *Cantico dei Cantici* for soprano, mezzo-soprano, and orchestra, was conducted by Arturo Toscanini.

For the next few years Montemezzi lived in semi-seclusion, working hard on his compositions. An opera of his was performed publicly for the first time in 1905, *Giovanni Gallurese*, produced in Turin. It met with such favor that it was repeated seventeen times in twenty-nine days. Some critics remarked that its composer was among the most promising of the younger Italians. His second opera, *Hellera*, produced in Turin on March 17, 1909, was a failure.

Montemezzi became world-famous with his third opera, *L'Amore dei Tre Re*. He had approached the Italian dramatist Sem Benelli, for the operatic rights to *The Jest*, only to discover that they had already been disposed of. Benelli offered Montemezzi the substitute of a drama which he was then planning. "For four hours after that," Montemezzi recalled, "we walked about the city, arm in arm, while he told me in great detail about the story, characters, and atmosphere. He had not written a single word yet, but from what he told me I could easily visualize the beauty of the drama, and without delay I took him to Ricordi. We signed a contract then and there—and just six months later, *L'Amore dei Tre Re* was produced as a play in Rome."

It took Montemezzi more than two years to write his score. The powerful play moved

Montemezzi: mŏn-tä-mĕd′dzē

ITALO MONTEMEZZI

him profoundly and stimulated him in a way no other text had done. He filled his score with intoxicating lyricism, dramatic impact, grandeur, and beauty. The opera was finally presented at La Scala, in Milan, on April 10, 1913, and was an outstanding success. Ten months later it was seen at the Metropolitan Opera House in New York. Since then, it had been accepted as one of the great Italian lyric dramas of the twentieth century.

After *L'Amore dei Tre Re* he wrote *La Nave*, based on a tragedy of Gabriele d'Annunzio. Introduced at La Scala on November 3, 1918, it met such immediate acclaim that it was selected to inaugurate the 1919-20 season of the Chicago Opera Company with the composer conducting.

Montemezzi, content with the long-accepted traditions, has not opened any new vistas for Italian opera. But within the well-established form, he has brought a vein of lyric beauty, a dramatic feeling, and a gift for characterization and atmosphere which are truly outstanding. He has always felt that melody is the spine of good opera, and that music must always come from the heart. He once said to Verna Arvey: "Anyone can write whatever music he wants to write, modern or ultra-modern. But if he doesn't have that underlying emotion, it is not music for me. Without emotion, it is just notes. . . . If you do not have melody you do not have music—but the melody need not neces-

sarily be in the strict sense that Donizetti knew it. If you analyze rhythm, you find that it has a melody of its own. . . . A composer can be modern and melodic, too."

In 1920 Montemezzi was married to an American, Katherine Leith. At the time of their courtship he knew no English, and she virtually no Italian. They were married in Paris, where a son was born to them. After 1939 Montemezzi came to California to live there for a decade. In 1941 he appeared as guest conductor at the Metropolitan Opera House in performances of his masterwork, *L'Amore dei Tre Re*. Montemezzi returned to Verona, Italy, in 1949, and he died there on May 15, 1952.

MAJOR WORKS:

Choral Music—Cantico dei Cantici, cantata, 1900; Cantata in Memory of Ponchielli, 1911.

Operas—Giovanni Gallurese, 1904; Hellera, 1908; L'Amore dei Tre Re, 1912; La Nave, 1918; La Notte di Zoraima, 1930; L'Incantesimo, 1943.

Orchestral Music—Paolo e Virginia, tone poem, 1929; Italia Mia, tone poem, 1944.

ABOUT:

Ewen, D., The Complete Book of 20th Century Music; Opera News, January 10, 1949.

Carl Nielsen *1865-1931*

AUGUST CARL NIELSEN is generally regarded as the foremost Danish composer of the twentieth century. He was born in Nörre-Indelse, on the island of Funen, on June 9, 1865. His parents were humble peasant folk. His father, a house painter, played the violin at local weddings and other festivities in his spare time.

While recovering from the measles, in his childhood, Carl asked for and was given a small violin hanging on the wall. In short order he learned to play a few tunes. For several years he continued learning to play the violin by himself, and in his fifteenth year he was able to perform in a band at the Odense garrison. A few of his friends, convinced that he had talent, raised a subsidy to send him to Copenhagen for music study. He went there in May 1883, presented himself to Niels Gade, director of the Conservatory and a famous composer, and showed him a string quartet he had written. This quartet

Nielsen: nĕl's'n

CARL NIELSEN

opened for him the doors of the Conservatory, where he remained for the next few years, a pupil of Gade, Rosenhoff, and Tofte.

Soon after his graduation from the Conservatory, Nielsen won the Ancker stipend, which enabled him to travel for a year in France and Italy. When he returned to his native land, Nielsen played in the Royal Orchestra for a period of five years, from 1890 to 1895. Before this, however, his career as composer had begun when the Suite for Strings was published in 1888. This composition, and his other early works— among them the String Quartet in C minor and the Symphony No. 1—are the writings of a young romanticist who speaks emotionally with spacious melodies and rich-textured harmonies.

But Nielsen was soon to outgrow the romantic tradition. In the third movement of his Symphony No. 2, entitled *The Four Temperaments,* true polyphonic music makes its first appearance both in Nielsen's works and in Danish music. In his Symphony No. 3, *Sinfonia Espansiva,* tonal independence was to be combined with rhythmic freedom. After 1922, with his Symphony No. 5, Nielsen completely shook off "the last vestige of traditional dust," as one of his Danish critics remarked. His later music was to be linear.

The Symphony No. 5, *Sinfonia Semplice,* is one Nielsen's most important works. When this work received its American pre-

miere on January 3, 1951, at a concert of the National Symphony Orchestra, the conductor on that occasion, Eric Tuxen, provided the following analysis: "The spiritual content . . . must be seen against the background of the doubt, anxiety, and unrest that seized the minds of people after World War I. Through its entire evolution, from a quite simple interval movement to the most violent eruptions, the first movement is borne by a peculiar cosmic notion of life. One perceives a gigantic fight between the principles of good and evil, the latter especially being characterized by the snarling and persistent attempts of the snare drum to disturb and tear the melodic structure. The victory of light over the powers of darkness heralded already at the end of the first movement is completed in the second, with its manful belief in will and vitality in all their manifestations."

Vagn Kappel describes the style of Nielsen's mature works as follows: "It might, on the whole, be said that the composer did not break with the major-minor mode; he rather built into that system a new melodious feeling akin to church modes. The feeling of pentatonic is extremely strong and distinct in his music. Moreover, chromaticism plays a great part in his more important instrumental compositions. . . . A distinctive feature of his instrumental melody is a tendency to allow the tune to weave, for a long time, around a central tone. These new harmonies have some relation to impressionism, which inspired him, by its combined chords, its unfunctional harmonies, even if the latter contradicted his sense of logic."

Nielsen was the director of the Royal Orchestra from 1908 to 1914. He also appeared as guest conductor in many parts of Europe. From 1915 to 1917 he served as director of the Copenhagen Conservatory and conductor of the Musikverein. The recipient of many national honors, Nielsen was made a Knight of the Dannebrog and a member of the Royal Academy of Stockholm. He died in Copenhagen on October 2, 1931.

A five-day festival of Nielsen's music was held in Copenhagen in 1953.

MAJOR WORKS:

Operas—Saul and David, 1901; Masquerade, 1905.

Chamber Music—First String Quartet, op. 5, 1890; First Sonata for Violin and Piano, op. 9, 1895; Second String Quartet, op. 13, 1898; Third String Quartet, op. 14, 1898; Second Sonata for Violin and Piano, op. 35, 1912; Woodwind Quintet, op. 43, 1923; Fourth String Quartet, op. 44, 1906.

Choral Music—Hymnus Amoris, op. 12, 1896; An den Schlaf, 1904.

Orchestral Music—Suite for String Orchestra, op 1, 1888; Symphony No. 1 in G minor, op. 7, 1894; Symphonische Suite, op. 8, 1894; Symphony No. 2, Four Temperaments, op. 16, 1901; Helios Overture, op. 17, 1904; Saga Dream, op. 21, 1907; Sinfonia Espansiva, 1911; Symphony No. 4, The Inextinguishable, op. 29, 1916; Concerto for Violin and Orchestra, op. 33, 1911; Pan and Syrinx, orchestral fantasy, op. 49, 1918; Symphony No. 5, Sinfonia Semplice, op. 50, 1922; Symphony No. 6, 1925; Concerto for Flute and Orchestra, 1926; Concerto for Clarinet and Orchestra, 1931.

ABOUT:

Kappel, V., Contemporary Danish Composers; Simpson, R. Carl Nielsen: Symphonist.

Courtesy of Musical Courier

VITĚZSLAV NOVÁK

Vítězslav Novák *1870-1949*

VÍTĚZSLAV NOVÁK was born in Kamenitz, Bohemia, on December 5, 1870. The death of his father, a doctor, put the burden of supporting the family on his shoulders while he was still very young. The necessity of earning a living, however, did not interfere with his education. He attended high school, then enrolled in the University of Prague for the study of law. He also attended the Prague Conservatory where his teachers included Dvořák in composition and Jiránek in piano.

Dvořák was the first to recognize Novák's creative talent and was influential in convincing him to give up law for music. Another intensive period of study followed, during which time Novák started writing music. Some of his early piano works came to the attention of Johannes Brahms, who was so impressed with them that he used his influence with the house of Simrock to get them published. Novák's earliest works, written between 1892 and 1895, and embracing the *Souvenirs* and *Serenades* for piano, the orchestral overture *Corsair* (inspired by Byron), and the Concerto for Piano and Orchestra, were greatly influenced by the Germanic romanticism of Brahms and Liszt.

Soon after the turn of the twentieth century, Novák entered a second creative phase, that of national Bohemian music. His works

now acquired a Slavic personality, rich with languorous folk melodies and vital folk rhythms. The best known of his works in this vein are the symphonic poem *In the Tatra*, and the *Slovakian Suite*, for orchestra.

Subsequently Novák became impressionistic, though impressionism did not preclude the expression of weighty ideas. The most ambitious compositions of his period were *The Tempest*, a fantasia for soloists, chorus, and orchestra, and the piano cycle, *Pan* (later orchestrated).

Regardless of his style, Novák always revealed personal idiosyncrasies in his writing. In an illuminating analysis of Novák's music, Vladimir Helfert pointed out the following stylistic mannerisms: "Novák invented a new manner of using motives which lends to his work an individual character. This characteristic he combined with fresh ideas of harmony, and an original type of melodies. These qualities enabled him to enrich Czech music with new forms. In the invention of harmonies, Novák successfully relied on the impressionism of Debussy. In this respect too he was modern, for he gave Czech music thereby a new orientation. . . . But it would be a mistake to think that Novák merely transplanted French impressionism to Bohemia. His strong individuality gave this impressionism other values in quite an in-

Novák: nô'väk

dividual and original manner. Novák used only the methods of impressionism in the treatment of his harmonies, but he did not succumb to it in his creative methods in general, for Novák's strictly logical construction has nothing in common with impressionism. . . . Novák's type of melody, new to Czech music, is based to a great extent on the folk music of eastern Moravia and Slovakia. Even in this respect, however, Novák is original. The great wealth of rhythm and melody contained in Slovak popular music was never before used to any great extent by Czech composers. Novák was the first to do so by consciously using the melodies and the rhythmical imagery of Slovak folk songs in his own compositions.

Novák also distinguished himself as a teacher. In 1909 he became professor of composition at the Prague Conservatory. Nine years later he was appointed professor of the Master School, and one year after that, director. His many pupils included some of Czechoslovakia's most gifted musicians—among them Alois Hába, Jirák, and Křička.

In 1946 Novák received the title of National Artist from the Republic of Czechoslovakia. He died in Skuteč, Slovakia, on July 18, 1949.

MAJOR WORKS:

Ballets—Signorina Gioventù, op. 58, 1928; Nicotina, op. 59, 1929.

Chamber Music—Quartet in C minor, for piano and strings, op. 12, 1897; String Quartet in G major, op. 22, 1899; Trio in D minor, quasi una Ballata, op. 27, 1902; String Quartet in D major, op. 35, 1905; Sonata for Viola, Cello, and Piano, op. 68, 1942.

Choral Music—The Tempest, fantasia for soloists, chorus, and orchestra, op. 42, 1910; The Bride of the Dead, for chorus and orchestra, op. 48, 1913; Force and Resistance, for male chorus, op. 51, 1917; Three Czech Songs, for male chorus, op. 53, 1918.

Operas—The Sprite of the Castle, op. 49, 1914; Karlstein, op. 50, 1916; The Lantern, op. 56, 1922; John the Fiddler, op. 57, 1925.

Orchestral Music—Maryša, overture, op. 18, 1898; In the Tatra, symphonic poem, op. 26, 1902; Slovakian Suite, op. 32, 1903; The Eternal Longing, symphonic poem, op. 33, 1904; Serenade in D major, for small orchestra, op. 36, 1905; Serenade for Small Orchestra, 1905; Toman and the Dryad, op. 40, 1907; To the Czechoslovak Victors, 1918; South Bohemian Suite, 1937; De Profundis, symphonic poem, op. 67, 1941; May Symphony, for chorus and orchestra, 1945.

Piano Music—Bagatelles, op. 5, 1899; Souvenirs, op. 6, 1894; Serenades, op. 9, 1895; Eclogues, op. 11, 1896; In the Twilight, op. 13, 1897; Three Bohemian Dances, op. 15, 1897; My May, op. 20, 1898; Sonatina Erotica, op. 24, 1900; Winternight Songs, op. 30, 1903; Slovakian Suite, op. 32, 1903; Pan Suite, op. 43, 1910; Erotikon, op. 45, 1911; Six Sonatinas, op. 54, 1919; Youth, op. 55, 1920.

Gösta Nystroem *1890-*

GÖSTA NYSTROEM is one of Sweden's most distinguished symphonic composers. He was born in Silfberg, in Dalecarlia, Sweden, on October 13, 1890. His father was a man of great culture whose interests ranged from botany and science to painting and music. He brought to all of his children a love of beauty in art and nature. The influence of his father on Gösta was far-reaching. A passion for painting and music and a deep-rooted love of nature were the dominating influences in Gösta Nystroem's life.

Gösta received his first piano lessons from his father. He also started studying the organ by the time he was twelve years old, achieving such proficiency that while still in his boyhood he was able to substitute for the regular organist at the church services. In his fifteenth year music study was begun in all seriousness in Stockholm, where his teachers included Lundberg and Bergenson. Later music study took place at the Academy of Music with Andreas Hallen.

For a long time Nystroem divided his interest and devotion equally between music and painting, and he revealed talent in both. In Copenhagen and Stockholm he gave some exhibitions of his paintings, which were well received. He went on to Paris for additional study and work in art, remaining there for twelve years.

En route to Paris, Nystroem lost all his luggage, which had contained virtually all the music he had written up to that time. The loss, which at first was a severe shock to him was soon accepted stoically as he began assimilating new ideas and experiences in Paris; he had lost interest in the kind of music he had written. Up to the time of his arrival in Paris, he had written in the romantic style of the late nineteenth-century German composers. His prolonged stay in Paris made him impatient with romanticism,

Nystroem: nü'strûm

Deux Sœurs

GÖSTA NYSTROEM

and he turned to impressionism. This impressionist phase, which resulted in several symphonic poems and the Symphony No. 1, was, however, transitory. After a period of study with Vincent d'Indy and Sabaneyev, Nystroem's style became contrapuntal, with the voices moving in complete independence of each other; greater restraint, objectivity, and purity entered his writing. The Concerto for Strings and the *Sinfonia Breve* revealed "a simplified idiom," as Moses Pergament wrote, "distinguished by polyphonic texture, greater certainty of form, and a complete release from vague color effects."

The works of his full maturity—the *Sinfonia Espressiva* and the *Sinfonia del Mare* —are still contrapuntal, but with a pronounced injection of the romantic spirit. Pergament points out that a greater feeling, atmosphere and increasing pathos are apparent as Nystroem evolves a "completely up-to-date medium of expression charged with new mentality and with contemporary conceptions of sound and color."

It is Pergament's opinion that the *Sinfonia del Mare*, written in 1946 on a commission from the Swedish Radio, is not only Nystroem's most important work to date, but one of the weightiest musical compositions by a Swedish symphonist. "Inspired by and written close to the sea, it is content to give a suggestive hint of the infiniteness of the horizon and the eternal movement of the sea. . . . Within such a structure there is ample room for all that dwells in the human heart. . . . Here is the will to live and struggle for life, but here is also—in the profoundly moving elegiac and funereal passages—much in it that expresses intense sorrow over the tragedy of living and the bitterness of life's limitations."

MAJOR WORKS:

Ballet—Young Men and Six Princesses, 1951.

Opera—The Blind, radio drama, 1949.

Orchestral Music—Tower of Babel, symphonic poem, 1928; Lyric Suite, 1929; Concerto for String Orchestra, 1930; Symphony No. 1, 1941; Sinfonia Breve, 1941; Concerto for Viola and Orchestra, 1941; Sinfonia Concertante, 1945; Sinfonia del Mare, 1948.

Carl Orff 1895- 1982

CARL ORFF is one of Germany's major composers of dramatic music. He was born in Munich on July 10, 1895. Highly secretive about his personal life, he has permitted only the barest facts about himself to be made public. His family was cultured and encouraged him to pursue the study of music. He was graduated from the Akademie der Tonkunst in Munich in 1914, and after that, for a period of four years, he served as a coach and conductor in various German theatres. In 1921 he began another intensive period of study, this time privately with Heinrich Kaminski. After 1925 he taught at the Gunther School of Music and conducted the orchestra of the Bavarian Theatre. He achieved some success in 1925 with his adaptation of Monteverdi's *Orfeo*, produced in Mannheim.

Orff believes that the music of the classical and romantic traditions has come to the end of its development. He has disowned all works written before 1935—including choral, instrumental, and orchestral music—because they were in the older traditions. He also feels that the stage provides the ideal avenue for artistic expression—but only if it discards the appurtenances of stagecraft, costuming, and scenery and reverts to the essentials of production.

Courtesy of Musical America
CARL ORFF

Orff carries out his theories by devoting himself to the theatre and by writing for it with the most elementary, even primitive, techniques and means. His first major work in this vein was *Carmina Burana*, based on anonymous medieval poems of the thirteenth century. Orff scored this work for soprano and baritone solos, small chorus, large chorus, and orchestra. While he intended it for stage presentation, he left the problems of scenery, staging, and costuming entirely to the discretion of the performing organization. *Carmina Burana* was introduced in Frankfort in 1937 and was well received.

Carmina Burana is the first of three works of a trilogy entitled *Trionfi*. The second in this group is *Catulli Carmina*, described as a "dramatic ballet," based on poems of Catullus. The musical accompaniment to this ballet is almost entirely a cappella choruses; only the prelude and postlude require an instrumental background, the instruments used being four pianos and percussion. *Catulli Carmina* was introduced by the Stuttgart Opera in 1952, at which time one critic described the score as "lively and musical," with the "rich expression of the melodic line . . . sometimes moving."

The concluding opera of this trilogy is *Trionfo d'Aphrodite*. The entire trilogy was performed for the first time at La Scala early in 1953.

Most of Orff's texts reach into the remote past, not only to medieval poetry, but also to Bavarian legends and ancient Greece. "I do not feel them as old," Orff has explained, "but rather as valid. The timely element disappears, and only the spiritual power remains. My entire interest is in the expression of spiritual realities. I write for the theatre in order to convey a spiritual attitude."

Die Kluge, based on an old fairy tale, was immensely successful when introduced in 1943. But *Antigone*, heard at the Salzburg Festival in 1949, inspired a mixed response. There were those who considered it a work of major significance, daring for its simplicity; others considered it merely an ingenuous work. Discussing the technique of *Antigone*, Everett Helm wrote as follows in *Musical America*, giving us an insight into Orff's creative methods in general: "In this work . . . the melodic, rhythmic, and harmonic means are primary. The major part of the opera consists of a kind of rhythmic declamation, employing rapid repeated notes, a sort of intoned recitation that has nothing to do with traditional free recitative. Some passages are sung without accompaniment (although always in rhythm) or with only an occasional punctuating chord by the orchestra—short rhythmic motives that are repeated many times. Harmonically, the style can be reduced essentially to tonic and dominant, and there are long stretches in which no change of harmony occurs. Dissonance is used sparingly; counterpoint, save of a rhythmic nature, is nonexistent."

Die Kluge was followed by *Der Bernauerin*, seen at the Munich Festival during the summer of 1950. It was the only modern opera on the program. Described by the composer as "a Bavarian piece," it is based on an old legend. The opera is, in the words of Virginia Pleasants, "a play with accompanying musical effects. . . . At no time is there an aria or anything else of a conventionally operatic character. The main figure . . . once sings a simple little melody, much like Ophelia's song in *Hamlet*. For the rest, communication among the principal characters is accomplished by unaccompanied spoken dialogue."

Orff has interested himself in music education for children, and has produced an authoritative text for that field called *Das Orff-Schulwerk.* In 1950 he was appointed professor of composition at the Musikhochschule in Munich.

MAJOR WORKS:

Ballet—Catulli Carmina, dramatic ballet, 1943.

Operas—Der Mond, 1936 (revised 1945); Carmina Burana, 1937; Die Kluge, 1942; Astutuli, 1946; Die Bernauerin, 1947; Antigone, 1949; Trionfo d'Aphrodite, 1952.

ABOUT:

Musical America, October 1950; New York Times, March 29, 1953.

Lorenzo Perosi *1872-*

Courtesy of Musical Courier
LORENZO PEROSI

LORENZO PEROSI, outstanding composer of contemporary Italian church music, was born in Tortona, Italy, on December 20, 1872. He was the son of the musical director of the Tortona Cathedral. For ten years Perosi studied music with his father, combining it with religious studies. He also attended, for brief periods, the Musical Lyceum in Rome and the Milan Conservatory, and took a course in church music with Haberl.

In 1890 Perosi became organist at Montecassino. One Christmas eve he was playing the organ there, when, suddenly and impetuously, he threw aside the music before him and started to improvise. This appeared to him as a message from God that he had been endowed with divine musical powers.

In 1894 Perosi became choirmaster of St. Mark's Cathedral in Venice, and two years after that he was ordained a priest. On December 14, 1898, he was appointed musical director of the Sistine Chapel by Pope Leo XIII. It was largely due to Perosi's efforts that there took place a revolution in Italian church music. For his distinguished services to Italian church music, Perosi was constituted "Perpetual Master of the Pontifical Chapel" by a special decree of the Pope on June 20, 1905.

Meanwhile, Perosi became known as a composer. In 1897 a trilogy of oratorios—including *The Last Supper,* the *Sermon on the Mount* and the *Crucifixion*—was heard at the Italian Church Music Congress in Milan. A second trilogy of oratorios (*Trans-figuration, The Raising of Lazarus,* and *The Resurrection*) was heard between 1897 and 1899. When the last work of this trilogy, *The Resurrection,* received its American premiere on June 9, 1950, the critic of the *New York Times* wrote as follows: "In unity of idea and of form, in fineness and solidity of texture of sound, in the fitness of the orchestral accompaniment, in dignity, reserve, and dramatic effectiveness, the work definitely takes its place among the best oratorios of recent times."

Perosi has written copiously, producing hundreds of works which have enriched contemporary choral literature, and particularly contemporary church music. Writing swiftly, as he once explained, was both a habit and a necessity. "I must produce without interruption, spontaneously . . . and under the impulse of a fresh inspiration. I rebel at the tiresome work of revision and correction."

Romain Rolland once described those qualities, both good and bad, in Perosi's music that gives it its special distinction: "His works abound in faults; but their qualities are so rare, and his soul shines so clearly through them, and such fine sincerity breathes in them, that I have not the courage to dwell on their weakness. So I shall content myself with remarking in passing that the orchestration is adequate and awkward,

Perosi: pā-rō′zē

and that . . . though he shows great ease in composition, he is often too impetuous. . . . The dramatic tendency of these oratorios is very marked. . . . It is not, however, Perosi's dramatic genius that strikes me in his work; it is rather his peculiar mournfulness, which is indescribable, his gift of pure poetry, and the richness of his flowing melody."

In 1917 Perosi first revealed symptoms that led to a nervous breakdown and forced him to abandon creative work temporarily. It was at this time, too, that (as Albert Spalding wrote in his autobiography, *Rise to Follow*) Perosi fell into disfavor with the Church authorities "because of certain heresies; had he not refused to officiate at Mass because he no longer believed in transubstantiation?" By 1922 Perosi was so ill that he was confined to a mental hospital. Under treatment, he recovered sufficiently by 1923 to be able to prepare a revised version of *The Resurrection* for a performance in Rome.

Since that time, Perosi has, at periodic intervals, been affected by recurrences of his mental disturbances. At other periods he has been well enough to continue composition. In 1949 he ventured into a new field, that of the theatre, by completing an opera, *Il Nazareno,* in the style of the old Italian *sacra rappresentazione.*

On December 27, 1952, Perosi was awarded a gold medal by the Pope in a special ceremony at which the composer directed his most important oratorio, *The Nativity,* which he had written more than a half century earlier. This performance was attended by Pope Pius XII, the first time the Pope had emerged to hear a concert.

Major Works:

Choral Music—The Last Supper, 1897; The Sermon on the Mount, 1897; The Crucifixion, 1897; The Transfiguration, 1898; The Raising of Lazarus, 1898; The Resurrection, 1898; The Nativity, 1899; The Entry of Christ into Jerusalem, 1900; The Slaughter of the Innocents, 1900; Moses, 1901; The Last Judgment, 1904; Stabat Mater, 1904; Transitus Animae, 1908; Dies Iste, 1910; Vespertina, 1912; Requiem; 30 masses; 120 motets.

Opera—Il Nazareno, 1949.

Orchestral Music—Symphony; Scherzo; Concerto for Violin and Orchestra; Dormi non Piangere, symphonic poem; La Festa del Villaggio, symphonic poem; Concerto for Piano and Orchestra; Tema Variato; National Suite.

About:

Rolland, R., Musicians of Today.

Hans Pfitzner *1869-1949*

HANS ERICH PFITZNER, the last of the German romantic composers of opera, was born in Moscow on May 5, 1869. His parents were of German origin. As a child, Hans was brought back to Germany where his father was employed as violinist in the orchestra of the Frankfurt Stadttheater and as music director of Hoch's Conservatory in Frankfurt. Hans received his first music instruction from his father. In his eighteenth year he entered the Hoch Conservatory where his teachers included Kwast (piano) and Knorr (composition). More than a decade later, in 1899, Pfitzner married Kwast's daughter.

In 1892-93, Pfitzner taught the piano at the Coblenz Conservatory, and from 1894 to 1896 he was one of the conductors at the Municipal Theatre in Mayence. Meanwhile, in 1893, he presented in Berlin a concert of his own works which was a major event and he became a major success; the critics predicted a rich future for the "budding genius."

In 1897 Pfitzner settled in Berlin. He taught composition at the Stern Conservatory. From 1903 to 1906 he was first Kapellmeister in the Theater des Westens. In 1907-08 he conducted the renowned Kaim Orchestra in Munich, resigning this post to become music director of the Strasbourg Conservatory. In 1910 he was appointed first conductor of the Strasbourg Opera.

He returned to Munich in 1916, and henceforth distinguished himself as teacher, composer, and conductor. But in 1920 he was back in Berlin, where he now served as director of the master class of composition at the Berlin Academy of Fine Arts. The last two decades of his life were spent principally in Munich where, for a period, he was professor at the Munich State Academy of Music.

His first opera, *Der Arme Heinrich,* was introduced in Mayence on April 2, 1895, the composer conducting. It was an outstanding success. The composer received a dozen curtain calls and was bedecked with genuine laurel wreaths. Humperdinck wrote in the *Frankfurter Zeitung* that this premiere was "an event of a significance far transcending local interest," and Max Steiner reported in the *Mainzer Tageblatt* that it was the most

Pfitzner: p'fĭts'nĕr

significant opera since Wagner. Within the next decade, the opera was performed in most of the major cities in Germany; as late as 1927 it was successfully revived in Berlin.

He did not duplicate this success with his second opera, *Die Rose vom Liebesgarten,* produced in Elberfeld on November 9, 1901. But with *Palestrina*, in 1917, he achieved the greatest triumph of his career as composer. Often called the last of the German romantic operas, *Palestrina* was concerned with the legendary saving of the art of contrapuntal music from banishment by the church by Palestrina's *Missa Papae Marcelli.* Some writers have pointed out that in this opera the composer identified himself with his protagonist: Pfitzner used the victory of Palestrina over the Council of Trent as symbolic of his own artistic victory over some of his bickering critics.

Palestrina was introduced in Munich on June 12, 1917. It was so successful that, despite the obstacles presented by World War I, it was sent on tour. It was subsequently heard in many of the leading opera houses of central Europe. Disciples of the Wagnerian music drama embraced the work; others also praised its nobility and spiritual grandeur. "In ethical pathos, in welding poetic and musical talents in a single work, it is the last example of successful Wagnerism," wrote Adolf Weissmann. Edward J. Dent said: "The whole work has a dignity and an asceticism which are rare in modern music."

Its archaic flavors, its heavy-handed Germanic writing, and its occasional dullness and stuffiness have caused the ultimate withdrawal of *Palestrina* from the living operatic repertory. Occasionally, however, the three orchestral preludes which preface the three acts are heard at symphony concerts, and they represent the best writing in the entire opera.

Though Pfitzner continued to write abundantly, he never repeated the success of *Palestrina*. But he was the recipient of many honors. In 1920 he was made Bavarian General Music Director, and five years later he was decorated with an Award for Merit by the Prussian Academy of Arts and Sciences. Hans Pfitzner societies were organized in several German cities. Pfitzner was active as a conductor up to the time of World War II.

HANS PFITZNER

He also wrote several books; a three-volume collection of his writings appeared between 1927 and 1929.

When Hitler came to power, Pfitzner immediately allied himself with the new order. In 1933 he refused to conduct at the Salzburg Festival because of the expressed antagonism of the Austrian Chancellor, Dollfuss, to Hitler. After that, he identified himself completely with the ideals, artistic and political, of the Third Reich. Official Nazis honored him, and several adulatory books about him were published.

During the War, Pfitzner suffered great deprivations. When the war ended, he lived in a Munich home for the aged. He was found there by the president of the Vienna Philharmonic, who transferred him to Austria where, until his death he was supported by the Vienna Philharmonic Orchestra.

Pfitzner died in Salzburg on May 22, 1949.

MAJOR WORKS:

Chamber Music—Sonata in F-sharp minor, for cello and piano, op. 1, 1890; Trio in F major, op. 8, 1896; Quartet in D major, op. 13, 1903; Piano Quintet in C major, op. 23, 1908; Sonata in E minor, for violin and piano, op. 27, 1918; Quartet in C-sharp minor, op. 36, 1925; Quartet in C minor, op. 50, 1942. ·

Choral Music—Der Blumen Rache, ballade for contralto, women's chorus and orchestra, 1888; Columbus, eight-part a cappella chorus, op. 16, 1905; Zwei Deutsche Gesänge, for baritone, men's chorus and orchestra, op. 25, 1916; Gesang der Barden,

1906; Von Deutscher Seele, cantata, op. 28, 1921; Das Dunkele Reich, for soprano, baritone, chorus, and orchestra, op. 38, 1929.

Operas—Der Arme Heinrich, 1893; Die Rose vom Liebesgarten, 1908; Palestrina, 1916; Das Christelflein, 1917; Das Herz, op. 39, 1931.

Orchestral Music—Scherzo, 1887; Herr Oluf, ballade for baritone and orchestra, op. 12, 1891; Die Heinzelmännchen, for bass and orchestra, op. 14, 1903; Incidental Music to Das Christelflein, op. 20, 1906; Concerto in E-flat major, for piano and orchestra, op. 31, 1922; Concerto in B minor, for violin and orchestra, op. 34, 1925; Symphony in C-sharp minor, op. 36a, 1933; Concerto in G major, for cello and orchestra, op. 42, 1935; Symphony, op. 46, 1941.

Vocal Music—more than 100 songs.

ABOUT:

Abendroth, W., Hans Pfitzner; Kroll, H., Hans Pfitzner; Valentin, E., Hans Pfitzner.

Riccardo Pick-Mangiagalli *1882-1949*

RICCARDO PICK-MANGIAGALLI was born in Strakonitz, Bohemia, on July 10, 1882; but he was a naturalized Italian and is regarded as an Italian composer. His musical education took place at the Verdi Conservatory in Milan with Appiani (piano) and Ferroni (composition). He was an outstanding student. After leaving the Milan Conservatory he went on to Vienna for additional study.

Courtesy of Musical Courier
RICCARDO PICK-MANGIAGALLI

Pick-Mangiagalli: pĕk män-jä-gä'lē

His musical career began on the concert stage, as pianist. He achieved success throughout Europe. But composition always interested him more than the piano, and he soon abandoned the stage entirely. His first works were for the piano. In 1913 his ballet *Il Salice d'Oro* was produced at La Scala in Milan and was so successful that it was given on fourteen consecutive nights. His greatest success came in 1918, *Il Carillon Magico*, a choreographic symphonic poem, produced at La Scala in Milan. So well was it received that it was soon seen in many leading opera houses, including the Metropolitan Opera House in New York, in 1920.

Il Carillon Magico remained the composer's best and most celebrated work. Guido M. Gatti provides the following analysis in the *Musical Times* (May 1921): "The comedy, distinctive in action, in gesture, and scene . . . has given rise to equally distinctive music with clear lines and decided movements: music melodiously constructed and solidly built, with fine rhythmic and instrumental effects following each other with lavish prodigality. . . . Certain elementary predominant colors, the blues of the sky or the emerald greens of the meadows, certain decorative arabesques, slender lines which seem to bring the figures in close proximity within an airy but tenacious net, are translated into the music of *Il Carillon Magico* with admirable precision."

In 1931 Pick-Mangiagalli wrote *L'Ospito Inatteso*, the first "radiophonic" opera for the Milan-Turin-Genoa network, the premiere taking place on October 25, 1931.

He also composed several fine works for the orchestra, some of them introduced in the United States by Arturo Toscanini. The best include *Sortilegi*, for piano and orchestra; *Notturno e Rondo Fantastico*; and *Piccola Suite*.

Pick-Mangiagalli never identified himself with the more progressive branch of Italian composers. He avoided experimentation, preferred the more traditional means, and emphasized contrapuntal writing.

He died in Milan on July 8, 1949. From 1936 until his death, he had served as director of the Milan Conservatory.

MAJOR WORKS:

Ballets—Salice d'Oro, 1913; Sumitra, 1917; Il Carillon Magico, 1918; Mahit, 1923; Casanova a Venezia, 1929; Variazioni Coreografiche, 1934.

Chamber Music—Sonata for Violin and Piano, op. 8; String Quartet, op. 18, 1909.

Operas—Basi e Bote, 1927; L'Ospito Inatteso, 1931; Il Notturno Romantico, 1935.

Orchestral Music—Ballata Sinfonico, op. 12; Notturno e Rondo Fantastico, op. 28, 1914; Humoresque, for piano and orchestra, op. 35, 1934; Sortilegi, symphonic poem for piano and orchestra, op. 39, 1917; Two Preludes, 1921; 4 Poemi, op. 45, 1924; Piccola Suite, 1926; Preludio e Fuga, op. 47, 1926; Three Intermezzi, 1932; Preludio e Scherzo Sinfonico, 1938.

Gabriel Pierné *1863-1937*

HENRI CONSTANT GABRIEL PIERNÉ was born in Metz, France, on August 16, 1863. He attended the Paris Conservatory, where he was a classmate of Debussy; his teachers included Lavignac, Marmontel, Durand, César Franck, and Massenet. Pierné was an outstanding student and won many prizes. In 1882 his cantata *Edith* received the Prix de Rome.

After returning to Paris from his three-year stay in Rome, Pierné succeeded César Franck as organist at the Sainte-Clotilde church. He held this post for eight years. In 1903 he entered upon a career as conductor. From 1903 to 1910 he served as assistant conductor of the Colonne Orchestra. When Colonne died, in 1910, Pierné became his successor. For nearly a quarter of a century, Pierné directed annual concerts in Paris. He was a major influence in bringing about performances of and recognition to many young French composers and outstanding French musical works. After his resignation as conductor in 1932, Pierné was made honorary president of the Colonne Orchestra.

As a composer, Pierné's primary interest was the creation of beauty. Content with old methods and traditions, he rarely concerned himself with new ways of saying things. He was an extraordinary craftsman; his writing has the characteristic Gallic qualities of grace, refinement, and sensitivity.

He first became known through his oratorio *The Children's Crusade*, which he wrote in 1902 and which was introduced with great success by the Colonne Orchestra under Colonne on January 18, 1905. This oratorio, which was based on an old Flemish legend, won the City of Paris prize of 10,000 francs.

Henri Manuel
GABRIEL PIERNÉ

A second oratorio, *Children at Bethlehem*, was also a huge success.

Pierné wrote his most successful stage work in 1913: the ballet *Cydalise et le Chèvre-pied*. Its first performance was long delayed because of World War I, but it was finally introduced at the Paris Opéra on January 15, 1923. At that time, Emile Vuillermoz wrote in the *Revue Musicale*: "Pierné has written . . . a score of extraordinary youthfulness and allurement. . . . The score abounds in coquetries of excellent quality, and is of a vivacity and freshness which will enchant the public." This ballet is now occasionally represented at symphony concerts by a sprightly and amusing little excerpt entitled "The Entrance of the Little Fauns."

Pierné's style was thus described by Charles Malherbe: "The talent of Gabriel Pierné is above all else touched with elegance and grace; without pain, he has elevated himself to the heights of the subject he handles; he has become almost a classicist with his works for harp and his Piano Concerto; he has attained dramatic intensity with certain scenes of *Vendée*, and finds in his *La Nuit de Noël* the precise note and the true emotion. Endowed with a fertile imagination, with a supple spirit, Gabriel Pierné sketches melodies full of charm, and reveals himself expert in giving these melodies shape and form because, within him . . . is con-

Pierné: pyĕr-nā'

cealed a very substantial science, together with an intimate knowledge of the classics and a profound understanding of counterpoint."

Pierné died while vacationing at Ploujean, in Brittany, on July 17, 1937.

MAJOR WORKS:

Ballets—Le Collier de Saphirs, 1891; Les Joyeuses Commères de Paris, 1892; Bouton d'Or, 1893; Le Docteur Blanc, 1893; Salomé, 1895; Cydalise et le Chèvre-pied, 1913; Impressions de Music-Hall, 1927; Images, 1935; La Grisi, 1935.

Chamber Music—Pastorale Variée dans le Style Ancien, for wind instruments, op. 30; Sonata in D minor, for violin and piano, op. 36; Piano Quintet, op. 41; Piano Trio, op. 45; Sonata da Camera, for flute, cello and piano, op. 48, 1926; Variations Libres et Finale, for flute, violin, viola, cello, and harp, op. 51, 1932.

Choral Music—L'An Mil, symphonic poem for chorus and orchestra, 1898; The Children's Crusade, 1902; The Children at Bethlehem, 1907; St. Francis of Assisi, 1912; La Nuit de Noël.

Operas—La Coupe Enchantée, 1895 (revised 1901); Vendée, 1897; La Fille de Tabarin, 1901; On ne Badine pas avec l'Amour, 1910; Sophie Arnould, 1927; Fragonard, 1927.

Orchestral Music—Fantaisie-ballet, for piano and orchestra, op. 6; Ouverture Symphonique, op. 10, 1910; Suite d'Orchestre, op. 11; Concerto in C minor, for piano and orchestra, op. 12, 1887; Marche Solenelle, op. 23; Pantomime, op. 24; Scherzo-Caprice, op. 25; Poème Symphonique, for piano and orchestra, op. 37; Konzertstück, for harp and orchestra, op. 39; Fantaisie Basque, for violin and orchestra; Les Cathédrales, suite.

ABOUT:

Hill, E. B., Modern French Music; Séré. O., Musiciens Français d'Aujourd'hui.

Willem Pijper *1894-1947*

WILLEM PIJPER was born in Zeist, Utrecht, in Holland, on September 8, 1894. Because his health was so frail, Willem was not able to attend school until his fourteenth year; at that time he entered the Latin Grammar School, where he stayed for three years. Meanwhile, he had received some training in music from his father. When he was seventeen, Willem Pijper abandoned all academic study for music. He became a pupil of Johan Wagenaar at the Utrecht Music School and before very long completed a creditable string quartet.

After passing his examinations at the Utrecht Music School in 1915, Pijper wrote his first symphony. Here the influence of the post-romantic school in Germany was noticeable, particularly that of Mahler. In 1918 Willem Mengelberg directed the premiere of this symphony. But Pijper was not satisfied to live in the past. Between 1918 and 1922 he impatiently discarded the more traditional styles and techniques and adopted an advanced idiom. He wrote polytonal music, and he adopted a method utilizing germinal ideas (he called these "germ cells") out of which his music was evolved with inflexible logic.

Pijper's most important work was written in 1926, the Third Symphony, which the Concertgebouw Orchestra under Monteux introduced on October 28 of the same year. This work has been heard extensively throughout Europe and in this country, and is still the work by which its composer is most frequently represented on symphony programs.

Pijper's style was analyzed by M. D. Calvocoressi in *The Gamut* as follows: "His themes are definitely tonal or modal, diatonic in character. And although he resorts freely enough to polytonal harmonies, and occasionally to other polytonal combinations, his music, in spirit, color, and tone, is altogether different from the French polyphonists. It comes no nearer to the atonality school of Schoenberg or to that of Bartók. I should incline to say that his incursions into the realm of atonality and polytonality are determined by special purposes of coloration or accentuation, by whims of a moment which the general purpose of the works in which they occur *justifies*."

Pijper was one of Holland's leading music teachers and critics. From 1918 to 1923 he was the critic of the *Utrechts Dagblad*, in which capacity he acted as spokesman for the most important of the younger and more progressive Dutch composers. In 1925 he helped found one of Holland's most important music journals, *De Muziek*, which he edited for many years. His career as teacher also began early. From 1918 to 1921 he taught harmony and composition at the Amsterdam High School. In 1925 he was appointed professor of composition at the Amsterdam Conservatory, and from 1930 to the time of his death he was the director of the Rotterdam Conservatory.

Pijper: pī'pĕr

WILLEM PIJPER

Pijper died at Leidschendam, near The Hague, on March 19, 1947. At the time of his death, he was working on an opera. When Pijper died, Paul Sanders wrote of him: "For the first time since the death of J. P. Sweelinck, two centuries ago, was the attention of the world drawn to the creative forces of Dutch music by the appearance of Pijper's work on the international concert stage."

The distinguished conductor Pierre Monteux wrote the following personal note on Pijper in the program notes of the Philadelphia Orchestra: "He was extremely erudite, and had the profound culture which stems from the classical education common to European schools. He possessed a sharp wit, and his repartee was at times sour and biting if not bitter. He was a great liberal, and an ardent Francophile, loving all things of France—its literature, its music, its paintings. He was a magnificent teacher and many are the young composers in Holland today who owe knowledge of their *métier* to this master. For he was a master, having in music—to my mind—what Erasmus so ably propagated in the world of learning and letters. The reactionaries hated him, and the young of spirit, ardent for the advancement of art in their country, adored him. I can see him now as he came up the walk to our home in Belgium on one of his numerous visits. Tall, pale, and very slender, his face

the face of a true ascetic, his eyes seemed to burn with inward enthusiasm for this long awaited moment—the opportunity of talking long hours of music, art and politics with those he knew loved and revered him."

MAJOR WORKS:

Chamber Music—Trio No. 1, 1913; String Quartet No. 1, 1914; Sonata No. 1 for Violin and Piano, 1919; Sonata No. 1 for Cello and Piano, 1919; String Quartet No. 2, 1920; Septet, 1920; Trio No. 2, 1921; Sonata No. 2 for Violin and Piano, 1922; Quartet No. 3, 1923; Sextet, for flute, oboe, clarinet, bassoon, horn, and piano, 1923; Sonata for Flute and Piano, 1925; Trio, for flute, clarinet, and bassoon, 1927; String Quartet No. 4, 1928; Quintet, for flute, oboe, clarinet, bassoon, and horn, 1929; String Quartet No. 5, 1946.

Choral Music—Two Ballades (Paul Fort), 1921; Sixteen Dutch Songs (two albums) 1924-35; Herr Danielken, 1925; Chansons, for male chorus and orchestra, 1932.

Opera—Halewijn, 1920.

Orchestral Music—Rhapsody for Piano and Orchestra, 1915; Fêtes Galantes (Verlaine), for voice and orchestra, 1916; Divertimento, for piano and strings, 1916; Symphony No. 1, 1917; Symphony No. 2, 1921; Incidental Music to Antigone, 1922; Incidental Music to The Bacchantes, 1922; Symphony No. 3, 1926; Concerto for Piano and Orchestra, 1927; Epigrammata, 1928; Incidental Music to The Tempest, 1930; Concerto for Cello and Orchestra, 1936 (revised 1947); Incidental Music to Phaeton, 1937; Concerto for Violin and Orchestra, 1939; Hymns, for baritone and orchestra, 1943.

Piano Music—Sonatina No. 1, 1917; Sonatina No. 2, 1925; Sonatina No. 3, 1926; Sonata, 1930; Sonata for Two Pianos, 1935.

Vocal Music—Four Songs, 1916; Two Songs, 1923.

ABOUT:

Eolus, January 1929; Gamut, July 1928.

Ildebrando Pizzetti *1880-*

ILDEBRANDO PIZZETTI was born in Parma, Italy, on September 20, 1880. When he was a child of two, his family moved to Riggo, where Pizzetti received his first piano lessons from his father, a piano teacher. When it was decided that music would be Pizzetti's career, the boy was sent back to his native city, in his sixteenth year, to attend the Conservatory. He was an outstanding student, and during this period he completed two operas and several orchestral works.

Pizzetti: pĕt-tsāt'tē

Wide World Photo
ILDEBRANDO PIZZETTI

He received his diploma from the Parma Conservatory in 1901. For a brief period he worked as assistant conductor at the Parma Opera. In 1908 he entered upon a career as teacher. After a year at the Parma Conservatory, he became professor of theory and composition at the Conservatory in Florence. In 1921 he was appointed director of the Milan Conservatory, and in 1936 he succeeded Respighi as professor of composition at the Santa Cecilia Academy in Rome. He was soon made director of the Santa Cecilia Academy; he resigned from this post in 1952 to dedicate himself completely to composition.

Despite his long and distinguished career as a teacher, and in this capacity his influence has been considerable, Pizzetti is known primarily as one of the most celebrated Italian composers of our time. Soon after leaving the Parma Conservatory as a student, he entered a competition for new operas conducted by the publisher Sonzogno. His opera, *Le Cid,* was disqualified because of an inadequate last scene. This disappointment was so great that for several years Pizzetti refused to write anything else for the theatre. He devoted himself instead to orchestral and chamber-music works.

The incidental music he wrote in 1905 for D'Annunzio's *La Nave* brought on the first phase of his career as a composer. During this period, Pizzetti was strongly influenced by D'Annunzio, and produced his incidental music to *La Pisanella,* the remarkable cycle of songs, *I Pastori,* and most important of all the opera *Fedra. Fedra,* completed in 1913, was introduced at La Scala in Milan on March 20, 1915. It was not at first successful. The action was too static, and the music seemed too cerebral and restrained. Eventually, however, *Fedra* proved to be one of Pizzetti's most popular works and most frequently performed operas. The wonderful unity of play and music—the music capturing the classic beauty of the text—became more understandable with repeated hearings.

The D'Annunzio phase was succeeded by the biblical period. Pizzetti now completed several important choral works and the opera *Debora e Jaele,* the texts derived from the Bible. *Debora e Jaele,* introduced at La Scala under Toscanini's direction on December 16, 1922, is the crowning work of this period. As Guido M. Gatti wrote: "All Pizzetti is in it. . . . In it all sides of his personality have found their highest degree of expression—the poet, the thinker, the man. In this opera is the final fruitage of his conception of art and life; all that was shadowed forth in *Fedra,* but could not find there full expression because fettered by another's words, is here presented in the most convincing manner. The musician was no longer in bondage; we feel that he has freed himself from the shackles he wore in *Fedra,* and that the dramatic conception that found theoretical expression in his writings has passed through the fires of emotion and been made to bend, as regards certain features, to the sole esoteric law of creative genius."

The biblical period was followed by one in which the composer was inspired by Italian history in the writing of his choral and operatic works. The most celebrated of his historical compositions is the opera *Fra Gherardo,* introduced successfully at La Scala on May 16, 1928, and seen at the Metropolitan Opera House one year after that.

In his operas, Pizzetti prefers expressive declamation to outright lyricism. His primary concern is to project the drama, and he molds his music to the contours of his text. As H. T. Parker wrote in his review of *Fra Gherardo*: "With Mussorgsky, Pizzetti agrees that a musical speech can compass the contours, the shadings, the emphasis of the spoken word and so become semi-humanized discourse."

Some of the finest and most stirring pages in his operas are for chorus. Castelnuovo-Tedesco has written that it is the choral passages of his operas, together with his other nontheatrical choral works, which make him the foremost Italian polyphonist since the sixteenth century. Though Pizzetti has written many fine works for orchestra, some of them introduced in the United States by Toscanini, he remains at his best in his dramatic, choral, and vocal music.

Pizzetti visited the United States in 1930, appearing as pianist and conductor in performances of his works. In 1950 he received the international Italia Prize for his one-act opera, *Ifigenia*.

MAJOR WORKS:

Chamber Music—String Quartet in A, 1906; Sonata in A, for violin and piano, 1919; Sonata in F, for cello and piano, 1921; Trio in A, 1925; Quartet in D major, 1932-33.

Choral Music—Requiem, 1922; De Profundis, for seven mixed voices, 1937; Epithalamium, cantata, 1939; Cantico di Gloria, 1948.

Operas—Fedra, 1912; Debora e Jaele, 1921; Lo Straniero, 1925; Fra Gherardo, 1927; Orseolo, 1935; L'Oro, 1942; Vanna Lupa, 1947; Ifigenia, 1950, Cagliostro, 1952.

Orchestral Music—Incidental Music to La Nave, 1905; La Pisanella, suite, 1913; La Sacra Rappresentazione di Abram e d'Isaac, incidental music, 1917; Concerto dell' Estate, 1928; Rondo Veneziano, 1929; Introduction to Agammemnon, 1931; La Rappresentazione di Santa Uliva, incidental music, 1933; Canti della Stagione Alta, for piano and orchestra, 1933; Concerto in C, for cello and orchestra, 1934; As You Like It, incidental music, 1938; Symphony in A, 1940; Concerto in A, for violin and orchestra, 1944; Canzone di Beni Perduti, 1949.

Vocal Music—I Pastori, 1908; La Madre al Figlio Lontano, 1910; San Basilio, 1912; Il Clefta Prigione, 1912; Passeggiata, 1915; Two Dramatic Neapolitan Lyrics, 1916; Three Sonnets of Petrarch, 1922; Tre Canzoni, for voice and string quartet, 1926; Five Lyrics, 1933.

ABOUT:

Ewen, D. (ed.) The Book of Modern Composers; Gatti, Guido M., Ildebrando Pizzetti; Musical Quarterly, January 1923.

Marcel Poot *1901-*

MARCEL POOT was born in Vilvorde, near Brussels, Belgium, on May 7, 1901. He writes: "Although I was very mediocre, I began studying music at an early age. My father, director of a Brussels theatre, had me join the clarinetists of a local band in which he was saxophonist. Less apt than my young friends, I soon had to give up this position. From then on dates my unpopularity in Vilvorde.

"My father, however, was determined to make me a musician. We then tried the piano. The town organist taught me scales and the Czerny exercises. This did not amuse me at all. But the laborious study continued until I was able to play with my professor overtures by Suppé arranged for four hands. My father then decided to enroll me at the Brussels Conservatory. The first time I was turned down. But another period of work with Czerny, and I was finally admitted. The teaching of the academicians did not succeed in making me love my instrument any more than I had up to now. However, from this time on, I began to undertake the writing of my first compositions, which I hid.

"We have arrived at the year of 1916. I was introduced to Paul Gilson, an authentic artist with an encyclopedic knowledge. He initiated me to the science of orchestra-

MARCEL POOT

Poot: pōt

tion and encouraged me in my composing. My road was now before me. Several hard years of work followed, after which I completed my first orchestral work, *Charlot,* three symphonic sketches inspired by the films of Charles Chaplin.

"Unfortunately, the opportunities for young composers to be heard were virtually nonexistent. Several of my friends decided to band together to protect themselves. Thus was born the school known as the 'Synthesists.' This title permitted us to exclude all well-determined programs in our music and to work each according to his own temperament but with respect for established forms and traditions. Arthur Prévost consented to direct a concert of our works before an irritated audience. That performance made a good impression. From that moment on it opened up for us the doors to other concerts. Most of my companions have since gone their own way. If at the present time the group is scattered, its formation at least permitted several Belgian composers to make themselves known, notably De Bourguignon, Bernier, Brenta, Schoemaker, and several others.

"The winning of the Rubens Prize in 1930 enabled me to go to Paris to work with Paul Dukas."

Poot has written a variety of works, including symphonies, ballets, an opera, orchestral pieces, chamber-music compositions together with functional works for the radio and motion-pictures. In his music, traditional forms are synthesized with contemporary techniques and idioms. Poot's writing is vigorous, rich in orchestral and harmonic colors, dramatic in its rhythmic pulse.

Poot has served as professor of harmony and counterpoint at the Brussels Conservatory. In 1943 he was nominated for the post of Inspector of the Belgian music schools, an offer which he turned down. He has also been music critic of *Le Peuple* and editor of *La Revue Musicale Belge,* a magazine he had helped found with Paul Gilson.

He has this to say about his personal life: "I smoke, like beer and wines of all kinds. I love the country, but for a long time now have preferred the city with its vibrant life. Like all normal people, I have a telephone, typewriter, automobile, and I play tennis. Rest assured that I do not earn my living from my compositions. Besides teaching at the Brussels Conservatory, I am a member of the jury of auditions of the Belgian Radio."

MAJOR WORKS:

Ballets—Paris et les Trois Divines, 1933; Camera, 1938.

Chamber Music—Three Pieces for Trio; Piano Quartet; Five Bagatelles, for string quartet; Octet, for clarinet, horn, bassoon, and five strings, 1949.

Choral Music—Le Dit de Routier.

Opera—The Imaginary Lake, 1943.

Orchestral Music—Poème de l'Espace, 1929; Jazz Music, 1930; Symphony; Ballade, for string quartet and orchestra; Impromptu in the Form of a Rondo, for string orchestra; Ouverture Joyeuse, 1934; Allegro Symphonique, 1937; Légende Épique, for piano and orchestra, 1938; Triptyque; Musique Légère; Sinfonietta, 1946; Fantasia, for chamber orchestra; Konzertstück, for cello and orchestra.

Piano Music—Sonata; Six Easy Pieces; Six Recreational Pieces; Suite; Variations; Rhapsody, for two pianos.

Vocal Music—Trois Petits Poèmes Nègres.

Francis Poulenc 1899-

FRANCIS POULENC was born in Paris on January 7, 1899. Since his parents insisted that he get a complete academic education, music was for a long time relegated to a position of minor importance in his life. His pronounced musical talent so impressed his friends that they raised a fund to pay for his lessons. He studied the piano with Ricardo Viñes, and harmony and theory privately from textbooks.

He was drafted into the French army in 1917 and remained in service until after the Armistice. Returning to the study of music, he became a pupil of Charles Koechlin in composition, at the same time completing the first work of his to be published, *Rapsodie Nègre.* Several other chamber-music works followed, together with an excellent cycle of songs on a text of Jean Cocteau, *Cocardes.* Louis Durey pointed out "the great musicianship and rich novelty" in these songs, "which often remind one of Mozart by the freshness of their invention, and the elegant and refined sobriety of style."

Poulenc first became known when the critic, Henri Collet, linked his name with those of Milhaud, Durey, Auric, Honegger,

Poulenc: pōō-lă̄nk'

and Tailleferre, in proclaiming the new school of the "French Six" (see Auric). Of the Six, Poulenc was most true to the principles of economy, simplicity, and a directness which was a reaction to German romanticism and French impressionism. Influenced on the one hand by Mozart, and on the other by the latter-day Stravinsky, Poulenc adopted a neo-classical style. He preferred to devote himself to miniatures. When he essayed the larger forms, he was always terse in his statements and compact in his form and transparent in his texture. Graceful workmanship was combined with charm and wit, and with a freshness that provides his music with a feeling of spontaneity. In this vein he produced several characteristic works: the delightful ballet with interpolated popular French songs, *Les Biches,* introduced by the Diaghilev Ballet in Monte Carlo in 1924; the *Concert Champêtre,* for harpsichord and orchestra, written for and introduced by Wanda Landowska in 1929; and the Concerto in D minor, for two pianos and orchestra, first heard at the International Society for Contemporary Music Festival in Venice in 1932.

During World War II Poulenc was an active member in the French Resistance movement. During this period his political consciousness invested his music with increasing intensity and expressiveness. In 1943 he wrote a poignant Sonata for Violin and Piano, inspired by and dedicated to the Spanish poet, Federico García Lorca, killed by the Falangists. In place of his one-time Gallic witticisms, there are here both vehemence and pervading sadness. Another work of compelling force is the *Figure Humaine,* for unaccompanied double chorus, based on a poem of Paul Éluard. This composition was written while Paris was occupied by the Nazis, and expressed musically the French resistance to Nazi tyranny, culminating in a powerful song to liberty.

Poulenc has produced many songs which rank with the finest in contemporary French music. Virgil Thomson goes so far as to say that Poulenc "is without a rival as a world master of the concert song. No other composer since Fauré has written for voice and piano so copiously, so authoritatively, with such freedom of musical thought, such variety of expression."

FRANCIS POULENC

In 1947 Poulenc was the center of storm and criticism when his opera-burlesque, *Les Mamelles de Tirésias,* was introduced at the Opéra Comique. The existentialist libretto of Claude Rostand included such intriguing items as a character who changed his sex and one who gave birth to 40,000 babies. This unusual text and tongue-in-cheek score created both shock and delight. The American premiere took place on June 13, 1953, at the second annual Festival of Creative Arts in Waltham, Massachusetts, Leonard Bernstein conducting.

Poulenc visited the United States for the first time in 1948.

MAJOR WORKS:

Ballets—Les Biches, 1924; Les Animaux Modèles, 1942.

Chamber Music—Rapsodie Nègre, for voice, flute, clarinet, string quartet, and piano, 1917; Sonata for Two Clarinets, 1918; Le Bestiare (Apollinaire), for voice, flute, clarinet, bassoon and string quartet, 1918; Cocardes, for voice, viola, cornet, trombone, drum, and triangle, 1919; Sonata for Clarinet and Bassoon, 1922; Sonata for Horn, Trumpet and Trombone, 1922; Trio for Piano, Oboe, Bassoon, 1924-25; Aubade, choreographic concerto for piano and eighteen instruments, 1929; Sonata for Violin and Piano, 1943.

Choral Music—Chanson à Boire, 1922; Un Soir de Neige, chamber cantata; Mass in G major, 1937; Four Motets; Figure Humaine, 1943; Stabat Mater, 1951.

Operas—Le Gendarme Incompris, 1920; Les Mamelles de Tirésias, 1947.

Orchestral Music—Concert Champêtre, for harpsichord (or piano) and orchestra, 1928; Concerto in D minor, for two pianos and orchestra, 1932; Concerto in G minor, for organ, strings, and timpani, 1938; Le Bal Masque, for baritone and chamber orchestra; Sinfonietta, 1947; Concerto for Piano and Orchestra, 1949.

Piano Music—Sonata, for four hands, 1918; Mouvements Perpetuels, 1918; Six Impromptus, 1920 (revised 1924); Promenades, 1921; Improvisations; Intermezzi; Suite Française, 1935.

Vocal Music—Cinq Poèmes de Ronsard, 1924; Metamorphoses; Banalités; Chansons Villageoises; Mais Mourir; Trois Chansons de F. García Lorca, for baritone and piano, 1947.

ABOUT:

Chesterian (London), November-December 1935; New York Times, November 7, 1948.

Serge Prokofiev *1891-1953*

SERGE PROKOFIEV was born in the district of Ekaterinoslav, in Ukrainian Russia, on April 23, 1891. His mother, a fine pianist, introduced him to music early in his life. Prokofiev began composing when he was only five. His first piece, for the piano, called *Galop Hindou,* was inspired by a famine in India which he had heard his parents discuss. After he had been taken by his father to see an opera, he tried writing one, completing the words and music of *The Giant* in his eighth year. From 1900 to 1902 he was occupied by a second opera, *Desert Islands.* By the time he was twelve, he had completed his first orchestral work, a symphony for four hands, a set of twelve piano pieces, and a third opera, *Feast During the Plague.*

With several of these scores under his arm, he went to Taneiev for advice and criticism. Taneiev told him: "You must develop a more interesting harmony. Too much of your music employs the tonic, dominant, and subdominant." But Taneiev recognized talent and advised Prokofiev to begin studying with Glière.

Prokofiev entered the St. Petersburg Conservatory in his thirteenth year, and for the next ten years he studied with Rimsky-Korsakov, Tcherepnin, and Liadov. He now wrote numerous works, some influenced by Reger, some by Scriabin, and some which ventured towards original goals. His first published works included the Piano Sonata No. 1; Four Etudes, for piano; *Suggestion*

Diabolique, for piano; Sinfonietta, for orchestra; the First Piano Concerto; and an opera, *Magdalene.*

In many of these works Prokofiev was already beginning to express dissatisfaction with traditional writing. As he felt surer of himself, he experienced the need to experiment with unorthodox chords, unconventional melodies, and new tonalities. His teachers were horrified at the kind of music he was trying to write. In one of his pieces he utilized unresolved seconds; in another, two different keys were used simultaneously. When Taneiev saw some of this music, he—who had originally criticized Prokofiev for being too conventional—now found him too daring. "I have merely followed your advice, master," Prokofiev told him. "I proceeded to develop a more interesting harmony as you advised me."

In the spring of 1914 Prokofiev was graduated from the Conservatory with diplomas in composition, piano, and conducting. He also won the Rubinstein Prize with his Second Piano Concerto, though some of the older academicians (including Glazunov) had voted against him. When Prokofiev played his Concerto at a public concert, the music proved to be too advanced for the listeners. "The audience is puzzled," wrote the critic of the *St. Petersburg Gazette.* "Some are indignant. The young composer's Concerto concludes with a mercilessly dissonant combination of brass instruments. There is a regular riot." At about this time, too, one of Prokofiev's songs ("The Ugly Duckling") was sung in public. Maxim Gorki's comment was: "He must have written this about himself."

What is interesting about these early Prokofiev works is not only their adventurous search for new kinds of musical expression but their mannerisms and traits which also identify Prokofiev's later mature style. In these early works, as in the later ones, we find a powerful rhythmic momentum, tart harmonies, an indulgence in chromaticism, impish melodies, and a partiality for whimsy.

Soon after leaving the Conservatory, Prokofiev went on a holiday to London. He met there the impresario of the Ballet Russe, Serge Diaghilev, who commissioned him to write a ballet score for his company. Mean-

Prokofiev: prŭ-kôf′yĕf

while, World War I broke out. As the only son of a widow, Prokofiev was exempt from military service. Back in Russia, he could devote himself to composition.

The ballet Prokofiev was writing for Diaghilev utilized a text in which the characters were the Scythians (an ancient race) and their gods. This did not appeal to Diaghilev and he rejected it. Prokofiev, however, was so taken with the theme that he decided to write an orchestral suite about it. The *Scythian Suite* was introduced in St. Petersburg on January 29, 1916, Prokofiev conducting. The music was too revolutionary for the tastes of both critics and audience. Glazunov cupped his hands over his ears to drown out the dissonant sounds, and then fled out of the auditorium. One of the violinists in the orchestra was quoted as saying to a friend: "My wife is sick and I must buy medicine, otherwise I would never consent to play this crazy music."

The *Scythian Suite* involved Prokofiev— and the famous critic Leonid Sabaneyev—in a scandal which created considerable stir at the time. The work had originally been scheduled for an earlier performance, but at the last moment had been withdrawn from the program. Sabaneyev, who did not attend that concert, wrote a review violently attacking the new Prokofiev work. The fact that there existed only a single copy of the score, and that that copy was in Prokofiev's possession, emphasized the amusing point that Sabaneyev had written his attack without having heard or being familiar with a single note of the music. This incident was widely publicized and created a furor and did much to bring the composer a great deal of attention, and even sympathy.

If Diaghilev was unsympathetic toward the subject of the Scythians, he was more partial to another ballet text with which Prokofiev was engaged. Steeping himself in Russian folklore, Prokofiev had come upon a whimsical tale of a buffoon, and adapted it for the purposes of a ballet. He completed this work, *Chout*, in 1915. The war delayed the premiere of the ballet until six years later. When introduced by the Ballet Russe in Paris, on May 17, 1921, it was a huge success.

Prokofiev's style, long foreshadowed in earlier works, was fully integrated and

SERGE PROKOFIEV

crystallized in the First Violin Concerto, two piano sonatas, and the *Classical Symphony*. Nicolas Nabokov wrote: "After the publication of the First Violin Concerto . . . little has changed in either the style or technique of Prokofiev's music." Nabokov goes on to analyze this style, which is so highly personal. "Prokofiev loves, for instance . . . to play a little game of melodic construction which could easily be discovered in any one of his pieces. The game consists of taking a conventional rhythmic figure, tying it up with a conventional melodic pattern, so obvious as to border sometimes on triviality, and then afterwards forcing this melodic line into a harmonic frame which seems disconnected, surprisingly arbitrary, and produces the feeling that the melody has been refreshed by having been harmonically mishandled. Another little game in Prokofiev's thematic structure is the abruptness and unexpectedness of his leaps. . . . These characteristics contribute a great deal to the joking, sarcastic nature of much of his music. . . . In a certain sense a similar game is carried on within his harmonic texture. Chords, generally very simple chords, are related in such an entirely unexpected fashion that the ear has always a new element of harmonic surprise to cope with it."

Soon after the Revolution in Russia, Prokofiev was provided with funds by the publishing house of Serge Koussevitzky to undertake an American tour. He came here by way of Japan (where he gave three concerts) and Honolulu, making his first American appearance in a recital in New York City on November 20, 1918. The critics liked his playing, but not his piano works, which they described as "Bolshevism in art" and "Russian chaos."

In Chicago, Prokofiev was commissioned by Campanini, director of the Chicago Opera, to write a new work for his theatre. Prokofiev completed his work, *The Love of Three Oranges*, on schedule, but Campanini found the opera too difficult for performance and refused to live up to his contract. Two years later, when Mary Garden took over the direction of the opera company, *The Love of Three Oranges* was seen on the stage of the Chicago Opera, on December 30, 1921. Its ironic libretto, combined with an austere modern score, proved puzzling, and the opera was a failure. Its first revival took place in November 1949, by the New York City Opera Company, when it received unqualified acclaim.

Prokofiev now made Paris his permanent home, leaving that city for a few months each year to make concert appearances throughout the world of music. He continued writing major works in a provocative modern style, and their premieres were events of first importance. On June 7, 1927, there took place the premiere of his ballet *Le Pas d'Acier (The Age of Steel)* in Paris by the Ballet Russe. This was Prokofiev's first attempt to provide a musical interpretation of Soviet life. It was mildly received in Paris, but in London it was such a triumph that it had to be played eight times. Other major works of this period included three symphonies, the Fourth written in 1930 to honor the fiftieth anniversary of the Boston Symphony Orchestra; two piano concertos, including the excellent Fifth Piano Concerto, introduced in Berlin in October 1932; and two ballets—*Le Fils Prodigue* and *Sur le Borysthène*—produced by the Ballet Russe and Paris Opéra respectively.

In 1933 Prokofiev decided to return to his native land, to live there permanently and become a part of its cultural life. In the Soviet Union the nature of Prokofiev's music was to undergo a transformation, even though his basic style remained unaltered.

Henceforth he was to dedicate his art to propagandize or interpret Soviet ideologies, and to glorify Russian culture and traditions. One of the first works written after his return home was the delightful incidental music for the motion picture *Lieutenant Kije* —music that has become popular in the concert auditorium through the orchestral suite adapted by the composer. *Lieutenant Kije* was a satire of military heroism in the time of the Tsars; it inspired Prokofiev to write some of his brightest and wittiest music in his inimitable vein.

Other Prokofiev works were now to be derived from Russian backgrounds. The most important was the cantata *Alexander Nevsky*, which also originated as incidental music for the motion picture. In its revised and enlarged version, the cantata was introduced in Moscow on May 17, 1939, with outstanding success, and has since become accepted as one of Prokofiev's most original and vital works.

Meanwhile, Prokofiev also turned to the writing of music for children. In 1935 he produced several delightful piano pieces and after that some ingratiating children's songs. The most important and successful of his works for children came in 1936, the symphonic fairy tale *Peter and the Wolf*, intended to teach children the instruments of the orchestra. Identifying each character in his fairy tale with a different instrument of the orchestra—and with a subtle use of leading motives—Prokofiev wrote music with a youthful charm, wit, and spontaneity that made it popular with sophisticated concertgoers as well as with children throughout the world.

When the Nazi troops invaded the Soviet Union in 1941, Prokofiev was living in a Moscow suburb working on a ballet, *Cinderella*. He now dedicated himself to the war effort, writing military marches and popular songs to anti-fascist texts. "But soon events assumed such gigantic and far-reaching scope," he told an interviewer, "as to demand larger canvasses." The *Symphonic Suite: 1941* was a first major attempt to reflect the impact of war on his thinking. Works of greater importance, and more ambitious stature, followed. In 1942 he completed his Piano Sonata No. 7, sometimes known as the "Stalingrad Sonata," its momentum and power interpreting the heroism that turned the tide at Stalingrad. The Sonata won the Stalin prize. Three years later came the Fifth Symphony, Prokofiev's first in fifteen years. Dedicated to the spirit of man—a spirit ennobled by the harrowing experiences of war—the Symphony is one of Prokofiev's noblest works. He himself considered it "the culmination of a large period of my creative life." But the most ambitious of his works completed during the war was the opera *War and Peace,* almost as epical in concept and in its projection as the Tolstoy novel that inspired it.

Prokofiev was now regarded, and justly so, one of the great cultural figures in the Soviet Union, and one of its most important composers. He received many honors. At the height of his fame—and at the height of his creative powers—he was suddenly and inexplicably the object of a violent attack by his own government. He became a victim of a new music policy adopted by the General Committee of the Communist Party on February 10, 1948.

Three months earlier, there had taken place the premiere of a new Soviet opera, *Great Friendship,* by Vano Muradeli. Muradeli's cacophonous music aroused leading Communist officials to violent anger. Led by A. A. Zhdanov, these officials demanded a new orientation on the part of Soviet composers: away from modernism or cerebralism towards simplicity, away from the esoteric and towards a musical language that derived its character and its inspiration from the Russian past. In the public resolution of February 10, 1948, the Central Committee vigorously denounced some of the leading Soviet composers of the time—not only Prokofiev, but also Shostakovich, Khatchaturian, Miaskovsky, and Shebalin—for what was described as "decadent" tendencies in their musical thinking (the official phrase was "decadent formalism"). In the words of the resolution, these composers were condemned for "the negation of the basic principles of classical music" and for preaching "a sermon for atonality, dissonance, and disharmony, as if this were an expression of 'progress' and 'innovation,' in the growth of musical compositions which transform into cacophony, into a chaotic piling of sounds."

One week after the promulgation of this resolution, Prokofiev hotly exclaimed to his neighbor, at a meeting of Soviet musicians in Moscow: "They should stick to politics and leave music to musicians." But as it became increasingly apparent that this new tendency in Soviet thinking would not pass, Prokofiev wrote a long and detailed apology to Tikhon Khrennikov, head of the General Assembly of Soviet composers: "Elements of formalism were peculiar to my music as long as fifteen or twenty years ago. Apparently the infection caught from contact with some Western ideas." He concluded that in his future composition he intended to take a new direction, towards melody, simplicity, and polyphony. "In my new opera, *A Tale of a Real Man,* I intend to introduce trios, duets, and contrapuntally developed choruses for which I will make use of some interesting northern Russian folk songs. Lucid melody, and as far as possible, a simple harmonic language are elements which I intend to use." However, when this new opera was completed it did not please the authorities, nor did Prokofiev's Sixth Symphony. The opera was condemned by Khrennikov for its "modernistic and antimelodic style." The Symphony was the object of a particularly virulent attack by the Soviet critics.

But Prokofiev was eventually able to regain his position in the Soviet Union. He wrote an oratorio, *On Guard for Peace,* a condemnation of the Western "war mongers" and a paean to the Soviet "international peace movement." He wrote a vocal-symphonic suite, *Winter Bonfire,* which also adopted the realistic and easily assimilable style demanded by the new Soviet esthetics. Both these works were responsible for bringing Prokofiev the Stalin Prize in 1951. To further emphasize Prokofiev's return to the good graces of the authorities, there took place on April 23, 1951, a special concert to celebrate his sixtieth birthday. Prokofiev, who was ill at a resort (he had previously suffered two strokes), could not attend but heard the concert over the radio. When his Seventh Symphony was introduced in Moscow on December 20, 1952, it was hailed by critics and public alike as embodying the greatness of Soviet art. But when this symphony received its American premiere on

April 20, 1953, in Philadelphia, the critics found the work to be generally "mediocre in invention" and without integration.

When Prokofiev visited the United States, before World War II, he was described as follows by Alice Berezowsky in her book, *Duet with Nicky*: "He was tall and bald-headed and looked exactly like a well-to-do business man. His suit was a conservative English tweed; his tie a small patterned foulard. His unremarkable face was clean-shaven. Prokofiev sat eating and talking with a minimum of motion and without changing his poker-face expression. . . . Judged by his looks, Prokofiev might have been the author of the President's Annual Report of the Consolidated Utilities Corporation. There was an air of authority about him and the evidence of seasoned judgment in his remarks. Prokofiev is a man who knows exactly what he wants, formulates his aims with absolute clarity and has the talent, healthy vitality, and capacity for hard work to achieve them."

He has further been described by his friends as a hard-headed and practical man who was always efficient, neat, and punctual. His method of writing music—as reported in *Time* magazine—provided still another insight into his personality: "He composes with the cold matter-of-factness of a mathematician, and keeps stacks of copybooks in which he hoards themes for future compositions. He jumps from bed to jot one down; they occur to him while taking walks, and especially while riding trains. . . . When he has saved up enough little scraps of melody, he works out an idea for a large composition to use them in. . . . He works regularly between the hours of ten and noon every day. When he is seriously at work, he never listens to anybody else's music."

Away from music his principal interest was chess. Occasionally he liked to participate in a game of bridge or, when partners were not available, double solitaire. He did not drink or smoke, but ate a great deal of candy. By a first marriage he had two sons, neither of whom is musical. His second wife was Myra Mendelson, the librettist of *War and Peace*.

Serge Prokofiev died of a stroke in Moscow on March 4, 1953.

MAJOR WORKS:

Ballets—Chout, op. 21, 1921; Le Pas d'Acier, op. 41, 1925; L'Enfant Prodigue, op. 46, 1929; Sur le Borysthène, op. 51, 1930; Romeo and Juliet, op. 64, 1938; Cinderella, 1944; The Stone Flower, 1952.

Chamber Music—Overture on Hebrew Themes, for clarinet, string quartet, and piano, op. 34, 1919; Quintet for Wind and Strings, op. 39, 1924; String Quartet No. 1, op. 50, 1929; Sonata for Two Violins, op. 56, 1932; Sonata for Violin and Piano, op. 80, 1945; String Quartet No. 2, in F major, op. 92, 1941; Sonata for Violin and Piano (or Flute and Piano), in F minor, op. 94, 1944.

Choral Music—Seven, They are Seven, incantantion for tenor, chorus, and orchestra, op. 30, 1917; Mass Songs, op. 68, 1936; Cantata for the Twentieth Anniversary of the October Revolution, op. 74, 1937; Songs of Our Day, op. 76, 1937; Alexander Nevsky, cantata, op. 78, 1939; Ballad of the Unknown Boy, cantata, op. 93, 1944; On Guard for Peace, op. 124, 1950.

Operas—The Gambler, op. 24, 1917 (revised 1928); The Love of Three Oranges, op. 33, 1919; The Flaming Angel, op. 37, 1923; Simeon Kotko, op. 81, 1939; The Convent Wedding, op. 86, 1940; War and Peace, op. 91, 1948; Tale of a Real Man, 1948.

Orchestral Music—Concerto No. 1 in D-flat major, for piano and orchestra, op. 10, 1911; Concerto No. 2 in G minor, for piano and orchestra, op. 16, 1913; Concerto No. 1 in D major, for violin and orchestra, op. 19, 1913; Scythian Suite, op. 20, 1914; Classical Symphony, op. 20, 1914; Concerto No. 3 in C major, for piano and orchestra, op. 26, 1921; Symphony No. 2, op. 40, 1924; Divertimento, op. 43, 1929; Symphony No. 3, op. 44, 1928; Symphony No. 4, op. 47, 1930; Concerto No. 4, for left hand and orchestra, op. 53, 1931; Concerto No. 5 in G major, for piano and orchestra, 1932; Symphonic Song, op. 57, 1933; Concerto for Cello and Orchestra, op. 58, 1938; Lieutenant Kije, suite, op. 60, 1934; Concerto No. 2 in G minor, for violin and orchestra, op. 63, 1935; Romeo and Juliet, three suites, op. 64, 1937; Peter and the Wolf, for narrator and orchestra, op. 67, 1936; Russian Overture, op. 72, 1936; Symphonic Suite: 1941; Symphony No. 5, op. 100, 1944; Ode to the End of the War, op. 105, 1945; Symphony No. 6 in E-flat minor, op. 111, 1947; Symphony No. 7, 1952.

Piano Music—Four Pieces (including Suggestion Diabolique), op. 4, 1912; Toccata, op. 11, 1911; Ten Pieces for the Piano, op. 12, 1913; Sarcasmes, op. 17, 1914; Visions Fugitives, op. 22, 1917; Sonata No. 3 in A minor, op. 28, 1917; Sonata No. 4 in C minor, op. 29, 1917; Four Pieces, op. 32, 1918; Sonata No. 5, op. 38, 1923; Choses en Soi, op. 45, 1928; Six Pieces, op. 52, 1931; Two Sonatinas, op. 54, 1931; Three Pieces, op. 59, 1934; Pensées, op. 64, 1934; Musique d'Enfants, op. 65, 1935; Sonata No. 6, op. 82, 1940; Sonata No. 7, op. 83, 1942; Sonata No. 8, op. 84, 1944.

Vocal Music—The Ugly Duckling, op. 18, 1914; Five Poems, for voice and piano, op. 23, 1915; Five Songs, op. 27, 1916; Five Melodies without Words, op. 35, 1920; Five Songs, op. 36, 1921; Three Melodies to Pushkin's words, op. 73, 1936.

ABOUT:

Ewen, D. (ed.) The Book of Modern Composers; Nestyev, I., Serge Prokofiev: His Musical Life; Nabokov, N., Old Friends and New Music; Musical Quarterly, October 1944; Time, November 19, 1945.

Giacomo Puccini *1858-1924*

GIACOMO PUCCINI, descended from a long line of church musicians, was born in Lucca, Italy, on December 22, 1858. His father, who died when Giacomo was still a child, was the choirmaster and organist of a Lucca church. Since the Puccinis were very poor, after the death of the father, great sacrifices had to be made to ensure Giacomo's early musical education. His first studies in music took place at the Seminary San Michele, where he was an excellent, though frequently mischievous, pupil. Even then his passion was opera. On one occasion he walked thirteen miles to hear a performance of Verdi's *Aïda*. Another time, at the church where he was studying the organ, he horrified the priests by interpolating opera arias in his organ improvisations.

Through a subsidy by Queen Margherita, supplemented by a contribution from his great-uncle, Puccini was able to enter the Milan Conservatory in 1880. "I like Milan," he wrote to his mother. "I am not hungry. I eat a great deal, and I fill up on substantial soup. My appetite is satisfied. In the evenings I go to the Gallery for a stroll, then come home footsore: reaching my room, I do a little counterpoint. I do not play the piano because it is not allowed at night. After that I go to bed, where I read seven or eight pages of a novel. This is my life."

As a Conservatory student, Puccini wrote a symphonic work, *Capriccio Sinfonico,* which was performed at a Conservatory concert and which was subsequently published. One of his teachers, Ponchielli (composer of *La Gioconda*), was convinced that Puccini's gifts belonged in the theatre. He urged the young man to enter a competition for one-act operas then being sponsored by the publisher Sonzogno, and even provided a libretto. Puccini's opera, *Le Villi,* failed to win the prize (Puccini did not even get honorable mention). But it was good enough to be accepted for performance by the Dal Verme

Attilio Badodi
GIACOMO PUCCINI

Theatre in Milan. Its premiere on May 31, 1884, was so successful that La Scala accepted it for the following season and Ricordi published it.

Puccini's second opera, *Edgar,* was a failure when given by La Scala on April 21, 1889. But success returned on February 1, 1893, with the premiere in Turin of *Manon Lescaut* (based on the famous French story of Abbé Prevost). *Manon Lescaut* was a triumph. The audience, as the *Gazzetta del Popolo* reported, was "stunned and overcome by emotion." In performances that followed in London and Paris, *Manon Lescaut* established Puccini's reputation firmly throughout Europe. "Considering the chronological position of the opera," wrote D. C. Parker many years later, "it is surprising that there is so much of the mature Puccini in it."

Now famous, Puccini proceeded to write the first of his unqualified masterworks. Drawing from his own experiences as a bohemian in Milan, and inspired by the sketches of Henri Murger, Puccini completed *La Bohème,* probably his best-loved opera. It was introduced at the Teatro Regio in Turin on February 1, 1896, Toscanini conducting. Strange to report, the audience was at first indifferent to this great work, and the critics unfavorable; Carlo Bersezio of *Stampe* prophesied that the opera "will leave no great trace upon the

Puccini: po͞ot-chĕ′nē

history of our lyric theatre." But a third production of *La Bohème*, in Palermo, was a huge success. From then on—as the opera was seen in the different opera houses of the world—its permanent place in the operatic repertory was assured.

"Puccini has caught the fanciful grace of Murger's style with the dexterity of genius," wrote R. A. Streatfeild. "His music is thoroughly Italian in style, but he never strikes a false note. He dashes off the irresponsible gaiety of the earlier scenes with a touch which though light is always sure, and when the action deepens to tenderness, and even to pathos, he can be serious without falling into sentimentality and impressive without encroaching upon the boundaries of melodrama. *La Bohème* is one of the few operas of recent years which can be described as a masterpiece."

La Tosca came next, presented by the Teatro Constanzi in Rome on January 14, 1900. If the reaction of the audience was not so apathetic as it had been to *La Bohème,* it was surely not enthusiastic, either. Like *La Bohème, La Tosca* had to receive repeated performances before its dramatic and emotional impact was felt by the opera public. But in less than a decade it was seen in most of the opera houses of the world and had become a favorite.

These two operas brought Puccini to a position of first importance among the Italian composers of his day. He was acclaimed as Verdi's successor. He was now famous, rich, idolized. He bought a beautiful villa at Torre del Lago, henceforth his home, where he could indulge his passion for motoring, hunting, and entertaining his many friends.

In 1903, while driving from Lucca to Torre del Lago, Puccini was seriously hurt in an automobile accident. His leg broken, he was confined to an invalid's chair for the next eight months, and he frequently suffered intense pain. His agony, however, did not prevent him from working on a new opera, *Madama Butterfly.* It was performed by La Scala on February 17, 1904, and was one of the greatest failures Puccini experienced in his entire career. Some in the audience disliked the idea of a Japanese play with a Japanese heroine. Others thought the second act too long. Still others considered

Puccini's music bizarre. Puccini withdrew his opera after a single performance and subjected it to extensive revision. It returned to the stage on May 28, 1904, in Brescia, this time to enjoy a triumph of major proportions. Puccini took ten curtain calls.

In 1907 Puccini visited the United States to attend the Metropolitan Opera premiere of *Madama Butterfly.* He arrived in this country on the very evening of a performance of *Manon Lescaut* and could not reach the Metropolitan Opera House until almost the end of the first scene. When the audience learned of his presence, he was given a tremendous ovation. "I have never seen anything like it," he wrote to his publisher. The Metropolitan premiere of *Madama Butterfly* took place on February 11, 1907. After that performance, Puccini was commissioned by the Metropolitan Opera to write a new work for that theatre. Puccini selected as his text *The Girl of the Golden West,* an adaptation of a Bret Harte story, then enjoying a successful run on Broadway. It took him two years to write his opera. He returned to the United States in 1910 to attend its world premiere on December 10. The Metropolitan provided a gala performance. Caruso, Destinn, and Scotti were in the cast; Toscanini conducted. The opera was a major success, but since that time it has been relegated to a second position among Puccini's works.

After a hiatus of seven years, Puccini turned to writing a new opera: *La Rondine (The Swallow),* a comedy. After that came a trilogy of one-act operas which included *Il Tabarro (The Cloak), Suor Angelica (Sister Angelica),* and *Gianni Schicchi.* Puccini's last opera was *Turandot,* which he left unfinished; it was ultimately completed by Franco Alfano.

While working on *Turandot,* Puccini suffered from a throat irritation. The ailment was finally diagnosed as cancer, and Puccini had to go to Brussels for an operation. He suffered a heart attack and died on November 29, 1924. The news of his death reached Rome while a performance of *La Bohème* was being given. The opera was interrupted for the tragic news, after which the orchestra played Chopin's Funeral March. Puccini's body was brought back from Brussels (at government expense) and buried in his native city of Lucca.

Two years after Puccini's death, his opera *Turandot* was presented at La Scala by Toscanini exactly as he had left it—unfinished. Towards the end of the opera, in the middle of a scene, the curtain came down suddenly. Toscanini turned to the orchestra, tears streaming down his cheeks, and announced: "Here the Maestro died." Later performances of *Turandot,* however, were given in the Alfano version.

Ildebrando Pizzetti once referred to Puccini's works as *"opera di arte non grande."* Puccini himself recognized that his art was not on a grand scale. "I love small things," he once said, "and the only music I can or will make is that of small things . . . so long as they are true and full of passion, and humanity, and touch the heart."

Limited though his operas are, they are unquestionably the creations of a master. "There is never anything coarse, vulgar, or effusively banal in his approach," wrote Richard Specht, "but always a noble and fastidious delicacy, the quintessence, so to speak, of exquisite music. . . . His ideas are full of an inimitable elegance, a quivering grace, and a sure feeling for artistic tact and grace which colors even the smallest phrase with personality. . . . He has his own peculiar, unforgettable note, and further, a bitter-sweet, gently irritating aroma that is all his own, not only in his orchestration, but also in pure tone and harmony."

MAJOR WORKS:

Operas—Manon Lescaut, 1893; La Bohème, 1896; La Tosca, 1899; Madama Butterfly, 1903; The Girl of the Golden West, 1910; La Rondine, 1916; Il Tabarro, Suor Angelica, and Gianni Schicchi, three one-act operas, 1918; Turandot (completed by Franco Alfano), 1924.

ABOUT:

Del Fiorentino, D., Immortal Bohemian: An Intimate Memoir of Giacomo Puccini; Marek, G., Puccini: A Biography; Puccini, G., Letters (ed. by G. Adami).

Henri Rabaud *1873-1949*

HENRI RABAUD, the son of a professional cellist, was born in Paris on November 10, 1873. He studied at the Paris Conservatory, where his teachers included

Gedalge and Massenet. In 1894 he won the Prix de Rome. After the three-year stay in Rome, he founded orchestras in Rome and Vienna devoted to performances of French music.

He wrote his first major work in 1895, the Symphony No. 1, in E minor. Four years after that came his first success, a tone-poem, *La Procession Nocturne.* Based on a portion of the Faust legend, retold in a poem of Nikolaus Lenau, Rabaud's work is a sensitive portrait of Faust, alone on a midsummer night, watching a religious procession. It is impressionistic in its writing, outstanding both for its subtle atmosphere and its structural logic. Introduced by the Colonne Orchestra in Paris on January 15, 1899, it was an immediate success and has since that time become the most frequently performed of Rabaud's orchestral works.

Rabaud produced another major work, this time for the operatic stage. It was the delightful comic opera *Marouf,* based on a story in *The Thousand and One Nights.* When introduced at the Paris Opéra on May 15, 1914 (shortly before World War I), it was immediately acclaimed. Camille Bellaigue said it "was the last smile of French music before the war." Much of the charm of Rabaud's score comes from the subtle injection of oriental flavors. One of the most effective moments of the entire opera is found in the sensuous oriental ballet of the

HENRI RABAUD

Rabaud: ră-bō′

third act. *Marouf* was first seen at the Metropolitan Opera in New York on December 19, 1917.

Rabaud has also had a notable career as conductor. In 1908 he joined the conductorial staff of the Paris Opéra, rising to the position of principal conductor in 1914. Two years later, he became musical director of the Concerts du Conservatoire, holding this post with great honor for many years. In 1918 he succeeded Karl Muck as conductor of the Boston Symphony Orchestra when Muck was interned as an enemy alien. After returning to Paris, in 1920, Rabaud succeeded Gabriel Fauré as director of the Paris Conservatory. He also conducted frequently at the Opéra Comique.

Rabaud had elegance of style, refinement, good taste, and, on occasion, wit. He combined, as André Cœuroy once put it, "intelligence and flexibility." His music, Cœuroy added, was the product of a "penetrating mind, energetic without rigidity, bold without braggadocio, marvelously balanced, and certain enough of its own strength to indulge in every curiosity."

Rabaud died in Paris after a prolonged illness on September 12, 1949.

MAJOR WORKS:

Choral Music—Job, oratorio, 1900; Psaume IV, for soloists, chorus and orchestra, 1901; Hymne à la France Éternelle, 1916; L'Été.

Operas—La Fille de Roland, 1904; Le Premier Glaive, 1908; Marouf, 1914; Antoine et Cléopâtre, 1917; L'Appel de la Mer, 1922; Roland et le Mauvais Garçon, 1933.

Orchestral Music—Symphony No. 1, in E minor, 1895; La Procession Nocturne, 1899; Symphony No. 2, 1899; Eclogue, 1899; Divertissement sur des Chansons Russes, 1899; Concertino for Violin and Orchestra; Allegro de Concert, for violin and orchestra.

ABOUT:

Hill, E. B., Modern French Music.

Serge Rachmaninoff *1873-1943*

(*See American Composers Today*)

Maurice Ravel *1875-1937*

JOSEPH MAURICE RAVEL was born in the town of Ciboure, in the Basque region of France, on March 7, 1875. While still an infant he was brought to Paris, where the Ravels made their home. Stimulated by his father, a lover of art, Maurice started studying music early. His first teacher was Henri Ghys, perhaps best remembered as the composer of *Amaryllis*. Lessons began in 1882, and were later supplemented with harmony instruction from Charles-René at the Lycée.

Convinced of Ravel's talent, Ghys and Charles-René set out to prepare him for the Conservatory. He passed his entrance examinations easily in 1889. The next fifteen years were spent at the Conservatory with such teachers as Pessard, Gedalge, Charles de Bériot, and Gabriel Fauré. Though Ravel respected the classical rules taught him, and was a brilliant student, he did not hesitate to indulge in harmonic explorations beyond the periphery established by the text-book. While still in his first years at the Conservatory, he met Erik Satie, whose iconoclastic thinking had a profound effect. Ravel, too, was to be rebellious in his efforts at composition. The *Sérénade Grotesque* and the *Minuet,* both for the piano, were obviously patterned after Satie's unorthodox style.

In 1898 Ravel found a sympathetic teacher in Fauré. Faure understood Ravel's restlessness and impatience with tradition and encouraged him in his individual approaches. Ravel's music now showed increasing boldness and independence. Two of these works were publicly performed in Paris at concerts of the Société Nationale de Musique between 1898 and 1899: *Sites Auriculaires,* for two pianos, and the orchestral overture, *Shéhérazade*. And both works were dismal failures.

Ravel's first important works were not slow in coming. In 1902 Ricardo Viñes introduced at a concert of the Société Nationale de Musique two Ravel masterpieces for the piano: the *Pavane pour une Infante Défunte* and *Jeux d'Eau*. They were successfully received. In 1904 the Quartet in F, introduced by the Heyman Quartet, was an even greater triumph. Roland-Manuel described the Quartet as "a miracle of grace and tenderness, a marvelous jewel of polyphony which knew how to submit to the requirements of the classical form without manifesting any of its restrictions." Ravel

Ravel: ră-věl′

had come to the end of his apprenticeship; and he had already become famous.

In 1905 Ravel made a fourth attempt to win the Prix de Rome and failed. Many musicians and musicologists, including Romain Rolland, felt strongly that Ravel deserved the award, that indeed he was now the most gifted of the younger composers in France; they violently condemned the judges for partiality to other and less worthy men and for prejudice to Ravel. The battle over Ravel grew so violent—fought in newspapers and pamphlets—that the director of the Paris Conservatory, Dubois, had to resign, to be succeeded by Gabriel Fauré.

This was the first of two major battles fought over Ravel in Paris. The second came in 1907. By 1907 Ravel had written *Miroirs*, a set of delicate impressionistic pictures for the piano. The influence of Debussy upon *Miroirs* and other Ravel works was inescapable, even down to Ravel's choice of titles. Some musicians in Paris—failing to perceive Ravel's original approaches to impressionism—accused him of plagiarism. After the premiere of Ravel's *Histoires Naturelles* on January 12, 1907, his accusers united in their attacks. But, fortunately, other critics, like M. D. Calvocoressi and Georges Jean-Aubry, rose to Ravel's defense. They pointed out the differences, rather than the similarities, between Ravel and Debussy—Ravel's wit and masculinity and intellectualism, which set his music sharply apart from that of Debussy. In short, these critics insisted that though Ravel had been influenced by Debussy, he was no imitator, but a profoundly original creator.

The two vigorous battles involving Ravel made him one of France's most provocative and highly publicized composers; only Debussy was now more famous than he. Ravel was also to prove himself to be one of France's greatest creative figures. One masterwork followed another in rapid succession. In 1907 came two compositions interpreting Ravel's lifelong fascination for Spain, its song and dance: the *Rapsodie Espagnole*, for orchestra, and the effervescent one-act comedy opera, *L'Heure Espagnole*. This was followed a year later by the suite *Ma Mère l'Oye (Mother Goose)*, and *Gaspard de la Nuit*, for piano. And in 1911 he completed both the *Valses Nobles et Sen-*

Photo-Lipnitzki

MAURICE RAVEL

timentales, for piano, and what was his crowning achievement up to that time, the ballet *Daphnis et Chloé*. This last work, which had been commissioned by Serge Diaghilev, the impresario of the Ballet Russe, was introduced in Paris on June 8, 1912, with Nijinsky and Karsavina. The reaction to Ravel's music was mixed, but even those who praised it failed to recognize its importance as one of Ravel's greatest creations. As Edward Burlingame Hill wrote about this music: "He has attained large contours, breadth of mood and impressive climaxes with the same continuity of development and richness of detail as in his shorter pieces. Throughout, the music achieves a graphic delineation of character, and furthermore has a plastic quality which incites mimetic response." This score is most familiar to concertgoers through two orchestral suites adapted by the composer.

During World War I Ravel served at the front in a motor convoy. One of the first works he wrote after these war experiences (which affected his sensitive nervous system profoundly) was a piano suite, *Tombeau de Couperin*, dedicated to his friends who fell in battle.

When the war ended, Ravel bought a villa at Montfort-l'Amaury, in the Île-de-France region. He was as proud of it as of one of his major compositions, and took infinite pains with its decoration and furnishings. He never married, and it was said that his villa was mother, wife, and child to him all in one.

Ravel visited the United States for the first time in 1928 for a concert tour in programs comprising his works. His first American appearance took place in Boston, with the Boston Symphony Orchestra, on January 12, 1928. Returning to France, Ravel wrote what is undoubtedly his most popular work, *Boléro*, commissioned by the dancer, Ida Rubinstein. Built on a single theme, *Boléro* was a veritable *tour de force* of instrumentation; its mounting tension, achieved through a gradual increase of the dynamics and enrichment of the instrumentation, was to have a powerful impact on audiences. Introduced by Ida Rubinstein on November 20, 1928, it was a sensation. After that, *Boléro* took the music world by storm, even though it was presented at symphony concerts without the benefit of the accompanying dance. In America, introduced by the New York Philharmonic-Symphony under Toscanini, and thereafter played by every major orchestra, it assumed the status of a genuine "hit." Six different recordings appeared simultaneously; it was played in moviehouses and over the radio in its original form and in many transcriptions and arrangements. It was used in a Broadway revue and its title was bought for a Hollywood movie.

Ravel's last two works were two concertos for the piano, one for the left hand alone in somewhat of a jazz idiom, and the other for piano and orchestra, in the classic style of Mozart and Saint-Saëns. Ravel himself regarded these compositions as the finest of his career.

After 1932, Ravel's health disintegrated alarmingly as a result of an injury sustained in a taxi accident. He suffered intense pain, and before long began to lose his powers of coordination. It was finally decided that a brain operation was imperative. Ravel never regained consciousness after this operation. He died in a private hospital in Paris on December 19, 1937.

Ravel once expressed his musical credo to this writer in the following words: "I belong to no school of music and adhere rigidly to no current musical styles. I try to create beautiful ideas in music, and attempt to develop them to their logical, perhaps inevitable, end. Great music must always come from the heart; great music must always be beautiful."

A fastidious, even exquisite, workman, Ravel continually produced musical beauty with sensibility, grace, and refinement. He had an extraordinary virtuosity in composition. His music was always the last word in skillful construction. But it was, surely, much more than skillful technique. He had a manner and a charm all his own. He was perhaps at his most delightful and original in the make-believe world of enchantment—of fairies and animals and puppets and children, as in the *Mother Goose Suite* or the ballet *L'Enfant et les Sortilèges*. But whether he wrote in this vein or in a Spanish idiom or in the rhythm and spirit of the Viennese waltz, he was a creator who could always give voice to an expressive beauty. He was, as Guido Pannain put it so well, "the spiritual heir to the last half-century's poetic feeling in France, and at the same time . . . he is a connoisseur of contemporary life, of that Parisian quality of richness and evanescence in thought."

In a biography of Ravel, Madeleine Goss presents the following personal picture of the composer: "Ravel was . . . precise in every detail. Small, both in stature and in build, his slender figure was always dressed in the latest and most irreproachable style. No effort was too great for him to make in achieving the effect he sought, whether this was a matter of matching ties, socks, and handkerchiefs to a certain suit, or of working out the intricate detail of a composition. . . .

"As a whole, his life was colorless, almost devoid of so-called human interest; no violent emotions or overwhelming passions clouded the clear mirror which reflected his art. . . .

"As a story-teller, Maurice Ravel . . . was clever and amusing; he expressed himself well, with simple elegance and a certain dramatic ability. Everything he did, even to the relating of anecdotes, was influenced by his desire for perfection. He had an unusual gift for imitation, and could reproduce the call of birds and animals in a singularly realistic way. If someone paid him a compliment he would try to conceal his pleasure and embarrassment by turning aside with a humorous bird or animal cry. . . . With Debussy he had a common trait in his passion for cats. Ravel's innate reserve and shyness left him only when he was with children or with animals."

MAJOR WORKS:

Ballets—Daphnis et Chloé, 1911; L'Enfant et les Sortilèges, 1925.

Chamber Music—Quartet in F, for strings, 1903; Introduction and Allegro, for harp, string quartet, flute, and clarinet, 1906; Piano Trio in A minor, 1915; Tzigane, for violin and piano (also violin and orchestra), 1924; Sonata for Violin and Piano, 1927.

Opera—L'Heure Espagnole, 1907.

Orchestral Music—Rapsodie Espagnole, 1907; Daphnis et Chloé, two suites, 1911; Alborada del Gracioso (also for piano), 1912; Ma Mère l'Oye, suite (also for piano, four hands), 1912; La Valse, 1920; Boléro, 1928; Concerto in G major, for piano and orchestra, 1931; Concerto for Left Hand and Orchestra, 1931; Don Quichotte à Dulcinée, for baritone and small orchestra, 1932.

Piano Music—Sites Auriculaires, for two pianos, 1896; Pavane pour une Infante Défunte, 1899; Jeux d'Eau, 1901; Miroirs, 1905; Sonatine, 1905; Gaspard de la Nuit, 1908; Menuet sur le Nom d'Haydn, 1909; Valses Nobles et Sentimentales, 1911; Prélude, 1913; Le Tombeau de Couperin (also for orchestra), 1917; Sur le Nom de Gabriel Fauré, 1922.

Vocal Music—Shéhérazade, for voice and piano (also orchestra), 1903; Le Noël de Jouets, 1905; Cinq Mélodies Populaires Grecques, 1907; Les Grands Vents Venus d'Outre-mer, 1906; Histoires Naturelles, 1906; Quatre Chansons Populaires, 1910; Deux Mélodies Hébraïques, 1914; Ronsard à Son Âme, 1924; Rêves, 1927.

ABOUT:

Brook, D., Five Great French Composers; Demuth, N., Maurice Ravel; Goss, M., The Life of Maurice Ravel; Roland-Manuel, Maurice Ravel; Seroff, V. I., Maurice Ravel; La Revue Musicale, December 1938.

Alan Rawsthorne *1905-*

ALAN RAWSTHORNE was born in Haslingden, Lancashire, England, on May 2, 1905. Since his original intention was to become a dentist, he did not begin the study of music seriously until he reached his early twenties. In 1926 he entered the Royal Manchester College of Music, where he studied the piano, cello, and composition for four years. After that he took private

lessons in piano with Egon Petri. His studies ended, he was appointed, in 1932, to the staff of Dartington Hall, in South Devon, where for two years his varied musical duties included the writing of music for the School of Dance-Mime. In 1935 he settled in London and concentrated on composition. Three years later he first attracted attention when his Theme and Variations, for two violins, was introduced at the International Society for Contemporary Music Festival in London, on June 18, 1938. Three subsequent festivals of this Society introduced other Rawsthorne works: the *Symphonic Studies,* for orchestra, in 1939; *Cortèges,* for orchestra, in 1946; and the Concerto for String Orchestra, in 1950.

During World War II Rawsthorne served in the British army, his principal activity being the writing of music for army films. However, he found the time to do serious writing, too. He began the Concerto for Violin and Orchestra in 1940, but lost the sketches during an air raid. He had to reconstruct what he had thus far written, but his war duties delayed the final product, which was not completed until 1947. The composer explained that his intention in this work "is to combine the rhapsodical style of expression with the brilliance of a solo instrument." Hubert Foss described the work as "the now gentle, now disturbing, now friendly, now menacing Violin Concerto." It

ALAN RAWSTHORNE

was introduced at the Cheltenham Festival in 1948 and was dedicated to William Walton; in connection with this dedication it is interesting to remark that Rawsthorne quoted in his Concerto a theme from Walton's *Belshazzar's Feast.*

Several other major works engaged Rawsthorne during the war years. One of these was the *Cortèges,* for orchestra, first heard at a Promenade concert in London in 1945, before being presented at the International Society for Contemporary Music Festival. Another work was the Concerto for Piano and Orchestra, actually a prewar creation, but now revised and rescored. The Concerto was given in 1942 at a Promenade concert in London, with Louis Kentner as soloist and the composer conducting; the composer was given a forty-eight-hour leave from his army base to fulfill this engagement.

Later important compositions by Rawsthorne include the Symphony, the premiere of which was given by the Royal Philharmonic Society of London in 1950, and the Concerto No. 2, for Piano and Orchestra, heard at the Royal Festival Hall in London in June, 1951. Hubert Foss wrote that the Second Piano Concerto "exhibits the full range of Rawsthorne's musical mind in its present maturity and middle life. It is essentially conceived for the piano, with orchestral backing—a prolonged song for the pianist, with light and ingenious writing for the orchestra."

Though the severity of Rawsthorne's style and the freedom of his tonality suggest a disrespect for tradition, he owes a considerable debt to the music of the past. Wilfrid Mellers remarks that, from a formal standpoint, Rawsthorne "is unequivocally a baroque composer with his roots in the formal conceptions of Corelli and Bach. . . . His notions of form are architectural and decorative and have two main prototypes in the baroque music of the seventeenth and early eighteenth centuries—the variation and the concerto grosso, the latter comprising toccata technique . . . cantilena or aria, fugal elements related to the old fantasia technique, and the formalism of the dance. . . .

"While the chaconne of the First Piano Concerto is naturally the clearest example of Rawsthorne's connection with the baroque technique, the two-violin Variations, the string-quartet Variations, and even . . . the Symphonic Studies, are more freely based on the same notion of the variation form. In all, the principle of development is cumulative over an harmonic skeleton that is hardly more than latent; and in all, it is this skeleton which gives such tautness to the often very passionate melodic and figurative elements.

"About the nature of Rawsthorne's aria technique . . . his aria-like movements manifest always his combination of lyrical fervor with balanced architectural discipline."

Rawsthorne is married to the concert violinist Jessie Hinchliffe.

MAJOR WORKS:

Chamber Music—Theme and Variations, for two violins, 1937; String Quartet, 1939; Clarinet Quartet, 1948; Sonata for Cello and Piano, 1949.

Orchestral Music—Concerto for Clarinet and Orchestra, 1936; Chamber Cantata, for voice, harpsichord, and strings, 1937; Symphonic Studies, 1938; Concerto No. 1 for Piano and Orchestra, 1942; Street Corner Overture, 1944; Cortèges, 1945; Prisoners March, 1946; Concerto for Oboe and Orchestra, 1947; Concerto for Violin and Orchestra, 1947; Concerto for String Orchestra, 1949; Symphony, 1949; Concerto No. 2 for Piano and Orchestra, 1951; Concertante Pastorale, for flute, horn, and strings, 1951; A Canticle of Man, for baritone, chorus, flute, and strings, 1952.

Piano Music—Bagatelles, 1938; The Creel, for two pianos, 1940; Sonatina, 1949.

ABOUT:

Bacharach, A. L. (ed.) British Music of Our Time; Mellers, W., Studies in Contemporary Music; Monthly Musical Record (London), February 1948; Musical America, February 1952; Musical Quarterly, April 1949.

Max Reger *1873-1916*

MAX REGER was born in Brand, Bavaria, on March 19, 1873, the son of a schoolteacher. He was so precocious in music that inevitable comparison was made with the child Mozart. As an infant he revealed perfect pitch and a retentive memory. He was only six years old when he heard a march played by a band passing his window and repeated the entire piece from memory on the piano.

He was first taught the organ and harmony by his father, and after that the piano

Reger: rä'gĕr

by Adalbert Lindner. In his boyhood Reger made several appearances as pianist in local school auditoriums, and when he was thirteen he officiated as church organist. He heard an orchestra for the first time in his fifteenth year, when, on a visit to Bayreuth, he attended several Wagnerian music dramas. That experience was so thrilling that then and there he decided to become a composer. He began his career as composer with some songs and chamber music.

But since he had decided to make teaching his profession, he entered the Royal Training School, where he successfully passed the examinations in 1889. Some of his musical works came to the attention of the eminent musicologist, Hugo Riemann. Convinced of Reger's creative talent, Riemann convinced Reger to give up the idea of becoming a teacher and to specialize in music. On Riemann's advice, Reger entered the Sondershausen Conservatory in 1890 and studied composition, piano, and violin. When, one year later, Riemann left for Wiesbaden, Reger followed him there, lived with him, studied privately under him, and profited by his criticism and advice. In Wiesbaden, Reger began his long and fruitful career as teacher of music when he joined the faculty of the Wiesbaden Conservatory in the piano department.

In 1896 Reger had to abandon music to enter military service. The rigors of military duty completely undermined his sensitive health. For a while he was confined to a hospital. Released from the army, he returned to his father's house, where his health was so poor that for three years he required the continued attention of a physician. These were years of fruitful creation. Reger completed numerous songs and works for various chamber-music groups.

In 1901 he settled in Munich, where he became a teacher at the Academy, and where he devoted himself to conducting and concert appearances as pianist. These activities, and his creative work, destroyed his sensitive constitution. During a concert in April, 1906, he suffered a slight paralytic stroke which affected his right side. A rest cure at Prien, on Lake Chiem, rehabilitated his health sufficiently to allow him to travel to Russia and appear in St. Petersburg as conductor and pianist.

In 1907 Reger was appointed music director at the University of Leipzig. He held this post only for a single year. But to the end of his life he retained his appointment to the faculty at the Leipzig Conservatory, which also came in 1907. He received the title of professor from the King of Saxony, and after that honorary degrees from the universities of Jena and Berlin.

Though he had been extraordinarily prolific until 1907, he produced his most important works between that year and the time of his death. They included the Concerto in F minor, for piano and orchestra, the *Variations and Fugue on a Theme of J. A. Hiller*, *Romantic Suite*, *Variations and Fugue on a Theme by Mozart*, *Four Tone-Poems after Böcklin*, and the *Variations and Fugue on a Theme by Beethoven*, all for orchestra. He also produced notable songs, chamber music, and piano compositions.

Reger was primarily a neo-baroque composer who preferred writing in sixteenth and seventeenth century forms (toccatas, passacaglias, fugues, variations) in an appropriate contrapuntal technique.) He had a phenomenal technique which enabled him to construct monuments out of simple materials, through the fullest resources of harmony, counterpoint, rhythm, and instrumentation. One program annotator has described him as "probably the most learned practitioner in the field of musical theory to have

MAX REGER

appeared since Sebastian Bach." His music is usually complex in structure, detailed in its writing, and highly academic in its approach. It provides more intellectual than emotional pleasure. Reger was perhaps best in the variation form, which he favored, and in which his skill in transforming musical ideas had a virtuoso quality. The most frequently heard of his works is in this form —the *Variations and Fugue on a Theme by Mozart*, a series of nine variations and fugue on the opening melody of Mozart's A major Piano Sonata (K. 331) which Reger originally wrote for two pianos and later orchestrated. Reger himself directed the orchestral premiere of this work on February 5, 1915, in Berlin.

"He created problems and found their solutions," wrote André Cœuroy of Reger's music. "He personified abstract music; he was the man of Bach's polyphony, and of old forms brought back to life."

He was apostle of abstract, pure music. Nevertheless, in the last years of his life he produced several significant works that were either pictorial or programmatic. The best of these was the *Four Tone-Poems after Böcklin*. This work was a musical interpretation of four paintings by Arnold Böcklin. It is interesting to remark that one of the paintings that inspired Reger was also the source of a celebrated tone poem by Serge Rachmaninoff, *The Isle of the Dead*. Reger directed the world premiere of his *Four Tone-Poems* in Essen on October 12, 1913.

In 1911 Reger was appointed conductor of the famous Meiningen Orchestra which had previously been directed by Hans von Bülow and Richard Strauss. When war broke out in Europe, in 1914, Reger tried to enlist in the army but was turned down because of his poor health. He went to live in Jena, devoting himself to prolific composition, and continuing his duties at the Leipzig Conservatory and as a concert pianist. He died suddenly of a heart attack while on a brief visit to Leipzig, on May 11, 1916. He was found dead in bed, a cigar in his teeth, a newspaper in his hands.

Adolf Busch, the famous violinist, who knew Reger well, described him as a "humorous, generous, impulsive man who could not bear restraint or hear of anyone being oppressed. He was a poor business man and all his life struggled against the habit of drink. When he tried to cut down he at least had to go through the motions of drinking. He would drink eight cups of bouillon as he sat talking. Once he got sick on too much lemonade."

MAJOR WORKS:

Chamber Music—String Quartet in G minor, op. 54a; String Quartet in A major, op. 54b; Piano Quintet No. 2, in C minor, op. 64; Sonata in C major, for violin and piano, op. 72; String Quartet in D major, op. 74; Sonata in F major, for cello and piano, op. 78; Sonata in F-sharp minor, for violin and piano, op. 84; Sonata in B-flat, for clarinet and piano, op. 107; String Quartet in E-flat major, op. 109; Piano Quartet in D minor, op. 113; Sonata in A minor, for cello and piano, op. 116; String Sextet in F major, op. 118; String Quartet in F-sharp major, op. 121; Sonata in E minor, for violin and piano, op. 122; String Quartet in A minor, op. 133; Sonata in C minor, for violin and piano, op. 139; Trio for Strings, op. 141b, Clarinet Quintet, op. 146.

Choral Music—Gesang der Verklärten, op. 71; Chorales, op. 79; Psalm 100, op. 106; Motetten, op. 110; Die Nonnen, op. 112; Die Weihe der Nacht, op. 119; Hömischer Triumphgesang, op. 126; 8 Sacred Songs, op. 138; Der Einsiedler, op. 144a.

Orchestral Music—Variations and Fugue on a Theme by Beethoven (also for two pianos), op. 86; Sinfonietta (also for piano four-hands), op. 90; Suite in the Old Style (also for violin and piano), op. 93; Serenade (also for piano four hands), op. 95; Variations and Fugue on a Theme by J. A. Hiller, op. 100; Concerto in A major, for violin and piano, op. 101; Symphonic Prologue to a Tragedy, op. 108; Concerto in F minor, for piano and orchestra, op. 114; Eine Lustspiel Ouverture, op. 120; Concerto in the Old Style, op. 123; Romantic Suite, op. 125; Four Tone-Poems after Böcklin, op. 128; Ballet Suite, op. 130; Variations and Fugue on a Theme by Mozart (also for two pianos), op. 132; Vaterländische Ouverture, op. 140.

Organ Music—Chorale Fantasia on Wie Schön Leucht't Uns der Morgenstern (orchestrated by Busch), op. 40; Sonata in D minor, op. 60; 12 Monologues, op. 63; 12 Pieces, op. 65; 52 Easy Chorale Preludes, op. 67; 10 Stücke, op. 69; Variations and Fugue on an Original Theme, op. 73; 13 Preludes, op. 79b; 4 Preludes and Fugues, op. 85; Suite in G minor, op. 92; Introduction, Passacaglia and Fugue, op. 127; 9 Pieces, op. 129; 30 Little Chorale Preludes, op. 135a; Fantasy and Fugue in D minor, op. 135b; 7 Pieces, op. 145.

Piano Music—Silhouetten, op. 53; 6 Burlesken, for four hands, op. 58; Ten Little Pieces, op. 79a; Variations and Fugue on a Theme by Bach, op. 81; Aus Meinem Tagebuche, op. 82; 4 Sonatinas, op. 89; Introduction, Passacaglia and Fugue, for two pianos, op. 96; 6 Preludes and Fugues, op. 99; Episodes, two books, op. 115; Variations and Fugue on a Theme by Telemann, op. 134; Träume am Kamin, op. 143.

Vocal Music—More than 250 songs; duets for soprano and alto; An die Hoffnung, for alto and orchestra, op. 124; Hymnus der Liebe, for alto or bass and orchestra, op. 136.

ABOUT:

Hasse, K., Max Reger; Isler, E., Max Reger; Lindner, A., Max Reger; Reger, E., Mein Leben für und mit Max Reger; Monthly Musical Record (London), July 1916; Musical Times (London), June 1925.

Ottorino Respighi *1879-1936*

OTTORINO RESPIGHI, who was born in Bologna on July 9, 1879, came from a musical family. His grandfather had been violinist and organist in a Bologna church; his father taught piano at the Liceo Musicale.

Ottorino's father taught him the elements of music. After this, Respighi entered the Bologna Liceo, a pupil of Federico Sarti in violin and Luigi Torchi and Giuseppe Martucci in composition. He was graduated in 1899 with a diploma in violin-playing. But he had already proven his creative talent: an orchestral work, *Symphonic Variations,* was performed at the Liceo and was highly praised.

A period of travel followed Respighi's graduation from the Liceo. For a while, he lived in St. Petersburg, where he studied composition with Rimsky-Korsakov and played in the orchestra of the St. Petersburg Opera. After that, he visited Berlin to study composition with Max Bruch. His studies ended, Respighi began his professional career by giving violin recitals and playing the viola in the Mugellini Quartet between the years of 1903 and 1908.

But his main interest, all this while, was composition, and important performances of major works encouraged him in this direction. In 1902 his Concerto for Piano and Orchestra was heard in Bologna; on March 12, 1905, his opera, *Re Enzo,* was introduced, also in Bologna. On January 6, 1905, his *Notturno,* for orchestra, was performed in New York City.

His first crowning success as a composer came on March 11, 1917, when the Augusteo Orchestra in Rome gave the premiere of his tone poem, *Fontane di Roma (The Fountains of Rome).* In this set of four nature pictures Respighi revealed for the first time a pronounced gift for pictorial writing. Respighi completed in 1924 a second set of Roman pictures, this time entitled *Pini di*

OTTORINO RESPIGHI

Roma (The Pines of Rome), introduced by the Augusteo Orchestra in Rome on December 14, 1924. Here, Respighi was no longer interested in nature portraits; his aim was to express memories and visions aroused by familiar Roman scenes. A third series of Roman pictures, *Feste Romane (Roman Festivals),* was written in 1928, and given its first performance by the New York Philharmonic-Symphony Orchestra under Toscanini on March 17 of that year. In this symphonic trilogy about Rome, Respighi "realized a personal form of symphonic poem" — so wrote G. A. Luciani—"in which the descriptive and colorful element blends intimately with the lyrical and sentimental element, and in a line which persistently maintains its classicism in spite of a very modern technique."

Vivid pictorialism, calling for the fullest resources of modern orchestration, is only a single facet of Respighi's music. He has also written in a neo-classical vein. In many important works Respighi employed old modes and plain chants within classical structures. He wrote a Piano Concerto in the Mixolydian mode; and a Violin Concerto utilizing Gregorian chants. Other compositions rooted in the past are two series of *Old Airs and Dances for the Lute,* transcribed by him for orchestra, and the orchestral suite *The Birds,* based on pieces by such old masters as Pasquini, Jacques de Gallot, and

Respighi: rä-spē′ge

Rameau. Whether he wrote orchestral music in the harmonic and rhythmic and instrumental language of the twentieth century, or music dependent on styles and techniques of a distant past, Respighi was an important creative figure who helped to bring about in his native land a renaissance of symphonic music.

Despite his emphasis on orchestral music, Respighi did not abandon opera. After his apprenticeship as an opera composer, he produced a notable work, *Belfagor,* given by La Scala on April 26, 1923. Other successful operas followed, including *La Campana Sommersa (The Sunken Bell), La Fiamma (The Flame),* and *Maria Egiziaca (Mary of Egypt).* In his dramatic works, Respighi carried on the traditions of his predecessors, notably Verdi.

Respighi had a long and distinguished career as a teacher. In 1913 he was appointed professor of composition at the Santa Cecilia Academy in Rome. Ten years after that he was appointed its director, in succession to Enrico Bossi. He stayed in this directorial post only two years, preferring to concentrate on composition; but he continued to teach composition. In 1932 he was appointed to the Royal Academy of Italy.

He visited the United States several times. The first trip took place during the winter of 1925-1926, when he toured the country extensively in performances of his works; his American debut took place in New York City on December 31, 1925, when he appeared as soloist in his Piano Concerto. In 1928 he came a second time to attend the Metropolitan Opera presentation of his opera *The Sunken Bell,* and in 1932 he returned to hear Toscanini give the world premiere of *Mary of Egypt.*

In 1933 Respighi was one of ten leading Italian composers to sign a manifesto condemning modern music for its cerebralism and avoidance of "human content."

In 1936 Respighi was stricken by a heart attack. Though sick in bed, he worked on the orchestration of his last work, the one-act opera *Lucrezia* (which had to be finished by his widow, Elsa). He died in Rome on April 18, 1936, his funeral attended by most of the leading Italian musicians, and by the King of Italy, and Premier Mussolini.

MAJOR WORKS:

Ballets—Boutique Fantasque (based on Rossini melodies), 1919; Scherzo Veneziano, choreographic comedy, 1920.

Chamber Music—String Quartet in D major, 1907; Sonata in B minor, for violin and piano, 1917; Sonata No. 3 for Violin and Piano, 1919; Doric Quartet, 1924; Concerto a Cinque, for oboe, trumpet, double bass, and piano, 1933; Piano Quintet, 1935.

Choral Music—La Primavera, lyric poem, for soloists, chorus, and orchestra, 1923.

Operas—Re Enzo, 1905; Semirama, 1910; Belfagor, 1923; La Campana Sommersa, 1927; Maria Egiziaca, 1932; La Fiamma, 1933; Lucrezia, 1936.

Orchestral Music—Fountains of Rome, symphonic poem, 1917; Old Airs and Dances for the Lute, two series, 1917, 1924; Dance of the Gnomes, 1920; Concerto Gregoriano, for violin and orchestra, 1921; Concerto in the Mixolydian Mode, for piano and orchestra, 1924; Pines of Rome, symphonic poem, 1924; Church Windows, four symphonic impressions, 1927; Trittico Botticelliano, for small orchestra, 1927; The Birds, suite, 1927; Toccata, for piano and orchestra, 1928; Roman Festivals, symphonic poem, 1929; Metamorphosen, modi XII, theme and variations, 1930; Impressioni Brasiliane, 1931; Poema Autunnale for violin and orchestra, 1932; Concerto for Oboe, Horn, Violin, Double-Bass and String Orchestra, 1934.

ABOUT:

Ewen, D., The Complete Book of 20th Century Music.

Knudåge Riisager 1897-

KNUDÅGE RIISAGER, one of Denmark's most important composers, was born in Port Kunda, in Estonia, on March 6, 1897. His father was a successful engineer. In 1900 the Riisagers returned to Denmark, where Knudåge received his early education. He studied political economy at the University of Copenhagen, receiving his Bachelor of Arts degree in 1921. He received his musical training from various teachers: Otto Malling, director of the Copenhagen Conservatory; Peder Gram, a well-known composer; and Peder Möller, a violin virtuoso. Riisager's first significant work was a String Quartet, introduced by the Peder Möller Quartet on November 10, 1919.

After being graduated from the University of Copenhagen, Riisager went to Paris to continue his music study with Paul Le Flem and Albert Roussel and to absorb the newer tendencies in French music. He visited Paris twice more, returning from his third stay in the French capital a musical

Riisager: rē′sä-ēr

revolutionary both in his compositions and in his critical writings—a passionate advocate of all the new tendencies. At first, he aroused considerable opposition among leading Danish musicians, all of whom were faithful to the accepted musical traditions. It was some years before his progressive attitudes were acceptable.

Beginning with the *Introduzione di Traverso* and the Symphony No. 1, both completed in 1925, Riisager used polytonality and polyrhythm. This music was complex in design and acrid in style, and it failed to gain an appreciative audience. But the *Variations on a Theme by Mézangeau,* introduced in Copenhagen in 1926, was praised. And the Piano Sonata, heard at the International Society for Contemporary Music Festival in 1930, was a success.

Meanwhile, Riisager was earning his living as a government official. In 1926 he became secretary of the Ministry of Finance, rising to the position of chief of section in 1939. He resigned in 1950 to devote himself entirely to music.

In 1931 Riisager won the Ancker Endowment, which enabled him to visit Leipzig and study counterpoint with Hermann Grabner. Elements of baroque writing now penetrated his austere style, though the advanced tendencies were not abandoned. Among the important works completed after his Leipzig visit was a ballet, *Qarrtsiluni,* introduced as an orchestral suite in 1939, and presented in its original version at the Royal Danish Opera in 1942. The term "Qarrtsiluni" is from the Eskimo language meaning "something that is about to burst." The ballet text was also of Greenland origin, based on *The Gift of the Feast,* by the arctic explorer Knud Rasmussen. In his score, Riisager combined primitive rhythms with sophisticated harmonies and orchestration; the music is at turns demoniac in its strength and ecstatic in its intensity. "This ballet," wrote Peter William, "is one of the most original and thrilling works I have seen in years . . . perhaps the most exciting work in the whole [Danish] repertory."

A strong national feeling pervaded Riisager's music during the Nazi occupation of Denmark. After World War II, he wrote a stirring *Danish Hymn* to a sixteenth century text; a *Summer Rhapsody,* based on Danish

KNUDAGE RIISAGER

folk melodies; and a national opera buffa, *Susanne.* "Such a change of style," wrote Sigurd Berg, "does not necessarily have to be an indication of artistic cleavage, but may be regarded as a slowly developing inner strength, anchored in the soil from which the best in Danish music has sprung. That crossing of the Gallic and the Nordic spirit which Riisager represents gives him an undisputed position in Danish music."

Riisager is the chairman of the Danish Composers Society.

MAJOR WORKS:

Ballets—Benzine, 1928; Qarrtsiluni, 1937; Bird Phoenix, 1945; Etude, 1948.

Chamber Music—String Quartet No. 1, 1922; Sonata No. 2 for Violin and Piano, 1923; Sonata for Flute, Violin, Clarinet and Cello, 1927; String Quartet No. 2, 1927; Music for Wind Quintet, 1927; String Quartet No. 3, 1928; Concertino for Five Violins and Piano, 1933; Serenade for Flute, Violin and Cello, 1936; Concertino for Oboe, Clarinet, and Bassoon, 1940; Quartet for Flute, Oboe, Clarinet and Bassoon, 1941; String Quartet No. 4, 1942; Divertimento, for flute, oboe, horn, and bassoon, 1944.

Choral Music—Danish Hymn, for chorus and orchestra, 1942; Song for the Sun, for soloists, chorus, and orchestra, 1947.

Opera—Susanna, 1948.

Orchestral Music—Bellman Variations, for small orchestra, 1919 (revised 1945); Overture to Erasmus Montanus, 1920; Suite Dionysiaque, for chamber orchestra, 1924; Introduzione di Traverso, 1925; Symphony No. 1, 1925; Variations on a Theme by Mézangeau, 1926; Symphony No. 2, 1927;

Shrove Time, overture, 1930; Suite, for small orchestra, 1931; Marche Tatare, 1933; Concertino for Trumpet and Strings, 1933; Little Overture, for strings, 1934; For the Children's Party, 1934; Primavera, concert overture, 1934; Symphony No. 3, 1935; Sinfonia concertante, for strings, 1937; Three Danish Carols, 1937; Partita, 1937; Targut Dance, 1939; Symphony No. 4, "Sinfonia Gaia," 1940; Final Galop, 1941; Summer Rhapsody, 1943; Sinfonietta, for small orchestra, 1947; Archaeopteryx, 1949; Sinfonia Serena, for strings and tympani, 1950; Chaconne, 1950; Concerto for Violin and Orchestra, 1951.

Piano Music—Sonata, 1931; Two Pieces, 1933; The Merry Trumpet, 1933; Sonatine, 1950.

Jean Rivier 1896-

JEAN RIVIER was born in Villemonble, near Paris, on July 21, 1896. Both his parents were excellent musicians. His father was a flutist, and his mother a pianist. When Jean was still in his boyhood, his family moved to Paris, in the Latin Quarter. There the boy began his schooling. Though he started playing the cello and composing when he was still quite young, he had very little technical training. Rivier now regards all his early and haphazard activity with music a complete waste of time.

After completing his academic education, Rivier enlisted in the French Army, since this was the period of World War I. While serving at the front, he felt the need for

Photo J. D. Rivier

JEAN RIVIER

Rivier: rĕ-vyā'

musical expression so acutely that he wrote a Sonata for Cello and Piano on whatever scraps of paper he could find. He was badly gassed in action and had to spend three years after his demobilization in army hospitals. By 1922 he had recovered sufficiently to enter the Paris Conservatory and receive his first formal musical instruction. He remained at the Conservatory four years, winning prizes in counterpoint and fugue.

His musical schooling over, he started composition in earnest. Several important French conductors became interested in him. Albert Wolff was responsible for Rivier's receiving his first public performance for an orchestral work, when *Chant Funèbre* was given at a Pasdeloup concert. Walter Straram and Pierre Monteux also directed premieres of Rivier's music—the *Trois Pastorales, Burlesque,* for violin and orchestra, the overture *Don Quichotte,* the *Adagio for Strings,* and the Symphony in D major. These performances emphasized that Rivier was one of the most vital of the younger French composers.

Together with Henri Barraud, Jean Rivier helped found a school of young French composers known as the "Triton." These young men chose to travel on a path of moderation—between the group that wrote in the twelve-tone technique or in the mystical style of Messiaen on the one hand, and the neo-classicists, on the other.

In his musical esthetics, Rivier stands closer to the neo-classicists than to the mystics and atonalists. If he has any single principle it is that conciseness and economy are all-important in the creative process. He believes that a musical work must be only so long as its idea warrants—the shorter the better. He avoids involved developments and elaborate recapitulations, preferring to state his ideas succinctly and then progressing to the next thought. His passion for brevity was once vividly revealed at a rehearsal of one of his trios. Continually, during the rehearsal, Rivier kept deleting non-essentials from his music until the performing artists (the Pasquier Trio) were afraid that nothing would be left; thereafter, they rehearsed Rivier's works only in his absence.

"Jean Rivier's temperament," wrote Henri Sauguet, "dictates all manner of emotional gradations, from the climactic to the intimate and tender, and he is not notable for any special selectivity in his style, either idiomatically or formally. His formal *métier* is most unspecific: he will compose in any form from operetta to oratorio with equal assurance, following his own caprice and humor of the moment without inhibition."

Jean Rivier lives in an ultra-modern apartment in the Latin Quarter of Paris. His home is filled with exotic plants, paintings, and *objets d'art*. His wife is a talented musician, and their only son is a doctor. Rivier is vitally interested in all the arts. Indeed, he feels that it is not possible to understand music maturely without some knowledge of the allied arts. Most of his musical writing is done in the late spring and during the summer months, when he can work on his terrace.

MAJOR WORKS:

Chamber Music—String Quartet No. 1, 1924; String Trio, 1933; Suite, for oboe, clarinet, and bassoon, 1934; Sonatina for Viola and Cello, 1937; Grave e Presto, for four saxophones, 1938; String Quartet No. 2, 1939; Improvisation et Finale, for oboe and piano, 1943.

Choral Music—Psaume LVI, for soprano, chorus, and orchestra, 1937; Ballade des Amants Désesperés, for chorus and orchestra, 1945.

Orchestral Music—Chant Funèbre, 1927; Danse du Tchad, 1928; Trois Pastorales, for small orchestra, 1929; Burlesque, for violin and orchestra, 1929; Don Quichotte, overture, 1930; Adagio for Strings, 1930; Ouverture pour une Opérette Imaginaire, 1930; Symphony No. 1, in D major, 1932; Le Voyage d'Urien, 1932; Paysage pour Jeanne d'Arc, 1935; Concertino for Piano and Orchestra, 1935; Symphony No. 2 in C, for strings, 1937; Symphony No. 3 in G major, for strings, 1938; Concerto for Piano and Orchestra, 1940; Concertino for Viola and Orchestra, 1945; Symphony No. 4, for strings, 1947; Divertissement dans le Style Operette, 1947; Symphony No. 5, 1947; Rapsodie Provençale, 1948; Concerto for Violin and Orchestra, 1949; Ouverture pour une Tragédie.

ABOUT:

Musical America, October 1948.

Hilding Rosenberg 1892-

HILDING ROSENBERG was born in Bosjökloster, Sweden, on June 21, 1892. His first musical impressions came from hearing his mother sing. In his eighth year he joined the church choir and was compensated for his diligence by being allowed to ring the tower bells every Sunday and holy day. He showed his musical gifts by being able to play on the piano, without taking a single lesson, some of the chorales he heard in church. He also learned the violin without the help of a teacher. Despite this lack of formal training he became a capable musician. By the time he was seventeen, he was able to play the violin in an orchestra, give concerts on the piano, and write some functional compositions.

But he was aware of his technical limitations. In his twenty-fourth year Rosenberg entered the Stockholm Conservatory for his first systematic training, specializing in conducting and composing. He had the good fortune to make an impression on one of the professors, Richard Andersson, who took him under his wing. He introduced Hilding Rosenberg to the great musical literature of the past and present; he also saw to it that Rosenberg became acquainted with classical literature and philosophy.

Hearing Sibelius' Fourth Symphony made such a deep impression upon him that he decided to write a symphony of his own. Naturally, he imitated Sibelius' style. Later on Rosenberg discarded most of this symphony. His Second Symphony (which he designated as his First) was still derivative, though more from the German romantic composers than from Sibelius.

Instinctively, Rosenberg felt dissatisfied with the kind of music he was writing; he sensed that there were fresher, newer ways of creating music. To find out what the younger composers of other lands were doing, he went to Dresden, where he first heard and became impressed with the works of Arnold Schoenberg. It was as if a new world opened before him; Schoenberg's atonality excited Rosenberg with its freedom of form, its new sounds, its harmonic independence. From Dresden, Rosenberg traveled to Paris where he became familiar with other advanced musical tendencies. Henceforth Rosenberg was to leave classical and romantic traditions permanently. His technique became free and independent; he was restless in his search for new, novel idioms.

His first work in an advanced style was a String Quartet, completed in 1920. How revolutionary this music sounded to the

Rosenberg: rō'zĕn-bĕr-y'

HILDING ROSENBERG

Swedish public can be guessed by a brief review that appeared immediately after its premiere performance: "With the last item, the portals of Hell were opened for the whole audience. Neither personal authority nor public sympathy can be increased by four performers impersonating inmates of Konradsberg [a lunatic asylum in Stockholm] and interpreting the barbarous and obscure fantasies of a fifth."

But Rosenberg was still dissatisfied with his style. He wanted simplicity, conciseness, transparency, directness. Without abandoning such progressive techniques as linear counterpoint or atonality, he went after brevity of expression and compactness of design. It was in this final style that he produced the works which made him famous, beginning with the eloquent *Sinfonia da Chiesa*, Nos. 1 and 2, written in 1923 and 1924, and culminating with the powerful and majestic *Sinfonia Grave* and the Symphony No. 3, completed in 1935 and 1939, respectively.

Always a lover of the theatre, Rosenberg produced incidental music for more than a dozen plays, including *Oedipus Rex* and *Medea*. He also wrote more ambitious scores for the stage. In 1932 he completed his first opera, *Journey to America*. Seven years after that, he produced a second opera, *The Marionettes*. His finest work for the theatre was a ballet, *Orpheus in Town*—a fan-

tasy in which the sculptured Orpheus group of Carl Milles (found at the Stockholm Concert Hall), comes to life. *Orpheus in Town* was seen for the first time at the Stockholm Opera in 1938.

Moses Pergament regards Rosenberg's oratorio *The Revelation of St. John* as his "mightiest and most comprehensively authoritative composition." Pergament goes on to add that the "apocalyptic visions are arrayed in musical apparel of convincing dramatic effectiveness. The work also contains a large number of chorales for a cappella choir, as exemplary in their linear purity as in their original but entirely ecclesiastical harmonic style, not to mention their great atmospheric value. I do not hestitate to describe this work as one of the most significant in the international musical literature of the twentieth century." In 1948 Rosenberg visited the United States to direct the American premiere of *The Revelation of St. John*.

Even more ambitious than this oratorio is a cycle of four opera-oratorios, *Joseph and His Brethren*, derived from the novel of Thomas Mann. "A whole world takes place in this music," wrote Pergament, "just as it did in the poetic work: a world of thought and dreams, experience and wisdom, of good and evil wills. It is a world whose stupendous radius and teeming life give a good idea of the extent of the spiritual evolution which must lie behind the composer's determination to express all this in music.

MAJOR WORKS:

Ballet—Orpheus in Town, 1938.

Chamber Music—String Quartet No. 1, 1920; Sonata for Solo Violin, 1921; Trio, for flute, violin, and viola, 1921; Suite in D major, for violin and piano, 1922; Sonatina for Flute and Piano; String Quartet No. 2; String Quartet No. 3; Sonata for Violin and Piano; Trio, for oboe, clarinet, and bassoon; String Quartet No. 4; String Quartet No. 5, 1949.

Choral Music—The Holy Night, oratorio, 1936; Golgotha, oratorio; Revelation of St. John, oratorio, 1940; The Tender of the Garden, symphony-oratorio, 1943.

Operas—Journey to America, comic opera, 1932; The Marionettes, 1933; Isle of Felicity, 1944; Joseph and His Brethren, opera-oratorio, 1949.

Orchestral Music—Suite for Violin and Orchestra, 1922; Chamber Symphony, 1923; Sinfonia da Chiesa, No. 1, 1923; Sinfonia da Chiesa, No. 2, 1924; Concerto for Violin and Orchestra, 1924; Suite for Strings, 1927; Triple Concerto, 1928; Concerto for Cello and Orchestra, 1928; Sinfonia

Grave, 1935; Symphonie Concertante, 1935; Symphony No. 3, 1939; Concerto for Viola and String Orchestra, 1942; Ouvertura Bianca-Negra, for string orchestra, 1946; Concerto for String Orchestra, 1946.

ABOUT:

Music and Letters, July 1947.

Manuel Rosenthal *1904-*

MANUEL ROSENTHAL was born in Paris on June 18, 1904. His mother, who was of Russian birth, loved music intensely. It was at her insistence that Manuel began to study the violin in his ninth year. His father died soon after the end of World War I. Carrying on the profession of midwife, Rosenthal's mother was able to support her family and to see that her son acquired a thorough musical education. From 1920 to 1923 he attended the Paris Conservatory, specializing in the violin under Jules Boucherit. In his last year at the Conservatory, Rosenthal wrote a Sonatina for Two Violins and Piano which impressed Ravel so greatly that the master offered to give Rosenthal private lessons. There was a period of military service to be completed before Rosenthal could accept Ravel's offer (military service, for the most part, consisting of playing the cymbals in a band). When that was completed, Rosenthal started studying with Ravel, from whom he received virtually all of his training in composition, and from whose counsel he was to profit until Ravel's death. Meanwhile, in 1928, Rosenthal was awarded the fellowship of the American Foundation for the French Arts.

Rosenthal first received attention as a composer in the 1930's when he wrote an important orchestral suite, *Jeanne d'Arc*, successfully performed in Paris in 1936. Ravel had been interested in Joan of Arc as the subject of an opera, but his illness made it impossible for him to carry out his project. On the advice of Ravel, his teacher and friend, Rosenthal decided to compose an orchestral suite on the same subject. A work in five sections for narrator and orchestra, this suite discusses the most important stages of Joan's life; the music is compounded of dramatic and spiritual elements.

Richards

MANUEL ROSENTHAL

In 1937 Rosenthal's delightful one-act comedy, *La Poule Noire* was heard at the Paris Exposition with great critical acclaim. His next ambitious project was the oratorio *St. Francis of Assisi*, completed in 1939. Theatrical in style, this music is characterized by pictorial effects on the one hand and, on the other, by an idiom derived from ecclesiastical plain chants.

In 1937 Rosenthal was appointed associate conductor of the French National Orchestra. On September 3, 1939, he was mobilized as an infantry corporal. He saw action, received the Croix de Guerre for his bravery, and after being wounded by shrapnel, was captured by the Nazis. For three months he was confined to a Nazi hospital, and later he was transferred to a prisoner-of-war camp. There he conducted an orchestra made up of fellow prisoners and wrote little songs and operettas for their amusement. Released from prison and back in France, Rosenthal was hunted by the Gestapo for his clandestine activities in the French Resistance movement. He had to assume a false name and had to be constantly on the move. A meager income from various musical hack jobs kept him from starving. But the major part of his energy and activity belonged to his propaganda work, writing pamphlets, and supplying vital information to the Allies. But even in this difficult period,

Rosenthal: rō-zĕn-täl'

serious composition was not completely neglected. As he said: "Music was a form of escape. By concentrating on it I could forget the Germans and danger." One of the works completed at this time was the witty *Musique de Table*, for orchestra, a kind of hymn to gastronomy. Through musical means, Rosenthal described many succulent dishes including eels in red wine, roast beef, salad, cheese, and wine. "It carries," wrote Virgil Thomson, "the technique of coloristic design into realms of brightness, especially through the use of high, thin sounds."

After the liberation of Paris, Rosenthal became the musical director and conductor of the French National Orchestra. At the same time he appeared throughout Europe as guest conductor of many leading orchestras. On November 6, 1946, visiting the United States for the first time, he directed a concert over the Columbia Broadcasting System in a program including his own *Jeanne d'Arc*. On November 23 he appeared with the St. Louis Symphony conducting *Musique de Table* and on December 5 with the New York Philharmonic-Symphony in the first orchestral program in America devoted entirely to his works. His success in this country, both as conductor and as composer, was unqualified. "I don't know," wrote Virgil Thomson, "when one has encountered in these parts a musician so heady, so invigorating, so clean of taste, so thoroughly dependable of output both as author and as executant." Inspired by this first visit to the United States, Rosenthal wrote an orchestral tone poem, *Magic Manhattan*, introduced by the St. Louis Symphony under Golschmann on January 13, 1950.

After serving for a year as composer-in-residence at the College of Puget Sound in Tacoma, Washington, Rosenthal became the principal conductor and musical director of the Seattle Symphony. His contract was abruptly terminated in 1951 when he was denied readmission to this country by the immigration authorities.

MAJOR WORKS:

Ballets—Un Baiser pour Rien, 1929; Que le Diable l'Emporte, 1948.

Choral Music—St. Francis of Assisi, oratorio, 1937-39; Trois Burlesques, 1941; La Pieta d'Avi-

gnon, 1943; Cantate pour le Temps de la Nativité, 1944.

Operas—Rayon des Soieries, 1928; La Poule Noire, comedy, 1937.

Orchestral Music—Jeanne d'Arc, suite for narrator and orchestra, 1936; Sérénade en Quatre Mouvements, 1936; Les Petits Métiers, suite, 1936; La Fête du Vin, choreographic poem, 1937; Musique de Table, 1941; Christmas Symphonies, 1947; Magic Manhattan, 1948; Aesopi Convivium, theme and variations for violin, piano, and orchestra, 1948.

ABOUT:

New York Times, November 10, 1946; Newsweek, November 11, 1946.

Albert Roussel *1869-1937*

ALBERT CHARLES PAUL MARIE ROUSSEL was born in Tourcoing, France, on April 5, 1869. Both his parents died when he was still a child, and he was raised first by a grandfather and then by an uncle. As a boy, Albert Roussel's first love was the sea, and his ambition was to become a sailor. In 1884 he entered the Stanislas College in Paris. Three years later he enrolled in the Brest Naval School, where he completed his nautical studies. After that, he was employed as a midshipman on an armored gunboat, the *Styx*, bound for Cochin-China. His experiences aboard ship awakened in him a love for nature which remained with him for the rest of his life. He often said in later years that his best musical ideas came to him when he took weeks off in the country.

Having always dabbled in music, and growing increasingly fascinated by it, Roussel decided in 1894 to abandon the sea and to study music. After a period of instruction in the organ and in theory with Eugène Gigout in Paris, he wrote two madrigals, both of which were submitted in 1897 in a competition by the Société des Compositeurs under two different pseudonyms; both were selected anonymously to share the prize. Roussel directed the premiere of these madrigals in Paris on May 3, 1898. In the same year, he entered the Schola Cantorum, attending the composition class of Vincent D'Indy, who encouraged and inspired him. Other professors at the Schola Cantorum criticized him severely for his insistence on breaking the established rules of composi-

Roussel: rōō-sĕl'

tion. Nevertheless, Roussel was a brilliant student, and in 1902 he was appointed professor of counterpoint at the Schola Cantorium, a post he held for a decade.

In 1908 Roussel completed a symphony, *Le Poème de la Forêt*, in an impressionist style and reflecting his intense love of nature. During the winter of 1909-1910, he yielded again to the call of the sea. This time he embarked for the East as a passenger, visiting India and exploring the ruins of old cities. This voyage had an effect on his musical style. Oriental idioms and colors and subjects were now fused with his former impressionistic writing. He now achieved his first major success with a symphony for chorus and orchestra inspired by the sights and sounds of India, *Évocations*. Georges Jean-Aubry wrote: "Roussel's *Évocations* is one of seven or eight symphonic works composed during the past twenty years which will insure, for a long time to come, the future of French music."

The ballet-opera *Padmavati* was another work inspired by this trip to India; for, while exploring ruins, Roussel visited the setting where, in the thirteenth century, the legendary tragedy of the Hindu heroine, Padmavati, took place. It made such an impression on him that he adapted it into a scenario. This ballet-opera was produced at the Paris Opéra on June 1, 1923, and was a major success.

Meanwhile, on April 3, 1913, Roussel had been acclaimed for still another ballet, *Le Festin de l'Araignée (The Feast of the Spider)*, inspired by Fabre's *Studies of Insect Life*, and produced at the Théâtre des Arts. The orchestral suite which the composer prepared from this ballet has since become one of his most frequently performed works. "Using a miniature orchestra," wrote Edward Burlingame Hill, "he has yet found the means to illustrate the action, characterize its personages, with delicate and pungent humor, and yet rise to tense moments."

During the entire period of World War I, Roussel served as a driver in the motor division of the French army. He saw action at Verdun. His war experiences so undermined his health that for the rest of his life he was to suffer.

After World War I Roussel's musical style experienced still another transforma-

Photo-Lipnitzki
ALBERT ROUSSEL

tion. He discarded once and for all his bent for impressionism and orientalism and started writing in a neo-classic style demanding simplicity and objectivity. In this idiom he produced one of his finest works, the Suite in F major, for orchestra, completed in 1926 and introduced by the Boston Symphony under Koussevitzky on January 21, 1927. Within such old classical forms as the prelude, sarabande, and gigue, Roussel produced music which at turns is energetic and graceful, ebullient and restrained.

In the Suite in F major, and in his succeeding works, Roussel resolved, in the words of Arthur Hoerée, "the classical problem of equilibrium between form and style. His constant evolution, a sign of vitality, does not preclude a fundamental unity which is in itself esthetic."

In 1930, Roussel was invited by Mrs. Elizabeth Sprague Coolidge to Prague to hear a performance of his Trio, for flute, viola, and cello at a music festival. In the same year, Roussel received a commission from Serge Koussevitzky for a symphony to commemorate the fiftieth anniversary of the Boston Symphony Orchestra. This Symphony, Roussel's Third, was introduced by the Boston Symphony under Koussevitzky on October 24, 1930; the composer was in the audience.

Roussel's tendency to be classical and objective was further emphasized in this Symphony, in the Sinfonietta for Strings, completed in 1934, and in the highly acclaimed Fourth Symphony, in 1935. The Fourth Symphony represented Roussel at the height of his powers. Introduced on October 19, 1935, at a Pasdeloup concert in Paris, under Albert Wolff, this Symphony was so well received that its scherzo movement had to be repeated. The work has been heard frequently in the United States.

Roussel remained productive until the end of his life. Not even his last serious illness could keep him from his work. He completed the String Trio, and was at work on the final pages of another trio, this time for woodwinds, when death came on August 23, 1937, at his home in Royan.

Hoerée described Roussel as follows: "I seem to see before me a portrait by Velásquez. A long face, straight forehead, small keen eyes, thin nose, drooping moustache, and short pointed beard, courteous manners, moreover, and a profound aristocracy."

Besides music, Roussel was interestd in mathematics and astronomy; he enjoyed reading scientific treatises. "I love the sea, forests, life in the country, animals, the aimless existence of the country in preference to the enervating life of the cities," he once said. "I also love to discover in old cities, treasures which their artists of many centuries ago have left behind as a heritage."

MAJOR WORKS:

Ballets—Le Festin de l'Araignée, 1912; Padmavati, opera-ballet, 1918; Bacchus et Ariane, 1930.

Chamber Music—Sonata No. 1 for Violin and Piano, 1908; Joueurs de Flute, for flute and piano, 1924; Duo for Bassoon and Cello, 1925; Sonata No. 2 for Violin and Piano, 1924; Serenade, for flute, violin, viola, cello, and harp (or piano), 1925; Trio, for flute, viola and cello, 1929; Quartet in D major, 1931-32; Trio, for strings, 1937.

Choral Music—Les Évocations, symphony for chorus and orchestra, 1912; Psalm 80, 1928; Aeneas, 1935.

Operas—La Naissance de la Lyre, 1924; Le Testament de la Tante Caroline, 1933.

Orchestral Music—Le Poème de la Forêt, symphony, 1904-06; Pour une Fête de Printemps, 1920; Symphony No. 2, in B-flat minor, 1921; Suite in F major, 1926; Concerto for Piano and Orchestra, 1927; Symphony No. 3 in G minor, 1930; Sinfonietta, for strings, 1934; Symphony No. 4, 1934; Rap-

sodie Flamande, 1936; Concertino for Cello and Orchestra, 1936.

Piano Music—Suite, 1909-10; Sonatina, 1912.

Vocal Music—Two Madrigals, 1897; Four Poems of Henri de Régnier, 1907; Flammes, 1908.

ABOUT:

Hoerée, A., Albert Roussel; Musical Quarterly, October 1938.

Edmund Rubbra *1901-*

EDMUND DOMINIC RUBBRA was born in Northampton, England, on May 23, 1901. Music did not play an important part in his family's life. But his mother did have a good voice and knew enough of the rudiments of music to begin her son's piano education when he was eight.

The financial problems of his family compelled Edmund to leave school when he was fourteen and earn his living as a clerk. By this time music had become all-important. In his spare time he continued his musical studies by himself and made his first attempts at composition.

When he was sixteen he gave a recital devoted to the music of Cyril Scott. Scott was so flattered by this gesture that he offered to teach Rubbra composition. Rubbra studied with Scott until his nineteenth year, when he won the Open Composition scholarship for Reading University. One year later he received a scholarship for the Royal College of Music, where he remained for four years. His teachers included Holst and Vaughan Williams.

Rubbra is particularly famous for his symphonies. Wilfrid Mellers has gone as far as to say that "after Sibelius, Rubbra is the composer who had made the most significant contribution to the contemporary symphonic problem." His Symphony No. 1 was introduced in 1937 by the BBC Symphony. The BBC Symphony was also responsible for the premiere performances of his next two symphonies, in 1938 and 1940. In his first two symphonies certain stylistic traits, apparent in his later works, are in evidence—notably his interest in counterpoint and his partiality for economy. As Arthur Hutchings noted, Rubbra's first two symphonies "show the composer at great labor not to

Rubbra: rŏŏ'brĕ

EDMUND RUBBRA

overcrowd his canvas, to write contrapuntally but in large, gracious periods which will allow certain moments to stand out as high spots."

There was even greater conciseness and concentration in the Fourth and Fifth symphonies. But the music did not lack emotional impact. Ralph Vaughan Williams once wrote to Rubbra in a personal letter: "Now and again there comes a work with the power to make one fall in love with music all over again. In such a mood I found myself when listening to your symphony."

Rubbra's style is modeled, though more instinctively than consciously, on the lyrical polyphony and the free rhythms of the Elizabethan composers. But he adheres to no single school. If he is faithful to any belief it is in "the generating power of melody," as he told this writer, "and in the diatonic system that the Western European music has used for centuries." But he emphasizes that he is no reactionary.

In 1933 Rubbra married Antoinette Chapin, a French violinist; they have two children. During World War II, Rubbra served in the Royal Artillery. When the war ended, he was appointed Lecturer of Music at Oxford University. He has also appeared as pianist in the Rubbra-Gruenberg-Pleeth Trio, which has frequently performed over the London Radio.

Rubbra explains that his interests extend "far beyond the bounds of music." He has read extensively—philosophy, poetry, and general literature. He is also interested in painting. In 1947 he joined the Roman Catholic Church.

Major Works:

Chamber Music—Sonata No. 2 for Violin and Piano, 1933; Five Spenser Sonnets, for tenor and string quartet, 1936; Sonata for Cello and Piano, 1947; String Quartet in F minor, 1947; Lyric Movement, for string quartet and piano, 1947; Trio in One Movement, 1950.

Choral Music—Missa Cantuariensis, 1946; The Morning Watch, motet, 1946; Magnificat, 1948; The Dark Night of the Soul, 1948; Missa in Honorem Sancti Dominici, 1949; Te Deum, 1951.

Orchestral Music—Symphony No. 1, 1937; Symphony No. 2, 1938; Symphony No. 3, 1940; Sinfonia Concertante, for piano and orchestra, 1943; Soliloquy, for cello, strings, two horns, and timpani, 1944; Festival Overture, 1947; Five Medieval Latin Lyrics, for baritone and string orchestra, 1948; Symphony No. 5, 1949.

Vocal Music—Three Psalms, for voice and piano, 1947.

About:

Bacharach, A. L. (ed.) British Music of Our Time; Mellers, W. Studies in Contemporary Music; Musical Quarterly, January 1942.

Camille Saint-Saëns *1835-1921*

THOUGH Saint-Saëns wrote his most important works before 1900, he was highly productive up to the end of his long life; he must, then, be grouped with the composers of the twentieth century.

He was born in Paris on October 9, 1835, coming from humble peasant stock. His precociousness was phenomenal. He began studying the piano when he was only two-and-a-half; when an attempt was made to stop his lessons he created such a fuss that they had to be continued. At five he was composing songs and piano pieces, and made a public appearance as pianist. At six, his greatest delight was to read through an entire opera score. Inevitably he was compared, and justifiably, with Mozart. Ingres, the famous painter, presented the boy with an inscribed medallion on which Mozart's face was painted.

A systematic period of study began in his seventh year with Camille-Marie Stamaty in

Saint-Saëns: săN säNs′

CAMILLE SAINT-SAËNS

piano and Pierre Maleden in theory. Such was his progress that, on May 6, 1846, Saint-Saëns gave a remarkable piano recital the program of which included concertos by Mozart and Beethoven.

In 1848 he was enrolled in the Paris Conservatory. He continued to amaze everyone with his gifts. In 1851 he won first prize in the organ class of Benoist. One year later, as a pupil of Halévy, he won another prize for the *Ode à Sainte-Cécile,* which was performed. His single failure was the Prix de Rome, and the reason he did not get the award was that the authorities considered him too young (he was seventeen).

Soon after he left the Conservatory—he was graduated in 1853—Saint-Saëns was appointed organist in a small Parisian church and had his First Symphony performed in Paris. His Second Symphony (later called by the composer the First Symphony) was heard three years after that, won the prize of the Société Sainte-Cécile, and was a great success. In 1857 Saint-Saëns received his most important appointment up to that time, that of organist at the Madeleine church. And in 1861 he joined the piano faculty of the École Niedermeyer.

A man of extraordinary, and seemingly inexhaustible, energy and drive, Saint-Saëns was henceforth to devote himself to his duties as concert pianist, church organist, teach-

er, and composer—and all with equal industry. But there were other important activities, too. In 1871 he helped found the celebrated Société Nationale de Musique, which was dedicated to the performances of new and unfamiliar French music and in the direction of which he had a hand. He edited the music of other composers (including a comprehensive edition of the works of Rameau) and wrote theoretical treatises on harmony and melody. Beyond all this, he was a student of astronomy, physics, archeology, and natural history. He painted and did creative writing. He was an omnivorous reader of the classics and enjoyed learning new languages.

He was, in short, a man of immense culture; but he was never stuffy or stodgy. His social evenings at home every Monday were celebrated throughout Paris, and primarily for the charm and amiability of the host. A brilliant conversationalist, he spiced his talk with engaging humor and irony. He had a flair for mimicry, and frequently delighted his guests with his impersonation of Marguerite in *Faust* or his parodies of early Italian operas.

He was described by Georges Servières as "of short stature. His head was extremely original and the features characteristic: a great brow, wide and open where, between the eyebrows, the tenacity of the man reveals itself; hair habitually cut short, and brownish beard turning gray; a nose like an eagle's beak, underlined by two deeply marked wrinkles starting from the nostrils; eyes a little prominent, very mobile, very expressive."

His prominence and significance as a composer dates from 1871, when he wrote his first tone poem, *Le Rouet d'Omphale,* and a comic opera, *La Princesse Jaune,* given by the Opéra Comique on June 12, 1872. In 1873 Pablo Sarasate introduced his Concerto No. 1 for Violin and Orchestra, and in 1875 the *Danse Macabre* received its premiere performance. Meanwhile, he had written his greatest opera, *Samson et Dalila,* which was refused by the directors of the Paris Opéra on the grounds that it was too severe in style and too Wagnerian. The premiere of *Samson et Dalila* took place in Weimar on December 2, 1877, and it was a success of the first magnitude; thirteen years after that it was permanently established in the repertory of the Paris Opéra. As one of the greatest creations in the French lyric theatre, its success throughout the music world was inevitable.

In 1881 Saint-Saëns was elected to the Institut de France. It was said of him in salutation at the time, "If it were necessary to characterize Saint-Saëns in a few words we should call him the best musician in France." His artistic stature grew with the premieres of his opera *Henry VIII*, at the Paris Opéra in 1883, and the Symphony No. 3 in C minor (one of his best works) in 1886.

Saint-Saëns' extensive travels brought him to the United States for the first time in 1906, and for a second visit in 1915. He continued traveling in all parts of the world until the end of his life. He toured South America in his eighty-first year, and was a visitor in Algiers and Greece when he was eighty-five.

Saint-Saëns gave his last concert as pianist in Dieppe on August 6, 1921, and directed his last orchestral concert two weeks later. He died suddenly in Algiers, where he had gone for his health, on December 16, 1921. His body was brought back to Paris, where impressive funeral services were conducted with the great personages of France's political and musical life participating.

Discussing the technique and style of Saint-Saëns' works, M. D. Calvocoressi pointed to "his lucidity, his versatility, his sense of proportion, and the perfection of what he achieved within the limits of his outlook—limits carefully thought out, deliberately adopted which he never fell short of nor overstepped." Calvocoressi goes on to say: "His qualities of emotion and imagination were inferior to his capacity for building and working out, but what his works lack in glow and profundity they almost make up for in technical interest and beautiful finish, in fineness of the proportion and perfection of texture."

"Of all composers, Saint-Saëns is most difficult to describe," wrote Arthur Hervey. "He eludes you at every moment—the elements constituting his musical personality are so varied in their nature, yet they seem to blend in so remarkable a fashion. . . . Saint-Saëns is a typical Frenchman. . . . He

is preeminently witty . . . It is this quality which has enabled him to attack the driest forms of art and render them bearable. There is nothing ponderous about him."

MAJOR WORKS:

Ballet—Javotte, 1896.

Chamber Music—Piano Quintet in A minor, op. 14, 1865; Piano Trio No. 1 in F Major, op. 18, 1869; Sonata for Cello and Piano, op. 32, 1873; Piano Quartet, op. 41, 1875; Septet, op. 65, 1881; Sonata for Violin and Piano in D minor, op. 75, 1885; Havanaise, for violin and piano, op. 83; Piano Trio No. 2 in E minor, op. 92, 1892; Sonata No. 2 for Violin and Piano, in E-flat, op. 102, 1896; String Quartet No. 1, op. 112, 1899; Sonata No. 2, for cello and piano, op. 123, 1905; Fantaisie for violin and harp, op. 124, 1907; Triptych, for violin and piano, op. 136, 1912; String Quartet No. 2, op. 153, 1919; Sonata for Oboe and Piano, op. 166, 1921; Sonata for Clarinet and Piano, op. 167, 1921; Sonata for Bassoon and Piano, op. 168, 1921.

Choral Music—Mass, op. 4, 1852; Christmas Oratorio, op. 12, 1863; Les Noces de Prométhée, cantata, op. 19, 1867; Le Déluge, oratorio, op. 45, 1876; Les Soldats de Gédéon, op. 46; Requiem, op. 54, 1878; La Lyre et la Harpe, op. 57, 1879; Hymne à Victor Hugo, op. 69, 1881; Les Guerriers, op. 84; Chant d'Automne, op. 113; La Gloire de Corneille, cantata, op. 126, 1906; Psaume CL, op. 127; La Gloire, cantata, op. 131; Ave Maria, op. 145; Hymne à la Paix, op. 159, 1919.

Operas—La Princesse Jaune, 1872; Samson et Dalila, 1877; Le Timbre d'Argent, 1877; Étienne Marcel, 1879; Henri VIII, 1883; Proserpine, 1887; Ascanio, 1890; Phryné, 1893; Les Barbares, 1901; Hélène, 1904; L'Ancêtre, 1906; Déjanire, 1910.

Orchestral Music—Symphony No. 1 in E-flat major, op. 2, 1853; Concerto No. 1, in D, for piano and orchestra, op. 17, 1858; Concertstück in A minor, for violin and orchestra, op. 20, 1859; Concerto No. 2 in G minor, for piano and orchestra, op. 22, 1868; Introduction and Rondo Capriccioso, for violin and orchestra, op. 28, 1870; Concerto No. 3 in B-flat major, for piano and orchestra, op. 29, 1869; Le Rouet d'Omphale, tone poem, op. 31, 1871; Concerto in A minor, for cello and orchestra, op. 33, 1873; Marche Héroïque, op. 34, 1871; Phaëton, tone poem, op. 39, 1873; Danse Macabre, tone poem, op. 40, 1874; Concerto No. 4 in C minor, for piano and orchestra, op. 44, 1875; Suite, op. 49, 1877; La Jeunesse d'Hercule, tone poem, op. 50, 1877; Symphony No. 2 in A minor, op. 55, 1878; Concerto No. 2 in C, for violin and orchestra, op. 58, 1879; Suite Algérienne, op. 60; Concerto No. 3 in B minor, for violin and orchestra, op. 61; Jota Aragonesa, op. 64, 1881; Rapsodie d'Auvergne, for piano and orchestra, op. 73, 1884; Le Carnaval des Animaux, for two pianos and orchestra, 1886; Symphony No. 3 in C minor, with organ, op. 78, 1886; Incidental Music for Antigone, 1894; Concerto No. 5 in F major, for piano and orchestra, op. 103, 1895; Incidental Music to Déjanire, 1898; Incidental Music to Parysatis, 1902; Concerto No. 2 for Cello and Orchestra, op. 119, 1902; Incidental Music to Andromaque, 1903; Ouverture de Fête, op. 133, 1910; Ouverture, op. 140; Incidental Music to On ne Badine pas avec l'Amour, 1917; Cypres et Lauriers, for organ and orchestra, op. 156, 1919; Odelette, for flute and orchestra, op. 162, 1920.

Organ Music—Three Rhapsodies on Breton Themes, op. 7, 1866; Three Preludes and Fugues, op. 99, 1894; Fantaisie No. 2, op. 101, 1895; Marche Religieuse, op. 107, 1897; Seven Improvisations, op. 150, 1898; Fantaisie No. 3, op. 157, 1919.

Piano Music—Six Bagatelles, op. 3, 1856; Variations on a Theme of Beethoven, for two pianos, op. 35, 1874; Six Études, op. 52, 1877; Third Mazurka, op. 66, 1883; Album, six pieces, op. 72, 1884; Souvenir d'Italie, op. 80; Suite, op. 90, 1892; Thème Varié, op. 97, 1894; Caprice Héroïque, for two pianos, op. 106, 1897; Six Études, op. 111, 1899; Six Études, for left hand, op. 135, 1912; Études, op. 152; Six Fugues, op. 161, 1920; Feuillet d'Album, op. 169, 1920.

Vocal Music—Mélodies Persanes, op. 26, 1870; Chanson de Grand-père, op. 53; Lola, op. 116, 1900.

ABOUT:

Brook, D., Five Great French Composers; Hervey, A., Saint-Saëns; Lyle, W., Camille Saint-Saëns: His Life and Work; Mason, D. G., From Grieg to Brahms; Rolland, R., Musicians of Today; Servières, G., Saint-Saëns.

Erik Satie *1866-1925*

ERIK ALFRED LESLIE SATIE was born in Honfleur, near Le Havre, on May 17, 1866. His mother, who was of Scottish descent, wrote pieces for the piano. His father was both a composer and publisher.

Erik began studying music in his eighth year with a local organist, who instilled in him a love for old polyphonic music. After a brief period of study with the organist, Guilmant, Satie entered the Paris Conservatory in 1879. At the Conservatory his musical preferences included medieval plain chants and old modal music. At the same time he showed an inquisitiveness about new techniques and idioms, frequently startling his teachers with his excursions into dissonance and unorthodox tonalities. Most of his teachers regarded him as indolent. He used to say facetiously that his harmony professor thought that his talent lay in his piano playing, while his piano professor thought that his talent was essentially creative. He remained at the Conservatory for only a single year, and after that shifted for himself in whatever direction an unbridled and undisciplined temperament would lead.

He started writing piano pieces unorthodox in their harmonic construction. The first, *Ogives,* came in 1886, and was soon followed by *Sarabandes, Gymnopédies,* and *Gnossiennes.* Here the style was precise, unemotional, economical; all nonessentials were dispensed with. Jean Cocteau put it well when he said that in these pieces Satie showed the greatest audacity of all, the audacity of being simple. But he had another kind of audacity, too: to use parallel chords and chords of the ninth which forcefully foreshadowed the later harmonic writing of Debussy.

Satie earned his living by playing the piano in a Montmartre cabaret, *Chat Noir.* It was during this period that he met and became a friend of Debussy, whom he influenced greatly with his ideas and theories of music. (Debussy orchestrated two of the pieces from *Gymnopédies.*)

Satie's early piano pieces not only exploited unorthodox harmonies and rhythms, and such unusual practices as barless notation, but they also bore quaint titles. With an impish humor he entitled some of his pieces *Desiccated Embryos,* or *Flabby Preludes for a Dog,* or *Three Pieces in the Shape of a Pear,* or *Airs to Make You Run Away.* He also filled these pieces with printed instructions that developed his impish manner. One of his phrases received the description "like a nightingale with a toothache," while in another the performer was instructed to "put his hands in his pockets."

But the rebel was not merely indulging in quixotic moods. He was a serious artist fighting against the romantic tradition dictating that composers take themselves and their art with religious sanctimony. He was a serious artist who was in conflict first with the pretentious structures and the even more pretentious style of Wagner and Mahler, and after that with the preciousness of Debussy and his followers. With his economical writing in slight forms, and with his queer titles and instructions, he was parting company with the excessive emotionalism, the pompous attitudes, and the elaborate styles of his immediate predecessors and some of his contemporaries. Through his novel approaches Satie was preparing the way for the neo-classicists, and for those French composers who were to make music a more human and direct esthetic experience for its audiences.

Satie: să-tē′

Satie became notorious in Paris not only for his unorthodox music but also for his eccentric personality. It was widely known that though he was frequently on the brink of starvation, he would squander his money recklessly when funds came his way; once, on receiving a small legacy, he spent it all on a dozen suits. It was known that he was a member of the Society of Rosicrucians, and a fervent disciple of a mystic named Peladan (for whose involved and obscure dramas Satie sometimes wrote incidental music). It was also rumored that he allowed no other human being to enter his home in Arcueil, near Paris.

On the eve of his fortieth birthday, Satie became dissatisfied with the music he had thus far written. He felt his technique was inadequate. To remedy this fault, he enrolled in the Schola Cantorum and for the next three years attended the classes of Vincent D'Indy and Albert Roussel. This period of study gave Satie the confidence to attempt compositions more ambitious than short pieces for the piano. In 1917 he wrote the score for a satirical ballet, *Parade*—in which he used the idioms of American jazz and which was introduced in Paris by the Ballet Russe on May 18 of that year. The year after that he completed his lyric drama, *Socrate*. Neither the audiences nor critics reacted more kindly to his larger works than they had done to his small pieces. The premiere of *Parade* created a scandal. So hostile were the critics that Satie was provoked into sending one of them (Poueigh) an insulting letter. Sued by the infuriated critic, Satie was sentenced to eight days in jail for "public insults and defamation of character." The sentence was, however, suspended. Several years later, Darius Milhaud was to write: "The performance of Satie's *Parade* will stand in the history of French music as a date equally important with that of the first performance of *Pelléas et Mélisande.*"

The critics might denounce him and the audiences might misunderstand him. But his influence on his contemporaries was profound. The impact of his many innovations was felt by not only Debussy but also by Ravel and the members of the "French Six." In 1923 another school of composers came into existence through his influence, known

From a sketch by Picasso
ERIK SATIE

as the "Arcueilists," a group which included Sauguet and Desormière.

Satie's was influential music, but it was also music with esthetic interest. Paul Rosenfeld wrote: "This music is modest in expression, quiet, utterly without bombast, in every bar the product of the good taste which abhors the discharge of fireworks from the breast. . . . He sought to refresh musical art by going to demotic music for themes, rhythms, and instrumental effects. . . . He was one of the first see the possibilities for music found in the polyrhythms of American commercial jazz."

Constant Lambert analyzed Satie's style thus: "Melodically speaking we find the juxtaposition of short lyrical phrases of great tenderness with ostinatos of extreme and deliberate bareness. Harmonically speaking, Satie's methods differ as much from Debussy's static use of chords for their own sake as they do from Liszt's rhetorical use of chords as so many points in a musical argument. His harmonic sense . . . is rich and pleasing, but, like his lyrical sense, displays a curiously objective and unatmospheric quality. The strangeness of his harmonic coloring is due not to the chords themselves, but to the unexpected relationships he discovers between chords which in themselves are familiar enough. . . . His progressions have a strange logic of their own but they have none of the usual sense of concord and discord, no trace of the *point d'appui* that we usually associate with the word progression. They may be said to lack harmonic perspective in much the way that a cubist painting lacks a special perspective."

Erik Satie died in Paris on July 1, 1925. In *Notes Without Music*, Milhaud described the intense poverty of Satie's last years. "A narrow corridor, with a wash-basin in it, led to the bedroom into which Satie had never allowed anyone, not even his concierge, to penetrate. The idea of entering it upset us. What a shock we had on opening the door. It seemed impossible that Satie had lived in such poverty. This man, whose faultlessly clean and correct dress made him look rather like a model official, owned almost literally *nothing*; a wretched bed, a table covered with the most incongruous objects, one chair, a half-empty wardrobe. . . . On the ancient, broken-down piano, with its pedals tied up with string, there was a parcel whose postmark proved that it had been delivered several years before."

Olin Downes, who met Satie in the closing year of the composer's life, described him as "an amusing old man, a dilettante of the future, who wore a blue, shiny suit, a gleaming eyeglass, and misleading whiskerage, and who ate his food in a mincing and derisive manner."

MAJOR WORKS:

Ballets—Upsud, 1892; Parade, 1917; Relâche, 1924; Mercure, 1924.

Operas—Socrate, 1918; Le Piège de Méduse, 1921.

Piano Music—Ogives, 1886; Sarabandes, 1887; Gymnopédies, (two movements orchestrated by Debussy), 1887; Gnossiennes, 1889; Trois Morceaux en Forme de Poire, 1903; Véritables Préludes Flasques, 1911; Descriptions Automatiques, 1913; Desiccated Embryos, 1913; Peccadilles Importunes, 1913; Heures Séculaires et Instantanées, 1914; Avant-Dernières Pensées, 1915; Études, 1915.

ABOUT:

Milhaud, D., Notes Without Music; Myers, R., Erik Satie; Templier, P. D., Satie; Van Vechten, C., Interpreters and Interpretations; La Revue Musicale, June 1952.

Henri Sauguet 1901-

HENRI SAUGUET was born in Bordeaux on May 18, 1901. The first music to interest him was the plain chants he sang

as a choirboy in the local church. But his most vital boyhood experience in music came in his fifteenth year from hearing some of Debussy's works. "This was the *coup de foudre* determining my career," he said. "Henceforth, my one all-abiding ambition was to become a composer. From this time on, too, I was fascinated by all contemporary music, sometimes to the exclusion of the classics."

He started studying the piano and organ with local teachers, and in his sixteenth year he began lessons in harmony. Faced with the practical problem of earning a living, he filled the position of clerk in various business houses, and for a year was secretary of the prefecture of Tarn-et-Garonne. Not until his twenty-sixth year was he able to concern himself exclusively with music.

Sauguet visited Paris for the first time when he was twenty to hear a performance of Schoenberg's *Pierrot Lunaire*. A year later he returned to Paris, this time to remain for an extended period and to study with Charles Koechlin. At about this time he joined with Desormière, Max Jacob, and Clignet in forming a school of composers calling itself the "Groupe d'Arcueil," whose dean was Erik Satie, then living in the Arcueil district of Paris. Satie's influence on Sauguet was profound; through Satie, he came to know the most advanced French music of the day.

He wrote the score of an opera-bouffe, *Le Plumet du Colonel*, which was introduced in 1924 in Paris. This was Sauguet's first work to receive a major performance. His first success came in 1927 with the ballet *La Chatte*, produced by the Ballet Russe in Paris, and received so well that it was given more than a hundred times. After that, Sauguet produced other successful ballets, including *David* (written in 1928 for Ida Rubinstein, who introduced it at the Paris Opéra that year) and *La Nuit*, introduced in London in 1930.

Sauguet's style is a compromise between impressionism and medievalism. His sensitive atmosphere is derived from Debussy. It blends with modal harmonies and melodic lines suggesting the plain chant. Occasionally, the influence of Honegger and Poulenc is also apparent, in his economy and precision. Sauguet has never lost his fascination

Photo-Lipnitzki

HENRI SAUGUET

for modern music. "What is happening in our time is to me most exciting of all," he says. He feels that the music of the past has had virtually no significant effect on his own artistic evolution.

For many years, Sauguet distinguished himself as the music critic of *L'Europe Nouvelle* and the journal *Écho de Paris*. He also helped to found several literary magazines, including the *Revue Hebdomadaire, Candide*, and *Tout à Vous*.

Sauguet lives on the sixth floor of an old and weatherbeaten house on the outskirts of Paris. His apartment is cluttered with collections of exotic fabrics, statuettes, a great many paintings, and *objets d'art*. Besides music, Sauguet is most interested in art, and his personal collection provides testimony to his discriminating taste. Another of his interests is acting; he has made several appearances on the stage. He has a country house in the Bordeaux region where he does most of his composing.

Sauguet visited the United States for the first time in the spring of 1953. On April 24 there took place in New York an all-Sauguet concert under the sponsorship of the International Society for Contemporary Music. "The native wit and movement, the Gallic point and esprit, and the warm, directly melodic nature of Mr. Sauguet's art were extensively revealed," wrote Olin Downes.

MAJOR WORKS:

Ballets—La Chatte, 1927; David, 1929; La Nuit, 1930; Fastes, 1933; Les Forains, 1945; Les Mirages, 1947; La Rencontre, 1948; Cordelia, 1951.

Chamber Music—String Quartet No. 1, 1940; Trio, for oboe, clarinet, and bassoon, 1947; String Quartet No. 2, 1948.

Choral Music—Les Ombres du Jardin, cantata, 1938; Les Saisons: Symphonie Allégorique, for chorus and orchestra, 1949.

Operas—Le Plumet du Colonel, opera-bouffe, 1924; La Contrebasse, opéra-comique, 1930; La Chartreuse de Parme, 1939; La Gageuse Imprévue, 1944.

Orchestral Music—Divertissement de Chambre, for small orchestra, 1931; La Voyante, cantata for solo voice and small orchestra, 1932; Concerto for Piano and Orchestra, 1934; Symphonie Expiatoire, 1945; Concerto for Violin and Orchestra, 1953.

Piano Music—Français (two books).

Vocal Music—La Voyante, song-cycle; La Chèvre-Feuille, song-cycle.

ABOUT:

New York Times, April 19, 1953.

Florent Schmitt 1870-

FLORENT SCHMITT was born in Blâmont, in the department of Meurthe-et-Moselle, France, on September 28, 1870. His parents, while not professional musicians, were devoted to and practitioners of the art, and saw to it that their son received training. They also insisted on a thorough academic training. Schmitt was raised with the classics and German romantics, and his favorite subjects at school were Latin, geography, and algebra.

In his seventeenth year he decided to become a musician. He went to Nancy to study with local teachers in preparation for his entrance examinations for the Paris Conservatory. Two years later he was enrolled in the Conservatory. His studies with Dubois, Lavignac, and Gedalge were interrupted by the prescribed military service (during which Schmitt played the flute in the band). When his period of service was over, Schmitt returned to the Conservatory and entered the composition class of Massenet and Fauré. In 1896 Schmitt tried for the Prix de Rome and failed. A year later he won second prize. He persisted each year until, in 1900, he won first prize with the

Schmitt: shmēt

Photo-Lipnitzki

FLORENT SCHMITT

cantata *Semiramis*; actually even then many of the members of the jury voted against Schmitt, but Fauré worked so conscientiously in gathering the necessary votes that Schmitt was able to win by a narrow margin.

During the years Schmitt lived in Rome as winner of the Prix de Rome, only a few months were spent at the Villa Medici. "I distinguished myself by the fact that I got into more trouble than probably any other holder of the Prix de Rome." The rest of the time was spent in traveling throughout Europe, Scandinavia, North Africa, and the Near East. Indignant letters from the Conservatory authorities followed him wherever he went and, at intermittent periods, brought him back to Rome long enough to appease them.

In 1906 Schmitt set the Fourty-seventh Psalm (Psalm 46 in the Vulgate) for chorus, soloists, organ, and orchestra. It is still regarded as one of his masterworks, music of nobility and majesty. When introduced in Paris on December 27, 1906, it was condemned by many for its advanced idiom. The reactionary critics and anti-modernists spoke bitterly about its dissonances, abrupt modulations, and bizarre orchestration.

One year after this, came another of Schmitt's famous works, *La Tragédie de Salomé*, inspired by a poem of Robert d'Humières. The score was originally intended for a "mute drama" for the dancer

Loie Fuller, seen in Paris on November 9, 1907. Schmitt adapted the score into a symphonic poem, and it is in this version that the music has been extensively performed. Sensuous in style, romantic in its fervor, and exciting in its emotional surges and exotic colors, *La Tragédie de Salomé* is one of Schmitt's finest orchestral compositions.

At the same time he was writing an important chamber-music work, the beautiful Quintet in B minor, which he began in 1905 and completed three years after that. When introduced in Paris on March 26, 1909, the Quintet was severely criticized for its inordinate length; one critic described it as "the longest quintet in history." But a minority report was rendered by M. D. Calvocoressi, who found it to be "one of the most moving and revealing creations of the past few years."

When Schmitt returned to Paris from his travels he took an active part in its musical life. As a composer he did not identify himself either with the Debussyites (then in vogue) or with the *avant-garde* (beginning to emerge). In his writing and thinking he remained independent of schools and trends. He did use his expanding influence, however, to further the cause of the modern composer, and he did not hesitate to hurl himself into the maelstrom of every *cause célèbre,* on the side of the attacked composer. He was one of the first musicians in Paris to speak enthusiastically about Satie. He defended Stravinsky at the tempestuous premiere of *The Rite of Spring*, and sided with Schoenberg when the *Five Pieces for Orchestra* created a furor in Paris.

Schmitt's music, wrote M. D. Calvocoressi, is "free from the abstract intellecualism and formalism that are so dangerous to all arts, and reveals a temperament loving sounds and rhythms for their own intrinsic beauty; it possesses that inwardness, that effusive lyricism through which it at times differs from the music of the impressionist school. . . . He does not scruple to use, at times, the simplest and so to speak the most massive dynamic effects; he shuns neither grandiloquence, nor insistence, nor any of the plain, if effective, means of classical art, never to be met with in the works of a Debussy or a Ravel. But with him they are never mere rhetorical expedients, and nowise resemble the stereotyped airs and graces of the post-classicists. In fact, that straight-forward idiom, that epic diction, being natural to Schmitt in some of his moods, appear in his music alive and original."

From 1922 to 1924 Schmitt was the director of the Lyons Conservatory. In 1932 he visited the United States, appearing as pianist in concerts of his works. Four years later he was elected a member of the French Academy.

Florent Schmitt spends winters in Paris (at the home of Mme. Frederick Moreau, who guards him jealously from the distractions and annoyances of the outside world). In summers he occupies his own house in St. Cloud. His diversions, today as yesterday, include travel, long walks, attending five o'clock teas of friends, and going to the theatre and movies. He possesses extraordinary vitality and has magically retained his enthusiasms. His conversation is usually spiced with cynical humor.

MAJOR WORKS:

Ballets—La Tragédie de Salomé, 1907; Le Petit Elf Ferme-L'Œil, 1924; Oriane et le Prince d'Amour, 1933.

Chamber Music—Quintet in B minor, for piano and strings, op. 51, 1908; Lied et Scherzo, for double wind quintet, op. 54, 1910; Sonata for Violin and Piano, op. 68, 1919; Suite en Rocaille, for flute, violin, viola, cello, and harp, 1934; Hasards, suite for piano, violin, viola, and cello, op. 95, 1939; Quartet, for saxophones, op. 102, 1941; String Trio, op. 105, 1944; Quartet, for flutes, op. 106, 1944; Quartet, for three trombones and tuba, 1946; String Quartet, op. 112, 1948.

Choral Music—Psaume 47, op. 38, 1906; Chant de Guerre, op. 63, 1914; Five Motets, op. 60, 1917; Fête de la Lumière, 1937; À Contre-Voix, 1942.

Orchestral Music—Musique de Plein Air, op. 44, 1906; La Tragédie de Salomé, suite, op. 50, 1907; Trois Rapsodies, op. 53, 1904; Légende, for violin (or viola, or saxophone) and orchestra, op. 66, 1918; Antoine et Cléopâtre, two suites, op. 69, 1920; Mirages, op. 70, 1921; Danse d'Abisag, op. 75, 1925; Salammbô, symphonic episodes, op. 76, 1925; Rondo Burlesque, op. 79, 1927; Symphonie Concertante, op. 82, 1931; Trois Danses, op. 86, 1935; Enfants, eight pieces for small orchestra, op. 92, 1938; 4 poèmes de Ronsard, for voice and orchestra, op. 98, 1940; Janiana, symphony for string orchestra, op. 101, 1941; Habayssée, for violin and orchestra, op. 110, 1947; Trois Monocantes, 1948; Scènes de la Vie Moyenne, 1949.

Piano Music—Soirs, ten preludes, op. 5, 1896; Trois Valses Nocturnes, op. 13, 1902; Puppazzi, eight pieces, op. 36, 1907; Pieces Romantiques, op. 42, 1908; Crépuscules, op. 56, 1911: Ombres, op. 64, 1917; Mirages, op. 70, 1921; Clavecin Obtempérant, op. 107, 1945.

ABOUT:

Ferroud, P. O., Autour de Florent Schmitt; Chesterian (London), March 1932.

Arnold Schoenberg *1874-1951*

(See *American Composers Today*)

Franz Schreker *1878-1934*

FRANZ SCHREKER was born in Monaco on March 23, 1878. As a child he was brought to Vienna, where he began his music study at the Conservatory. Though he was a brilliant student, winning highest honors in composition, he often came into conflict with the school authorities. On one occasion he broke the rules against extra-curricular activity by organizing a music society for the purpose of giving public concerts; on other occasions he antagonized his teachers by his repeated espousal of advanced and iconoclastic tendencies.

He wrote his first opera, *Flammen,* at the age of twenty (it was not performed until almost two decades later). Failing to get recognition, he earned his living at musical tasks other than composition. In 1911 he founded (and after that directed) the Philharmonic Choir. He now devoted himself to the cause of contemporary music by giving first performances to many provocative works, including Schoenberg's *Gurre-Lieder* in 1913. Because of his association with the most radical and provocative tendencies in music, Schreker was dismissed in 1913 from

FRANZ SCHREKER

Schreker: shrā'kĕr

the faculty of the Academy of Prussian Arts, a post he had held for a few years, by order of the German Ministry of Education.

Meanwhile, on August 12, 1912, there took place in Frankfurt the premiere of an opera, *Der Ferne Klang*. It was a failure. Though its chromatic writing betrayed its indebtedness to the Wagnerian style then in vogue, the opera already undertook experiments with naturalism and with a vigorous and modern harmonic and instrumental language. When this opera was heard in Paris it was well received. Henri Quittard wrote in *Le Figaro*: "It is certain that the composer must be counted from this day as one of the most original and most interesting writers of our epoch." However, the premiere of his one-act opera, *Das Spielwerk und die Prinzessin*, created such a scandal in Vienna in 1913 that the director of the opera house had to remove it suddenly from the repertory.

Schreker's success was not established until after World War I. The first performance of his opera *Die Gezeichneten*—in Frankfurt in 1918—was the first indication that the tide had turned. By this time Schreker's identity as an opera composer was completely realized. He blended Wagnerian tendencies with expressionistic devices, merged naturalism with mysticism. The dramatic element was pronounced, but lyricism was not sacrificed. The melodies, for all their freedom of movement, had lyrical charm, at the same time serving the immediate demands of the play. The orchestration, now refined and sensitized, and now rich-textured, seemed (as César Saerchinger once wrote) to "atomize the whole musical substance into a delicate spray."

Die Gezeichneten was followed by an even greater success: *Der Schatzgräber*, introduced in Frankfurt in 1920. From this time on, Schreker was frequently heard in the opera houses of Europe; before 1924, his works were given more than two hundred performances in Germany and Austria. His works inspired the emergence of a school of German musical thought which regarded Schreker as its leader and prophet. "In Germany and Austria," wrote A. Machebey, "Schreker is the champion of the reaction against Wagner. . . . But his culture is entirely romantic, his music entirely dependent

on the old technique; in the melodies, expressive chromaticism is exploited; the harmonization is fundamentally Wagnerian—a feature which is underlined by the quality of the scoring. Here and there, however, atonal tendencies are discernible, even in his comparatively early works. And in the later works these tendencies gain ground, although his musical education will always prevent his reaching the final stage of full atonality."

In 1920 Schreker became director of the Akademische Hochschule für Musik in Berlin. For the next decade his influence as a teacher was felt strongly by many of the younger German musicians who studied with him. In May 1933, because the Nazi authorities were making his position uncomfortable, he decided to take an "indefinite leave-of-absence." He never returned to the Academy. He died in Berlin on March 21, 1934.

Like Wagner, Schreker wrote the texts for all his operas.

Major Works:

Ballet—The Birthday of the Infanta, 1908.

Choral Music—Psalm 116, for female chorus and orchestra, op. 6; Schwanengesang, for chorus and orchestra, op. 11.

Operas—Flammen, op. 10, 1902; Der Ferne Klang, 1911; Das Spielwerk und die Prinzessin, 1916; Die Gezeichneten, 1916 (revised 1920); Der Schatzgräber, 1920; Irrelohe, 1924; Der Singende Teufel, 1928; Christophorus, 1932; Der Schmied von Gent, 1932.

Orchestral Music—Ekkehard, overture, op. 12, 1902; Romantic Suite, 1903; The Birthday of the Infanta, suite, 1908 (revised 1923); Ein Tanzspiel, Rokoko, 1908; Fantastic Overture; Kammersymphonie, for twenty-three instruments, 1921.

About:

Bekker, P., Franz Schreker.

Cyril Scott 1879-

CYRIL MEIR SCOTT was born in Oxton, Cheshire, on September 27, 1879. His father, a Greek scholar, directed his son early to academic study. Music always appealed strongly to Cyril Scott: as a child he played the piano by ear and began making up his own melodies. His mother, a talented pianist, insisted that he study music formally. Study began in Germany at the Hoch

Conservatory, and four years after that continued privately with Ivan Knorr.

Returning to England from Germany, Scott settled in Liverpool, where he earned his living by teaching the piano. He also worked intensively on composition. In 1900 Hans Richter conducted the premiere of his *Heroic Suite* in Liverpool, and in the same year Richter introduced his First Symphony in Darmstadt. Scott subsequently destroyed these and other early works. Much more representative of the kind of music he wanted to write were the Piano Quartet in E minor, introduced in London in 1901 (the ensemble included Fritz Kreisler as first violinist), and the Second Symphony, directed by Henry J. Wood in London in 1903.

Scott was also writing and publishing some of the songs and smaller pieces for piano which made him famous. The best piano numbers included *Danse Nègre, Water Daffodil,* and *Lotus Land;* among his best songs were *Lullaby, The Blackbird Song,* and *Daffodils.* These small piano compositions and songs became so well known throughout the world of music that for a long time Scott was believed to be exclusively a composer of miniatures.

But his larger works had a definite impact on contemporary music. He was the first English composer to write in a pronounced modern style. His works contained many experimental techniques—such as shifting meters, dissonances, unorthodox modulations, strange progressions—adventurous for those years. Many composers have expressed their indebtedness to Scott's original style. "When I first went to London around 1900," wrote Percy Grainger, "Cyril Scott seemed to me to be the leading English compositional thought. It was largely his musical ideas and innovations that his fellow composers discussed and drew esthetic nourishment from." Eugene Goossens said: "Cyril Scott was the first English composer who was at once truly English and truly modern." And Claude Debussy wrote: "His rhythmic experiments, his technique, even his style of writing may at first appear strange and disconcerting. Inflexible severity, however, compels him to carry out to the full his particular system of esthetics and his only."

Tatler Studio

CYRIL SCOTT

Scott scored a great personal success with his Concerto for Piano and Orchestra, introduced in 1916 at a British music festival directed by Sir Thomas Beecham. (This Concerto was again heard in 1921 at the first concert of the British Music Society in London.) Other major works followed: *La Belle Dame sans Merci,* introduced in 1916 and successfully revived at the Leeds Festival in 1934; the opera *The Alchemist,* its premiere taking place in Essen, Germany, on May 28, 1925; and the *Festival Overture.* More recently, Scott has written the *Ode to the Great Men,* introduced in 1936, and the Concerto for Oboe and Orchestra, completed in 1946.

George Lowe has described Scott's style as follows; "The vocabulary in which he chooses to express himself is one of considerable originality both rhythmically and harmonically. He has no belief in imprisoning himself within the bounds set by theorists, but believes that art should be allowed to articulate freely, and he takes all sorts of licenses so long as they are not incompatible with his ideas of good taste."

Scott expounded his musical beliefs to this writer: "I consider that music without some sort of melody or motive cannot be lasting. The secret of satisfactory musical creation and form lies in variation. Moreover, musical form cannot be dispensed with.

As to narrowing down musical creation to theories and labels, this in my opinion denotes a lack of inspiration and a backward step.

"Although the dictum must be taken with some reservation, for opinions differ as to what is beauty and what is ugliness, yet the true artist is he who succeeds in inventing new forms of beauty. It is not very difficult to invent new forms of ugliness but far from easy to invent new forms of beauty as did the masters of music. Of course, for the sake of variety and strength, it is essential to have periods of discordancy as a foil to the concordant parts, especially in operatic creations, but where there is nothing but discordancy the result is monotony. For my own part, in my more serious creations, I have not been afraid of discord, but neither have I been afraid of melody as a necessary contrast."

At the age of twenty-four, Scott took up the study of mystical and occult philosophy, which affected both his life and outlook. Since then he has been a pronounced mystic, with a leaning towards Yoga theosophy and Vedantic philosophy.

In 1921 Scott toured the United States extensively, playing the piano, conducting orchestras, and lecturing on modern music. He has written several books, including *Music: Its Secret Influence Throughout the Ages,* an autobiography entitled *My Years of Indiscretion,* a study in adult education, and several books on occult philosophy (the last published anonymously).

During World War II Scott lived in Devonshire, in circumstances which made composing impossible. He then confined himself almost exclusively to his literary work, writing poems, plays, and an opera libretto, *Maureen O'Mara.*

About some of his other interests Scott writes: "I like to paint. I also like to go to some lonely place (preferably on the mountains) and find a quiet spot with a lovely view, and there write a libretto or a book. When I paint, I do not paint from nature but out of the imagination."

MAJOR WORKS:

Ballets—The Incompetent Apothecary; The Dance of the Red Death; Karma.

Chamber Music—Sonata for Violin and Piano, 1910: Tallahassee Suite, for violin and piano; Piano Quintet; First String Quartet; Second String Quartet; Piano Quartet; Piano Trio; Trio, for violin, viola, and cello; Divertimento, for string quartet; Rapsodie Arabesque, for flute, harp, violin, viola, and cello; Ballad, for cello and piano; Scotch Pastoral, for flute and piano; Idyllic Fantasy, for voice, oboe and cello.

Choral Music—Princesse Maleine, 1907; Nativity Hymn, 1910; La Belle Dame sans Merci, 1916; Ode to the Great Men, 1936; Summerland; Mystic Ode.

Operas—The Alchemist, 1924; The Shrine, 1925; The Saint of the Mountain.

Orchestral Music—Heroic Suite, 1900; Symphony No. 1, 1900; Three Symphonic Dances (revision of Symphony No. 2); Aubade, 1911; Festival Overture; Christmas Overture; Two Poems, 1913; Two Rhapsodies; British War March, 1914; Concerto for Piano and Orchestra, 1915; Two Passacaglias on Irish Themes, 1916; Concerto for Violin and Orchestra; Concerto for Cello and Orchestra; Concerto for Two Pianos and Orchestra; Concerto for Harpsichord and Orchestra; Concertino for Two Pianos and Small Orchestra; Symphony; The Muses; Concerto for Oboe and Orchestra, 1946.

Piano Music—Sonata, 1910; Indian Suite; Russian Suite; Jungle Book Impressions; Sonata No. 2; Ballad; Pastoral Suite; Fantaisie Orientale, 1937; Variations on an Oriental Theme, for two pianos; more than a hundred pieces, including Danse Nègre, Lotus Land, etc.

Vocal Music—Numerous songs for voice and piano including Lullaby, The Blackbird Song, and Daffodils, etc.

ABOUT:

Bacharach, A. L. (ed.) British Music of Our Time; Hull, A. E., Cyril Scott; Scott, C., My Years of Indiscretion.

Alexander Scriabin *1872-1915*

A LEXANDER NICOLAEVITCH SCRIABIN was born in Moscow on January 6, 1872. His mother, a talented pianist, died when he was less than two years old. The child was entrusted to the care of his grandmother and an aunt, both of whom —though oversolicitous and overprotective— allowed him to develop academically and musically according to his own inclinations. The boy learned by himself to read, write, and play the piano. On one occasion, after attending an opera, he built a little theatre with which he performed miniature dramas of his own writing by taking all the roles.

His interest in music threw other pastimes into the background. The piano became something of an obsession. He would kiss it

Scriabin: skrē-ä′bĭn

as if it were a human being, and would become emotionally disturbed when it was repaired or tuned. He was indefatigable in his practicing, and would spend tireless hours at improvisation. One day his aunt brought him to Anton Rubinstein. Rubinstein, impressed by the boy's talent, advised the boy to follow his own musical impulses, a suggestion which seemed both intelligent and practical.

In 1882, at his own request, he was enrolled in the Military School in Moscow. He was an excellent student and was popular with both his teachers and his classmates. At the same time, he studied the piano intensively with G. E. Conus. Subsequent music study included that of theory with Taneiev and piano with Zverev.

By the time he completed his studies at the Military School, Scriabin became convinced that he wanted to become a professional musician. He entered the Moscow Conservatory in 1888, and for several years studied with Arensky, Taneiev, and Safonov. He now devoted himself so slavishly towards developing his piano technique that some of the muscles of his right hand became paralyzed. This did not prevent him from competing for, and winning, the Gold Medal in piano playing. Nor did it arrest his intensive practicing. Ultimately full flexibility returned.

Scriabin left the Conservatory precipitately, and without a diploma, because he felt that undue partiality was being shown to a fellow-student, Rachmaninoff, at his expense. He now began his career as concert pianist with moderate success. He also had his first few works for the piano published by Jurgenson. These publications, and one of his recitals in 1894, attracted the interest of the powerful publisher Belaiev. Recognizing Scriabin's talent, Belaiev decided not only to publish everything Scriabin wrote but also to finance his musical career. The first works by Scriabin published by Belaiev appeared in 1895: Twelve Etudes and a Sonata.

In his earliest piano pieces Scriabin wears the mantle of Chopin. Here Scriabin is the romanticist in search of tonal beauty. But as Alfred J. Swan noted, Scriabin was no mere imitator. "He is Chopin's rightful successor, **and, as such, carried** to an extreme certain **peculiarities of** Chopin's style. What lay in

ALEXANDER SCRIABIN

the background with Chopin comes to the fore with Scriabin: the music grows in nervousness. . . . The tissue becomes closer and more compact, the writing neater and more scrupulous than even Chopin's."

In 1896 Belaiev organized an extensive concert tour for Scriabin. He gave recitals in Russia, Germany, France, Belgium, and Holland and scored a great success. The critic of the *Libre Critique* in Paris described him as "equally great as composer and pianist . . . an enlightened philosopher." The success of this tour further convinced Belaiev of Scriabin's immense gifts. He arranged a special annuity of about 515 rubles a year to enable him to devote more time to composition.

In 1897 Scriabin married the pianist Vera Isakovitch. Henceforth she was to devote a great part of her concerts to his music, and she often appeared with her husband in two-piano recitals of his works. Between 1898 and 1903 Scriabin taught at the Moscow Conservatory, but he did not like teaching, resented the fact that it kept him from composing, and finally gave it up completely. At about this time, Belaiev died, bringing to an end the annuity which he had been paying the composer. Fortunately, another patron appeared—one of his own pupils—to provide him with a generous yearly subsidy. Financially independent for the time being, Scriabin left Russia in 1904 for long tours. He now fell in love with a young girl and gifted pianist, Tatiana Schloezer, sister of the celebrated critic Boris de Schloezer, and for her he left his wife permanently. Though his wife Vera refused to give him a divorce, she seemed to harbor no bitterness against her husband and continued to do everything in her power to propagandize his music.

In November of 1906 Scriabin came to the United States on a concert tour. When Tatiana Schloezer arrived to join him, a scandal developed, since it was publicized that they were not married. To avoid prosecution on the grounds of moral turpitude, Scriabin and Tatiana left the United States suddenly without completing the projected tour.

Beginning with the turn of the twentieth century, Scriabin was more and more absorbing himself with mysticism. He associated himself with a group of mystics, "The Philosophical Society," and was greatly impressed by its teachings. A few years later, he turned to philosophy, becoming a passionate admirer of Nietzsche, and identifying himself with the Superman. From philosophy he progressed to theosophy.

This immersion in mysticism and theosophy affected his music. He started to evolve a musical system of his own, the basis of which was the so-called "Mystic Chord," constructed from the interval of the fourth. His musical writing was becoming increasingly involved and rarefied as he tried to make his works express his mysticism.

This new tendency in his music became particularly evident in his third symphony, *The Divine Poem,* intended to describe the evolution of the human spirit through pantheism to the affirmation of the divine ego. Scriabin completed this work in 1903, and it was introduced in Paris, under Nikisch's direction, on May 29, 1905. "A piece of wonderful music," A. Eaglefield Hull described it, "full of rich themes, well developed, and combined with mastery of counterpoint and modern harmony of a hue the like of which had not been heard before. It is musically logical, full of contrast, design, and color. At times the texture is quite simple; at other moments, of great complexity. Altogether it is a work of great originality and high poesy —an epoch-making work in the handling of modern harmony."

In his next symphony, entitled *Poem of Ecstasy,* Scriabin described the ecstasy of unfettered activity in the creative field. He completed it in 1907, and played parts of it for a group of distinguished musicians. One of them, Rimsky-Korsakov, said: "He's half out of his mind." But the Symphony received the second Glinka Prize, and found many supporters when introduced in New York on December 10, 1908, and repeated a month later in St. Petersburg.

In 1908 Scriabin met the brilliant young conductor Serge Koussevitzky, who was also the director of a new publishing house devoted to Russian music. Since Belaiev's death, Scriabin had been looking for a new publisher and patron; and young Koussevitzky was on the look-out for a new exciting personality to promote. Koussevitzky proposed to publish all of Scriabin's music, and —as a conductor—to propagandize his music widely. In 1910 when Koussevitzky embarked with his orchestra on his famous trip along the Volga, Scriabin went along as piano soloist in his own Piano Concerto. On March 15, 1911, Koussevitzky gave the world premiere of Scriabin's last symphony, and most ambitious orchestral work: *Prometheus.* This was a complex and not often clear musical delineation of the struggle of Man against the Cosmos, with Man endowed by Prometheus with the creative will through a divine spark. An involved work, it was made even more complicated by its demand for a color-keyboard which threw colors on a screen while the music was being played. The color apparatus was not used when Koussevitzky introduced the work, but it made its appearance during the American premiere of the Symphony in 1915.

A break between Scriabin and Koussevitzky took place soon after the Russian premiere of *Prometheus.* Each one was too much of an individualist to be able to work harmoniously with the other. Notwithstanding this permanent rift, Koussevitzky never relaxed his activity—not only in Russia, but later in Paris and Boston—to bring a greater understanding to Scriabin's music through repeated performances.

Scriabin was now evolving from the writing of mystical works to the creation of a monumental world-philosophy to which he gave the name of "The Mystery." His "Mystery" was to consist of a union of social, religious, philosophic, and artistic thought in summing up the history of man from the dawn of time to the final, and inevitable, cataclysm. (After the cataclysm, Scriabin felt, a new era would come, and a nobler race of men.) Every means was to be used; not only sight and sound, but also smell; Scriabin even planned employing a new language of sighs and exclamations to express the heretofore unexpressible. To Scriabin, his "Mystery" was the last will and testament of a dying civilization before the emergence of a new and greater one.

For many years, Scriabin planned his Mystery. He wanted it performed in India in a special temple built for that purpose and before worshipers. He went to an agency to get all the information he could about travel to and accommodations in India. But all that Scriabin succeeded in writing of the Mystery was the text and some musical sketches for a preamble which he called "Propylaea" —"Propylaea" being the entrance to the Acropolis in Athens.

When war broke out in 1914, Scriabin was jubilant, for he was convinced that this was the cataclysm that he had so long foreseen. He was also convinced that he was delegated by Fate to become the new Messiah to lead the way out of the cataclysm and into the brave new world. But his premature death brought his grandiose visions to a sudden end. Death was caused by an infection from a furuncle and took place in Moscow on April 27, 1915.

Besides his symphonies, Scriabin produced a library of music for the piano, including sonatas, etudes, and preludes. We can trace here the growth of his style from romanticism through harmonic and rhythmic experimentation to its final refinement, rarefication, and mysticism. During the period of experimentation, "his innovations consisted mainly in creating new chords," wrote Leonid Sabaneyev in *Modern Russian Composers.* "This enthusiasm was a sort of sport with him. Scriabin wished to outdistance his contempories in creating chords with the greatest number of notes." In the last period, Scriabin's style—once again in Sabaneyev's description—reached "an extraordinary exquisiteness and refinement, his harmony a rare complexity along with a saturation of

psychologic content. Side by side with this, we observe a dissolution of rhythm, a reduction of melody to the minimum, a severance of the musical web and line which turns into a series of spasmodic exclamations and destroys the impression of unity and wholeness."

Major Works:

Orchestral Music—Concerto in F-sharp major, for piano and orchestra, op. 20, 1894; Symphony No. 1, in E minor, op. 26, 1891; Symphony No. 2, in C major-C minor, op. 29, 1903; The Divine Poem (Symphony No. 3), op. 43, 1905; The Poem of Ecstasy (Symphony No. 4), op. 54, 1908; Prometheus: The Poem of Fire (Symphony No. 5), op. 60, 1910.

Piano Music—10 sonatas; 24 etudes; 85 preludes; 12 poems; 9 impromptus; 21 mazurkas; 4 nocturnes; 2 waltzes; etc.

About:

Hull, A. E., Scriabin; Swan, A. J., Scriabin.

Dmitri Shostakovich *1906-*

DMITRI SHOSTAKOVICH was born in St. Petersburg (now Leningrad) on September 25, 1906. Both his parents were musical, his mother having graduated from the St. Petersburg Conservatory. She began teaching her son the piano when he was nine years old. Soon realizing he required better instruction than she could give him, she enrolled him in the Glasser Music School where, in his initial year, he wrote his first work, the *Theme and Variations,* for piano. The piece was never actually put down on paper. But, a few years later, when Shostakovich gave piano recitals, he sometimes played it as an encore.

From the Glasser Music School, Shostakovich went on to the Leningrad Conservatory, in 1919, to study the piano with Nikolaev and composition with Maximilian Steinberg. During his first year at the Conservatory he completed a set of eight piano preludes which made a deep impression on Glazunov, director of the Conservatory. It was not long before Shostakovich was to see one of his works published: *Three Fantastic Dances,* issued in 1926, in which the influences of Schumann and Chopin are evident. Before his graduation from the Conservatory, Shostakovich also made several successful appearances as a pianist.

Shostakovich: shŏs-tă-kô'vĭch

Courtesy of Musical Courier

DMITRI SHOSTAKOVICH

Life was not easy for him. The Revolution caused widespread deprivation and suffering. Besides this, the death of Shostakovich's father intensified the poverty of the family so that it was often denied even basic necessities. Furthermore, Shostakovich was suffering from tuberculosis of the lymphatic glands, a condition which necessitated repeated visits to a sanatorium. These problems might, at times, interrupt his activities at the Conservatory and his composing, but they could not arrest his development.

In 1926 Shostakovich was graduated from the Conservatory. For his graduation exercise he completed the First Symphony, which was introduced by the Leningrad Philharmonic, under Nicolas Malko, on May 12, 1926. It was well received. Though derivative of Tchaikovsky and Prokofiev, the symphony was a brilliant achievement, remarkable for its rhythmic vitality, freshness of melodic material, and virtuosity in orchestration. When the symphony was heard in Moscow a few months later it was an even greater success. In 1927 Bruno Walter directed the symphony in Berlin (the first time it was heard outside the Soviet Union) and it was acclaimed. It was given in the United States in 1928 by Leopold Stokowski. Since then it has become the most popular of all Shostakovich's symphonies.

He did not do any writing immediately after leaving the Conservatory. As he put it, he first wanted to "overhaul a great part of the musical baggage I had acquired." And it was several years before he duplicated the striking success of his First Symphony. In the spring of 1927 he wrote a new symphony to commemorate the tenth anniversary of the October Revolution; it was a failure. The Third Symphony, performed two years later, was also a failure. An opera, *The Nose* (based on a Gogol story), performed in 1930, was denounced as "decadent" and "bourgeois" by the Association of Proletarian Composers.

In 1930 Shostakovich won first prize in a national competition for a ballet on Soviet themes with *The Age of Gold*. This work also was received coldly when it was introduced that same year, but only because its libretto was confused; Shostakovich's music was liked for its trenchant wit and delightful impudence. From this ballet score, two excerpts have survived: "Polka" and "Russian Dance."

In the next few years, Shostakovich was able to establish himself as one of the most important composers in the Soviet Union. His ballet *The Bolt,* produced in Leningrad in 1931, was a major success. His twenty-four preludes for piano, completed in 1933, increased his artistic prestige, and his Concerto for Piano and Orchestra, written in the same year, contributed to his growing fame. On January 22, 1934, his most ambitious work up to that time—the opera *Lady Macbeth of Mzensk*—was produced in Leningrad. It was a triumph. The critics were effusive in their praises, and the audiences were so taken with the new opera that for two years it played to capacity houses. It was hailed as the greatest opera to come from the Soviet Union, and in 1935 it was presented in Cleveland and New York.

Shostakovich intended his opera as a tribute to the emancipation of the Russian woman. "I tried to make the musical language as simple as possible," he explained at the time. "All vocal parts in my opera are built on broad cantilena, making use of all the resources of the human voice." But he did more than this, too. He allowed his instinctive bent for satire complete freedom of expression.

With the success of both the opera and its composer seemingly uncontested and secure, Shostakovich was suddenly and mysteriously subjected to a violent attack from a *Pravda* editorial, which described his opera as "a mess instead of music," and its music as "crude, primitive, vulgar." Hardly had the repercussions of this bitter denunciation died down when Shostakovich was excoriated again, this time for the music of his ballet *The Limpid Stream.* "It jingles, it means nothing; the composer apparently has only contempt for our national songs"—so wrote an editorialist. Two such vitriolic attacks in succession, and from a source like *Pravda,* could mean only one thing: Shostakovich had fallen out of grace with the Soviet authorities.

But those who suspected that Shostakovich's career had come to a sudden end were wrong. In 1937 he completed the Fifth Symphony, which was performed on November 21, 1937 and received a thunderous ovation. The critics, apathetic to Shostakovich for two years, were rhapsodic; one of them—Andrei Budyakovsky—did not hesitate to describe the symphony as "a work of great depth . . . a milestone in the composer's development." The Fifth Symphony is, indeed, one of Shostakovich's most powerful and consistently inspired works. In place of his usual attitudes of satire and grotesquerie, we have wind-swept emotions, intense feelings, majesty of expression and within a form of cathedral-like spaciousness. Its slow movement is among the most moving pieces of music Shostakovich had written up to this time.

Having reestablished himself as a successful composer, Shostakovich succeeded in winning the Stalin Prize, for his Piano Quintet, in 1940. Once again he was one of the most highly esteemed and honored of Soviet composers. But, after the invasion of the Soviet Union by the Nazis in 1941, he also became a national hero. He joined the fire-fighting brigade at the Conservatory (he tried to join the Red Army but was turned down), and at the same time enlisted his music in the war effort. One of his first endeavors, and the most ambitious, was a symphony interpreting the impact of the war on the Soviet people, and particularly the effect of the Leningrad siege on the citizens of that city. He completed the symphony—his Seventh—in the town of Kuibyshev, where he had been sent when the government was transferred there from Moscow. And there the Symphony was introduced on March 1, 1942. It was a triumph, and it once again brought its composer the Stalin Prize.

The Symphony was now heard throughout the Soviet Union, to be acclaimed whereever it was heard. Success followed outside the Soviet Union, too: in London, it inspired an ovation on June 29, 1942; in the United States, it was introduced over the radio under Toscanini's direction on July 19, 1942, and shortly after that performed by most of the leading American orchestras. Much of the overpowering effect of the music was due to the momentous struggle in which the free world was engaged in 1942, and the promise of ultimate victory it gave. Later hearings confirmed what some of the critics suggested even in 1942—namely, that the symphony was specious in its dramatic effect and blatant, and that as music, apart from propaganda, it had little permanent value.

Shostakovich's Eighth Symphony came one year after the Seventh. It was intended by the composer as an optimistic work pointing to the beauty of life, but—since the Soviet Union was still at war—it had tragic overtones as well. It was introduced in Moscow on November 4, 1943, and met with only moderate success.

The optimism and gaiety Shostakovich hoped to express in his Eighth Symphony is found in the Ninth, introduced in Leningrad on September 3, 1946. It is one of Shostakovich's finest symphonies, and its feeling of exuberance and joy is truly intoxicating: its Largo movement, like the slow movement of the Fifth, is a deeply and personally felt piece of music. Both audience and critics liked this new Shostakovich symphony; D. Rabinovitch described it as "intensely moving and at times soul-stirring." But Soviet officials were less kindly disposed. They dismissed it for its "ideological weakness."

But an attack of a much more serious nature was soon to be leveled against Shostakovich. On February 10, 1948, the Central Committee of the Communist Party severely took to task some of the leading Soviet composers for their "subservience to bourgeois decadence" and their "formalism" (see Prokofiev). Shostakovich was also under fire.

With perhaps not too commendable resiliency, Shostakovich proceeded to change his esthetic aims and musical style to conform with the principles laid down by the Central Committee. He also made a public confession that he was guilty of all serious faults pointed out by his accusers. And he did not fail to return to the good graces of the authorities. In March 1949 he was selected as one of a committee of seven to represent the Soviet Union at the Cultural and Scientific Conference for World Peace held in the United States. And a few months after his return to his native land he won the Stalin Prize for a third time—for the oratorio *The Song of the Forests*, first heard on November 26, 1949.

Whether he is extravagantly praised or just as extravagantly denounced—and frequently with justification on each occasion—Shostakovich is one of the most significant composers of the twentieth century. It is very true that he lacks self-criticism and that often he combines powerful creation with second-hand ideas and clichés. But if a composer is to be judged by his best music, Shostakovich is a powerful and original voice. He has a scintillating irony and an infectious wit; and in moments of greater repose, he can be noble and genuinely majestic. His greatest works—the First, Fifth, and Ninth Symphonies; the Piano Quintet; the Second String Quartet; his best piano preludes; and the Piano Concerto—are among the finest works produced in our time. Works such as these are—as Ivan Martynov wrote—"allied to the best and most progressive works of Western European art. . . . Only this will reveal the full significance of Shostakovich's art which has inherited the best traditions of the Russian classics and is so strongly linked with the strivings of the most advanced artists of our times. This too reveals the truly modern character of Shostakovich's music and explains its exceptional popularity throughout the world. The art of this master is indeed profoundly national and intimately connected with the whole of Soviet culture. It is interlaced, nonetheless, with the best and most progressive elements of world art and is, therefore, cosmopolitan, and international in

nature. The significance and timeliness of their content, their refreshing originality, eloquence of expression and progressive character place the mature works of Shostakovich among the most outstanding creations of world culture."

Shostakovich has always conceived of his music not as "an end in itself but a vital weapon in the struggle." He goes on to say: "There can be no music without ideology. . . . Lenin himself said that 'music is a means of unifying broad masses of people.' . . . Even the symphonic form . . . can be said to have a bearing on politics." On another occasion he said: "The aim which I assign to my work is that of helping in every way to enlighten our remarkable country."

His wife has described his work methods: "He demands no 'special' working conditions. He just sits down at his writing desk and writes—morning, noon, evening. . . . If it isn't singing or shouting, noises do not affect him at all. The door of the room where he works is usually open. . . . He composes swiftly, writing the score straight through, usually without changes or deletions. Dmitri has a great capacity for work and once having started a composition he is wholly engrossed. . . . Once the work is finished he cools down, to so speak, to warm up again and become entirely engrossed with the next work. He almost never reverts to what he has already written and therefore already experienced. It is far simpler for him to write a new than to remold a finished work."

MAJOR WORKS:

Ballets—The Age of Gold, op. 22, 1930; The Bolt, op. 27, 1931; The Limpid Stream, op. 39, 1935.

Chamber Music—Two Pieces for String Octet, op. 11, 1925; Sonata for Cello and Piano, op. 40, 1935; String Quartet No. 1, op. 49, 1938; Piano Quintet, op. 57, 1940; Trio in E minor, op. 67, 1944; String Quartet No. 2, op. 69, 1945; String Quartet No. 3, op. 73, 1947.

Choral Music—Song of the Forests, oratorio, 1950.

Operas—The Nose, op. 15, 1930; Lady Macbeth of Mzensk, op. 29, 1932.

Orchestral Music—Symphony No. 1, op. 10, 1925; Symphony No. 2, op. 14, 1927; Symphony No. 3, op. 20, 1929; Concerto for Piano and Orchestra, op. 35, 1933; Symphony No. 4, op. 43, 1936; Symphony No. 5, op. 47, 1937; Symphony No. 6, op. 54, 1939; Symphony No. 7, op. 60, 1941; Leningrad, suite for chorus and orchestra, op. 61, 1942; Symphony No. 8, op. 65, 1942; Symphony No. 9, op. 70, 1945; Ballet Suite No. 1, 1950.

Piano Music—Sonata, op. 12, 1926; Twenty-four Preludes, op. 34, 1932-33; Sonata No. 2, op. 64, 1943; Twenty-four Preludes and Fugues, 1951.

Vocal Music—Six Songs, to words by Japanese poets, op. 21, 1930; Four Songs to Pushkin's texts, op. 46, 1936.

ABOUT:

Nabokov, N., Old Friends and New Music; Martynov, I., Shostakovich: The Man and his Work; Seroff, V. I., Dmitri Shostakovich: The Life and Background of a Soviet Composer; Musical Quarterly, October 1942.

Jean Sibelius *1865-*

JEAN CHRISTIAN SIBELIUS was born in Tavastehus, Finland, on December 8, 1865, the son of a regimental doctor. He started the study of the piano in his ninth year, showing marked aptitude and fascination for improvisation. One year later he wrote his first piece of music, *Water Drops,* a duet for violin and cello. When he was eleven, he entered the Finnish Model Lyceum. He was a shy and introspective boy, given to prolonged day-dreaming. "There goes Sibelius, off into another world," his teacher would announce.

He began taking lessons on the violin when he was fifteen. At the same time he learned all he could about harmony, theory and counterpoint from textbooks, and acquired enough of knowledge of composition to complete a trio and a piano quartet.

After his graduation from the Lyceum, he was sent to the Helsingfors University for the study of law. But music meant much more to him than law studies, which he neglected for musical activities. After a single year at the University, he gave up law for good to concentrate on music. He attended the Helsingfors Conservatory, where his teachers included Busoni (then on a visit to Finland to teach at the Conservatory) and Wegelius. He made such rapid progress that he was given a scholarship for further study in Germany. In 1889 he went to Berlin, where he studied with Albert Becker. After a brief return to Finland, to become engaged to his sweetheart, Aino

Finnish Travel Information Bureau
JEAN SIBELIUS

Järnefelt, he went on to Vienna to complete his music study with Karl Goldmark and Robert Fuchs. Contact with the German romantic tradition, then so much in vogue both in Berlin and in Vienna, led him to write on octet and an orchestral overture in a similar manner.

But he deserted German romanticism immediately after his return to his native land in 1891. During the closing decade of the nineteenth century, Finland was suffering oppression at the hands of its Russian rulers. The ruthless despotism of Nicholas II robbed the Finnish people for their freedom. Newspapers were suppressed; patriots were imprisoned. This attempt to crush the Finnish people inevitably aroused and inflamed their patriotic ardor. Underground movements arose to keep alive the messages of truth and freedom, to bolster the national pride. The spirit in the air infected Sibelius upon his return from Germany. He now found his mission as a composer: to make his works serve the cause of Finnish liberation, to make it express his own intense national feelings. Thus he produced the first of his works with a Finnish personality. It was a five-movement symphonic poem called *Kullervo,* and it was introduced in Helsingfors on April 28, 1892, under the composer's direction. It was an immense success, for it spoke a message that was secretly nursed in

Sibelius: sĭ-bā'lĭ-ōōs

every true Finnish heart. With *Kullervo,* Sibelius emerged as a national composer.

On June 10, 1892, Sibelius married Aino Järnefelt. Marital obligations intensified the long-existing need to earn a livelihood. He taught theory at the Conservatory and at the orchestral school of the Philharmonic Society and he played the violin in a string quartet. He accelerated his creative activities at the same time. In 1892, he completed the first of his celebrated tone poems: *En Saga.* With the broad, passionate principal theme, the vigorous rhythms that sometimes had barbaric strength, and the bleak harmonies and sonorities, *En Saga* sounded a new voice in Finnish music.

After *En Saga,* Sibelius wrote the *Karelia Suite,* and a set of four legends inspired by the Finnish epic poem, the *Kalevala,* and centered around one of the mythical heroes, Lemminkäinen. This set included one of the most poignant orchestral tone poems written by Sibelius, *The Swan of Tuonela,* which is performed independently of the other three legends.

The most popular work produced by Sibelius before 1900 was the patriotic tone poem, *Finlandia.* Here is how it came to be written: As a reaction to a new wave of tyranny in Finland in 1899, a series of entertainments was organized to raise money and to voice a protest. For these entertainments, Sibelius wrote a suite called *Finland Awakes,* the last section of which was named *Suomi,* the Finnish name for Finland. In France, this last section was played under the name of *La Patrie,* and in Germany under *Vaterland.* This patriotic music had such an intoxicating effect on Finnish citizens that before long Nicholas II suppressed its performance throughout Finland. Not until 1905, when Russia was compelled to make far-reaching concessions to the Finns, was it heard again in Finland. Now retitled *Finlandia,* the work was played far and wide, expressing the national pride of a people that would be free.

Sibelius' position as the leading composer of Finland was acknowledged even before he wrote *Finlandia.* In 1897 he became the first Finnish composer to be given an annual government grant in order that he might be able to give up all his activities for composition.

Sibelius completed another significant work in 1899—his First Symphony. It was introduced in Helsingfors on April 26, 1899, at an all-Sibelius concert. The Second Symphony, written in Italy, was completed two years later and introduced in Helsingfors on March 8, 1902. In these two symphonies—which have never lost their popular appeal with audiences everywhere—Sibelius is almost Russian in his partiality to dramatic and emotional statements, in the Slavic character of his poignant melodies, and in his peasant energy. They may lack the subtlety of expression found in later symphonies, but their dramatic impact is inescapable.

Greater restraint of feeling, an increasing economy of means, a more tight-lipped control is found in the symphonies that Sibelius wrote after 1902. Five more appeared between 1907 and 1924, and in them Sibelius achieves that full mastery of symphonic technique, that sublimity of concept, that powerful conciseness and that national identity which are the identifiable traits of his symphonic style. "For any parallel to the mature symphonic work of Sibelius," wrote J. H. Elliot, "one turns to the sagas of the Northern races, so naturally and deeply is the music informed by the spirit, national and heroic, from which the legends arose. The general atmosphere is that of the wild, solitary, fabulous; and even where the moods of the music are predominantly triumphant —as, for instance, in the Third and Fifth Symphonies—the bursts of barbaric splendor and the building-up of powerful and vivid climaxes retain a certain austerity not to be accounted to the conscious joys of victory. Rather do they appeal as an exaltation in the abstract of some noble impulse which has striven and achieved.

"The moods of the music are not painted by arbitrary means or expressed in classical symbols; they are implicit in the substance, the very conception, of the music's esthetic. The despair and desolation of the wonderful Fourth Symphony hang in the air like tangible things: they do not agitate the personal feelings after the manner of Tchaikovsky's *Pathétique.* . . . Sibelius attains to a level of emotional implication more profound, more nearly objective. His music, moreover, lives on one plane and retains a unity of expression despite its multifarious changes of spirit. . . . Sibelius gives each symphony an individual character while sustaining the whole compass of his art upon a level that is remote, noble, and aloof."

Constant Lambert remarked that Sibelius advanced "the symphonic form more than any composer since Beethoven. Unhampered by the oppressive tradition which has virtually driven the Germans from a sentimental diatonicism to its mechanical reaction of intellectual atonality, he has produced a series of works which would, one imagines, be far more acceptable to Beethoven himself than the elaborate scaffoldings the Germans have erected in his name."

H. H. Mischa-Leon has pointed out that Sibelius' method of thematic development is original. "As a general rule, his symphonic movements are built up from fragmentary germs, or groups of notes, which grow and expand until the climax is reached with the complete presentation of the theme in its full splendor."

It is quite true that Sibelius has produced his best music within the symphonic form. But in the years preceding World War I he completed several highly successful works in other media as well—notably the popular salon piece, *Valse Triste*, and the romantic Concerto for Violin and Orchestra, both in 1903; the symphonic-fantasy, *Pohjola's Daughter*, in 1905; and the introspective string quartet (appropriately entitled *Voces Intimae*) in 1909.

Just before the outbreak of World War I, Sibelius paid his only visit to the United States. He was invited by Carl Stoeckel, a music patron, to conduct his own music with the Litchfield County Choral Union at the Norfolk Festival of Music. Sibelius' American debut took place on June 4, 1914, when he directed an all-Sibelius concert which included *Pohjola's Daughter* and *The Swan of Tuonela*. He was given a magnificent reception. Two weeks later, Yale University conferred on him the honorary degree of Doctor of Music. In making the presentation, the president of the university said: "Still in the prime of life, he has become by the power and originality of his work, one of the most distinguished of living composers. What Wagner did with Teutonic legend, Dr. Sibelius has done in his own impressive way with the legends of Finland as embodied in her national epic. He has translated the *Kalevala* into the universal language of music, remarkable for its breadth, large simplicity, and the infusion of a deeply poetic personality."

The period of World War I was a trying one for the composer and his family. Immediately after the Revolution in Russia, civil war broke out in Finland between the "Red" and "White" Guards. The Red Army twice invaded Sibelius' home, terrifying its occupants. We have descriptions of Sibelius trying to soothe his family by playing the piano for them.

Shortly after World War I, Sibelius toured Europe conducting concerts of his works. After 1924 he went into complete retirement. Henceforth he traveled little, except for periodic visits to Helsingfors, and wrote less. He secluded himself in his beautiful villa, Ainola, in the little town of Järvenpää, his home since 1904. Here, surrounded by the forests he loves and in scenes of incomparable natural beauty, he has had the privacy and seclusion he requires for contentment. Up to the time of World War II pilgrims from all parts of the world would beat a path to Järvenpää to pay homage to Sibelius. They did not need an address to reach their destination. They merely boarded the northern train out of Helsingfors and told the conductor they wanted to visit Sibelius. Since Järvenpää is too small a town to have a station, all trains stop there only when passengers specify they are visiting the master. To his visitors, Sibelius has always been a gracious host. He loves to be surrounded by the company of people and he likes to hear first-hand news of the outside world. But these visits have proved to be very taxing, and since World War II, Sibelius' wife has been protecting him from his admirers. In this she is aided by her countrymen, who do everything they can to discourage strangers from going to Villa Ainola. Nowadays, when a conductor is asked to stop the train at Järvenpää, he informs the passenger, politely but firmly, that visitors are no longer permitted at the Sibelius home.

Sibelius is not a falsely modest person. He knows he has produced great music and is proud of the fact. But honors of all kinds embarrass him profoundly. There is nothing he detests more than to talk about his own music. Asked about one of his works, he becomes flustered, waves his hand impatiently, and shakes his huge head brusquely. Then he changes the subject.

He is essentially a simple man whose only indulgence is smoking expensive cigars. His greatest pleasure comes from his gardens and from walking in his forests. Before World War II, he used to enjoy visiting the town tavern surrounded by neighbors and joining them in the drinking of *schnapps,* a smoke, and small-town talk.

The years of World War II were, to be sure, difficult ones, since Sibelius knew the agony of seeing his beloved land ruthlessly attacked by the superior Soviet forces. But he did not suffer physically. The grim realities of war hardly penetrated into Järvenpää, and throughout the war there was enough food for the entire family.

He is the most famous man in Finland. An attempt was made in 1940 to erect a statue in his honor, but this project had to be abandoned when Sibelius protested loudly. However, the Finnish government issued a postage stamp with his picture, the first time that a living composer has thus been honored. His seventy-fifth, eightieth, and eighty-fifth birthdays have been celebrated throughout Finland with festive concerts and other events befitting a national hero. The outside world, too, has honored him on these occasions with performances of his works.

MAJOR WORKS:

Chamber Music—Voces Intimae, string quartet, op. 56, 1909; Four Pieces, for violin or cello, and piano, op. 78, 1915; Sonatina in E-major for violin and piano, op. 80, 1915; Novelette, for violin and piano, op. 102, 1923; Four Pieces, for violin and piano, op. 115, 1929; Three Pieces, for violin and piano, op. 116, 1929.

Choral Music—The Origin of Fire, op. 32, 1902; The Captive Queen, op. 48, 1906; Five Part Songs, for a cappella male chorus, op. 84, 1915; Our Own Land, op. 92, 1918; Song of the Earth, op. 93, 1919; Hymn of the Earth, op. 95, 1920; Ritual Chorus, op. 107, 1925; The Song of Vainö, op. 110, 1926; Musique Religieuse, op. 113, 1927.

Orchestral Music—Kullervo, tone poem, op. 7, 1892; En Saga, tone poem, op. 9, 1892 (revised 1901); Karelia Overture, op. 10, 1893; Karelia Suite, op. 11, 1893; Four Legends (including The Swan of Tuonela), op. 22, 1899; Symphony No. 1 in E minor, op. 39, 1899; Finlandia, tone poem, op. 26, 1899 (revised 1900); Romance in C major, for string orchestra, op. 42, 1901; Symphony No. 2

in D major, op. 43, 1901; Valse Triste, op. 44, 1903; Pelleas and Melisande, suite, op. 46, 1905; Concerto in D minor for Violin and Orchestra, op. 47, 1903 (revised 1905); Pohjola's Daughter, fantasia, op. 49, 1905; Belshazzar's Feast, suite for small orchestra, op. 51, 1906; Symphony No. 3 in C major, op. 52, 1907; Night Ride and Sunrise, tone poem, op. 55, 1908; In Memoriam, funeral march, op. 59, 1909; Symphony No. 4 in A minor, op. 63, 1911; The Bard, tone poem, op. 64, 1913; Oceanides, op. 73, 1914; Symphony No. 5 in E-flat major, op. 82, 1915; Symphony No. 6 in D minor, op. 104, 1923; Symphony No. 7 in C major, op. 109, 1924; Tapiola, tone poem, op. 112, 1925.

Piano Music—Sonata in F, op. 12, 1893; Ten Pieces, op. 24, 1894-1903; Ten Pieces, op. 58, 1909; Three Sonatinas, op. 67, 1912; Four Lyric Pieces, op. 74, 1914; Thirteen Pieces, op. 76, 1914; Five Pieces, op. 85, 1916; Six Pieces, op. 94, 1919; Six Bagatelles, op. 97, 1920; Eight Short Pieces, op. 99, 1922; Five Romantic Pieces, op. 101, 1923; Five Characteristic Pieces, op. 103, 1924; Esquisses, op. 114, 1929.

Vocal Music—Seven Songs, op. 17, 1899; Six Songs, op. 36, 1899; Five Songs, op. 37, 1898-1902; Five Songs, op. 38, 1904; Six Songs, op. 50, 1906; Eight Songs, op. 57, 1909; Two Songs from Shakespeare's Twelfth Night, op. 60, 1909; Eight Songs, op. 61, 1910; Six Songs, op. 72, 1915; Six Songs, op. 86, 1916; Six Songs, op. 88, 1917; Six Songs, op. 90, 1917.

ABOUT:

Abraham, G. (ed.) The Music of Sibelius; De Törne, B. S., Sibelius: A Close-Up; Ekman, K., Jean Sibelius; Gray, C., Jean Sibelius; Newmarch, R., Jean Sibelius.

Christian Sinding *1856-1941*

CHRISTIAN SINDING was born in Kongsberg, Norway, on January 11, 1856. After studying piano and harmony with Lindemann in Trondheim, he went to the Leipzig Conservatory, where he remained from 1874 to 1877 and was a pupil of Reinecke (piano), Schradieck (violin), Jadassohn (composition) and Kretzschmar (musicology). Back in Norway, Sinding settled in Christiana (now Oslo), where he earned his living by teaching the piano and making a few concert appearances. In 1880 he was given a modest government stipend enabling him to afford further music study in Berlin, Dresden, and Munich and to direct his musical energies into composition. In 1884 his first major work was published, a Piano Quintet, severely criticized at the time for its harmonic audaciousness. Sinding's reputation as a composer, however, was made with his early compositions for the piano,

Sinding: sĭn'dĭng

both in the large and the small forms. Eugen Stegnitz remarked, these piano works are noteworthy for "the way in which the thematic material as a nursery of new musical organisms is turned to best advantage, the luxuriantly-flowing, ever-expressive and refined melody, and finally the spontaneous but always highly interesting themes." One of Sinding's early piano pieces is his most popular work, the sentimental *Rustle of Spring, (Frühlingsrauschen)* op. 32, no. 3.

In 1890 Sinding became the recipient of a new government stipend, this time large enough to enable him to give up all his activities except composition. This was testimony of the high position he had begun to occupy in the musical life of his native land. When Grieg died in 1907, Sinding was acknowledged to be the leading living Norwegian composer. In 1915 he was awarded a life pension of four thousand crowns a year, and on the occasion of his sixtieth birthday, in 1916, he was given an additional thirty thousand crowns.

For many years, Sinding spent part of every year in Berlin, where he was highly esteemed and where he was a member of the Academy of Arts. Between 1921 and 1923 he was a member of the faculty at the Eastman School of Music. He died in Oslo, on December 3, 1941.

Jenö Arbo has written that Sinding's music is "independent of any school. His style has often a Scandinavian strain, without its being always possible to characterize it as specifically Norwegian; but its sharp-cut rhythms, bold harmonies and vigorous tendency are characteristic of his Norwegian temperament. . . . Sinding's music is more epic than dramatic. He favors a heroic *al fresco* style which is manly and passionate in its form of expression. Side by side with the typical Sinding characteristics (restless modulation, violent harmonic movements, rhythmic monotony), we see the influence of Wagner, especially as regards melody and harmonization."

M. M. Ulfrstad makes an interesting comparison between Sinding and his distinguished predecessor Grieg: "Grieg's style was a combination of national melody with Schumann technique. Sinding's style became a combination of national melody with Wagnerian technique. His music is optimistic,

Courtesy of Musical Courier
CHRISTIAN SINDING

virile, and of epic strength and breadth. Whilst Grieg's music was an echo from the mountains, thin, mournful moods and poetic idylls, Sinding's is an echo from the sea that dashes against the rocks. In his music are heard the storm, the thunder of the waves, and the daring of the Vikings."

MAJOR WORKS:

Chamber Music—Piano Quintet in E minor, op. 5; Suite for Violin and Piano, op. 14; Piano Trio No. 1, op. 23; Sonata in E major, for violin and piano, op. 27; Scènes de la Vie, suite for violin and piano, op. 51; Piano Trio No. 2, op. 64; String Quartet in A minor, op. 70; Sonata in F major, for violin and piano, op. 73; Cantus Doloris, variations for violin and piano, op. 78; Piano Trio No. 3, op. 87; Suite in G minor, for violin and piano, op. 96; Sonata in D minor, for violin and piano, op. 99.

Opera—Der Heilige Berg, 1914.

Orchestral Music—Concerto in D-flat major, for piano and orchestra, op. 6; Suite in A minor, for violin and orchestra, op. 10; Symphony in D minor, op. 21; Épisodes Chevaleresques, suite, op. 35; Rondo Infinito, op. 42; Concerto in A major, for violin and orchestra, op. 45; Légende, for violin and orchestra, op. 46; Concerto in D major, for violin and orchestra, op. 60; Symphony in D major, op. 85; Romanza in D major, for violin and orchestra, op. 100; Symphony in F major, op. 121.

Piano Music—Alte Weisen, op. 1; Variations in E-flat minor, for two pianos, op. 2; Suite, op. 3; Five Pieces, op. 24; Seven Pieces, op. 25; Six Pieces, op. 31; Six Pieces, op. 32 (including the famous Rustle of Spring); Six Characteristic Pieces, op. 33; Two Duets, for two pianos, op. 41; Fifteen Caprices, op. 44; Burlesques, op. 48; Mélodies Mignonnes, op. 52; Morceaux Caractéristiques, op. 53; Five Etudes, op. 58; Waltzes, for four hands, op. 59; Eight Intermezzi, op. 68; Six Studies, for four hands, op. 71; Eight Intermezzi, op. 72; Eight Intermezzi, op. 82; Studien and Skizzen, op. 83; Sonata in B minor, op. 91; Fatum, variations, op. 94; Nordische Tänze und Weisen, for four hands, op. 98.

ABOUT:

Monrad-Jorganssen, D., Christian Sinding.

Richard Strauss *1864-1949*

R ICHARD STRAUSS was born in Munich, Germany, on June 11, 1864. His mother was the daughter of the prosperous Munich brewer, Pschorr; his father, Franz Strauss, was a celebrated horn player who was in the orchestra when Wagner helped rehearse *Tristan and Isolde* for its world premiere. It is interesting to point out—particularly in view of the son's later devoted espousal of Wagner and the music dramas—that Franz Strauss detested Wagner's music and did everything in his power to discredit it. Many intrigues in Munich against Wagner were both organized and led by him. On one occasion, he revealed his contempt for Wagner openly by suddenly rising during a rehearsal and leaving the orchestra, saying bitterly that he simply would not play such music.

Richard's mother began teaching him the piano when he was only four years old.

RICHARD STRAUSS

By the time he was six, the child started composing pieces for the piano. From then on he was often found sketching tunes on scraps of paper, even at school. His gift for music was apparent. His mother decided to place her son in more experienced hands. Under the instruction of August Tombo, and later under Benno Walter and F. W. Meyer, Strauss made remarkable progress.

His musical studies were combined with a thorough academic education first at the high school and, after 1882, at the University of Munich. By the time he entered the university, Strauss was an established composer with several important performances to his credit. In 1880 three songs were performed in Munich by a well known singer, Maysenheim. In 1881 a string quartet was introduced by an ensemble headed by his teacher, Benno Walter, and his Symphony in D minor was given its first performance under the direction of Hermann Levi.

While attending the university, Strauss first became a passionate Wagnerite. Up to this time he had echoed his father's prejudices. But additional hearings of Wagner's music dramas opened his eyes, and ears, and from then on his allegiance to Wagner was undivided.

Through his publisher in Berlin, Strauss had some of his early works brought to the attention of Hans von Bülow, the celebrated conductor at Meiningen. Hans von Bülow was impressed with the promise these pieces revealed and henceforth did what he could to promote the musical career of the young man. First he introduced Strauss's *Serenade for Thirteen Wind Instruments* in Meiningen. Then he commissioned Strauss to write several new works for his concerts. (The result was the Concerto for Horn and Orchestra and the *Suite for Thirteen Wind Instruments.*) In 1885, von Bülow appointed Strauss as his assistant in Meiningen, and one year later he designated the young man as his full-time successor as the conductor of the Meiningen Orchestra.

This was Strauss's apprenticeship with the baton. For the remainder of his life he was to combine his activity as composer with that of conductor, and to achieve striking successes with his performances. He was finally to become world-famous for his interpretations not only of his own works but also of the masterworks of Wagner and Mozart.

The final works in the first period of Strauss's career as a composer included a second Symphony, in F minor (introduced not in Europe but in the United States, by Theodore Thomas, on December 13, 1884) ; a Piano Quartet (awarded the Berlin Ton-künstlerverein Prize) ; and a Sonata for Violin and Piano. In this initial phase, Strauss was true to the established conventions of German romanticism. His music was derivative, sometimes from Brahms, sometimes from Wagner.

A meeting with the poet-musician Alexander Ritter, and the intimate exchange of ideas brought about by their friendship, was the turning point in Strauss's life. Ritter (who married Wagner's niece) was a staunch believer in the Wagnerian faith. He convinced Strauss that he must forsake German romantic tendencies and embrace the principles set forth by Wagner. Ritter wanted Strauss to write music that was dramatic and programmatic, instead of absolute and pure, and within a flexible mold, such as Liszt had created in his tone poems. Strauss later confessed: "His influence was in the nature of a storm wind."

His thinking clarified by his conversations with Ritter, Strauss stood ready to free himself from his subservience to Brahms and to write a new kind of music, more in line with Wagner's theories and esthetics. After a brief trip to Italy, in 1886, Strauss completed the first of his works to betray his new ideals: a symphonic fantasy entitled *Aus Italien*, which gave dramatic expression to the impact Italy had made upon him. For the first time he attempted dissonant writing, in an effort to arrive at greater realism; at the same time he built up a musical structure that was elastic and supple. Introduced in Munich, on March 2, 1887, *Aus Italien* was a fiasco.

There was no turning back for Strauss, however his audiences might reject his music; on the contrary, he was now to proceed with greater courage and daring in the direction he had chosen. In 1887, he completed his first tone poem, *Macbeth*. During the next decade he completed half a dozen other **tone poems which now** startled, now shocked, **now excited the entire** world of music, and which made their composer the most provocative figure in music. These tone poems made him famous, but they also proved him to be one of the most original and gifted composers of his generation; to this day, these tone poems are his greatest and most celebrated orchestral works. *Don Juan* came in 1888; *Death and Transfiguration (Tod und Verklärung)* in 1889; *Till Eulenspiegel's Merry Pranks (Till Eulenspiegels Lustige Streiche)* in 1895; *Thus Spake Zarathustra (Also Sprach Zarathustra)* in 1896; *Don Quixote* in 1897; and *A Hero's Life (Ein Heldenleben)* in 1898.

As Lawrence Gilman wrote, these tone poems "intruded into the snug and homely milieu of the concert room of the nineties with somewhat the effect of a lightning bolt at a family reunion." There was always, in Strauss's music, the unusual and the unexpected: the bold dissonances; the amazing use of realistic effects; the overrich orchestration, which sometimes called for instruments rarely found in the traditional symphony orchestra, and sometimes even of Strauss's own invention. Music such as this inevitably inspired either indignation or satire. Debussy once described one of the tone poems as "an hour of music in an asylum." One music critic characterized *Till Eulenspiegel* as "a vast and coruscating jumble of instrumental cackles about things unfit to be mentioned."

The shock and the surprise, of course, are gone. Neither Strauss's dissonances nor realism can startle audiences long since accustomed to greater indiscretions by more daring iconoclasts. But the wonder of this music remains, its pages of luminous poetry and of majestic speech, its passion and fire. In these tone poems Strauss seemed "to touch life with generous daring," as Lawrence Gilman wrote, "and at every side—at its loveliest and noblest, at its most disordered and pitiable and grotesque. He had learned how to convey experience still drenched in its essential colors, pungent with veritable odors, rich with all its implications. But Strauss, the orchestral tone poet, concerned himself less with the voicing of elemental emotions through heroic types than with the expression of human experience through the most direct and realistic processes of musical psychologizing. Unlike Beethoven in his dramatic overtures, Liszt and Tchaikovsky in their symphonic tone painting, Strauss was little concerned with the voicing of elemental emotions through symbolic figures. It was not Grief or Desire that engrossed him, but Don Quixote's grief, and Don Juan's desire."

Even before he started to write these remarkable tone poems, Strauss began to produce some of the best *Lieder* to be written since Schubert. As early as 1882 and 1883 he produced masterpieces: *Allerseelen* and *Zueignung*, for example. Before the century was over he had written a whole series of songs which deservedly put him in the noble company of the greatest *Lieder* composers of all time—songs like *Morgen*, and *Traum durch die Dämmerung*, and *Wiegenlied*. Gift of melody was here combined with a most astute capacity to project moods, and with an uncommon ability to suggest the subtlest nuances of the poem in tones.

Having written his most notable tone poems and songs by 1900, Strauss was to dominate a new world, that of opera. He had written his first operas in the closing decade of the nineteenth century. Imitative of Wagner, his first opera—and the one that followed it—were failures. But on December 9, 1905, Strauss's unqualified masterwork for the operatic stage was performed. On that day, in Dresden, there took place the premiere of *Salome*, based on the play of Oscar Wilde.

With *Salome*, Strauss again became the most controversial figure in the music of his day. The premiere in Dresden was an immense success; Strauss had to take more than twenty curtain calls. The critics were rhapsodic in their praises of Strauss's virtuosity as an orchestrator, the power and elemental passion of his musical conception, and the overwhelming dramatic impact of the final scene. But this acclaim was merely the lull before a storm. It was not long before a tempest erupted in many different parts of the music world. In Berlin, *Salome* was first barred by the Kaiser himself; then, when performed, it was described as degenerate and disgusting. In London, the censors would not permit its performance. In New York, at the Metropolitan Opera, it aroused such moral indignation that the

opera had to be removed from the repertory after a single performance. It was also withdrawn in Chicago, after the protests became vociferous.

But *Salome* has outlived its attackers. Time has made possible a more tolerant view towards Wilde's lascivious play about the love of Salome for John the Baptist, and for Strauss's equally sensual score. It was now apparent that here was one of the most vital and original operas to be written since Wagner's day—a work whose emotional effect on an audience is overpowering. Its place in the permanent operatic repertory is now assured.

With his next opera, *Elektra*, Strauss collaborated for the first time with the Austrian poet Hugo von Hofmannsthal, henceforth to provide the librettos for most of Strauss's operas. With even greater realism than in *Salome*, music and text portrayed the neurotic and demoniac Elektra in an artistic work that was at turns morbid and passionate, gruesome and spellbinding. When *Elektra* was introduced—in Dresden, on January 25, 1909—a correspondent for the *New York Times* reported: "It is a prodigious orchestral orgy. . . . The marvelous imitative effects of the orchestra are blood-curdling, drastic and gruesome to the last degree. It is fortunate for the hearers that the piece is no longer, for else it would be too nerve-wracking." Some of the German critics regarded the work as too "lurid," "violent," "harrowing." But a few recognized and acknowledged its power. Alfred Kalisch remarked that "the mind has to travel far back to search for anything at all comparable to it in musical mastery and almost elemental emotional power."

Elektra, like *Salome*, is one of the towering works in twentieth-century opera. Strauss completed one more unqualified masterwork for the stage, but one in a vein far different from the operas that preceded it. It was the comic opera, *Der Rosenkavalier*, following the traditions of German comic opera established by Mozart and further glorified by Wagner in *Die Meistersinger*. Hugo von Hofmannsthal produced a witty and nostalgic book set in the Vienna of Maria Theresa. For this play Strauss produced one of his most ingratiating, and at times deeply moving, scores. The waltzes from the opera have become favorites at symphony concerts. But they are by no means the most outstanding pages in the work. The Marschallin's monologue, in which she contemplates approaching advanced age, the beautiful Serenade in an eighteenth-century Italian style, the love duet of Sophie and Octavian, and the closing trio represent Strauss at his very best.

Der Rosenkavalier was completed in 1910 and successfully introduced at the Dresden Opera (Max Reinhardt was the stage director) on January 26, 1911. In the next few years Strauss produced several more charming works, though none of the stature of *Der Rosenkavalier*. The best of these included his delightful incidental music for Molière's *Le Bourgeois Gentilhomme* (in the classic style of the eighteenth century), a captivating opera, *Ariadne auf Naxos,* and *Ein Alpensinfonie.*

There could no longer be any question that Strauss was the most celebrated composer of the twentieth century; and a good case could be built up that he was also the most important. Fifty years old, he was the acknowledged master, apparently destined for still greater artistic and personal triumphs.

He was to receive those personal triumphs because he had written operatic, orchestral, and vocal works which had become classics, and because he was one of the great conductors of the time. But further artistic acclaim was to elude him. Though for the next generation he was to write many works and in virtually every form, the flame that had once burned so hot had become subdued. His one-time elemental passion and irresistible force were gone. What took their place were technical adroitness, wit, sophistication, and a certain amount of charm. After World War I, Strauss was sometimes a clever composer, and sometimes an appealing one; but he had ceased to be a great composer. He took to repeating mannerisms that had once made him successful. On the occasion of Strauss's seventieth birthday, Ernest Newman had to remark sadly that "Strauss *was* a genius." In the closing years of his life, Strauss reverted to the style of his apprentice years, writing concertos for the horn and for the oboe which reminded the listener of the early Brahmsian effusions of his Violin Sonata and Piano Quartet. In his last opera, *Die Liebe der Danae*—given its world premiere at the Salzburg Festival in the summer of 1952—Strauss imitated Wagner, even as he had done many years before in his very first opera.

But though he produced little after World War I to equal the genius and daring of his masterworks, he remained one of the giant figures in contemporary music. The works of his early manhood are indestructible; their importance cannot be overestimated. As Newman wrote in the London *Sunday Times:* "He laid the foundations, in the great sweeping melodies of his youthful *Don Juan*—which were something without parallel at that time in German or any other music—for a new melodic style, that of musical prose, which is at its best as wonderful as the finest musical metric, surpassing this, indeed, in sweep of line, variety of phrase-articulation, and shifting of actual footfall. . . . In *Salome* and *Elektra* in particular he proved that tonal harmony is still capable of new subtilizations. . . . Finally, in each of his best orchestral works he cast his structure unerringly in a form appropriate to the subject. . . . The mere fusion of them all into an organic musical work would of itself have been a technical feat of the first order; but more astonishing even than that is the imaginative power that somehow made a psychological unity of it all, a poignant expression of resignation and nostalgia. Yes, he was of the royal line, even if some queer kind of indolence and cynicism in him made him too content to play the part of the Old Pretender."

When the Nazis came to power in 1933, Richard Strauss—who embraced the new order—was made President of the Third Reich Music Chamber. He offered no resistance to the policies of the Chamber of Culture when it removed non-Aryan musicians from German musical life. Upon the ejection of Bruno Walter from his post with the Leipzig Gewandhaus, Strauss assumed his place. He also conducted in Bayreuth after Toscanini announced he would not conduct there for the Nazis. But this honeymoon of Strauss and the Nazi powers was brief. The break came when he insisted on collaborating with a Jew—Stefan Zweig—in the writing of his opera, *Die Schweigsame Frau.* He resigned his official position and went into seclusion and retirement at his Bavarian home in Garmisch-Partenkirchen. He lived there, and in Switzerland, during the turbulent years of World War II.

When the war was over, Strauss returned to his musical activities by completing several large works. They included a Concerto for Oboe and Orchestra, the *Metamorphosen* for twenty-three solo strings, and a Double Concerto, for clarinet, bassoon, strings, and harp. Despite his advanced age, he visited London in 1947 to conduct a concert of his own works at a festival dedicated to him. He was given a rousing ovation. Shortly before his death, his eighty-fifth birthday became an occasion for world-wide celebration. He died at his Bavarian home on September 8, 1949.

Walter H. Breuer, who visited Strauss after World War II, recorded his impressions in the *Musical Digest*: "I was surprised at the magnificent physique of Richard Strauss at his age. He is very tall, hardly bowed and still has a very distinguished and handsome appearance. As we talked, he would get up and move around the room with great agility, picking up photographs to show me. Occasionally, he became exceedingly animated in his conversation, in which his wife Pauline assisted. . . . Strauss has long slender hands of a remarkable blend of physical and spiritual beauty, terminating in probably the longest and most perfectly shaped fingers I have ever seen. In contrast to most musicians' more or less rounded heads, Strauss has an unusually elongated shape of head with a well developed frontal portion. Like most outstanding personalities, Strauss' eyes have a striking fascination about them. . . .

"Strauss still dresses in excellent taste and reflects the unobtrusive nonchalance of the grand seigneur. . . . There is a sincere, convincing politeness in his manner. . . . He is still vitally interested in the happenings of the music world. . . . In his ardent interest in the goings-on of the modern world and his flexibility in accepting completely revolutionary ideas, Strauss is a fine example of a mellowed wisdom and adaptability of a great mind that has succeeded in remaining young in spirit and, thus, is still able to cope with and derive zest from a young, modern life at the culmination of his own times."

There were two Strausses, and not one, each diametrically opposed to the other. The one was the lord of the music world, the aristocrat who lived in the grand manner, and who impressed those around him with his immense culture as well as refinement and impeccable taste. The *other* Strauss was known only to his most personal friends, a man capable of pettiness and opportunism, a man who was fantastically parsimonious, a man who was dominated by and in continual terror of his wife.

Strauss once explained his method of composition in the following lines: "I compose everywhere . . . walking or driving, eating or drinking, at home or abroad, in noisy hotels, in my garden, in railway carriages. My sketch book never leaves me, and as soon as a motive strikes me I jot it down. One of the most important melodies for my . . . opera [*Der Rosenkavalier*] struck me while I was playing a Bavarian card game. . . . But before I improvise even the smallest sketch for an opera, I allow the texts to permeate my thoughts and mature in me for at least six months so that the situation and characters may be thoroughly assimilated. Then only do I let my musical thoughts enter my mind. The sub-sketches then become sketches. They are copied out, worked out, arranged for piano and rearranged as often as four times. This is the hard part of the work. The score I write in my study, straightway without troubling, working at it twelve hours a day."

He wrote down his ideas on loose sheets, all of them stored in a closet as "people put their savings in a bank." Strauss added: "With the flight of time, interest accumulates. Likewise as time flies, the outlined ideas develop within me. One fine day I take all the sheets out of the closet and an opera grows out of it."

Strauss regarded *Till Eulenspiegel* as his finest tone poem, *Der Rosenkavalier* as his best opera, and *Traum durch die Dämmerung* as his most inspired song.

Strauss visited the United States twice, the first time in 1904 when he toured the country with the Wetzler Orchestra of Germany. At the first concert of this tour, on March 21, 1904, he introduced his *Sinfonia*

Domestica. Strauss returned to the United States in 1921, when he appeared as guest of many major orchestras in programs of his own works.

MAJOR WORKS:

Ballets—Eine Joseph-Legende, op. 63, 1914; Schlagobers, op. 70, 1924.

Chamber Music—String Quartet in A major, op. 2, 1881; Sonata for Cello and Piano in F major, op. 6, 1882; Piano Quartet in C minor, op. 13, 1884; Sonata in E-flat, for violin and piano, op. 18, 1887; Duett-Concertino, for clarinet, bassoon, harp, and strings, 1947.

Operas—Feuersnot, op. 50, 1900; Salome, op. 54, 1905; Elektra, op. 58, 1909; Der Rosenkavalier, op. 59, 1910; Ariadne auf Naxos (including Bourgeois Gentilhomme), op. 60, 1912 (revised 1916); Die Frau ohne Schatten, op. 65, 1917; Intermezzo, 1925; Die Aegyptische Helena, op. 75, 1928; Arabella, op. 79, 1933; Die Schweigsame Frau, op. 80, 1935; Der Friedenstag, op. 81, 1938; Daphne, op. 82, 1938; Midas, 1939; Die Liebe der Danae, op. 83, 1940; Capriccio, 1941.

Orchestral Music—Concerto for Violin and Orchestra, op. 8, 1881; Concerto No. 1 for Horn and Orchestra, op. 11, 1884; Symphony in F minor, op. 12, 1884; Burleske, for piano and orchestra, 1886; Aus Italien, op. 16, 1886; Don Juan, op. 20, 1888; Macbeth, op. 23, 1887; Death and Transfiguration, op. 24, 1889; Till Eulenspiegel, op. 28, 1895; Also Sprach Zarathustra, op. 30, 1896; Don Quixote, op. 35, 1897; Ein Heldenleben, op. 40, 1898; Sinfonia Domestica, op. 53, 1903; Eine Alpensinfonie, op. 64, 1915; Divertimento (after Couperin), 1941; Concerto No. 2 for Horn and Orchestra, 1942; Sonatina No. 1, for sixteen wind instruments, 1943; Metamorphosen, for twenty-three solo strings, 1945; Concerto for Oboe and Orchestra, 1945; Sonatina No. 2, for sixteen wind instruments, 1945; 4 Letzte Lieder, for soprano and orchestra, 1948.

Vocal Music—Eight Songs, op. 10 (including Allerseelen and Zueignung), 1883; Six Songs, op. 17 (including Ständchen), 1886; Four Songs, op. 27 (including Ruhe Meine Seele, Cäcilie, Heimliche Aufforderung, and Morgen), 1894; Three Songs, op. 29 (including Traum durch die Dämmerung), 1895; Five Songs, op. 32, 1896; Six Songs, op. 37, 1897; Five Songs, op. 41 (including Wiegenlied), 1899; Three Songs, op. 43, 1899; Five Songs, op. 46 (including Morgenrot), 1900; Five Songs, op. 47, 1900; Five Songs, op. 48, 1900; Eight Songs, op. 49, 1901; Six Songs, op. 56, 1906; Krämerspiegel, op. 66, 1921; Six Songs on Shakespeare and Goethe, op. 67, 1919; Six Songs, op. 68, 1919; 5 Kleine Lieder, op. 69, 1919; Gesänge des Orients, op. 77, 1929.

ABOUT:

Armstrong, T. H., Strauss' Tone Poems; Ewen, D. (ed.) The Book of Modern Composers; Finck, H. T., Richard Strauss: The Man and His Works; Gysi, F., Richard Strauss; Schuh, W., Richard Strauss.

Igor Stravinsky *1882-*

(See *American Composers Today*)

Joseph Suk *1874-1935*

JOSEPH SUK was born in Křečovice, Bohemia, on January 4, 1874. Precocious in music, he was enrolled in the Prague Conservatory when he was eleven years old. There his teachers included Anton Bennewitz, and Antonín Dvořák. Dvořák exercised a pronounced influence upon Suk. While still a conservatory student, Suk started composing, and in these early works he imitated the personal style of Dvořák.

In 1891 Suk helped found the Bohemian Quartet, and for about a decade he was its second violinist. This Quartet was important in setting a new standard for chamber-music performance throughout Bohemia and in giving performances to Bohemian composers; it was due largely to this organization that Smetana's *Aus Mein Leben* achieved recognition. Suk's association with this group was significant in his own development as well, since it gave him an intimate understanding of chamber-music style, an understanding that served him well when he wrote quartets and quintets.

In 1898 Suk married Dvořák's daughter, Otilie. It was at about this time that Suk

JOSEPH SUK

Suk: sook

first became known as a composer. On October 1, 1900, there took place in Prague the premiere of his First Symphony, and it was outstandingly successful. In the same year another of Suk's works was performed and well received: the orchestral suite, *A Fairy Tale,* based on music that the composer had written a few years before for a play, *Raduz and Mahulena.* In 1903 one of Suk's finest works was heard, the *Fantaisie,* for violin and orchestra. In all this music, his indebtedness to Dvořák is pronounced; but, as Václav Stepan remarked, Suk's music has "greater gentleness, a softer sentiment, and a richer rhythm."

A double tragedy struck Suk in the years 1904 and 1905: the death of Dvořák followed by that of Suk's wife. Morbidity and brooding set in. In his composition a funereal atmosphere now prevailed, as his melodies became broader and elegiac. Otakar Sourek wrote: "He took up the struggle forced upon him by destiny. The range of his work expands from the narrow sphere of the individual to embrace the sterner problems of humanity, and he now strives to show how grief and suffering may be overcome through faith in life and in the individual will, while in his boldest flights he hymns universal love—the love of all for all."

The symphony *Asrael,* written in 1906 and dedicated to the memory of Dvořák and Otilie, is pervaded by gloom. But despair was followed by resignation, which is found in works like *A Summer Tale,* written in 1907, and the String Quartet which he completed in 1911. In the closing decades of Suk's life another transformation took place in his writing. He showed a greater disposition towards using modern rhythms, harmonies, and tonalities.

In discussing Suk's musical output, Hans Hollander remarked how Suk was influenced by Dvořák, particularly in his chamber music and piano pieces. "These works reveal the intimacy of his voluntary artistic kinship with Dvořák. . . . Even after Suk had turned his attention to program music . . . this exuberant melodist and reveler in tone color still faithfully cherished the spiritual legacy of the departed Dvořák, a legacy closely in keeping with the distinctively subjective character of his own artistry."

In 1922 Suk was appointed professor at the Prague Conservatory. He became its director eight years later. Two years before his death, Suk was elected a member of the Santa Cecilia Academy. He died in Benesov, on May 29, 1935.

MAJOR WORKS:

Chamber Music—Piano Quartet in A minor, op. 1, 1891; Piano Trio in C minor, op. 2, 1890; Piano Quintet in G minor, op. 8, 1893; Four Pieces, for violin and piano, op. 17, 1900; Elegy, for piano trio, op. 23, 1902; String Quartet No. 2, op. 31, 1911; Bagatelle, for flute, violin, and piano, 1917; Melody, for two violins, 1934.

Choral Music—Křečovice Mass, 1888; Songs for Female Chorus, op. 15; Three Songs, for unaccompanied chorus, op. 19, 1900; Male Choruses, op. 32; Epilogue, for solos, chorus and orchestra, op. 37, 1932.

Orchestral Music—Dramatic Overture, op. 4, 1891; Serenade in E-flat, for strings, op. 6, 1892; Tale of a Winter Evening, op. 9, 1894; Symphony in E major, op. 14, 1899; A Fairy Tale, suite, op. 16, 1900; Fantaisie, for violin and orchestra, op. 24, 1903; Fantastic Scherzo, op. 25, 1903; Praga, op. 26, 1904; Symphony in C minor, "Asrael," op. 27, 1906; A Summer Tale, op. 29, 1907; Maturity of Life, op. 34, 1917; Meditation on an Ancient Czech Choral, op. 35a, 1914; Sokol March, op. 35c, 1919; Legend of the Dead Victors, op. 36b, 1919.

Piano Music—Fantasy-Polonaise, op. 5, 1892; Pieces, op. 7, 1893; Moods, op. 10, 1895; Pieces, op. 12, 1895; Spring, 22a, 1902; Summer 22b, 1902; Before the Mother, op. 28, 1907; Through Life and Dream, op. 30, 1909; Cradle Songs, op. 33, 1913; Friendship, op. 36, 1920; Episodes, 1924.

ABOUT:

Musical Quarterly, July 1934.

Karol Szymanowski *1883-1937*

KAROL SZYMANOWSKI was born in Tymoszowka, near Elisavetgrad, in the Ukraine, on September 21, 1883. His father, a wealthy Polish landowner, made his home the rendezvous for artists and scholars. Thus, in his childhood and boyhood, Karol Szymanowski moved in a setting where the love of literature, music, and art was encouraged and nursed.

In his early youth he suffered injuries from a fall which impaired his health seriously. Consequently, he was unable to join other children either at school or in play. His education was received privately at home. His boyhood was lonely, and he had to find diversion in such solitary pastimes as making

Szymanowski: shĭ-mä-nôf′skē

music, reading, and introspection. He was particularly attracted to music. Without any formal instruction, and guided only by his instincts, he began to play the piano. Eventually, a local teacher (a distant relative) started to teach him theory. Szymanowski soon wrote a set of piano preludes modeled after Chopin, whom he admired more than any other composer. These preludes, completed in 1900 and the first of his works to be published, gave forceful evidence of his creative talent. "The lyric sincerity," wrote Zdzisław Jachimecki, "the charmingly poetic ideas, the beauty of melodic invention, the harmonic variety and, finally, the elegance of technique and finesse commanded universal attention."

Convinced that their son had talent, the Szymanowskis decided to send him to Warsaw for more study. He arrived in the Polish capital in 1903 and soon after that began studying with Noskowski. A piano sonata he wrote under Noskowski's guidance won first prize in a Chopin competition held in Lemberg. During this period Szymanowski also completed his first large work for orchestra, the Symphonic Overture in E major.

In 1905 Szymanowski left Warsaw for Berlin. There he was influenced by the music of such German and Austrian composers as Richard Strauss, Mahler, and Bruckner. His First Symphony, written in 1906, betrayed the effect that German postromanticism had upon him. But subjugation to a German style did not please him. After he left Germany, in 1908, his writing became more subjective, filled with restless moods and dramatic expositions; in this manner he completed the Second Symphony and the Second Piano Sonata.

Still dissatisfied with the kind of music he was writing, Szymanowski now turned to exotic idioms. Interest in mysticism and oriental philosophy led him to produce works which derived their atmosphere and colors from the East: the opera *Hagith*, completed in 1913; the *Love Songs of Hafiz*, written one year after that; and the Third Symphony, *The Song of the Night*, in 1916.

Up to the outbreak of World War I, Szymanowski divided his time between his homeland and travels in Europe. The war confined his movements within the borders of Russia and Poland and enabled him to come into contact with the music of Scriabin

KAROL SZYMANOWSKI

and the Russian nationalists. Still sensitive to outside influences, Szymanowski started to emulate the style of the Russians.

The Russian Revolution had far-reaching repercussions in Poland. The Szymanowski estate was plundered, and all the belongings of the family confiscated. Destitute, Szymanowski settled in Warsaw and earned a living through his music. He also appeared as a pianist, and frequently in performances of his own music, in Paris, London, and the United States (his American visit took place in 1921).

After the war, Szymanowski spent a few months in the Tatra ranges of the Carpathian mountains of Poland. There he heard native folk songs and dances which inspired him to utilize native idioms in his own music and thereby become a *Polish* composer. His first effort at a national style was a Mazurka, for the piano. "Today," he wrote after completing this piece, "I have developed into a national composer, not only subconsciously but with a thorough conviction, using the melodic treasures of the Polish folk."

He was now to produce the works that put him in the first position among the Polish composers of the period. The first was the ballet, *Harnasie*, written in 1926, based on a Polish legend from the Tatra mountains. The music was as authentically Polish as the text, deriving its brilliant harmonies, shifting tonalities, and languorous melodies from the peasant music heard in that region of the Carpathians. "The music," wrote H. H. Stuckenschmidt, "conjures up with the pose of genius the wild and lonely landscape of the Carpathians. . . . [It shows] Szymanowski as a masterly manipulator of nationalist melody and of intricate Slavonic rhythms."

Another masterwork with roots embedded in nationalism came two years later. It was the *Stabat Mater,* the composer's first attempt at liturgical music. Here Szymanowski combines the melodies and rhythms of his land with sixteenth-century polyphony, in a pictorially vivid and highly dramatic way. When his *Stabat Mater* was introduced in Warsaw the year it was written, it was highly praised; it became the first of his works to be honored in his own country.

In 1926 Szymanowski became the director of the Warsaw Conservatory. His always delicate health disintegrated through hard work and in 1929 he suffered a nervous breakdown. Resigning his post at the Warsaw Conservatory, Szymanowski went to a sanitarium. Invigorated by his stay there, he was able to accept the presidency of the Academy of Music in Warsaw and to complete two major and highly successful works, the Symphonie Concertante, for piano and orchestra, and the Second Concerto for Piano and Orchestra.

A relapse sent Szymanowski back into a sanitarium, near Lausanne, Switzerland. He died there of laryngeal tuberculosis on March 28, 1937. A few months before his death he had attended a very successful presentation of *Harnasie* at the Paris Opéra.

"The work of Karol Szymanowski," wrote his compatriot and fellow composer, Alexander Tansman, "does not merely mark a glorious page in Polish music; it has attached itself incontestably to the artistic heritage of the entire world, as very precious material; it is a robust branch of the musical tree of Europe. It is quite certain that the music of Szymanowski cannot please everyone; lovers of the 'picturesque,' of 'local color,' of extravagant sonorous effects will relish it only slightly; but for real musicians it presents a genuine interest by its very existence, because its undeniable originality

imposes itself upon musicians of a different esthetic. Freeing itself from a certain heaviness which weighs down his earlier works, Szymanowski learned to forge for his ideas a musical language that is very personal. He belongs, without doubt, to the group of the greatest musicians of our time."

MAJOR WORKS:

Ballets—Mandragora, op. 43, 1920; Harnasie, op. 55, 1926.

Chamber Music—Sonata in D minor, for violin and piano, op. 9, 1904; String Quartet No. 1, op. 37, 1917; String Quartet No. 2, op. 56, 1927.

Choral Music—Stabat Mater, op. 53, 1928; Litany, op. 59, 1937.

Operas—Hagith, op. 25, 1912; King Roger, op. 46, 1924.

Orchestral Music—Symphony No. 1, in F minor, op. 15, 1907; Penthesilea, for soprano and orchestra, op. 18, 1907; Symphony No. 2 in B-flat major, op. 19, 1908; Symphony No. 3, for tenor, chorus, and orchestra, "The Song of the Night," op. 27, 1916; Concerto No. 2 for Violin and Orchestra, op. 61, 1930; Symphonie Concertante, for piano and orchestra, op. 60, 1932; Concerto No. 2 for Piano and Orchestra, 1933.

Piano Music—Nine Preludes, op. 1, 1900; Sonata No. 1 in C minor, op. 8, 1905; Sonata No. 2 in A minor, op. 21, 1909; Métopes, op. 29, 1915; Twelve Studies, op. 33, 1917; Masques, op. 34, 1916; Sonata No. 3, op. 36, 1917; Four Polish Dances, op. 47, 1926; Twenty Mazurkas, op. 50, 1924-26; Two Mazurkas, op. 62, 1934.

Vocal Music—Love Songs of Hafiz, two cycles, op. 24, 26, 1910-14; The Songs of the Fairy Princess, op. 31, 1916; Four Songs (Tagore), op. 41, 1918; Songs of the Foolish Muezzin, op. 42, 1918; Slopiewnie, op. 45, 1922; Children's Rhymes, op. 49, 1923; Five Songs (Joyce), op. 54, 1926; Twelve Kurpian Songs, op. 58, 1930.

ABOUT:

Ewen, D. (ed.) The Book of Modern Composers; Pannain, G., Modern Composers; Chesterian (London), November 1927; Musical Quarterly, January 1922.

Alexander Tansman 1897-

ALEXANDER TANSMAN was born in Lodz, Poland, on June 12, 1897. He began studying music in his native city with local teachers. He was only fifteen when one of his works—*Symphonic Serenade,* for strings—was performed by the Lodz Symphony.

Intending to make law his career, he went to Warsaw to attend the University of War-

Tansman: täns'män

saw. But he did not neglect music, continuing to study privately with Piotr Rytel. Music soon became such an all-consuming interest that he decided to leave the University.

When Poland became an independent state during World War I, Tansman joined the Polish army. While in service he continued to write music. In 1919 he entered two of his compositions in a competition among Polish composers, winning first and second prizes. When the war ended, Tansman participated in two concerts of chamber music devoted entirely to his works, one in Lodz, the other in Warsaw. The proceeds from these concerts enabled him to visit Vienna, and after that to settle in Paris, henceforth his home.

His first years in Paris were marked by poverty and trying personal deprivations. But he was not unhappy. The vitality of Parisian musical life exhilarated him. He moved among some of the most prominent French musicians of the day—including Ravel and Schmitt—and was stimulated by them to write abundantly. The young but influential conductor Vladimir Golschmann recognized Tansman's talent. He arranged a concert of Tansman's works in Paris on February 17, 1920. A year later, Golschmann directed the premiere of Tansman's *Impressions* and *Intermezzo Sinfonico,* both for orchestra. Golschmann continued for many years to promote Tansman's music and was largely responsible for bringing him recognition. Most of Tansman's works for orchestra were either introduced or performed by Golschmann in Europe and America, and some of them were written for him.

Gradually, Tansman's music became increasingly French in its structural logic, refinement of style, and emotional restraint. But it did not lose its Polish identity. For a strong national strain permeated Tansman's writing almost from the beginning. The rhythms of Polish dances became an integral part of his idiom: he wrote many mazurkas and polonaises, in addition to sundry other works like the *Four Polish Dances,* for orchestra. In his Symphony in A minor and the Third String Quartet Polish dances are introduced in the Scherzo movements.

Having established his reputation in **Paris as one of the** most vital of younger

ALEXANDER TANSMAN

Polish composers, Tansman began a series of concert tours. He appeared in the triple role of composer, conductor, and pianist. In 1926 he visited Austria, and one year after that Germany. In 1927 he appeared for the first time in the United States. He made his debut in America on December 29, 1927, with the Boston Symphony Orchestra in a program including the premiere of his Second Piano Concerto.

Edward Lockspeiser described Tansman's style as follows: "A lyric quality is one of his salient characteristics. His melodic inventiveness, particularly in the slow movements, has a warmth and sensitiveness which are truly his own; and it is in the Lied (aria form), often employed by him for the Andante in works of the sonata-type that his melodic gifts are severely tested. . . . Tansman has rhythmic dynamism to a remarkable degree, but this forceful virility, sometimes brutal, but never vulgar, does not in any way detract from the beauty of the lyricism which helps to characterize his manifold personality."

On October 30, 1941, Tansman received the Elizabeth Sprague Coolidge medal for distinguished services to chamber music. Soon after this, Tansman arrived in this country, after harrowing experiences in France, where he had to elude the Nazis. He remained here for the war years. Soon after his arrival, several of his works—written during the trying period in war-torn France and reflecting his emotional disturbance at the time—were successfully performed in this country. One of these was the *Polish Rhapsody,* inspired by the brief but heroic defense of Warsaw in the first month of the war. Another work was the elegiac Fifth String Quartet. While living in this country, Tansman wrote many new works, including several compositions for chamber-music groups, piano pieces for children, a variety of other works for different media, and several scores for Hollywood motion pictures.

Tansman has explained his musical credo to this writer in the following words: "Musical composition is an independent and self-sufficient art and should, as far as symphonic music is concerned, be motivated exclusively by musical elements of melody, harmony, rhythm, and form, without trying to express literary or pictorial subjects. I think that before anything else, a composer has to follow his own ideas without any conscious concession to temporary theories (esthetic or technical), tastes or publicized trends. I am not a partisan of the utilitarian concept of music. It is fortunate for a composer if his work is pleasing. But the purpose of a composition should not be influenced in advance by this effort to please; the task of the composer is to say what he *must* say and not to follow an *à la mode* pattern. This does not mean that music has to be complicated or enigmatic to be original. On the contrary: simplicity goes hand in hand with honesty. But *artificial* simplicity often results in vulgarity and is often more "fabricated" and contrived than the most complex modern score.

"The development of musical composition goes more and more to the melodic outline, which after all is the basis of the music, the melody being shaped by its rhythmic design. The harmony remains as always a temporary means of expressing the musical idea; and the constructive element of form, unfortunately so often neglected in our time, is of primary importance. It does not matter if the form is classical, or a derivation from classicism; but it has to be present, seriously worked out. In my last works, I take very great pains with my constructive element

without which, I feel, music remains improvisation rather than art."

In 1937 Tansman married Colette Cras, daughter of the late Jean Cras, Admiral of the French Navy. One year after his marriage Tansman became a French citizen. His home is in Paris, to which he returned after World War II. He is an avid traveler and a profound admirer of the movies (his Second Piano Concerto was dedicated to Charlie Chaplin). His other diversions include playing tennis and billiards, and reading.

MAJOR WORKS:

Ballets—Sextuor, 1923; Le Cercle Éternel, 1929; La Grande Ville, 1932; Bric-à-Brac, 1939.

Chamber Music—Suite Divertissement, for violin, viola, cello, and piano, 1929; Serenade for Piano, Violin, and Cello, 1930; Serenade for String Trio, 1938; Piano Trio No. 2, 1939; String Sextet, 1940; String Quartet No. 5, 1940; Divertimento, for oboe, clarinet, trumpet, cello, and piano, 1944; Sonatine, for violin and piano, 1944; String Quartet No. 6, 1945.

Operas—La Nuit Kurde, 1926; Poisson d'Or, opera buffa, 1940.

Orchestral Music—Danse de la Sorcière, 1922; Sinfonietta, for small orchestra, 1924; Concerto No. 1 for Piano and Orchestra, 1925; Symphony in A minor, 1926; Symphonic Overture, 1926; Concerto No. 2 for Piano and Orchestra, 1926; Toccata, 1929; Sonatine Transatlantique, 1930; Triptyque, for string orchestra (also for string quartet), 1930; Four Polish Dances, 1931; Symphonic Movements, 1932; Partita, for string orchestra, 1933; Concerto for Viola and Orchestra, 1936; Two Intermezzi, 1936; Concerto for Violin and Orchestra, 1938; Polish Rhapsody, 1940; Symphony No. 4, 1940; Symphony No. 5 in D minor, 1942; Concert Piece, for left-hand piano and orchestra, 1943; Symphonic Etude, 1943; Symphony No. 6 with chorus, 1943; Serenade No. 3, 1943; Short Suite, for instrumental group and orchestra, 1944; Symphony No. 7, 1945; Concertino for Guitar and Orchestra, 1945; Partita, for piano and orchestra, 1945; Ricercari, 1949; Sinfonia Piccola, 1952.

Piano Music—Four sonatas; mazurkas; polonaises; etc.

ABOUT:

Schwerké, I., Alexander Tansman.

Alexander Tcherepnin *1899-*

A LEXANDER TCHEREPNIN—son of the celebrated Russian composer and conductor Nicolas Tcherepnin—was born in St. Petersburg on January 20, 1899. He was introduced to the study of music early in life and he proved to be highly precocious. His

Tcherepnin: chĕ-rĕp-nēn'

father was his first teacher. Later he studied at the St. Petersburg Conservatory, where his teachers included Liadov and Sokolov. While still a boy, Tcherepnin wrote several songs that were published, and when he was fourteen he played a group of his piano pieces at a benefit concert.

In his nineteenth year, Tcherepnin received an important appointment, as musical director of the Kammerspiel Theatre in Tiflis. He did not hold that position long. Since the Tcherepnins were not sympathetic to the new Bolshevik regime in Russia, they fled by boat to Marseilles, and from there made their way to Paris, which they made their new home. In Paris Alexander continued his music study at the Conservatory, principally with Vidal (composition) and Isidor Philipp (piano). One day, Philipp glanced at some of Tcherepnin's music and was so impressed that he was henceforth to use his influence in furthering the young man's career. When he left the Conservatory, Tcherepnin found influential sponsors ready to promote him as a concert pianist. In 1922 Tcherepnin gave an immensely successful piano recital in London which marked the beginning of his virtuoso career.

Tcherepnin first attracted attention as a composer when he introduced his First Piano Concerto with the Monte Carlo Orchestra. He scored an even greater success with an opera, *Ol-Ol*, based on Andreyev's *The Days of Our Life*, and introduced in Weimar on January 31, 1928. (It was performed in New York City in 1934.) Willi Reich wrote of this opera: "The text . . . is a lively picture of student and soldier life of old Russia. To this material Tcherepnin added some striking music admirably adapted in willful primitiveness to the action in hand, and spreading around the tragic conflict of life the true atmosphere of peasant thought and peasant ways."

In 1933 Tcherepnin undertook a world tour as composer-pianist. He came for the first time to the United States in 1934 and made a coast-to-coast tour. From 1934 to 1937 he lived in China and Japan. During this period he interested himself in oriental music and oriental composers. He helped promote the careers of promising young composers and he edited a collection of Chinese and Japanese music in European nota-

ALEXANDER TCHEREPNIN

tion. His own music was affected by this contact with the Orient, as he began writing in oriental scales.

When the Sino-Japanese War broke out, Tcherepnin came to this country and lived here for one year. He then returned to Paris and after World War II gave concerts for American troops in France. After the war he made numerous concert appearances throughout Europe and the Near East. In 1948 he returned to the United States to conduct a master class in piano at the San Francisco Music and Art Institute. After that he joined the faculty of the De Paul University Music School in Chicago.

On August 13, 1952, the world premiere of his opera, *The Farmer and the Fairy*, took place at the Aspen Music Festival, in Aspen, Colorado. The text is based on an ancient fable. In reviewing the opera, Quaintance Eaton wrote in *Musical America*: "Tcherepnin has employed the pentatonic scale for his fable, exemplifying, as he says, an uncomplicated way of life. . . . To tell the simple story the composer has devised a set of songs connected by orchestral tissue of the colorful texture provided by a large percussion section, used in the five-tone manner which gives oriental flavoring throughout, plus the occasional Slavic reference that seems to be inescapable. The narrative is sometimes humorous. . . . The Tcherepnin opera provided considerable visual amusement."

Tcherepnin's music is touched with either a Russian or an oriental atmosphere. It is always technically sure, and it exploits modern rhythmic and harmonic devices. An unusual technical characteristic of his music is the use of a nine-tone scale (not his own invention, but intimately identified with him). Nicolas Slonimsky explains that this scale "consists of three repeated progressions of a semitone, a whole tone, and a semitone" and that it is most effective in giving voice to "grotesque situations in satirical music, or utter anguish in expressionist compositions."

MAJOR WORKS:

Ballets—Training, 1922; Ajanta's Frescoes, 1923; Fahrend Schuler mit dem Teufelbannen, 1937; Trepak, 1938; The Legend of Razin, 1941; La Femme et Son Ombre, 1948.

Chamber Music—String Quartet No. 1, 1922; String Quartet No. 2, 1926; Piano Quintet; 3 sonatas for cello and piano, 1924-28.

Choral Music—2 cantatas, 1945.

Operas—Ol-Ol, 1925; Die Hochzeit der Sobeide, 1930; Die Heirat, 1935; The Farmer and the Fairy, lyric legend, 1952.

Orchestral Music—Concerto No. 1 for Piano and Orchestra, 1919; Prélude pour un Entrainement de Boxe, for chamber orchestra, 1922; Romance, for violin and salon orchestra, 1922; Concerto No. 2 for Piano and Orchestra, 1923; Concerto da Camera, 1924; Three Pieces, for chamber orchestra, 1925; Mystère, for cello and chamber orchestra, 1925; Magna Mater, 1927; Symphony No. 1, 1927; Concertino, for violin, piano and strings, 1930; Concerto No. 3 for Piano and Orchestra, 1932; Russian Dances, 1933; Suite Georgienne, for piano and string orchestra, 1939; Symphony No. 2, 1951.

Piano Music—2 Toccatas, 1922; 7 Etudes, 1938; Expressions, 1951.

Ernst Toch *1887-*

(See *American Composers Today*)

Vincenzo Tommasini *1878-1950*

VINCENZO TOMMASINI was born in Rome on September 17, 1878. Since his father had respect for a well-rounded education, Vincenzo had to combine the study

Tommasini: tōm-mä-zē′nē

of music with an academic training. He acquired the elements of music at the Liceo Santa Cecilia under such instructors as Falchi, Pinelli, and Mazzarella. At the same time he attended the University of Rome, where he specialized in philology and Greek literature. While attending the University he wrote scholarly articles for philological journals and an introduction for a new edition of Xenophon's *De Re Equestri*.

In 1902 Tommasini left Italy for a long and extended trip. He spent a year in Berlin studying with Max Bruch. Then he visited Paris, London, and New York. The musical associations in these centers enriched his outlook and brought him to maturity. Before 1902 he had been imitating the styles of other composers in his music; after 1902 he started to evolve a personal style which combined a romantic outlook with modern techniques and idioms.

He completed his first major work in 1910. It was the String Quartet in F major, about which Guido M. Gatti wrote: "The themes of the first movement are really beautiful. . . . They always retain their ego; their emotion is always alive and vivid. . . . This fine emotion, half sentient, half mystic, which pervades Tommasini's themes can be discerned in all his compositions, and the more we study the musician's work, the more clear and luminous does it become. His score may be arduously wrought to the last stage of nobility and refinement, but his fundamental thought, the root of his emotion, remains simple and glowing with life."

Tommasini's climb to success was now rapid. In 1913 he won first prize in a national competition sponsored by the city of Rome for a one-act opera. His entry, *Uguale Fortuna*, was successfully given by the Teatro Costanzi. On November 16, 1916, Arturo Toscanini directed the first performance of one of Tommasini's finest works for orchestra at the Augusteo in Rome: *Chiari di Luna*, a sensitive tone picture rich with poetic imagery. *Chiari di Luna* placed its composer in the fore of those younger Italians concerned with the creation of a distinguished Italian symphonic art.

One year later Tommasini scored his greatest triumph up to that time with his ballet *The Good-Humored Ladies*—an adaptation of music by Domenico Scarlatti to a text based on Goldoni's comedy. *The Good-Humored Ladies* was introduced in Rome by the Diaghilev Ballet Russe on April 12, 1917, and immediately became one of the most popular numbers in the repertory.

Later works by Tommasini established him as a major creative figure in contemporary Italian music. Among these were the *Paesaggi Toscani* (based on authentic Tuscan folk melodies), the *Carnival of Venice*, and the *Prelude, Fanfare and Fugue*, all for orchestra.

Alfredo Casella summarized Tommasini's importance in Italian music by saying that Tommasini's works summed up "the whole of the movement which has given to Italy a characteristic school of instrumental music. Like his contemporaries, Respighi, Pizzetti, Malipiero . . . he had to wage war against the persistent and exclusive devotion of the Italians to operatic music, which, having accomplished the destruction of the native instrumental tradition, violently opposed every attempt to revive a nonoperatic style. . . . In this movement Tommasini played a considerable part.

"His first compositions were based on classic examples. He was next influenced to some extent by French impressionists, but eventually freed himself from their sway, and his latest works are typically Italian in style and character. The nationalism is perceptible even in the earlier ones, and is especially manifested in certain features common to all modern Italian music, chief of which are (1) a scheme of construction so absolutely one with the fundamental idea as to appear its logical and inevitable development; (2) a harmony which arises from the free movement of the parts; (3) musical ideas which tend to be contained within a melodic line. These three characteristics are almost invariably found in Tommasini's compositions."

Analyzing the style of Tommasini's most important works, M. Zanotti-Bianco finds that they are "dreamy, melancholy, restrained in emotion, graceful, light, and ironical. In the combination of these qualities, lies his personality. He is not an innovator, but he

VINCENZO TOMMASINI

remains in the current of new achievements. He constructs his music with sureness and with technical knowledge that is free from pedantry, and his art is essentially Italian."

Tommasini had many and varied interests in addition to music, ranging from horses to classical literature. He produced some skillfully wrought verses in Greek. Of his method of writing music he said: "I am in the habit of reworking each thing I compose many times. Sometimes I will put aside a work for several months before beginning to work upon it anew. I find that I can achieve the most felicitous expression only through constant revision."

Tommasini died in Rome on December 24, 1950.

MAJOR WORKS:

Ballet—The Good-Humored Ladies, 1917.

Operas—Medea, 1906; Uguale Fortuna, one-act opera, 1913.

Orchestral Music—La Vita è un Sogno, 1901; Poema Erotico, 1909; L'Hymne à la Beauté, 1911; Suite, 1912; Chiari di Luna, 1915; Il Beatoregno, 1921; Paesaggi Toscani, 1922; Two Songs with Orchestra, 1925; Prelude, Fanfare, and Fugue, 1927; Carnival of Venice, 1928; Napoli, fantasy, 1930; Concerto for Violin and Orchestra, 1934; Three Symphonic Marches, 1940.

ABOUT:

Ewen, D., The Complete Book of 20th Century Music.

Joaquín Turina *1882-1949*

JOAQUÍN TURINA Y PÉREZ was born in Seville, Spain, on December 9, 1882. He began to study music in his native city with the organist and choirmaster of the cathedral. He then entered the Madrid Conservatory, where he specialized in the piano with José Tragó. In 1905 Turina went to Paris and enrolled at the Schola Cantorum. His musical studies ended there with various teachers, one of whom—Vincent D'Indy —had a profound influence upon him.

Turina remained in Paris for a decade. His close association with most of the leading young French composers inevitably affected him, and he began to write music in their style and idiom. Fortunately, his meeting with and friendship for his celebrated compatriot Isaac Albéniz turned his thinking in the direction of musical nationalism. He was able to combine French impressionistic tendencies with Spanish folk idioms.

Turina came to the attention of the Parisian music public with a Piano Quintet which the Quatuor Parent introduced in 1907. Four years after this another excellent chamber-music work was given in Paris, his String Quartet, introduced by the Quatuor Touche. Both these works are distinguished by a sureness of form, articulateness, and keen sensitivity. These qualities

are also found in Turina's next important work—the one in which his musical personality revealed itself fully developed for the first time. It was *La Procesión del Rocío*, a musical description of a religious procession in Seville, written in 1912, and introduced that year by the Orquestra Sinfónica in Madrid. *La Procesión del Rocío*, which Debussy likened to a luminous fresco, made its composer an important figure in the Spanish nationalist school; to this day, it remains one of his most notable works.

Turina returned to Spain in 1914, settling in Madrid. From then until the time of his death he played a major role in his country's musical life. He was the pianist of an important chamber-music ensemble, the Quinteto de Madrid. He was professor at the Madrid Conservatory. He directed performances of the Ballet Russe in Spain. He wrote music criticism. And he was a member of the Spanish Academy of Arts.

But his principal significance rested with his creative work. Beginning with the premiere of his opera, *Margot*—in Madrid in 1914—his place with the foremost Spanish nationalist composers was never in dispute. Several of his works are among the proudest achievements of this school of composers. These include *La Oración del Torero,* for string quartet; the *Sinfonía Sevillana*, which won first prize in a competition conducted by the San Sebastian Casino in 1920; and the *Danzas Fantásticas*, a glorification of authentic Andalusian rhythms.

Pedro Morales divided Turina's music into three groups. "First, those bearing no distinctive mark of nationalism; second, those in which it predominates; and third . . . in which the idiom is a blending of Spanish and foreign elements."

In his most important music, Turina is —according to Leigh Henry—"a musical impressionist of fine sensibility, both spiritually and musically. His music however, differs in constructive methods from that of those generally termed impressionists. He tends towards the rather literary type of poetic expression exemplified in Albéniz' *Iberia* or in *Images* of Debussy, but his treatment of sound and rhythm is more objective in the strictly aural sense, and more full of feeling for pure musical design than that of the elder

JOAQUIN TURINA

Turina: tōō-rĕ'nä

Spaniard. Viewed as a whole, the general character of his work is subjective and impressionistic and has a certain flavor of romanticism."

Joaquín Turina died in Madrid on January 14, 1949.

MAJOR WORKS:

Chamber Music—Piano Quintet, 1907; String Quartet, 1911; Escena Andaluza, for violin, piano, and string quartet; La Oración del Torero, for string quartet, 1925; Poema de una Sanluquena, suite, for violin and piano.

Operas—Margot, 1914; Navidad, 1916; La Adúltera Penitente, 1917; Jardín de Oriente, 1923.

Orchestral Music—La Procesión del Rocío, 1912; Evangelio de Navidad; Sinfonía Sevillana, 1920; Danzas Fantásticas, 1920.

Piano Music—Sonata Romántica; Mujeres de España; Tres Danzas Andaluzas; Cuentos de España; Jardines de Andalucía.

Vocal Music—Rimas de Bécquer; Poema en Forma de Canciones; Tres Arias.

ABOUT:

Chase, G., The Music of Spain.

Ralph Vaughan Williams *1872-*

R ALPH VAUGHAN WILLIAMS, dean of present-day English composers, was born in Down Ampney, Gloucestershire, on October 12, 1872. He received a thorough academic and musical schooling. His academic education took place at Charterhouse and Trinity College, Cambridge, his musical studies at the Royal College of Music in London (with Stanford and Parry) and in Berlin with Max Bruch.

His education ended with the acquisition of a doctorate at Cambridge in 1901. He then began his professional career as a musician by becoming organist of the St. Barnabas Church in South Lambeth. He filled this post for three years, and during this period he wrote a few minor works for orchestra and several hymns, but nothing demonstrating any particularly outstanding creative talent.

The turning point in his life came in or about 1904 when he first became acquainted with English folk music, particularly the folk songs of the Tudor period. This music so fascinated him that he started to dig deeper into the field of English folk music. He became a member of the Folk-Song Society, and as one of this group made intensive research into native English songs (particularly those heard in Norfolk) and set some of them to new harmonizations. His revitalization of such gems as "The Turtle Dove" and "Down in Yon Forest" has become deservedly celebrated, and did much to restore them to popularity.

This complete immersion in English folk songs had an inescapable effect on his composition. Vaughan Williams started writing a new kind of music in which the folk song played a prominent role. In 1904 he completed *In the Fen Country,* for orchestra. Between 1905 and 1907 he wrote three Norfolk Rhapsodies in which the folk melodies native to King's Lynn in Norfolk are incorporated. The best-known of these Rhapsodies is the first, in E minor, in which· the following folk-songs appear: "The Captain's Apprentice," "A Bold Young Sailor," "The Basket of Eggs," "On Board a '98," and "Ward the Pirate."

He had now found his direction as a composer. But he was still dissatisfied with his technique, and he felt that additional study was needed. He went to Paris in 1908 and for eight months studied privately with Maurice Ravel. It was not long after his return from this period of study that he wrote his first important work: *Fantasia on a Theme by Thomas Tallis.* Taking a tune from the Metrical Psalter of the sixteenth-century English church composer Thomas Tallis, Vaughan Williams wrote an impassioned work for strings in which the antiphonal character of sixteenth-century church music was retained. The *Fantasia* was introduced at the Three Choirs Festival in Gloucester on September 6, 1910. To this day, it is one of Vaughan Williams' most frequently performed orchestral compositions.

Other works, completed between 1909 and the beginning of World War I, revealed that he had arrived at a full mastery of his technique and full maturity of style. They included the song-cycle based on poems of A. E. Housman, *On Wenlock Edge;* the opera *Hugh the Drover;* and most important of all, the *London Symphony.*

The *London Symphony* was written in 1913 (though it was later revised twice by

Joseph Muller Collection—William Rothenstein
RALPH VAUGHAN WILLIAMS

the composer) and received its first performance in London on March 27, 1914. Though
the composer originally avoided a program,
he did not discourage later annotators from
providing a detailed description of the symphony in which the four movements become
four pictures of London life. "The West-
minister chimes hum on the air and suddenly
London wakes," wrote Scott Goddard.
"Then turn to the uneasy sighs at the end of
the Scherzo or to the rending wail that begins the last movement. This is a different
London and a musician not viewing it but
pondering over it. It is a town haunted by
the countryside it devours. The Nocturne
(the second movement) recalls walking home
along Piccadilly in the small hours of a summer's morning when, petrol fumes at their
weakest, the light winds from the country
blow across the Green Park. . . . The errand
boys whistle tunes such as Swift might have
heard while bathing in the Thames before
his house in Chelsea, tunes that have a country air and a folk-song turn of phrase."

Vaughan Williams was forty-two years
old when World War I broke out. Though
he was exempt from military service because
of his age, he enlisted in the Territorial
Royal Army Military Corps and for three
years served as an orderly in hospitals in
France and Macedonia. Determined to fill
a more active part in the war, he took and

passed examinations for a commission in the
Artillery, and saw service on the battlefields.

The war over, Vaughan Williams returned to musical activity and assumed a
leading place in English music. He joined
the faculty of the Royal College of Music,
where for the next three decades he taught
composition. He was appointed conductor of
the Bach Choir, which he directed for a six-
year period. And he wrote many works
which were successfully performed and
which assured him a position of first importance among twentieth-century composers.
One of these was the quiet and contemplative *Pastoral Symphony*, written in 1921,
and introduced by the London Philharmonic
Orchestra on January 26, 1922. Another was
the opera-oratorio, *Shepherds of the Delectable Mountains*, completed in 1922. Other
significant compositions included the Mass in
G minor, in 1923; the suite for viola, small
chorus, and orchestra entitled *Flos Campi*, in
1925; the Violin Concerto in D major, also
in 1925; and the oratorio *Sancta Civitas*, in
1926.

In these works Vaughan Williams' style
was characterized, in the words of Philip
Heseltine, "by strong melodic invention and
a most original fund of contrapuntal re-
source in which there is nothing even faintly
reminiscent of scholasticism. With the purely harmonic development of the twentieth
century, Vaughan Williams shows but little
sympathy. . . . We certainly find extremely
novel combinations of sounds in some of the
later compositions, but they are almost invariably conditioned by the movement of the
individual parts, of which the line is often
seen in a higher dimensional aspect, so to
speak, through the addition to each note of
the two other notes necessary to complete
the common chord."

As Scott Goddard remarked in *Music
and Letters*, this music had a far-reaching
impact on Vaughan Williams' contemporaries. "Vaughan Williams has influenced
English composers in various directions and
in varying degrees. His inclination towards
folk song, . . . his singularly down-right use
of contrapuntal devices, the richness of the
resultant harmony—all these he has increased in intensity and made personal to
himself; and their effect on his contemporaries is undoubted."

Vaughan Williams came to the United States for the first time in 1922 on an invitation to direct a concert of his works at the Norfolk Music Festival. He paid a second visit to this country a decade later. At that time he delivered several lectures and gave a course on national music at Bryn Mawr College.

Among his most important works in the decade preceding World War II were the masque *Job,* the opera *Riders to the Sea* (based on the famous play of Synge), the Fourth Symphony in F minor, and *Five Tudor Portraits.* These works, like those that preceded them, are varied in their style. On the one hand, Vaughan Williams is devoted to older musical styles and melodies, as in *Job* and the *Five Tudor Portraits;* on the other hand, he can be austerely modern, as in the stark harmonies of the F minor Symphony and the bold declamatory style of *Riders to the Sea.* Some of his works—like the *Pastoral Symphony* and *The Lark Ascending*—have about them what Eric Blom once described as "the quiet enchantment of the most secluded rural England"; this is the music of a composer with either romantic or impressionist tendencies. Yet other works are the writings of a sound contrapuntist.

The common denominator of Vaughan Williams' music is, without doubt, its English identity, its deep-rooted nationalism. He himself has written: "Many young composers make the mistake of imagining they can be universal without at first having been local. Is it not reasonable to suppose that those who share our life, our history, our customs, our climate, even our food, should have some secret to impart to us which the foreign composer, though he be perhaps more imaginative, more powerful, more technically equipped, is not able to give us? This is the secret of the national composer, the secret to which he only has the key, which no foreigner can share with him and which he alone is able to tell to his countrymen."

The nationalism of Vaughan Williams, in the words of Hubert Foss, "grows from the earth. It comes from the people; its roots are in what they wanted to sing then, though it may not be what they want to hear now. His nationalism is not negative; sometimes it is more positive than his esthetic thought and his musical appeal to the public.

It is never superimposed; not once in his career has he been an Englishman consciously. There is no *pastiche,* no strutting, no attitudinizing. Vaughan Williams does not deliberately mispronounce foreign words."

As the most famous English composer after the death of Elgar, and as one of the acknowledged masters in contemporary music, Vaughan Williams has been frequently honored. In 1935 he received the Order of Merit. His seventieth birthday was not ignored in 1942 even though at the time England was engaged in a life-and-death struggle with Nazi Germany. Six concerts of his principal works were broadcast over the BBC and many English composers wrote works in homage to him. His eightieth birthday, which came after the war, was an occasion for world-wide tribute.

Though an old man, Vaughan Williams continued to produce major works both during and after World War II; the best of these are among his greatest creations. In the Fifth Symphony and the Concerto for Oboe and Orchestra, completed between 1941 and 1942, there are serenity and repose which are amazing when one recalls they were written during the first grim years of the war; it was almost as if the composer were escaping from gruesome reality to the peace and contentment of his inner life. His Sixth Symphony, which came in 1947, and which is one of his greatest works in any form, has greater turbulence and restiveness in the first three movements, together with a feeling of immense tragedy. But the concluding movement is perhaps the most tranquil music ever put on paper. "The symphony progresses deeper and deeper to the inmost recesses of the consciousness," wrote Olin Downes. "We know of no other symphony whose finale is so sensitive and intimate in its nuances, so completely of the spirit. . . . It was as if the reveries of centuries had amassed themselves about his heart."

Still another masterwork produced by Vaughan Williams after the war was the opera (or as the composer designated it, "morality") *Pilgrim's Progress,* introduced in London on April 26, 1951. This work, which blends mysticism with deep poetic feeling, was regarded by Vaughan Williams as the culminating point of his creative life;

as if to emphasize this very point, he embedded in it portions of earlier works, including his one-act opera, *The Shepherds of the Delectable Mountains,* written in 1922. Reviewing the opera for the London *Daily Express,* Cecil Smith wrote that it was "the noblest new work produced on any of the world's lyric stages since the end of the war."

Stephen Williams sketched the following personal portrait of Vaughan Williams in the *New York Times:* "He looks like a farmer. Indeed, one commentator has likened him to 'a large shaggy sheepdog, lovable, kindly, intelligent and untidy.' He is a man entirely without self-consciousness: a big, heavy, lumbering figure, usually dressed in rough tweeds, who looks as though he is on his way to judge the shorthorns at an agricultural show.

"On state occasions he wears evening dress. No—this is a ridiculous overstatement. He doesn't wear evening dress; he grudgingly allows it to cover his massive body. And while he sits, his head hunched down between his shoulders, the white tie gradually glides toward his left ear and the stiff shirt-front buckles and ruckles up against his chin. Occasionally he glances down at it as if to say, 'What the devil's all this?'

"He speaks his mind, and it is a fine and richly stored mind, well worth speaking and hearing. He has a disarming honesty. Once, after listening to one of his own works, he exclaimed: 'Well, if that's modern music I don't like it.' And another time when an orchestral player questioned the accuracy of a note in his scores, he looked at him quizzically. 'Yes,' he said, 'it looks wrong, and it sounds wrong—but it's right.'

"In a word, 'V.W.' is England. He typifies England just as solidly and ruggedly as did Chaucer or Samuel Johnson, or . . . Bunyan."

A few months after his eightieth birthday, Vaughan Williams married his secretary, Ursula Wood.

MAJOR WORKS:

Ballet—Old King Cole, 1923.

Chamber Music—Piano Quintet; On Wenlock Edge, song cycle for tenor, string quartet, and piano (A. E. Housman), 1909; Fantasy Quintet, for Strings, 1914; String Quartet in G minor, 1921.

Choral Music—Toward the Unknown Region, 1905; A Sea Symphony, 1910; Five Mystical Songs, for baritone solo and chorus, 1911; Fantasy on Christmas Carols, for baritone solo and chorus, 1912; Mass in G minor, 1923; Sancta Civitas, 1926; Five Tudor Portraits, for contralto and baritone solos and chorus, 1936; Flourish for a Coronation, 1937; Thanksgiving for Victory, 1945; Fantasia on the Old 104th, for piano solo, chorus, orchestra, and organ, 1950; An Oxford Elegy, for speaker, chorus, and orchestra, 1952.

Operas—Hugh the Drover, 1914; The Shepherds of the Delectable Mountains, 1922; Sir John in Love, 1929; Job, a masque, 1930; The Poisoned Kiss, 1936; Riders to the Sea, 1937; Pilgrim's Progress, 1950.

Orchestral Music—Three Norfolk Rhapsodies, 1907; Fantasia on a Theme by Tallis, for strings, 1909; A London Symphony, 1914 (revised 1920); The Lark Ascending, for violin and orchestra, 1914; A Pastoral Symphony, 1922; Flos Campi, suite for viola, chorus and orchestra, 1925; Concerto in D major, for violin and orchestra, 1925; Fantasy on Sussex Folk Tunes, for cello and orchestra, 1930; Concerto for Piano and Orchestra, 1933; Suite for Viola and Orchestra, 1934; Symphony in F minor, 1935; Concerto for Oboe and Orchestra, 1941; Serenade to Music, 1944; Symphony No. 5 in D major, 1945; Symphony No. 6 in E minor, 1948; Symphony No. 7, "Antarctica," 1952.

ABOUT:

Dickinson, A. E., An Introduction to the Music of Ralph Vaughan Williams; Foss, H. J., Ralph Vaughan Williams; Howes, F., The Dramatic Works of Ralph Vaughan Williams; Music and Letters (London), January 1937.

Sir William Walton *1902-*

SIR WILLIAM WALTON was born in Oldham, Lancashire, England, on March 29, 1902. He came from a family of musicians. Both his parents were singing teachers and his father, in addition, was choirmaster of the Oldham church. William joined that choir when he was only five years old. Before long he began taking lessons on the violin, and in his tenth year received a scholarship for the Christ Church Cathedral Choir School, Oxford. He started writing music when he was thirteen and shortly afterward began studying theory and harmony by himself. At Christ Church, which he entered in his sixteenth year after receiving a degree of Bachelor of Music, he applied himself so completely to music and music study—and was so negligent in all other courses—that he was finally expelled.

He could now concentrate on his musical interests. Settling in London, he lived with the Sitwell family, whose members encouraged him to undertake serious composition. His first major works were a Piano Quartet and a String Quartet. The String Quartet was successfully performed at the International Society for Contemporary Music Festival in Salzburg in 1923. The Quartet for Piano and Strings was published by the Carnegie Trust Fund.

But Walton became famous as a result of an unconventional and provocative piece of music. In 1922 he completed a work for reciting voice and seven instruments called *Façade*, a setting of twenty-one abstractionist poems of Edith Sitwell. It was heard in London on June 12 of the following year at a private concert. Two years later, Walton revised and expanded the work, and in this new version it was introduced in London on April 27, 1926, in a novel manner. Unseen, Edith Sitwell recited her poems with her voice emerging through a megaphone-shaped mouth painted on the curtain; the instrumentalists were also concealed. And Walton's music was just as unconventional as the performance. It revealed an uncommon feeling for burlesque humor, mock sentimentality, whimsy, and parody. It was wonderful fun and it created a sensation. "As a spirited and lively work," wrote Hubert J. Foss, "it is without a modern English rival, so full of pace and vivacity and humor is it. Its chief technical interest lies first in its brilliant rhythmic pattern which, touched by the tricks of jazz writers, far exceeds mathematically anything they have ever heard of; and secondly, in its ability to state a plain and obvious melody in a significant way without accompaniment. . . . *Façade* is an amusement of the high-jinks kind, but well shows that music to be amusing must first be satisfactory, and (particularly) skillful as music." *Façade* is best known to present-day concert audiences through two orchestral suites prepared from the score by the composer.

The works following *Façade* had a more traditional approach and a more serious content. Two were particularly successful and did much to give Walton a significant position in contemporary English music. One was the picturesque concert overture *Portsmouth Point,* portraying a waterfront scene with nautical-sounding tunes and dances. It was first heard at the International Society

SIR WILLIAM WALTON

for Contemporary Music Festival in Zurich on June 22, 1926, and after that given by most of the important symphony orchestras in Europe and America.

Even more successful was the cantata *Belshazzar's Feast,* introduced at the Leeds Festival on October 10, 1931. The text, adapted from the Bible by Osbert Sitwell, begins with the prophecy of Isaiah. Though this was Walton's first attempt at choral writing, it was outstanding for the nobility of the style and the spaciousness of design. "If Walton never again wrote a note, good, bad, or indifferent, he has in *Belshazzar's Feast* definitely staked a claim to a position of importance," wrote J. H. Elliot. "No words could do justice to this music; its force and power, its unhesitating rightness as musical and dramatic statement and, above all, the blazing artistic conviction which drives the whole conception forward, mark it as one of the most remarkable achievements of any English composer."

Later works by Walton—and they are of outstanding musical significance—included his Symphony and the Concerto for Violin and Orchestra, both written before World War II. In these works, Walton's tendency, as Edwin Evans pointed out, was "to surround his material with a wealth of contrapuntal arabesque and a profusion of rhythms. But it is such clean writing that clarity suffers but rarely. . . . Walton has acquired [such] confidence that, when he is so disposed, he can allow a subjective emotion to rise to the surface without any fear that it will float there like an oil stain."

During World War II Walton served in the Ambulance Corps in London. He was assigned by the Army to write music for several documentary films. He was also to complete several concert works and ballets, notably the comedy overture *Scapino* (written on a commission from the Chicago Symphony Orchestra to commemorate its fiftieth birthday) and the ballets *The Quest* and *The Wise Virgins*. During this war period he also produced scores for important English motion-pictures, including *Major Barbara, Henry V,* and *Hamlet*.

In 1949 Walton married Susana Gil Passo in Buenos Aires, and soon after this he achieved complete financial independence through a legacy left him by one of his closest friends. In 1951 Walton was knighted by the Crown for his distinguished services to English music.

MAJOR WORKS:
Ballets—The Wise Virgins, 1940; The Quest, 1943.

Chamber Music—Piano Quartet, 1919; First String Quartet, 1922; Toccata, for violin and piano, 1923; Second String Quartet, 1947; Sonata for Violin and Piano, 1950; Two Pieces, for violin and piano, 1951.

Choral Music—Belshazzar's Feast, cantata, 1931; In Honor of the City of London, 1937.

Opera—Troilus and Cressida, 1953.

Orchestral Music—Façade, for reciting voice and seven instruments (also for orchestra), 1922 (revised 1926); Portsmouth Point, concert overture, 1925; Siesta, for chamber orchestra, 1925; Sinfonia Concertante, for orchestra with piano obbligato, 1927; Concerto for Viola and Orchestra, 1929; Symphony, 1935; Crown Imperial, coronation music for George VI, 1937; Concerto for Violin and Orchestra, 1939; Scapino, comedy overture, 1940; Orb and Sceptre, coronation music for Elizabeth, 1953.

ABOUT:
Bacharach, A. L. (ed.) British Composers Today; Howes, F., The Music of William Walton; Tovey, D. F., Some English Symphonists.

Anton Webern *1883-1945*

THE trinity of the twelve-tone technique included Anton Webern, Arnold Schoenberg, and Alban Berg. Webern was born in

Webern: vā'bĕrn

Vienna on December 3, 1883. After completing his preliminary schooling in the Austrian towns of Graz and Klagenfurt, he entered the University of Vienna in 1902, specializing in music as a research student under Guido Adler. He received his doctorate of philosophy at the University in 1906.

After graduating from the University, Webern earned his living by conducting in small opera houses and theatres. A meeting with Arnold Schoenberg, in 1904, was the decisive influence in his life. For four years Webern studied privately with Schoenberg and under Schoenberg's guidance made his first serious attempts at composition.

His first important work was the Passacaglia, for orchestra, completed in 1908. It was more or less traditional in form and style. Gerald Abraham described it as follows: "The thought is clear, continuous and comparatively expansive; and the scoring, if transparent, is solid, even rich, in conventional doubling."

But as Schoenberg was drawn more and more away from Wagnerian post-romanticism to atonality, and after that to the twelve-tone technique, Webern followed him with the devotion and dedication of a true disciple. The *Five Pieces for Orchestra,* which was completed by Webern in 1913, were in Schoenberg's most austere and revolutionary atonal manner. When introduced in Vienna on March 31, 1913 (at a concert featuring works of Schoenberg and his disciples), it created a scandal.

During World War I Webern served in the Austrian army. Later he settled in the Mödling section of Vienna, near Schoenberg and the other Schoenberg disciples. He helped Schoenberg found—and he subsequently supervised the programs of—the Society for Private Musical Performances in Vienna so that the works of the Schoenberg school could be presented under the favorable conditions denied them in the public concert auditoriums. (Only enthusiasts of the Schoenberg style attended these concerts; professional critics were excluded.) Beginning with *Three Sacred Songs,* written in 1924, Webern adopted the twelve-tone idiom of his teacher.

In 1925, Webern was commissioned by the League of Composers in New York to write a symphony. The unorthodox work Webern created (in the twelve-tone idiom) aroused in turn mild amusement and hostility when the symphony was introduced in New York on December 18, 1929. As *Musical America* reported, the audience "broke into slightly horrified amusement. . . . Alexander Smallens, directing the premiere with one hand, tried less successfully to keep his audience silent with the other."

Other works by Webern were also attacked when they were first heard. It is not difficult to understand why his compositions created such an unpleasant stir. They are the last word in musical expressionism. Webern carries economy, brevity, precision as far as they can possibly go. Some of Webern's pieces are only a few seconds in duration. His melodies are often nothing more than fragments. His harmony and counterpoint are at times so simple that they consist only of a few isolated tones. The dynamics are also restricted, and usually only of the delicate kind. "He endeavors to deploy," wrote Edwin Evans, "within a narrow space the utmost possible range of expression, employing thereto all the available resources of the instruments concerned."

"In order to speak relevantly of Webern and his music," wrote Heinrich Jalowitz, "one would have to be able to write exactly as he composes, to capture the inexpressible in the softest, most sensitive imagery, to discover better means of communication than the usual forms of reasoning, with their attendant danger of exaggeration and misunderstanding. . . . The impulse to create comes to him from experiences of nature and visions which cannot be expressed except in music—echoes of a world so thoroughly his own that only tones never heard before can translate them. He uses the new alphabet created by Schoenberg on the basis of the old, but speaks his own highly individual language."

Erwin Stein explains that Webern's language is "suffused with an extraordinary tender and intimate feeling. He is the composer of the *pianissimo espressivo*. Most of his compositions . . . are extremely transparent in sound, and his melodies are highly, sometimes ecstatically, expressive."

In the period before World War II Webern was active as a conductor, particularly

ANTON WEBERN

of works of the modern German and Austrian school. He started to direct a symphony orchestra over the Austrian Radio in 1927, and in 1929 he served as a guest conductor with the British Broadcasting Company. In 1932 he was invited to conduct two concerts of contemporary Austrian and German music in Barcelona.

Webern also devoted himself to teaching —he was an indefatigable propagandist for the Schoenberg style and esthetic principles.

Webern remained in Austria during the period of the Anschluss and World War II. An account of his tragic death, in 1945, was given at the time by the *Wiener Kurier*: "On September 15, in Mittersill in the Pinzgau, near Salzburg, Webern, while visiting his son-in-law, Benno Mattel, met a tragic and as yet not fully explained death. About ten o'clock in the evening he was standing in front of his son-in-law's house enjoying a last cigaret before retiring when there was a sudden series of shots. Webern staggered into the house and said to his wife, 'I've been hit.' He died soon afterwards."

Webern's son-in-law was arrested, and for a while was falsely accused of being the murderer. But an intensive police examination revealed the fact that Webern, while strolling near his son-in-law's house, was ordered by an American soldier to stand still. He misunderstood the order and continued to advance towards the soldier and was shot.

MAJOR WORKS:

Chamber Music—Five Pieces for String Quartet, op. 5, 1909; Four Pieces for Violin and Piano, op. 7; Six Bagatelles, for string quartet, op. 9, 1913; Three Pieces for Cello and Piano, op. 11; String Trio, op. 20, 1927; Saxophone Quartet, op. 22, 1930; Piano Quartet, 1937; String Quartet, op. 28, 1938.

Choral Music—Two Choral Songs (Goethe), op. 19; First Cantata, op. 29, 1940; Second Cantata, op. 31, 1945.

Orchestral Music—Passacaglia, op. 1, 1908; Six Pieces, op. 6, 1909 (revised 1929); Two Songs with Orchestra (Rilke), op. 8; Five Pieces for Orchestra, op. 10, 1913; Four Songs with Orchestra, op. 13; Symphony, for chamber orchestra, op. 21, 1925; Orchestral Variations, op. 30, 1943.

Vocal Music—Songs after Stefan George, op. 3, 4, and 5; Six Songs with Chamber Music, op. 14; Five Sacred Songs, op. 15, 1924; Five Latin Canons, op. 16, Three Sacred Folk Songs, op. 17, 1924.

ABOUT:

Ewen, D., The Complete Book of 20th Century Music; Monthly Musical Record (London), December 1946; Modern Music, January-February 1931.

Kurt Weill *1900-1950*

(See *American Composers Today*)

Jaromir Weinberger *1896-*

(See *American Composers Today*)

Ermanno Wolf-Ferrari *1876-1948*

ERMANNO WOLF-FERRARI was born in Venice on January 12, 1876. His mother was Italian and his father German. From his father, a famous painter, Wolf-Ferrari appeared to inherit a gift for art. As a boy he was sent to Rome for art study and eventually succeeded in producing some noteworthy canvases. A pilgrimage to Bayreuth, the shrine of the Wagnerian music drama, changed the course of his life. Hearing Wagner's music convinced him that he wanted more than anything else to be a composer. However, in view of this early passion for Wagner, it is interesting to note that a later hearing of *Siegfried* brought on what some have described as a "psychosomatic shock." A serious illness followed, and when Wolf-Ferrari recovered he became almost pathologically opposed to anything Wagnerian.

He started music study by himself in his fifteenth year. His progress was so rapid that in 1893 he was permitted to go to Munich, where he studied with Rheinberger. Wolf-Ferrari began to compose in Munich. When he returned to Venice in 1899, his biblical cantata, *La Sulamita* was performed. One year later his first opera, *Cenerentola,* was introduced, though with very little success, at the celebrated Teatro Fenice in Venice. When this opera was repeated in Germany in 1901 it made a more favorable impression.

His talent for the theatre first became evident with *Le Donne Curiose,* a farce based on a play by Goldoni, introduced in Munich on November 27, 1903. The infectious score revealed that its composer was a worthy successor to the long line of famous composers of the Italian opera buffa.

From 1902 to 1909 Wolf-Ferrari served as director of the Liceo Benedetto Marcello in Venice. He resigned to devote himself more completely to writing operas. He now produced two works which are acknowledged to be his masterworks. The first was an engaging one-act comic opera, *The Secret of Suzanne,* successfully introduced (in a German translation) in Munich on December 4, 1909. A rather silly little play, revolving around Suzanne's terrible secret that she smoked cigarettes, inspired Wolf-Ferrari to write some of his gayest and most infectious music.

In marked contrast to the levity of *The Secret of Suzanne* was his next successful opera, *The Jewels of the Madonna,* heard in Berlin (again in a German translation) on December 23, 1911. With a remarkable change of pace, Wolf-Ferrari here wrote a tragic opera in which the music is outstanding for its realism, tension, and dramatic impact.

William Saunders contrasts the strength and weaknesses of Wolf-Ferrari's two celebrated operas as follows in *The Monthly Musical Record* (August 1918): "His airs do not display a great power of melodic invention, but interspersed as they frequently are in a welter of discordant cacophony, they actually sound to better advantage than they would otherwise have done. A great fault in

Wolf-Ferrari: vôlf′ fär-rä′rē

ERMANNO WOLF-FERRARI

these melodies of his, also, is a too frequent use of cadence. His clever borrowings and employment of popular airs and folk themes, on the other hand, supply a welcome variety. . . . His writing and scoring of dance themes, also . . . falls little, if at all, short of genius. His choral writing, again, is seldom at fault, and generally reminds one of the

best examples of Verdi. . . . And lastly he is a past master of orchestration."

In 1912 Wolf-Ferrari visited the United States to supervise the American premiere of *The Jewels of the Madonna* at the Chicago Opera. Though he wrote a great deal of music after 1912—and not exclusively in the field of opera—he never equaled the inspiration or success of his two most distinguished operas.

Wolf-Ferrari died in Venice on January 21, 1948.

MAJOR WORKS:

Chamber Music—Piano Quintet, op. 6; Piano Trio, op. 7; Sonata No. 2, for violin and piano, op. 10; String Quartet, 1940.

Choral Music—La Sulamita, cantata, 1899; The Daughter of Jairus, mystery, op. 3, 1900; La Vita Nuova, oratorio, op. 9, 1902.

Operas—Cenerentola, 1899; Le Donne Curiose, 1903; I Quattro Rusteghi, 1906; The Secret of Suzanne, 1909; The Jewels of the Madonna, 1911; L'Amore Medico, 1913; Gli Amanti Sposi, 1925; Veste di Cielo, 1927; Sly, 1927; La Vedova Scaltra, 1930; Il Campiello, 1935; La Dama Boba, 1937.

Orchestral Music—Chamber Symphony, op. 8, 1901; Idillio, concertino for oboe, string orchestra and two horns, op. 16, 1932; Suite Veneziana, op. 18, 1936; Arabeschi, 1937; Divertimento, 1938.

ABOUT:

Grisson, E., Ermanno Wolf-Ferrari; Stahl, E., Ermanno Wolf-Ferrari.

APPENDIXES

APPENDIX I

COMPOSERS GROUPED BY NATIONALITY

Austrian
Berg ✓
Einem
Mahler ✓
Webern ✓

Belgian
Absil
Gilson
Jongen
Poot

Czechoslovakian
✓ Janáček
✓ Novák
Suk

Danish
Nielsen
Riisager ·

Dutch
Andriessen
Badings ✓
Dresden ✓
Pijper

English
Bantock ✓
Bax ✓
Bliss
Britten ✓
Delius
Elgar
Goossens
Holst ✓
Ireland ✓
Jacob
Rawsthorne
Rubbra
Scott
Vaughan Williams ✓
Walton

Finnish
Sibelius ✓

French
Aubert ✓
Auric ✓
Barraine ✓
Barraud
Charpentier ✓
Debussy ✓
Delannoy
Dukas
Fauré ✓
Françaix
Ibert
Indy ✓
Le Flem
Lesur
Martinon
Messiaen ✓
Migot ✓
Milhaud ✓
Pierné
Poulenc ✓
Rabaud
Ravel
Rivier
Rosenthal
Roussel
Saint-Saëns
Satie
Sauguet
Schmitt

German
Orff ✓
Pfitzner ✓
Reger
Schreker
Strauss ✓

Hungarian
Dohnányi ✓
Kodály ✓

Italian
Alfano ✓
Casella ✓

Dallapiccola
Giordano ✓
Malipiero
Mascagni ✓
Montemezzi
Perosi
Pick-Mangiagalli
Pizzetti
Puccini ✓
Respighi
Tommasini
Wolf-Ferrari ✓

Norwegian
Sinding

Polish
Szymanowski
Tansman

Rumanian
Enesco

Russian
Glazunov
Glière
Kabalevsky ✓
Khatchaturian ✓
Medtner ✓
Miaskovsky
Prokofiev
Scriabin
Shostakovich ✓
Tcherepnin

Spanish
Albéniz
Granados ✓
Turina

Swedish
Alfvén
Atterberg
Nystroem
Rosenberg

Swiss
Honegger ✓
Martin

APPENDIX II

MAJOR SCHOOLS OF COMPOSERS AND SPECIFIC IDIOMS AND STYLES

(WITH REFERENCE TO SKETCHES IN WHICH THEY ARE DISCUSSED)

Arcueilists: Satie (also Sauguet).
Armenian national music: Khatchaturian.
Atonality: Berg (also Webern).
Bohemian national music: Janáček (also Novák).
English national music: Vaughan Williams.
Finnish national music: Sibelius.
French Six: Auric (also Honegger, Milhaud, Poulenc).
Hungarian national music: Kodály (also Dohnányi).
Impressionism: Debussy (also Delius, Ravel).
La Jeune France: Messiaen (also Lesur).
Melodies of the language: Janáček.
Mystery: Scriabin.
Naturalism (or Realism): Charpentier (also Strauss).
Neo-baroque: Reger.
Neo-classicism: Casella (also Francaix, Respighi).
Neo-mysticism: Messiaen.
Neo-romanticism: Mahler (also Scriabin, Strauss).
Norwegian national music: Sinding.
Polish national music: Szymanowski (also Tansman).
Proletarian music: Shostakovich (also Glière, Kabalevsky, Miaskovsky, Prokofiev).
Rumanian national music: Enesco.
Spanish national music: Albéniz (also Granados, Turina).
La Spirale: Le Flem.
Swedish national music: Alfvén (also Atterberg).
Synthesists: Poot.
Triton: Rivier (also Barraud).
Twelve-tone technique: Berg (also Dallapiccola, Webern).
Verismo: Mascagni (also Puccini).

APPENDIX III

A SELECT BIBLIOGRAPHY

Abraham, Gerald. Eight Soviet Composers. London: Oxford University Press, 1943.

Bacharach, A. L. (editor). British Music of Our Times. London: Pelican Books, 1946.

Bauer, Marion. Twentieth Century Music. 2d ed. New York: G. P. Putnam's Sons, 1947.

Brook, Donald. Composers' Gallery. London: Rockcliff Publishing Corp., 1946.

Brook, Donald. Five Great French Composers. London: Rockcliff Publishing Corp., 1947.

Calvocoressi, M. D., and Abraham, Gerald. Masters of Russian Music. New York: Alfred A. Knopf, 1936.

Chase, Gilbert. The Music of Spain. New York: W. W. Norton & Co., 1941.

Copland, Aaron. Our New Music. New York: McGraw-Hill Book Co., 1941.

Dyson, George. The New Music. New York: Oxford University Press, 1926.

Ewen, David (editor). The Book of Modern Composers. 2d ed. New York: Alfred A. Knopf, 1950.

Ewen, David. The Complete Book of 20th Century Music. New York: Prentice-Hall, 1952.

Foulds, John H. Music Today. London: Ivor Nicholson and Watson, 1934.

Fraser, Andrew A. Essays on Music. London: Oxford University Press, 1930.

Graf, Max. Modern Music. New York: Philosophical Library, 1946.

Gray, Cecil. A Survey of Contemporary Music. London: Oxford University Press, 1924.

Howard, John Tasker. This Modern Music. New York: Thomas Y. Crowell Co., 1942.

Křenek, Ernst. Music Here and Now. New York: W. W. Norton & Co., 1939.

Lambert, Constant. Music Ho! New York: Charles Scribners' Sons, 1934.

Leibowitz, René. Schoenberg and His School. New York: Philosophical Library, 1949.

Mellers, Wilfrid. Studies in Contemporary Music. London: Dennis Dobson, 1947.

Moisenko, Rena. Realist Music—25 Soviet Composers. London: Meridian Books, 1949.

Newlin, Dika. Bruckner, Mahler, Schoenberg. New York: Columbia University Press, 1947.

Pannain, Guido. Modern Composers. New York: E. P. Dutton & Co., 1933.

Rosenfeld, Paul. Discoveries of a Music Critic. New York: Harcourt, Brace & Co., 1936.

Sabaneyev, Leonid. Modern Russian Composers. New York: International Publishers, 1927.

Salazar, Adolfo. Music in Our Time. New York: W. W. Norton & Co., 1946.

Saminsky, Lazare. Music of Our Day. 2d ed. New York: Thomas Y. Crowell Co., 1939.

Shera, Frank. Debussy and Ravel. London: Oxford University Press, 1938.

Slonimsky, Nicolas. Music Since 1900. 3d ed. New York: Coleman-Ross Co., 1949.

Swan, Alfred J. Music 1900-30. New York: W. W. Norton & Co., 1929.

Thompson, Oscar (editor). Great Modern Composers. New York: Dodd, Mead & Co., 1941.

Tovey, Donald Francis. Some English Symphonists. London: Oxford University Press, 1941.

Trend, J. B. Manuel de Falla and Spanish Music. New York: Alfred A. Knopf, 1929.

Weissmann, Adolph. The Problems of Modern Music. New York: E. P. Dutton & Co., 1925.